NORTH-EAST INDIA

INTERPRETING THE SOURCES OF ITS HISTORY

NORTH-EAST INDIA

INTERPRETING THE SOURCES OF ITS HISTORY

Edited by

RANJU BEZBARUAH
PRIYAM GOSWAMI
DIPANKAR BANERJEE

INDIAN COUNCIL OF HISTORICAL RESEARCH
New Delhi

ARYAN BOOKS INTERNATIONAL
New Delhi

NORTH-EAST INDIA: INTERPRETING THE SOURCES OF ITS HISTORY

ISBN-10: 81-7305-295-6
ISBN-13: 978-81-7305-295-8

The views expressed in this volume are those of the authors and are not necessarily those of the editors or the publishers.

First Published in **2008** by

INDIAN COUNCIL OF HISTORICAL RESEARCH
35, Ferozeshah Road, New Delhi-110 001

and

ARYAN BOOKS INTERNATIONAL
Pooja Apartments, 4B, Ansari Road, Darya Ganj, New Delhi-110 002 (India)
Tel.: 23287589, 23255799; Fax: 91-11-23270385; E-mail: aryanbooks@vsnl.com

Computer Typeset and Printed in India at
ABI Prints & Publishing Co., New Delhi

Preface

It is indeed a matter of great pleasure and satisfaction on our part to have been associated with the efforts of the ICHR to bring to light source materials for the reconstruction of the history of North-East India. The articles incorporated in this volume are selections from those presented by scholars in the National Seminar on Sources of History of North-East India, organized by the ICHR in collaboration with its North East Regional Centre, at Guwahati in March 2002. The seminar was the first of its kind, being devoted wholly to sources of the history of the region.

The Brahmaputra Valley of Assam has a rich tradition of recording the past. The *Kalika Purana* and the *Yogini Tantra*, a large number of inscriptions, the *Buranjis, the Carit Puthis*, Memories official correspondences, along with a vast array of oral traditions constitute the major sources for the study of the region. The Barak Valley of Assam, Manipur and Tripura are equally rich in recording the past in one from or another. The Manipuri *Puyas* are immensely important as source material for the reconstruction of the history of the Valley. In reconstructing the history of most of the tribes inhabiting the region in pre-colonial times, one has to depend primarily on oral traditions, though for the colonial and post-colonial periods oral traditions are amply supplemented by archival documents. All these sources are, however, yet to be properly interpreted and compiled to enable scholars to study North-East India's history as part of mainstream Indian history.

The papers presented in the seminar and selections incorporated in this volume are by no means a comprehensive catalogue of the whole gamut of the source-materials for the study of North-East India's past. They merely highlight certain sources chosen by individual scholars. Nevertheless, they represent practically all the states of the region and are ready materials for other scholars to fall back upon. Forty-one papers were presented at the Seminar and twenty-seven papers have been incorporated in this volume. An Editorial Board with Ranju Bezbaruah, Priyam Goswami, and Dipankar Banerjee as co-editors, and J.B. Bhattacharjee, S.D. Goswami, S.D. Dutta as members, screened, scrutinized and edited the papers into their present from. However, the views expressed by the contributors are wholly their own.

We take this opportunity to thank the authorities of the ICHR for entrusting this onerous responsibility upon us. We are also grateful to the officials and staff of both the ICHR, New Delhi, and the North East Regional Centre, Guwahati, for extending to us their support in a variety of ways. Professors J.B. Bhattacharjee, S.D. Goswami, and S.D. Dutta who spared their valuable time in selecting the papers for this volume also deserve our thanks.

We believe that if this volume helps scholars in finding further clues to the sources of the history of North-East India even partially, the purpose of this volume will be amply served.

Editors

Contents

List of Contributors

J.B. Bhattacharjee

Professor in History (Retd.), NEHU, Shillong, Meghalaya & Former Vice-Chancellor, Assam University, Silchar, Assam.

S.K. Bose

Library of Numismatic Studies, Block - BF 70, Sector I, Salt Lake City, Kolkata - 700 064.

S. Dutta

Professor in History, Arunachal University, Rono Hills, Doimukh, Arunachal Pradesh - 791 112.

Amrendra Kr. Thakur

Reader in History, North Eastern Hill University, Shillong - 793 022, Meghalaya.

D.K. Ganguly

Aban Pally, Santiniketan, Bolpur - 731 235, West Bengal.

P.C. Sarma

Director, Vivekananda Kendra Institute of Culture, M.G. Road, River Side, Uzan Bazar, Guwahati - 781 001.

J.V. Hluna

Head, Department of History, Pachhunga University College, Aizawl, Mizoram - 796 001.

Paromita Das

Reader, Department of History, Gauhati University, Guwahati - 781 014.

Nisipad Dev Choudhury

Secretary, Kamrup Anusandhan Samity, Ambari, Guwahati - 781 001.

R.D. Choudhury

Former Director General, National Museum of India, Janpath, New Delhi - 110 011.

Anima Choudhury

Lecturer in History, Chaygaon College, Chaygaon, Kamrup (Assam).

Sangkima

Principal, Aizawl West College, Aizawl, Mizoram.

Romesh Buragohain

C/o N. Gogoi, Bhagadattapur, near Chaturbhuj Namgharh, Beltola, Guwahati - 781 028.

Radha Das

Lecturer in History, Gauhati University, Guwahati - 781 014.

I.S. Mumtaza

Reader in History, Gauhati University, Guwahati - 781 014.

N. Lokendra

Professor in History, Manipur University, Canchipur, Imphal - 795 003.

Rena Laisram

Lecturer in History, Gauhati University, Guwahati - 781 014.

N. Joykumar Singh

Professor in History, Manipur University, Canchipur, Imphal - 795 003.

Mahadev Chakravorty

Professor in History, Tripura University, Agartala - 799 004, Tripura.

F.A. Qadri

Professor in History, North Eastern Hill University, Shillong - 793 022, Meghalaya.

Priyam Goswami

Professor in History, Gauhati University, Guwahati - 781 014.

Lopita Nath

Lecturer in History, Cotton College, Guwahati - 781 001.

S.D. Goswami

Professor in History, Dibrugarh University, Dibrugarh - 788 004, Assam.

D.R. Syiemlieh

Professor in History, North Eastern Hill University, Shillong - 793 022, Meghalaya.

Dipankar Banerjee

Reader in History, Gauhati University, Guwahati - 781 014.

Indira B. Gupta

Deputy Director (Publication), Indian Council of Historical Research, New Delhi - 110 001

Ranju Bezbaruah

Professor in History, Gauhati University, Guwahati - 781 014.

Shiela Bora

Professor in History, Dibrugarh University, Dibrugarh - 788 004, Assam.

1
Keynote Address

J.B. Bhattacharjee

North-East India is no longer a *terra incognito* a Indian historiography, as many rightly thought it to be till 1960s. Thanks to the efforts of the University, the departments of history, the North East India History Association (NEIHA), and similar organisations and institutions that a large number of historians of the region, including a few from outside the region, have individually and collectively substantially contributed to the various aspects of the history of North-East during the last thirty years. The publication of the five-volume *Comprehensive History of Assam*, edited by H.K. Barpujari, nearly a decade ago, which integrated the findings of the researches till then, gives a good account of the progress of historical research in the North-East. On an average, at least ten books and more than a hundred substantive papers are now published in a year. NEIHA holds its session every year, and its proceedings are published regularly. The quality of research also can legitimately claim an all-India standard. The need is to sustain the enthusiasm that has been noticed in recent years among the scholars of the region.

Notwithstanding what I have just said, this seminar should be important for a two-fold purpose, viz., (i) to measure the depth and breadth of the use of sources that were identified years ago; and (ii) to share information about the newly-identified sources. I shall particularly expect the reporting of some newly-identified sources, for I always hear young scholars complaining of the paucity of data, irrespective of the theme they initially pick up by their own choice. This may be primarily because of the limitation of scope of the sources that are used (and they obviously created the gap areas) and because new sources of information (particularly of the pre-colonial period) have not been added for some time. Sir Edward Gait's report on the *Progress of Historical Research in Assam* (1898) listed some important sources which were readily available, and the efforts of the local scholars (K.L. Barua, P.N. Bhattacharya, S.K. Bhuyan and K.P. Singha to name a few) led to the identification of invaluable source-materials in the early decades of the 20th century. Serious reviews of these sources (particularly conventional ones) are found in Vols. II, III & IV of the *Sources of the History of India,* published by the Institute of Historical Studies, Calcutta (1974, 1978 & 1982). These reviews covered the sources which were contemporarily used by the scholars.

In fact, most of the literary and epigraphic sources pertaining to the pre-colonial period (ancient & medieval) were unfolded till 1960s and very little have been added since then. The inscriptions (including the copper plates) were reported in the *Journal of the Asiatic Society* and various issues of the *Epigraphic Indica,* and now available in two excellent compilations (*Copper-plates of Sylhet,* 1967, ed. by K.K. Gupta and *Inscriptions of Ancient Assam,* Guwahati, 1978, ed. by M.M. Sharma). The important archaeological sites were noticed in the reports of Archaeological Survey of India in the colonial period, while Ambari (Guwahati), Pilak (Tripura), Malinithan, Bhismaknagar, Balukpung, Ita (Arunachal Pradesh), Bhaitbari (Meghalaya) are among the few sites excavated in post-1960s. The Department of Anthropology, Guwahati University, made an important beginning in the explorations of pre-historic sites in Garo Hills and North Cachar Hills in the same period. The coins of the medieval monarchies were also mostly catalogued in museums and/or reported in numismatic bulletins and in the *Journal of the Numismatic Society* or *Asiatic Society* till 1960s, and only few could be added after that. The Harikela coinage, some later Gupta coins, and a hoard of local coins found at Dhula Padung (all pertaining to an ancient period) are among the post-1960 finds. The chronicles of Assam, Manipur and Tripura are widely used for a long time. The *Prachya Sasannavali* (compiled and edited by Maheswar Neog, Guwahati, 1974) is a source-book which has been found handy by many researchers. Therefore, the fact remains that new sources for the pre-colonial history of the North-East have not come to light for a long time. This seminar may explore the possibility of alternative and supplementary data which can be helpful in filling up the gaps in the political, social and economic history of the pre-colonial period.

The archival records continue to be the main source of information for the modern period. The historians of the region have been using the Assam Archives (formerly Secretariat Record Office), West Bengal Archives, National Archives of India, and the India Office Library & Records (London). Some scholars have used the District Record as well (though in a very small way). The private papers (particularly those in the Cambridge South Asia Archives, Cambridge and the Nehru Memorial Museum & Library, New Delhi) have also been used by some of our scholars, besides newspapers, records of the political parties, tea, oil, coal and railway companies and the Tea Board, contemporary literature in local languages, and the memoirs, autobiographies and reminiscences of the administrators and freedom-fighters. The missionary papers have of late been found to be very useful. The records preserved in the mission headquarters and archives in England, Italy, Germany and the United States, besides those in India, are being used by the historians. *The American Missionaries and North-East India* (a documentary study, Guwahati, 1986) by H.K. Barpujari is an example of how important the missionary sources for social, cultural, intellectual and economic history are. Similarly, memoirs of some of the early Italian and German missionaries in North-East India (translated and published by the Sacred Heart College, Shillong) are indeed mines of information. The accounts and reports of the British officials, eg Buchanan Hamilton's *An Account of Assam* (1807-14), R.B. Pemberton's *Descriptive Account of Assam* (1840), W.J.M. Mills' *Report on Assam* (1853), W.W. Hunter's *Statistical Account of Assam* (1878), and many others of the kind, have been reprinted more than once and these are still being used by the researchers. In fact, the sources on the modern period are so wide in range and varied that the real problem lies in identifying and handling them rather than the dearth of them. However, the archival records are generally the official versions of events and development and hence, there is always a need for alternative sources of information. The alternatives (to supplement, authenticate or to complement) are also available, provided the researchers are adequately trained and equipped to trap them. As of now, I see need for larger use of district and sub-divisional records for micro-level studies. Unfortunately, these records are in a bad state of preservation and the record rooms hardly provide any facility to the researchers. Similarly, the records of the municipalities and other local bodies and the traditional authorities and educational and cultural institutions should also be explored to supplement the information we get from the official archives. In this seminar, we may discuss these and several other possibilities as we sit down to serious business.

I have emphasised on several occasions that in the North-East we should explore non-conventional oral sources as an alternative and/or supplementary to the conventional recorded sources, and for this, we might interact with sister disciplines in social sciences like social anthropology, sociology and socio-linguistics for interdisciplinary study of social forces and social development and take advantage of the tools and techniques of field research in those disciplines. The oral sources (folklore, folksongs, beliefs and superstitions, ceremonies, hymns, ritual practices, and those of the kind) are always important for peoples' history (or history from below) as they reflect on the problems, needs and aspirations of the masses at various points of time. The oral history societies in Britain and the United States have done excellent work in developing methodologies for research in oral history. In the North-East, these are particularly important because most of the communities in the region were in pre-literacy in the pre-colonial period and the languages were reduced to writing only in the later years of the 19th century or even after that. Therefore, the conventional recorded indigenous sources are not accepted for the earlier period. Aware of this predicament, the British officers did a commendable job in recording and compiling the oral traditions of the various tribes in the North-East. E.T. Dalton's *Descriptive Ethnology of Bengal* (1872) and monographs like Gordon's *The Khasis* (1907), Playfair's *The Garos* (1909), Mutton's *The Angami Nagas* (1926) and *The Sema Nagas* (1928) or Mills' *The Ao Nagas* (1928), to name only a few of those great works of the monographers, contain so many tales and traditions which are important for historical analysis. Some excellent collection of folklore have been brought out by our own scholars since 1950s. S.N. Barkakati's *The Folktales of Assam* (1956) and P.D. Goswami's *Ballads and Tales of Assam* (1960) are indeed outstanding collections with scholarly interpretation in unique literary style. Some oral history projects and a large number of Ph.D. and M. Phil. dissertations in the School of Social Sciences at NEHU have yielded excellent results in reconstructing the history of the North-Eastern tribes. May I recommend to this seminar that the oral history of North-East India is taken up more seriously by us.

Finally, I need not repeat the words of the great historians to remind ourselves that the interpretation of a source is as important as the source of information, and this integral segment of the historians' craft, calls for rigorous training in historical method. R.G. Collingwood called the history constructed by excerpting and combining the testimonies of different authorities a 'scissors-and-paste history' and he said, "it is not really history at all, because it does not satisfy the necessary conditions of science" (*The Idea of History*, CP, Oxford, 1993 edition, p. 257). As we talk of the sources, the interpretation of those will legitimately deserve our attention in this seminar.

2

On a Coin of Jaintiapur

S.K. Bose

Numismatic evidences constitute important source-materials for the reconstruction of the history of the Jaintia kingdom.

The origin of the Jaintia kingdom remains a matter of conjecture and inference.[1] The terrain was bounded on the east by the rivers Keerowah and Kapili, separating it from Cachar. To the north, the Kapili drained into the Kallang, the latter segregating the Jaintia kingdom from Assam. The state of Khyriem was to the west, and this western boundary then diverted south-easternly to reach Surma river, which found its southern border except in the region of Satbak Purgana.[2]

No one knows what united the Syntengs, or the inhabitants of Jaintia Hills under one king. This is quite unlike their neighbours in the hills – the Khasis – who had adopted a democratic system to elect Chiefs to rule their petty states.[3]

The keys to the past being very few, the story of the Jaintia kingdom has so far been reconstructed on the basis of the history narrated traditionally, the chronicles of the Ahoms and the Koches, a few copper-plates of the late medieval period and most importantly, a limited number of coins struck by the Jaintia kings.[4]

An earlier reference of Jaintiapur has been made in the revenue assessment of the Mughals. Todarmal, the Revenue Secretary of Emperor Akbar, had assessed the collection from the Jaintia plains to 27200 *dam* (Rs. 680/-). However, whether the Jaintias were at all under the Mughals is debatable. Blockmen opined that neither Jaintia nor Tripura could be conquered by the Mughals.[5]

In 1835, when the British annexed the Jaintia kingdom, it spread over an area of about 650 square miles. Lieutenant Fisher, in a report in August 1822, however, limited the size to 545 square miles.

Traditionally, the Jaintia subjects in the plains maintained a dynastic list of their rulers. Such a list is also recorded in the Ahom and the Koch chronicles. One such list was shown to the author by the last descendant of the Jaintia royal family, Rajkumari Ira Devi. She reportedly received it from the Royal priest, late Chandra Kumar Deshmukhya.[6] Such recordings could have been relied upon to construct a political history of Jaintia. Unfortunately, these do not bear dependable dates. In the given circumstances, late Jaintia coins seem to stand out as reliable documents to determine the royal lineage.[7]

However, a major problem in dating Jaintia rulers in this fashion is that most of the Jaintia coins are anonymous.[8] Unless supported by other corroborative evidence, the exercise remains a matter of some doubt.

The dynastic list mentioned above starts with Parbat Rai Brahman. According to Gait,[9] Parbat Rai might have extended the Jaintia kingdom towards the plains some time in the early 16th century. Unfortunately, no coin of Parbat Rai has yet been discovered.

An undated coin, with the legend *Sri Rupesya Banadasthan Jantapuramka Saupradhana* on the reverse, has recently been discovered.[10] From the translation of the legend, it appears that this particular coin was dedicated to the most handsome chief and ruler of the forest land and Jaintia inhabitants; thereby probably referring to Lord Shiva.[11] The basis for such a reference is a temple of Lord Shiva near Muktapur, built by king Borgohain I of Jaintiapur. The priest of the temple was one Rupanath; and the temple as well as the image of the Lord were alluded to by the same name.[12] As Borgohain had dedicated his kingdom to Rupanath and his consort Jaintesvari, no separate land was earmarked for the maintenance of the temple.[13] It may be conjectured that this very piece might have been issued by him. In that case, Borgohain I may be regarded as the first Jaintia king to have minted coins.

According to *Darrang Rajvansavali,* written after Naranarayana invaded Jaintiapur (c. 1563/1564), the Jaintia king was killed and his successor was banned from striking coins in his own name, but could do so in the name of Jaintiapur.[14] Gait viewed that this story may perhaps explain why so few Jaintia coins bear the name of the king in whose reign they were struck. The king is simply described on the coins as the most illustrious ruler of Jaintiapur.[15] A few historians, however, opined that the *Vansavali*, being a late work, may not be entirely reliable as a source of information on Jaintia coinage.[16]

On the basis of the Jaintia coins noticed so far and other reliable information available, we may accept the following chronology of the Jaintia rulers:

Name of the king	*Year of accession*	*Event-related year recorded*[17]	*End of the rule*
Parbat Rai	?		
Borgohain I	?		
Vijay Manik	1575		
Dhan Manik			1612
Yaso Manik		1618	1633
Chota Parbat Rai	1633		1640
Yasmat Rai	1640	1658	1660
Man Simha	1660		1669
Pratap Simha	1669		1670
Lakshmi Narayana	1670		1703
Ram Simha	1703		1708
Jay Narayana	1708		1731
Borgohain II	1731		1770
Chatra Simha	1770	1778	1782
Jatra Narayana	1782		1785
Bijay Narayana	1785		1790
Ram Simha	1790		1832

Information about a number of gold and silver coins were reported at Kolkata during the 1970s, however those were, possible not genuine; hence not taken into consideration.[18]

Gait has mentioned about a coin issued by one Jai Simha. The legend on the obverse reads, *Sri Sri Hara Gouri Charana Parayana* and the reverse, *Sri Srim Jai Bhupalasya Sake 1585*.[19] This piece is similar to any Jaintia coin both in fabric and style, though it is difficult to say with certainty that Jai Simha was a Jaintia ruler. No corroborative information in this regard has surfaced so far and he has not been mentioned in any chronicle. The Mughal general, Mir Jumala, was in Assam during Saka 1585 (AD 1663). It is possible that during that period of turmoil, Jai Simha had occupied a portion of Jaintia and struck his coin.[20] The above-mentioned coin was found with other Jaintia coins.[21] Interestingly, during 1663, the Jaintia king Man Simha had attended the coronation of the Ahom king, Chakradhvaja Simha.[22] Jai Simha might have seized this opportunity for some political gains.

The author has recently noticed an unusual two-rupee Jaintia coin of Borgohain II. This coin was found at Raha, in the modern Nagaon district in Assam, along with two more rupee coins of Ram Simha II (AD 1790-1832). Raha is not far away from Phulaguri, north of Kallang where, with the consent of the Ahom king, Pratap Simha, the Jaintia king Yaso Manik, organised a fair.

This was the first attempt made by a Jaintia ruler to initiate a commercial contact between the two kingdoms.[23] In fact, this region had three passes, viz, Gobha, Neli and Khala, connecting it to the Jaintiapur kingdom, which were utilised by the traders. Most interestingly, Borgohain II had actually travelled to the boundary near Raha at the end of AD 1768. He retreated when the Ahoms misunderstood the aim of such a venture and placed a cannon at their border.[24]

The two-rupee coin mentioned earlier may be described as below:

Metal-debased silver, size-round, diameter-30 mm, weight-14.7 grams, legend-Sanskrit, Scrit. Asamese-Bengali, denomination-two rupee, date-Saka 1653.

Obverse– In double circle with dots in between, a crescent with a dot inside at the top within the double circle, a *trisula* (trident) flanked by two human figures (Nandi and Bhringi ?), as well as a group of four dots in square shape above the legend, musket on left and sword on right, the legend flanked by a dagger and dots near the inner circle, a six-pointed star, a Hindu representation of six seasons at the bottom of the legend. The legend runs in four lines-

Sri Sri Sri
Va charana ka-
Mala madhuka-
Rasya

Reverse– A double circle with dots between, and horizontal line above the last line of the legend, two rows of five dots, one each above and below the legend, first line flanked by dots arranged in a triangle; two dots at right and half portion of the flower at left of the second line.

The legend runs in four lines-

Sri Sri Ja-
Yantipura Pu-

Randarasya Sa-
Ke 1653

Rhodes has recorded at least three one-rupee coins of Borgohain II weighing 7.54, 7.32, and 7.12 grams.[25] These coins bear between twelve and thirty-two dots. The two-rupee coin under discussion has thirty two dots. It is a debased silver coin. From the appearance of the earlier Jaintia coin, it can be concluded that the process of striking debased coins began from the period of Borgohain II and reached its peak during the reign of Ram Simha II. Use of debased metal in striking Jaintia coins was the result of a system by which the right to mint coins was sold by the ruler to the highest bidder. Two coins bearing the date 'Saka 1712' were sent to the Assay Master, Calcutta Mint in AD 1836. The findings show the value of the said coins according to the Company's standard, as 3 annas and 4 annas 3 pie only.[26]

It is recorded that Borgohain II was the first Jaintia king to have experimented to introduce quarter-rupee coin. As such, a two-rupee coin by the said ruler might have been a part of his experiments. This was certainly an attempt to raise his revenues, as the king used to receive most of the revenues in kind.

With this unique piece, till date, altogether three varieties of denominated coins have been noticed in the eastern part of our country, the other two being the two-rupee coin of Radha Kishore Manikya of Tripura (AD 1897) and the ten *tanka* coin of Jalal-ud-din Muhammad Shah, Sultan of Bengal, struck in AD 1420.

NOTES AND REFERENCES

1. E.A. Gait, *A History of Assam*, Guwahati, 1962 (reprint), p. 259.
2. S. Mumtaza Ali, *The History of Jaintia*, Dacca, 1954, p. 1.
3. E.A. Gait, 'Some Notes on Jaintia History', *JASB*, Vol. LXIV, pt. 1, 1895, p. 242.
4. *Ibid.*, p. 242.
5. A.C. Choudhury, *Srihatyer Itibritta*, Srihattya, BS 1317, Part 2, Chapter IV, p. 1.
6. Author's *Jaintia Mudrar Itihas*, Sanghriti, Shillong, 1992, p. 197.
7. N. Rhodes, *The Coinage of North-East India*, Hythe, 1994, Jaintiapur, p. 111.
8. A.W. Botham, *Catalogue of the Provincial Coin Cabinet-Assam*, Allahabad, 1930, p. 542.
9. E.A. Gait, *op. cit.*, p. 261.
10. N. Rhodes, *op. cit.*, p. 112.
11. N. Rhodes and V. Choudhury, 'An Enigmatic Jaintia Coin', *ONS Newsletter*, London, 1993, No. 135.
12. A.C. Choudhury, *op. cit.*, Part 2, Chapter IV, pp. 6-7.
13. *Ibid.*

14. N. Sarma (Ed.), *Darrang Rajvansavali,* Pathsala, 1973, p. 85. (This chronicle was written by poet Baladev Suryakhari Daibagya between 1791 and AD 1806.)
15. E.A. Gait, *op. cit.,* p. 243.
16. J.P. Singh, "Jaintia Coins and Koch Tradition: An Examination", *N.I. Bulletin,* London, May 1988, pp. 112-5.
17. Based on either chronicle or copper-plate.
18. Rhodes and Mitchiner, "A Series of Forged Coins from North-East India", *Numismatic Circular,* London, March-April 1981.
19. E.A. Gait, *op. cit.,* p. 245, PI. XXIV, No. 18.
20. Author's Jaintia, *op. cit.,* p. 199.
21. *JASB,* 1895, p. 245.
22. A. Choudhury CX, *op. cit.,* Part 2, Chapter IV, p. 12.
23. Lakshmi Devi, *Ahom-Tribal Relations,* Guwahati, 1968, p. 109; *Jayantia Buranji,* (Bhuyan S.K. Ed.) pp. 17 and 168.
24. Lakshmi Devi, N. 23, p. 133.
25. N. Rhode, *The Coinage, op. cit.,* p. 127.
26. *JASB,* 1895, p. 243.

3

Sources of History of Arunachal Pradesh: A Critical Survey

S. Dutta

INTRODUCTION

Before dealing with the theme of this paper it is necessary to give certain important characteristics of the land and the people. It would also be appropriate to point out certain limitations while dealing with the subject.

Arunachal Pradesh, the erstwhile North-East Frontier Agency, the land of the rising sun in the North-Eastern tip of India, spreads over approximately an area of 84,000 sq. kms. It is the abode of a large number of tribes totaling a population of about 10,91,117 (as per 2001 census-provisional) with their distinct culture, varied customs, language and colourful costumes. Lying along the southern slopes of the Eastern Himalayas it is the largest state in the North-Eastern region of India in terms of area, having a strategic location with international borders with Tibet (China), Myanmar and Bhutan of about 1628 kms, of which 1030 kms is with China, 441 kms with Myanmar and 157 kms with Bhutan.

Arunachal Pradesh has a very severe and rigorous topography. In the degree of hardship that depends on three main factors – the terrain, the climate and the degree of isolation (in terms of communication) from the rest of the world – Arunachal Pradesh is very badly placed. In the words of Waddell,

Driven into these wild glems by the advance of civilisation up the plains and lower valleys, these people have become hemmed-in among the mountains, where pressing on each other in their struggle for existence, they have developed into innumerable isolated tribes.[1]

K.A.A Raja, one of the pioneer Administrators of erstwhile NEFA and the first Lt. Governor of Arunachal Pradesh, has echoed a similar view:[2]

Numerous communities in the earlier stages of material culture had moved away, over centuries, into these hills. They moved in batches and stages depending on pressure exerted. Each batch was self-contained and lost contact with the present stock and the related groups in the course of migration. Every fresh arrival pushed those that followed it, from place to place, till they all reached their present habitats. These movements accelerated and intensified the diversification.

Geography has also influenced the cultural development of the province to a great extent. The northern region had little contact with the lower region, particularly the Brahmaputra Valley and so it had been greatly influenced by the Indo-Tibetan culture. The southern belt of the foothills has had similar contact with the plains of Assam with resultant cultural impact. But the middle zone has remained comparatively backward and both Tibetan and Assamese influence are visible in their way of life.[3]

Most of the tribes of Arunachal Pradesh can boast of a rich heritage. But because of lack of scientific data, particularly of the ancient period, understanding and study of the past pause a Himalayan problem before a modern-day researcher. Understanding and study of the past becomes easier if one can trace documents, relics, movements and archaeological evidences. But most of the languages spoken by the tribes of Arunachal Pradesh (more than fifty in number and most belonging to the Tibeto-Burman group), do not have scripts and written literature excepting those of the Monpas and the Khamptis who have written literature and documents in Tibetan script and language and Tai script and language respectively. Thus, Arunachal Pradesh, an island itself (popularly known as *terra-incognita*) till independence, was full of islands of various tribes separated for so many factors. Over the decades after independence, however, a common Arunachalee 'personality' has grown up, as the tribal people of Arunachal Pradesh have come into close contact with each other and the rest of the nation through various means of contact. The present democratic set up has contributed further to accelerate the process.

An evolution of names may be traced in case of the tribal groups of people in the North-East from the earliest blanket designations like *Nisada, Kirata* and *Astra* of the Vedic and Epic literature which made little distinction between the various people of the North-Eastern region of India including Assam, Arunachal Pradesh and other tribal states of the present time to later appellations for different groups of people noticed in the Ahom Buranjis and British records.[4] The names of different tribes used in the present paper are those which are being currently used by respective tribes in identifying them, since the names or appellations given to tribes by the outsiders were mostly unknown to the tribal people themselves.[5] However, in the excerpts quoted and wherever it was required to establish with distinction the contemporary historical context, the use of old names could not be avoided.

With this background in mind while dealing with the subject, I am aware of the limitations of dealing with such a vast subject like sources of the history of Arunachal Pradesh from the ancient period to the modern time in a single paper. My attempt, therefore, will be of macro-nature, leaving scope of micro-studies of each source-materials in details. Like in most other cases, the sources of the history of Arunachal Pradesh also may be broadly divided into the following categories: Archaeological sources, Oral sources and Literary sources.

Archaeological Sources

In spite of an unfavourable climate and seismic disturbances, we are fortunate to have a number of archaeological remains in Arunachal Pradesh, which help us in reconstructing the history of the state.

Stone Age tools and artifacts along with Neoliths and river terraces have been recorded by B.P. Bopardikar in his report of first ever scientific exploration in the Daphabhum area of Lohit district in 1969-70. SN Rao of Dibrugarh University detected some objects which seems to be Palaeoliths in the Kamlang Valley of Lohit district in 1971. Y.A. Raikar of the Research Department of the Govt. of Arunachal Pradesh discovered chips of semi-precious stones from Vijaynagar of Tirap district in 1971, which he considered to be relics of Microlithic culture. These reports appear to be significant in the background of discoveries of Stone Age relics from the adjoining regions of Assam, Meghalaya and other parts of North-East India.[6]

Neoliths have been found in plenty from all over Arunachal Pradesh chiefly as surface finds. All these indicate the potentiality of the area awaiting further research for pre-historic remains. In this respect the discovery of a Megalithic site at Jamini in West Kameng district is of much importance.[7] The fortification at Naksa Parvat situated in the Seijosa circle in the foothills of the East Kameng district excavated during 1980-82 is considered to be a somewhat later construction.[8]

Implements and utensils of the old period preserved in private household and monasteries indicate the life-pattern and industry of their respective periods. Well-known specimens of Tibetan and Burmese types made of silver, brass, copper and other metals are seen in most of the religious centres. Apart from these, gongs and other items of heirloom preserve in the households of non-Buddhist tribal folks occasionally having definite exchange value are also noteworthy in this context.[9]

Thus the results of various pre-historic exploration along with the discovery of vertebrate fossils strongly suggest habitation of pre-historic man inside the territory of present-day Arunachal Pradesh. Comparative study of materials and technology exhibit a close affinity of the Neoliths of Arunachal Pradesh with objects of Assam, Burma, Indo-China, China and Malay peninsula. The potteries from Parsin-Parlo in lower Subansiri district from stratified deposits reveal its affinity with Chinese and South-East Asian pottery. We have no direct proof of an Iron or Copper Age culture in Arunachal. The technology behind the manufacture of certain Neolithic tools, however, is thought to be involved in the use of metal implements and thus A.H. Dani believes that the Neoliths themselves were perhaps products of Chalcolithic Age. About the authors of the Paleolithic culture we cannot say anything definitely. However, proximity, ecological identity and similarity of remains suggest that they belonged to the same ethnic tribes who were responsible for the contemporary cultures of North-East India, Burma, South China and South-East Asian countries.[10] It seems that they would have been the Austric-speaking people who were supposed to have lived till their dispersal or miscegenation with later Mongoloid immigrants of North-East India, who penetrated from China and South East Asia in the Neolithic period.[11]

Architectural vestiges of Arunachal are exemplified by Buddhist monasteries, stupas and shrines, forts and hill-resorts noticed at Bhalukpung, Nakshaparvat, Itanagar, Bhismaknagar, Sisupalgad, etc and old Hindu shrines like Malinithan and Tamreswari temple. These furnish valuable materials for study of various aspects of religious, social and political life and history of the territory. Architectural characteristics of these monuments indicate varying degrees of impact and interaction of different cultural strains.[12]

Tawang, Zemithang, Kalaktong, Dirang, Rupa, Shergaon and other places of Tawang and West Kamang district and Mechuka, Tuting, Gelling and other sites of the upper parts of West Siang and Dibang Valleys are full of Buddhist *Gompas*, monasteries and *Chortens* (*stupas*) belonging to different sects of Vajrayana Buddhism constructed during different periods. Images preserved in monasteries and *Gompas* are traditionally ascribed to AD 11th-12th century or still earlier times. The Theravada monasteries and shrines of the Lohit and Tirap districts also contain numerous images of the Buddha, other deities and monks in metal, wood or stone. Some of these are assignable to the 17th century, while others belong to later times. From an 18th century *stupa* excavated at Vijaynagar of Tirap district, have been found a number of Buddha figures made of stone and metals.[13]

Beautiful icons of Hindu divinities have been discovered from the temple of Malinithan in the foothills of the West Siang district bordering Assam which are variously datable to different periods between the 10th and 14th centuries. The Tamreswari temple in Lohit district and Naksaparvat ruins of the East Kameng district also furnish specimens of stone sculpture. These structures, excavated mainly in the foothills near the southern boundary adjoining Assam, reflect a culture penetration from the adjoining areas of Assam or the broader field of East India. It is to be noted here that numerous specimens have not yet been thoroughly investigated or studied. But whatever sculptural and other material remains have been discovered and studied, a lot can be known about migration of various ethnic groups, their admixture and cultural contact with the world beyond its present geographical limits.

The earliest datable inscription is found from the Tamreswari in the Lohit district. It is said to have recorded building of a boundary wall around the temple by one Muktadharmanarayana, supposed to be a Chutiya king, in 1364 Saka (AD 1442), which throws some light on the political, religious and cultural history of the period. Next, mention may be made of the short legends inscribed in a number of bricks found from the Bhismaknagar Fort situated at a place not far from the Tamreswari temple. The Sadiya Snake Pillar inscription found at Sadiya in Assam near the border of Arunachal Pradesh written in Tai script and language records some contract made between the Ahom King and the Mishmis. Numismatic evidence is very rare in the state and coins found are of the neighbouring rulers, which might have been brought in course of trade relationship.

Thus, archaeological relics so far discovered in the state are not as prolific as in most other parts of the country. Still whatever little have come to light, especially in recent years, deserves intensive examination from various angles and inter-disciplinary studies are likely to resolve many knotty problems related to the pre-historic period of Arunachal Pradesh.[14]

Oral Sources

Myths and legends represent quite an interesting and important source for the preparation of the history of Arunachal Pradesh. Paucity of written literature, documents and other material-remains invest them with additional significance for having direct access into tribal mind and tradition. Every village and community of the state has a rich heritage of such legends regarding its ancestors, origin, migration, etc which exist mainly in the form of oral tradition. In the words of Robinson,

> History furnishes a very imperfect insight into the origin and descent of the tribes of the North East Frontier. We must, therefore, depend on the reflected light which is obtained by the comparison of languages, by the analysis of civil and religious institutions and mythological fables or by tracing clearly marked affinities in the manners and customs of different tribes.[15]

It would, therefore, not be an exaggeration to state that the history of Arunachal Pradesh is mixed with legends, folklore, folk songs and traditional accounts.

Oral traditions nowadays are universally accepted as one of the necessary complementary sources for recreating or reconstructing the past. In the words of Tomba Singh, "If history is the mother of the truth, folklore happens to be the mother of emancipation and reconstruction."[16] T Mibang has echoed a similar view in these words, "Oral information becomes the only reliable source in areas where the documentary evidences are inadequate and especially for a society like Arunachal where and of whom history is yet to be written."[17] He further states, "Ponung (folk dance accompanied with songs of the Adi tribe) rereflects the simple sun, the moon and the creation of the universe .... There may be certain fictitious plots in the tale to amuse and entertain the listeners. But then here certainly the genesis of Adi cultural life is referred to. It remains an account of the past connecting the missing link in our history."[18] Here a special mention may be made of the *Abangs* of the Adis, an Indo-Mongoloid tribe of Arunachal Pradesh. Verrier Elwin has called tribal myths as Puranas:

> In the tribal-Puranas, as we may call them, we find a strong sense of history, a pride in the descent of the race from a great ancestor, the record of a belief in the value of supreme self-sacrifice for the good of mankind.[19]

Most of the tribes of the state have such rich traditional sources. In fact Elwin's book *Myths of the North East Frontier of India* (1958) acquaints us with various myths of the tribals which are of great importance for the study of social history of the area.

Oral sources, however, have their limitations like subjectivity, personal biases and exaggeration. While using these sources, one should be careful to check and verify the facts in corroboration with other sources before arriving at any conclusion. In spite of its limitations, oral sources are a valuable supplementary source for an imaginative reconstruction of the past, especially for filling the gaps in our information. Although *Sources of the History of India,* Vol. VI (N.R.Ray, 1988) has compiled the archaeological and other literary sources relevant for use in the study of Arunachal Pradesh, it has not included the oral sources or data for historical research in Arunachal Pradesh. Though an initiative in this respect has been taken by scholars like Sachin Roy, T. Nyori, T. Mibang and others, much more has yet to be done in this field to set right some distortions made by even some current scholars.

Literary Sources

Literary source for convenience of our study, may broadly be divided into those of (a) ancient and medieval periods; (b) colonial periods; and (c) post-independence, post-Chinese aggression period.

Literary Sources of Ancient and Medieval Periods

Starting from the earliest phase of Indian literary history, there are implied references to the non-Aryan autochthons like the Nishadtas, Kiratas, etc and their settlements. Many of these accounts from the nature of their hints and description may well be construed as related to the areas and people presently representing the region called Arunachal Pradesh and its inhabitants. The early and later Vedic literature, because of distance and lesser contact of the Aryans with this area, only vaguely mentioned this region. In course of time, however, because of eastward migration of the Aryans, a greater knowledge about this area and people have been reflected in the *Mahābhārata*, the *Rāmāyaṇa*, the Puranas and the Tantras in the *Vishnu Purana*, the *Kalika Purana* and the *Yogini Tantra*.[20]

Other works of both indigenous and foreign origin occasionally reveal awareness about this region. Early foreign account of the Indian Subcontinent like those contained in the *Periplus of the Erythraean Sea and Ptolemy's Geography* are often found to incorporate references to the land of the Kiratas and the trade that was carried on with China.

In Hiuen Tsang's account (AD 7th century) an idea is given of the hilly region east of Bhaskarvarman's kingdom. It was full of folks living amidst forests infested with venomous snakes, herbs, etc and extended upto the border of China. Muhammad Kasim, a Muslim historian, in his account states that in the days of Aurangzeb, the Nishis (Dafalas) were entirely independent of the Assam Raja and plundered the country contiguous to their mountains whenever they found an opportunity. Shihabuddin Talish, who accompanied Mirjumla during his expedition to Assam (1662-63) left a detailed narrative on Assam.[21] In this he also incorporated available information about the tribal people residing in the region, now comprising the hills of Assam and Arunachal Pradesh.

The Ahom *Buranjis* (Chonicles) which provide elaborate accounts of medieval Assam contain references to people of Arunachal Pradesh. The relationship of the Arunachal tribes with Ahom monarchs have been recorded in detail which is useful for constructing the political history of medieval Arunachal Pradesh. Besides political relationship, the *Buranjis* also throw light on the economic history of the people of Arunachal Pradesh.

Even some of the Vaisnava literature of medieval Assam contain references about Arunachal and its people. The *Katha Gurucharita,* a biographical work of the medieval Vaisnava Saint of Assam, written in the later part of 18th century, gives an exhaustive list of communities of Assam and the neighbouring areas which includes the names of many tribal communities of Arunachal Pradesh. Similarly the *Sri Sri Aniruddhadevar Charita aru Mayamara Gosain Sakalar Vamsawali* (1933) refers to the participation of Nishi and Nishi-Bahatias with the Mataks againts the Ahom government in the Moamaria Rebellion.

Literary Sources of the Colonial Period

After the establishment of British supremacy in Assam in the first part of the 19th century, the North-Eastern Region gradually attracted the attention of a band of British adventurers and imperialists. The colonial intervention culminating into the establishment of British paramountcy over the hill men of the region and their incorporation into the colonial cobwebs was determined by the colonial interests in the Brahmaputra Valley and the commercial and strategico-political interests beyond the frontiers. By the beginning of the seventies of the 19th century, the economy of Assam had become promising and trade and industry had made a good start. Tea, petroleum, coal, rubber and timber became flourishing industries and items of business. As all the districts of Assam bordered on some hills inhabited by the tribes, further growth and consequent profit of the industries mentioned above greatly depended upon the administration's capacity to maintain law and order in the foothill areas. The tribes on the other hand, driven or restricted into the hills by British commercial interest in the foothills, sometimes had to fall upon the plains to draw their supplies, which they did traditionally. So there was the need of regulation of hill-plain relationship for the Britishers and for this they needed intimate knowledge of the tribes and their land.

As a result, the British administrators, travellers and explorers—some of them were also trained anthropologists—left behind systematic accounts of the tribes they studied. Their studies, however, were the results of politico-economic needs of the colonial State which reflected the 19th century outlook of these ethnographers with an unchanging attitude for the oriental societies in general and the societies of this region in particular "with a view to projecting the British rule as the legitimate agency of progress."[22] The resultant monographs and studies followed a set standard pattern in which the tribes were depicted as 'isolates', 'ignorants', 'savages', 'uncivilised', 'culturally backward', 'belligerents', etc.[23]

Today, very few students of historiography would seem to believe that the colonial rule was "governed by the motives of humanity" and that it attempted "to conciliate the hill-tribes". Here lies the significance of the call given by B.K. Roy Burman in which he cautions the historians of India "to examine the events documented by sources close to colonial administration with conscious intellectual tuning."[24] Amalendu Guha echoes a similar view in which he wishes the historians writing on this region to be largely unconventional by delineating the characteristics of the colonial ethnography.[25] Actually the term 'isolation' was used to create a hill-plain dichotomy and to negate the symbiosis that existed between the habitats of the hills and plains for centuries during the pre-colonial period. Similarly, by using the term 'savage' the tribes were depicted as the fossilised segments of humanity around whom the colonial construct of 'wanton aggression and impulsive behaviour' could be foisted.

Even after admitting the facts mentioned above, we are also to admit the fact that though not above reproach, like in other areas of the North-East, it is in fact the writings of the British historians, adventurists, anthropologists and sociologists, whose works can still be considered as the pioneering and scientific works on different aspects of Arunachal Pradesh. For the modern researchers the problem of considerable dimension is to check and counter-check such writings to make these presentable to the modern world. It appears proper here to mention some such important works which throw light on the different aspects of the State. These are:

Bucanon Hamilton (Francis), *An Account of Assam* (1807-1814); R.B. Pemberton, *Report on the Eastern Frontier of British India* (1835); Montgomery Martin, *The History, Antiquities, Topography and Statistics of Eastern India* (1836); John M'Cosh, *Topography of Assam* (1837); L.A. Waddell, *Tribes of the Brahmaputra Valley* (1837); William Robinson, *A Descriptive Account of Assam* (1837); E.T. Dalton, *Descriptive Ethnology of Bengal* (1979), now printed with title *Tribal History of Eastern India;* H.H. Rishly, *The Tribes and Castes of Bengal* (1872); W.W. Hunter, *A Statistical Account of Assam* (1979); J.F. Michell, *Report on the North East Frontier of India* (1883); Alexander Mackenzie, *The North East Frontier of India* (1884); E.A. Gait, *A History of Assam* (1905); L.W. Shakespear, *History of Upper Assam, Upper Burma and the North East Frontier* (1914); R.S. Kennedy, *Ethnographical Report on the Akas, Kwowas and the Mijis and the Membas of Tawang';* B.C. Ellen and E.A. Gait, *Gazetteers of Bengal and North East India;* Dorothy Woodman, *Himalayan Frontier,* C.U. Aitchison, *A Collection of Treaties, Engagements and Sanads;* G.A. Grierson, *Linguistic Survey of India;* R. Reid, *History of the Frontier Areas Bordering on Assam from 1883-1941; Reports on the Administration of North East India* (1912-22), etc. The list of course is not an exhaustive one.

Apart from the above works, various unpublished works like Political Proceedings, Secret Proceedings, Judicial and Revenue Proceedings, Official Correspondences, Census Reports, Military Reports concerning this area of the British period serve as primary sources for the study of the territory of Arunachal Pradesh. These unpublished documents can be studied in the National Archives, New Delhi; India Office Library and Records, London; West Bengal Government Archives, Kolkata; the Library of the Asiatic Society of Bengal and the National Library, Kolkata; Assam Secretarial Record Office, Itanagar Archive, etc.

Literary Sources of the Post-Colonial Post-Chinese Aggression Period

Even after independence the dominant trend of colonial historiography mentioned above about the tribes living in this frontier region or elsewhere in India took time for a perceptible change. Even upto 1970s such an attitude was clearly manifested in the historiography of this region, whereas in the writings of the sociologists and anthropologists such perceptible changes had occurred already. The historical writings took a broader time-span to adjust with the changing situation. One more point to be noted here is that this was a period of Sino-Indian clashes of 1962 which had aroused a great interest in the history of the North East Frontier Agency and that elicited a spate of writings on the subject and the region.

The post-colonial writings on the area require some reference here. Dr. Verrier Elwin's *A Philosophy for NEFA* (1957), the foreword of which was written by none other than Jawaharlal Nehru, is still considered as a classic on Arunachal Pradesh. His other important works on the state are: *Myths of the North East Frontier of India* (1998); *Democracy in NEFA* (1965) and *The Art of the North East Frontier of India* (1959). H.K. Barpujari's *Problems of the Hill Tribes of North East Frontier* is of immense importance to understand the history of Arunachal Pradesh. S.K. Bhuyan's *Anglo-Assamese Relations* (1949 2nd Edition, 1974) and Laxmi Devi's *Ahom Tribal Relations* (1968) have made considerable contributions in understanding the relationship of the different tribes of Arunachal Pradesh with the Ahom rulers and the people of Assam.

Other works on the state are: C. Von Furler Heimen-dorf, *Ethnographic Notes on the Tribes of the Subansiri Region* (1947); *Himalayan Barbery* (1955); *The Apa Tanis and their Neighbours* (1962); G Graham Bower, *Hidden Land* (1953); N.K. Rustomji, *Tribal Administration in the North East Frontier Agency* (1955), B.K. Roy Burman, *Demographic and Socio-Economic Profiles of the Hill Areas of North East India* (1961); P.N. Luthra, *Constitutional and Administrative Growth of NEFA* (1961); B.C. Chakravarti, *British Relations with the Hill Tribes of Assam Since 1858* (1964); J.N. Choudhury, *Arunachal Panorama* (1973); S.M. Dubey, *Modernization and Elites in Arunachal Pradesh* (1975); D.P. Choudhury, *The North East Frontier of India 1865-1914* (1978); L.N. Chakravarty, *Glimpses of Early History of Arunachal Pradesh* (1979); M.L. Bose, *British Policy in the North East Frontier-Agency* (1979); and *History of Arunachal Pradesh* (1997); Y.A. Raikar and S. Chatterjee, *Archaeology in Arunachal Pradesh;* Subid Chatterjee, *Comprehensive History of Arunachal Pradesh* (1991); Sachin Roy, *Aspects of Padam-Minyong Culture;* S. Dutta, *Students Movements in Arunachal Pradesh* (1998). Here again the list is not an exhaustive one.

The recent books from scholars from among the tribes of Arunachal Pradesh have thrown a lot of light on the history and culture of the region, which may be considered as insiders' scientific views on different aspects of the history and culture of Arunachal Pradesh. Noted among them are T. Nyori, *The History and Culture of the Adis* (New Delhi, 1993); T. Mibang, *The Social Changes among the Tribes of Arunachal Pradesh* (New Delhi, 1995); N.N. Osik, *The Anglo-Adi Relations* (1995).

The Directorate of Research of the Government of Arunachal Pradesh has taken a lead in bringing out various books, booklets and pamphlets on different tribes of the state and their culture, religion, language, etc which are the results of efforts of a group of dedicated Research Officers and Directors of the Department.

CONCLUSION

Since its inception in 1980, the North East India History Association (NEIHA) has been doing a yeoman's job in bringing to light through its proceeding volumes, the scholarly writings of the trendsetters of historiography of North-East India, including Arunachal Pradesh. These writings have provided the young scholars with new themes, perspectives and methodology of interdisciplinary approach, and delineating the research designs so as to have even conventional "sources close to colonial administration with conscious intellectual tuning" to unravel new facts of the history of the region.

The research papers in the NEIHA proceedings on the region show a significant shift from affirmation to negation of the dominant trend of colonial discourse outlined above. In this connection, we may quote from the presidential address of Prof. J.B. Ganguly, one of the prominent economists of the North-East, who has postulated that the colonial interference and the resultant changes have much to do with the "equality and poverty" presently manifesting in the area under discussion.[26] The research papers published in the NEIHA proceedings upto the 15th session on the state of Arunachal Pradesh have been published in an edited volume[27] which can be considered as a mine of information and scientific data for scholars and researchers on the history and culture of Arunachal Pradesh.

One point to be noted here is that most of the modern scholars have studied the political and administrative aspects of the colonial period of this region on traditional lines, viz, by narrating the policy of the British Government towards the tribes of Arunachal Pradesh. But the whole gamut of socio-economic and cultural aspects have yet to get adequate attention. "The migration and transformation of the tribes, their systems of land tenure, their traditional system of law and justice, system of warfare, trend of modernisation in their tradition-bound society, economic transition, impact of the two world wars, and search for identity in the recent scenario of Indian political changes require utmost research-oriented care."[28] Studies on the participation of the tribes in the Freedom Movement of the country and reasons for less-intensification of the movement in the area should also be studied scientifically.

Finally, the Acts, Regulations, etc of the independent Indian Union bearing on Arunachal Pradesh and Parliamentary Papers and decisions changing the status of the territory leading to its establishment as a full-fledged state may be perused for an up-to-date account of the political evolution and development of Arunachal Pradesh.

NOTES AND REFERENCES

1. L.A. Waddell, *The Tribes of the Brahmaputra Valley*, Delhi, 1986, 1st Edn. 1937, pp. 1ff.
2. K.A.A. Raja, 'Arunachal: The Evolution of Personality', *Arunachal News*, June 1975, p. 5.
3. M.L. Bose, *History of Arunachal Pradesh*, New Delhi, 1997, p. 16.
4. Subid Chatterjee, *A Comprehensive History of Arunachal Pradesh*, Calcutta, 1991, pp. 20ff.
5. *Census Report*, 1901, Vol. IV, Part. I, Chapter-XI, p. 120.
6. Chatterjee, *op. cit.*, p. 4.
7. Y.A. Raikar, 'Megaliths at Jamiri', *Arunachal News*, September 1979.
8. Y.A. Raikar and S. Chatterjee, *Archaeology in Arunachal Pradesh*, Shillong 1980,

p. 46; D.K. Bora, 'Archaeological Ruins of Naksa Parvat', Resarun IX, No. I, 1993, pp. 26f.

9. Chatterjee, *op. cit.*, p. 5.
10. E.G. Worman, 'The Neolithic Problem in the Prehistory of India', *Journal of Washington Academy of Sciences*, Vol. 39, No. 6, pp. 181-201.
11. B. Tripathy, *Archaeological Remain of Arunachal Pradesh* (MS).
12. Chattetterjee, *op. cit.*, pp. 5ff.
13. *Ibid.*
14. *Ibid.*, p. 30.
15. William Robinson, *A Descriptive Account of Assam*, p. 325.
16. T. Tomba Singh, 'Folk History and Historiography', *North East India History Association* (NEIHA), Proceeding Volume, 11th Imphal Session, 1990, p. 28.
17. T. Mibang, 'Interpreting History through Ponung', S. Dutta (ed.), *History, Culture and Economy of Arunachal Pradesh*, New Delhi, 1998, p. 34.
18. *Ibid.*, p. 31.
19. Verrier Elwin, *A Philosophy for NEFA*, 1988, p. 212.
20. Chatterjee, *op. cit.*, p. 11.
21. *Fathiyya-I ibbriyya,* Portion Translated by J.N. Sarkar, *Journal of Bihar and Orissa Research Society*, Patna, 1915, pp. l82ff.
22. Amalendu Guha, Presidential Address, *NEIHA Proceedings*, 2nd Session, Dibrugahr, 1981.
23. Verrier Elwin, *India's North East Frontier in the Nineteenth Century*, Madras, 1959, Introduction; Sanghamitra Mishra, 'The Nature of Colonial Intervention in the Naga Hills, 1840-80', *The Economic and Political Weekly*, Vol. XXXIII, 19th December, 1998.
24. B.K. Roy Burman, Prefatory Introduction to the new edition in Alexander Mackenzie, *History of the Relations of Government with the Hill Tribes of the North East Frontier of Bengal*, reprinted as the *North East Frontier of Bengal*, New Delhi, 1995.
25. Amalendu Guha, *op. cit.*
26. J.B. Ganguly, Presidential Address, 7th NEIHA Session, Pasighat, 1986.
27. S. Dutta (ed.), *History, Culture and Economy of Arunachal Pradesh*, Delhi, 1998.
28. P.K. Nayak, Trends in the Historiography of Arunachal Pradesh: A Brief Discussion, S. Dutta (ed.), *op. cit.*, p. 23.

4

Historical Studies of Arunachal Pradesh: An Overview

Amrendra Kr. Thakur

INTRODUCTION

The land and the people of North-East India have caught the attention of writers from ancient period. However, blanket terms like the Kiratas, Nisadas, Asuras, Dwellers on the high mountain ridges, etc of the Vedic and Epic literatures and other accounts of ancient period are unable to satisfy the scholars working on the origin and migration of various tribes of the region and on their identification. The archaeological evidences from the Brahmputra Valley and other areas are also not very helpful in this respect. It is only in the Ahom Buranjis and the Muslim chronicles that they were largely identified. The accounts and reports of the British period regarding the land and people of this region made the research easy for the scholars of independent India. It is in this perspective that this paper has been prepared on the problems and prospects in the historiography of present Arunachal Pradesh. Arunachal Pradesh, erstwhile North East Frontier Agency (NEFA), which spreads over approximately an area of 84000 sq. kms and lying along the southern slopes of the Eastern Himalayas, is bounded by Tibet and China in the north, Assam in the south, Myanmar in the east and Bhutan in the West. It provides today the best example of a cultural continuity that has survived a long and diversified history in which changes have occurred, old images of life have been altered and new elements and influence have been observed and amalgamated, enriching and variegating the cultural strands, without, however, mutilating them, because it lies at the tri-junction of the Indo-Chinese, Indo-Myanmar and the India sub-regions.

HYPOTHESES

The new generation of Indian historians has started reassessing the past with a scientific and unbiased attitude. It has become imperative for the reconstruction of the real history of the Indian people that systematic efforts should be made to prepare the detailed regional history based on various sources through a scientific analysis. The regional history is not a separate entity but a part of the national history. It provides the base for the structure of national history. Its ultimate aim is to explain the regional historical sources, regional variations in historical developments and proper reconstruction of the history of marginalia. The idea of the topography of region, extensive field work, local observations, wide surveys and intimate conversation with its inhabitants are essential requirements for the perfect study of the regional history.[1] Without pursuing this method the picture of the past Indian society will remain incomplete and to some extent confused. Efforts are being made in this direction but a lot is to be done.[2] It is with such ideals that the present paper has been prepared on sources of the history of present Arunachal Pradesh. In this context, it seems important to note that earlier historians working on the regional history of North-East India have also ignored both the regional diversity and the distinct features of different periods, tribes and regions of Arunachal Pradesh.

For the historical reconstruction of Arunachal Pradesh five categories of sources have to be consulted and utilised: (i) unpublished official records (ii) published papers and reports; (iii) modern literature in the form of books and articles in different journals; (iv) oral tradition and field studies; and (v) archaeological evidences. Regarding the relevance of different sources, it would be naturally difficult to pronounce any final judgement. To construct a historical account of Arunachal Pradesh all of them are important and, in fact, should be treated as complementary and supplementary to one another. Any account based on any single primary source could hardly be compete and authentic. These sources should not be tapped in isolation, in the reconstruction of the history in Arunachal Pradesh. For such an undertaking, one must have a forward looking and scientific approach and must formulate theories substantiated by facts. This approach to the handling of sources can alone carry conviction regarding the theories and other basic postulates of the reconstruction of historical past of Arunachal Pradesh. Facts collected from one source should be corroborated by the evidences of other sources and conclusions based on such utilisation of various sources would be factual, scientific and authentic. Such a check-up helps eliminate and differentiate legendary, fictitious, imaginary and motivated portions from the content of the main sources and the remaining part holds well as the ultimate reliable historical truth. Thus, sources should be considered complementary to one another. Studies made on such a model could alone present a comprehensive and balanced picture of the historical past of Arunachal Pradesh.

The published records of various departments provide valuable information on various topics. They are not repetitive in nature but complementary to each other. The records may further be classified as (a) Political Proceedings; (b) Secret Proceedings; (c) Correspondence with the Chief Commissioner, Assam; (d) Foreign Department Consultations; and (e) Tribal Areas Consultations, etc. It is important to mention that certain records preserved by the State Archives, Itanagar of which no copies are found in the National Archives, New Delhi, are a valuable treasure of information. Some records even of the post-independence period are very important for the study of Arunachal Pradesh. Some information is also available in the 19th and 20th century (especially pre-independence period) accounts prepared by or at the instance of the British administrators. While these bits and pieces are very useful, there is still much scope for fresh evaluation. The following accounts deserve mention here: A. Mackenzie's *Memorandum on North-East Frontier of Bengal,* 1869; *History of the Relations of the Government with the Hill Tribes of the North-East Frontier of Bengal,* 1884; Damant's Papers *Relating to the Frontier Tribes of North-East Frontier,* 1855; *the Hill Tracts Between Assam and Burma and on the Upper Brahmaputra,* 1873; R Reid's *History of the Frontier Areas Bordering on Assam (1883-1941),* 1942; L.W. Shakespear's *History of Upper Assam, Upper Burma and the North-East Frontier,* 1914; A. Hamilton's *In Abor Jungles,* 1912; R.B. Pemberton's *Report on the Eastern Frontier of British India,* 1835; Capt. G. Beresford's *Notes on the North- East Frontier of Assam,* 1881; C.U. Aitchison's *A Collection of Treaties, Engagements and Sanads Relating to India and Neighbouring Countries,* (Compiled) Vol.-I 1892. These sources from the British period are truly known for plentitude of facts. Since they suffer from bias and distortions for partisan attitude, they should be handled with caution.[3] Most of these were compiled by the functionaries of the British government and in many cases were creation of arm-chair historians. Above all, linguistic and cultural barriers further widened the gap between the rulers and the ruled. Notwithstanding such drawbacks, the usefulness of these official documents as the source material is immense indeed if used as complementary and supplementary to other sources.

Furthermore, the published works of a number of eminent scholars of social-sciences, administrators-turned-ethnographers or historians or lawyers, etc of post-independence period are significant for any study. These writings can make the cross-checking of the information contained in the government records and papers possible. In addition to the oft-quoted works on Arunachal Pradesh, Verrier Elwin's *A Philosophy for NEFA,* Shillong, 1959; *India's North East Frontier in the Nineteenth Century,* Bombay, 1959; *Myths of North East Frontier Agency,* Shillong, 1959; C. von Furer-Haimendorf's *Himalayan Barbary,* London, 1955; *A Himalayan Tribute: From Cattle to Cash,* Delhi, 1980; *Highlenders of Arunachal Pradesh,* Delhi, 1982; L.N. Chakravarty's *Early History of Arunachal Pradesh,* Shillong, 1954; J.N. Choudhury's *Arunachal Panorama,* Shillong, 1973; *Arunachal Through the Ages: From Frontier Tract to Union Territory,* Shillong, 1982; H.K. Barpujari's *Assam in the Days of the Company 1826-58,* Guwahati, 1980; *Problem of Hill Tribes,* Vol. 1-III; M.L. Bose; *History of Arunachal Pradesh,* New Delhi, 1997; S.K. Bhuyan's *Anglo-Assamese Relations (1771-1826),* Guwahati, 1949; L. Devi's, *Ahom-Tribal Relation,* Guwahati 1976; are quite significant for a historical study of Arunachal Pradesh. Some other important works are Major S.R. Johari's *Where India, China and Burma Meet,* Calcutta, 1962; Sheelendra Kumar's *Law and Administration of Justice in Arunachal Pradesh,* Lucknow, 1982; Chandra Shekhar Panchani's *Arunachal Pradesh: Religion, Culture and Society;* D.P. Choudhury's *The North-East Frontier of India (1865-1914),* Calcutta, 1978; P. Thankappan Nair's *Tribes of Arunachal Pradesh,* Guwahati, 1985; Nair K. Rustomji's *Imperilled Frontiers: India's North-East Borderlands,* New Delhi, 1983; B. Datta Ray's (edited) *The Emergence and Role of Middle Class in North-East India,* New Delhi, 1983; V. Elwin, B. Shastri and I. Simon's (edited) *Important Directives on Administration of NEFA,* Shillong, 1967; N.K. Barooah's *David Scott in North-East India (1802-31): A Study in British Paternalism,* New Delhi, 1970; Leo E. Rose and M.W. Fisher's *The North-East Frontier of India,* Barkley, 1967; D.D. Mali's *Revenue Administration in Assam,* Guwahati, 1985; S.K. Bhuyan's (ed.) *Tungkhungia, Buranji or History of Assam,* O.U.P., 1933; Meena S. Barkataki's *British Administration in North-East India 1826-74,* Delhi, 1985. In addition to these works, numerous articles and papers in various Indian and foreign journals and the proceedings of the *North East India History Association* and *Indian History Congress* and other professional bodies are also very important to be consulted for a systematic account of Arunachal Pradesh. In this regard the materials published in *Resarun, NEFA Information, Arunachal News and Arunachal Review* (Government Publications) are also quite informative. Here it is important to mention that the Chinese aggression brought significant changes in the historiography of Arunachal Pradesh. "It not only baffled the planners and administrators but also the historians and other social-scientists. Arunachal became the cynosure of their inspiration and investigation, the cockpit of historical sources and hypothesis".[4]

Though the classical works on Arunachal Pradesh are very important sources for any of its historical inquiry, they also need cautious use. Such is the case because the pitfalls in the writing of the British rule got adequately reflected in the subsequent writings. To the Europeans tribal people had been nothing but queer and exotic.[5] The necessity of colonial administration, nevertheless, made the bureaucrats study the life and culture of these people fairly intensively. But because of mental preoccupation, the alien subject population, particularly those under colonial subjugation, by and large, appeared only as savage, primitive, barbarous, etc. Lacking the experiences of heterogeneous realities, the very approach to the study of alien tribes became an exercise on cultural isolates. Some of the modern works were not devoid of the inadequacies of the ethnographic studies conducted largely under the influence of the British tradition. We inherited not only concepts, techniques, theories and methods of study but also the topics of study. Thus, studies of various socio-economic institutions of the tribes of Arunachal Pradesh were not very popular till recently. Now a significant trend has been the shift from generalised description of tribes to problem-oriented specialised studies.[6] Rather than being portrayed by an outsider as museum specimen the scholars are providing an insider's view of reality. Instead of encouraging research on esoteric aspects of tribal life by outsiders the systematic investigation of relevant elements of their life are on the card. All these are to provide a true picture of their past, free from any bias and prejudices. These are also to correct the distortions of facts and misrepresentation of reality in the writings of the outsiders.[7] It may be a clarion call in favour of indigenisation of a region.[8]

Though the use of oral data is discouraged by traditional historians in serious historical studies, in the context of Arunachal Pradesh they can be utilised for proper contextual setting. The authenticity of oral source has been doubted in the following lines.[9] "Oral history itself indulgently concerned with tangential issues"; "it locked into the irrelevance of the small scale"; "memory is notoriously unreliable and untrustworthy"; and "the form (of oral evidence) is not fixed, the chronology is frequently imprecise, the communication may frequently be unsupported", etc. Notwithstanding these shortcomings, oral source is a quite useful source for the historical reconstruction of Arunachal because in Arunachal practically there is no native writings. In this regard myths of genesis, family histories of masters and slaves, proverbs, etc can provide significant insider's views of the continuity and change in various social, economic, political and cultural institutions of Arunachal. The oral data has given voice in an humble way, to those who are voiceless in the documentary record.[10] Here oral source is to correct and comprehend other sources and perspective just as much as literary sources correct and comprehend it.

It is important to note that the job of a historian is not only to explain why things happened in the past but also to explain historical continuity of the subject. And presently, this methodology can be practised to study various socio-economic and political institutions. This methodology may be adopted on the line of historical-sociology than that on historical[11] only. To be more specific, the works towards the reconstruction of social history of Arunachal Pradesh can be also credited to the influence of postmodernism than that of the long tradition of objective researches on the marginals by historians.[12]

So far as the utilisation of archaeological source for the reconstruction of history of Arunachal Pradesh is concerned, till recently this branch was not very popular among scholars. Even in the first, seriously planned and well-represented book on the archaeology of North-Eastern India, Arunachal Pradesh remained almost unrepresented.[13] However, the Directorate of Research, Government of Arunachal Pradesh, has done some work as the reporting of some existing monuments scattered mostly in the foothills of Arunachal Pradesh. Reports related to stone tools, Neoliths and Megaliths implements and utensils have also been published almost regularly. Other reported areas have been Hindu shrines and Buddhist monasteries, stupas, etc and forts of Arunachal Pradesh. However, no visible progress is made towards the study of pre-colonial and colonial surface communication archaeology, network of Buddhist monasteries especially as politico-cultural centres and centre of trading activities. The other neglected area is the ethno-archaeology (construction of houses, industries, water and wind mills, weaving and dyeing of clothes, defence mechanism of individual house and village, special defence of the house of the chiefs or the village of the chief, etc). The systematic study of forts will certainly make some breakthrough towards pre-colonial socio-economic and political formation in Arunachal Pradesh. It may point towards the level of urbanisation in the past.[14] Here it is important to mention that some archaeological features, especially the aspects of ethno-archaeology, have witnessed the planned destruction during the British period. For the reconstruction of historical archaeology therfore one has to base the study on text-aided archaeology.[15] However, strong possibility is also in favour of archaeology-aided text.

Victim of Negative Writing

The rule of law has often been considered one of the greatest gifts of the colonial government to this subcontinent. This was the cornerstone of British policy. As far back as 1881, W.W. Hunter surveying England's work in India, envisioned a more secure, more prosperous India, where roads, railways, bridges, canals, schools and hospitals had been built; famines tackled, *thugi*, *dakaiti* and predatory castes suppressed; trade developed; barbaric social practices like widow-burning and infanticide abolished, for the relationship between itinerant and sedentary communities has always been not just problematic but bound together in a kind of mutual antagonism. Vagrancy, wanderlust, lack of stability and general purpose in life, restlessness and aimlessness – these are accusations that plague all itinerant communities. Nomadic communities are notoriously difficult to control and govern, to administer or tax. They were also romanticised in imagination and were feared and shunned as ferocious criminals and yet eulogised for their supposedly healthy outdoor life and independent spirit.[16] There were, thus, only negative recollections of their historic memory before the settlement and now only gratitude for what had been perpetrated on them by the Salvation Army.

The report mentioned below is clearly indicative of this negative writing on Arunachal Pradesh. It has reported[17] that "For the capturing of men and *mithun* has proved so easy a means of acquiring wealth, that Licha (a Nishi village) is not likely to forego the fruits unparalleled reputation in war... they boast openly of the non-fulfillment of their trade obligations. They intimidate not the Apa Tanangs (Apatanis) but also the Dafalas (Nishis) of the Upper Khru Valley, threatening to capture anyone who come southwards..."

Some reported cases of involvement of Licha in the capturing of men and *mithun* is important enough to be mentioned here. "Four years ago Nada Dezang of Haja went to look after his exphasis grazing Jorum and was captured by Licha men in the forest. He was kept by Dogur Teji and Techi Teji, two brothers, for one month in stocks. Pura Tope of Haja and Sarbi Toko, a Dafla of Toko, went to Licha and arranged the release for the ransom of one woman slave, one Tibetan bell, one brass plate and two daos... five years ago Kaso Peshe of Haja was captured by men of Licha. He is still held captive in Licha... Pura Tada of Haja was captured last year by Lichi Tada of Licha.

"Twenty years ago Licha Tajan... came to Duta as a friend and was offered hospitality by Koje Roza of Duta, where he married a girl from Gemi and had two sons. One day he killed a *mithun* in a hunting accident belonging to Doin Tanan of Haja. Roza agreed to pay the compensation to Doin Tanan if Tajan worked as his slave until the debt was paid... Tajan and his family members worked as slave for seventeen years until they left Duta never to return or never to repay his debt telling Roza that they were going to his wife's family, now living in Toko...

"Five years ago Lida Tegi of Licha came to Duta with a Dafla girl to whom he was not married and sought refuge in the house of Koji Roza... While hunting Tegi killed a *mithun* cow belonging to Dani Taga of Haja mistaking it for a wild pig. Roza paid compensation, thinking that sooner or later he would be able to make the Daflas his slaves. The compensation was 1 *mithun* bull, 1 cow, 5 seers salt, 4 Apa Tanang daos, 3 piece pork ... Five years ago Padi Layen of Bela sold a Dafla slave, Bamu Bada of Pemir, whom he had originally acquired in compensation for outstanding debts of rice, to Taga of Licha for 1 *mithun* cow and calf, 1 peace of cloth, 1 big pig...." Some of the above cited cases are from the sixty-three reported cases in which the Licha village was the aggressor. However, this is not the end of the phenomenon.

It is reported, "Some ten years ago, Haja and Duta joined in a raid against Linia and also joined by some men of the Dafla village of Jorun Linia had angered the Apa Tanangs by continually stealing their *mithun* and Jorum men by giving shelter to runaway slaves.... They decided to raid.... The raiders captured three women and one boy, the wives and child of Linia Buda. The women were subsequently ransomed, but the boy now lives as a slave in Haja." Last but not the least is another incident quoted to clearly understand the phenomenon. It has been reported, "Bela is, on the other hand, on friendly terms with Linia, but has an old feud with Dadun, a village north of Linia; many men of Bela have been captured by Dadun and many mithun stolen.... Several times peace treaties (dapo) were concluded, but the Apa Tanangs maintain that they were always broken by Dadun. Four years ago twenty men of the Reru Khel of Bela in conjunction with ten Daflas of Linia raided one of the settelments at Dadun and captured ten women and ten children.... Four other men and two boys were ransomed, but the people of Dadun made no attempt to ransom the other captive; they were all sold—some to Licha, some to Toko and Jorum and some to Table south of Panir River."

Dangerous Generalisation

In case of Arunachal Pradesh also we see that some distortions in the form of wrong generalisations are taking place because of lack of sufficient knowledge of regional variations of the North-East India on one hand and the tribes and regions of Arunachal Pradesh on the other. The opinion of BP Singh that, "All the tribes and sub-tribes have a profound distrust of and antipathy towards outsiders" is not based on objective analysis of socio-economic and political facts. It may be a fact for a few tribes and sub-tribes of this region but such a general observation for the whole region is not healthy for the social fabric. In Arunachal Pradesh non-tribals have become a part and parcel of the society and one of the important factors in the economic growth of the area. Another general remark by the same writer, about North-East India is also applicable to the social life of Arunachal Pradesh. He writes, ... in the foreseeable future in tribal factor, the relationship between Assamese-Hindus and Bengali-Hindus and Assamese-Hindus and Bengali-Muslims will dominate the cultural equations and politics of North-East India." Such type of socio-cultural polarisation is completely absent in Arunachal Pradesh. In an opinion directly meant for Arunachal Pradesh he writes, "There is no aristocracy in Arunachal Pradesh...."[18] The above observation of B.P. Singh is not correct because it has rightly been said regarding almost all tribes of Arunachal Pradesh that their society consisted of ... the chief, of nobles, the middle classes and slaves".[19]

It is needless to point out that such remarks are the outcome of the influence of colonial writers. In another book Singh has ignored the well-deserved aspects of culture, state and trade of North-Eastern India.[20] This theme has been discussed in detail in the context of pre-colonial Arunachal Pradesh on some other occasions by me.[21]

The impact of colonial historiography on the Indian historians was such that they also endorsed the approaches of imperial historians in their writings. On the basis of the review of the books observes Lahiri, "...gradually the whole of the North-eastern Fontier containing a variety of races and sub-races not to be found elsewhere in India was brought within *the pale of the enlightened British Administration*"[22] (emphasis added). The approach of Lahiri is also clearly expressed in the conclusion to one of his chapters, "Such was the country (Assam) that came under the possession of the East India Company after the treaty of Yandabo and here, truly speaking, for the first time in their long annals of victory and conquest in vast sub-continent of India the British seemed to step in as saviours rather than as conquerors. But Assam was a liability rather than an asset – the British Government had taken over a country with a meagre income, a scanty population and a troublesome frontier beyond which dwell a predatory neighbour." Thus, in view of Lahiri too, hill people have been troublesome and predatory to Assam. H.K. Barpujari worked extensively in his lifetime on the lines of "Problem of Hill Tribes".

Conclusion

On the basis of the above discussion, by way of conclusion it can be suggested that the influence of the colonial historiography was so immense that earlier generation of scholars working on the reconstruction of the history of Arunachal Pradesh could not think on different lines. The impact can be clearly seen over the first planned publication of government of Arunachal Pradesh on the early history of the area.[23] It mentions that "Nothing is known definitely about the conditions prevailing in the 18th century and prior to that, in the area lying to the north of Darrang," and almost similar views have also been expressed for the people of other areas. The opinion of K.A.A. Raja, the first Lt. Governor of Arunachal Pradesh has also colonial overtone. He writes, "Numerous communities in the earlier stages of material culture had moved away, over centuries, into these hills. They moved in batches and stages depending on the pressure exerted. Each batch was self-contained and lost contact with the present stock and related groups in the course of migration. Every fresh arrival pushed those that followed it, from place to place, till they all reached their present habitats. These movements accelerated and intensified the diversification.[24] A similar view has been expressed by L.A. Waddell during pre-independence period. He writes, "Driven into these wild glens by the advance of civilisation up the plains and lower valleys, these people have become hemmed- in among the mountains, where pressing on each other in their struggle for existence, they have developed into innumerable isolated tribes." Hence, it is high time to come out of the canopy of the colonial historiography and present an objective, scientific, secular insider's view of reality based upon the sources from "field to archives". The studies should also be in aid of the related concepts and theories and be linked with a critical appraisal of the stratification of literary materials and interpreted in conjunction with archaeological and anthropological evidences.

NOTES AND REFERENCES

1. For details of the importance of regional studies in reconstructing the true history, see the articles of V.C.P. Choudhury and some others in S. Katharine's (ed.), *Primary Printed and Manuscript for Sixteenth Nineteenth Century Studies Available in Bengal, Orissa and Bihar Libraries*, Calcutta, 1970, V.C.P. Choudhury *et al.* (ed.), *Indian Historiography: An International Controversy* (Hindi), Patna, 1982; C. Sharma (ed.), *Parochialism in Historiography* (Hindi), Patna, 1986, V.C.P. Choudhury, A.K. Thakur *et al.*, (ed.), *Swami Sahajanand Saraswati: From Religion to Revolution*, Patna, 1990 and A.K. Thakur, *India and the Afghans: A Study of Neglected Region*, pp. 1370-1576, Patna, 1992.
2. Some stray articles reflecting upon the various aspects of the past life of the people of Arunachal Pradesh have been coming up in proceedings and journals of various organisations and institutions associated with historical studies during the last decade or so. In addition, the Department of Research, Government of Arunachal Pradesh and many independent researchers in good number have published the ethnographic accounts dealing mainly with existing or just extinct features of life. However, very few comprehensive problem-oriented accounts, using the tools and techniques of other sister-disciplines too, have come up as yet.
3. For details see B.K. Roy Burman, the Prefactory Introduction to the New Edition of A. Mackenzie's *History of the Relations of Government with the Hill Tribes of the North East*

Frontier of Bengal, New Delhi, 1979 (1884), pp. 1-13. And the article of A.K. Thakur, *Historiography of Arunachal Pradesh: Problem and Perspective, Proceedings of North-East India History Association* (hereafter *PNEIHA*), Jagiroad Session, 1991, reproduced also in S. Dutta's (ed.), *Studies in the History, Economic, and Culture of Arunachal Pradesh*, Delhi, 1997, pp. 26-30.

4. P.K. Nayak, "Trends in the Historiography of Arunachal Pradesh: A Brief Discussion", *PNEIHA*, Shillong Session, 1993, reproduced also in S. Dutta (ed.), *op. cit.*
5. The same can also be found in A. Mackenzie's *The North East Frontier of Bengal*, Mittal, New Delhi, 1995 (*History of the Relations of Government with the Hill Tribes of the North East Frontier of Bengal*, Calcutta, 1884), pp. 367-68. The predisposing cause of the Aka raid of 1883-84 must be sought apparently in certain forest and boundary grievances; but the raid arose directly out of the Calcutta Industrial Exhibition. In fact, the Deputy Commissioner of Darrang deputed Lakhidhar, the Mauzadar of Baleepara to procure for the Exhibition specimens of agricultural and other implements of the Akas and to persuade some tribesmen to come down to be modeled. Lakhidhar, along with a servant and twelve elders and ryots of Baleepara, went straight to the Midhi's village and told Midhi that he had been sent to take down to Calcutta 'a Raja and a Rani with all their ornaments', for which he was ready to pay. The Akas hated Lakhidhar because he was also present when boundary of the Aka country was being demarcated in 1875 which was highly objectionable to the Akas. Anyway, the Akas professed to be furious at this demand alleging that they had given ornament on former occasions and they had only been partly paid; while the idea of sending a Raja and a Rani to the show was intolerable to them. Charging the Mauzadar with being the man who had robbed them of their land, sent him and his servant under guard to another village and kept them in confinement; and Ajit K. Danda, Tribal Enthography ICSSR, New Delhi, 1996.
6. For details see David R. Syiemlieh's *Survey of Research in History of North East India 1970-1990*, New Delhi, 2000; Ajit K. Danda, *op. cit.* And the introduction of A.K. Thakur, *Slavery in Arunachal Pradesh*, I.C.S.S.R. Project, 1999 (under publication).
7. For example, J.B. Bhattarcharjee's contention that 'the tribes of Arunachal Pradesh in India's North-East Frontier who did not experience state-building before the British colonisation in the last century...' (*Technology, Social Formation and Historical Inquiry*, Presidential Address, XVII Indian Social Science Congress, Bangalore, 1993) and K.S. Singh's attempt to universalise the elements of tribal state formation in India ("State Formation in Tribal Society: Some Preliminary Observations", *Journal of Indian Anthropological Society*, 6, 1971; have been contradicted by A.K. Thakur's "Peasantisation and State Formation in Arunachal Pradesh", *Proceedings of Indian History Congress* (hereafter PIHC), Bangalore, 1997; and 'state formation in Arunachal Pradesh" *NEHU Journal of Humanities and Social Science*, 1-1 1998. Further B.P. Singh's description of ehtnic problems of North-East India and specific observation on tribal society of Arunachal Pradesh (*The Problems of Change: A Study of North-East India*, OUP, 1987 and 147) have been proved to be wrong by A.K. Thakur's "Historiography of Arunachal Pradesh": *PNEIHA* 1991 and some other distortions in the

historiography of Arunachal Pradesh have been exposed by P.K. Nayak's "Trends in the historiography of Arunachal Pradesh": *PNEIHA* 1993. B.N. Jha through his paper "Politics of Posha: A Case Study of Pre and Post Independence Scenario in Arunachal Pradesh and Assam", *PIHC,* Madras Session, 1996, has proved wrong the claim of S.N. Mishra that 'Posha ... was finally abolished towards the end of the nineteenth century' in his article "Private Property Formation Among the Highland Tribal Communities of North-East India", Social Science Probings, Vol-X, No. 4, 1987, p. 386 and some details by the same author,"Arunachal Tribal Economic Formation and Their Dissolution", *Economic and Political Weekly,* XVIII, 42, 22nd October 1983.

8. Yogesh Atal, "The Call for Indigenisation", *International Social Science Journal,* Vol. XXXIII, No. 1, 1981.
9. For details see P. Thomson, "The Voice of the Past: Oral History", Oxford, 1978, J. Vansina, *Oral Tradition as History,* Madison, 1985, D. Henige, *The Chronology of Oral Tradition: Quest for a Chimera,* Oxford, 1974 and an article by G. Prins, "Oral Tradition".
10. P. Thomson, *op. cit.,* and Bernard S. Cohn, *An Anthropologist Among The Historians and Other Essays,* Delhi, 1996 (first published in 1987), pp. 24 and 73.
11. For details of this approach see Bernard S. Cohn, *op. cit.,* Victoria E. Bonnel, "The Uses of Theory, Concepts and Comparison in Historical Sociology", *Comparative Studies in Society and History,* Vol. 22, 1980 and E.P. Thompson, "Folklore Anthropology and Social History", *Indian Historical Review,* Vol - III, No. 2, Jan. 1977.
12. For details of the two schools see Peter N. "Social History: Encountering Postmodernism", *Journal of Social History,* Vol. 24, 1990; Elizabeth A. Smith and Ellen Somekawa, "Theorizing the Writing of History Or, I Can't Think Why It Should be so Dull, For a Great Deal of It Must be Invention", *Journal of Social History,* Vol. 22, 1988; John E. Toews, "Intellectual History after the Linguistic Turn: The Anatomy of Meaning and the Irreducibility of Experience", *American Historical Review,* 92, 1987, pp. 879-907; and the response, Richard H. Brown, "Positivism, Relativism, and Narrative in the Logic of the Historical Sciences", pp. 908-20, M.P. Foucault, *Marxism and History: Mode of Production versus Mode of Information,* Cambridge, U.K., 1984.
13. For details see J.P. Singh and Gautam Sengupta (ed.), "Archaeology of North Eastern India", New Delhi, 1991 and similar treatment of the aspects of archaeology has been given by T. Mibang in his article "Priorities in Historical Research" in Gurudas Das (ed.), *Research Priorities in North East India with Special Reference to Arunachal Pradesh,* New Delhi, 1991.
14. The discovery of about 250 coins of different sizes and denominations belonging most probably to the rulers of the Shah dynasty of Bengal from Bhalukpong fort complex, the gateway to Bomdila, Seppa and Tawang can also be an important pointer in this regard. Most likely, it served as central place of contact between the traders of Bengal and Assam on the one hand and Arunachal Pradesh, Bhutan and Tibet on the other. For details of the coins, see the Letter No. BPG/DEV/B/10/98

dated 24-8-1998 from the EAC, Bhalukpong to the Director of Research, Itanagar. Some other details can be found in my articles on trade in pre-colonial period discussed elsewhere.

15. For details see A.K. Thakur's "Text Aided Archaeological Study of Village Defence Technology of Arunachal Pradesh" paper presented during the North East India History Association, Tezpur Session, 2001.
16. For details of the approach see Meena Radhakrishna, *Dishonoured By History: Criminal Tribes and British Colonial Policy,* Hyderabad, 2001; S. Abraham, "Steal or I'll Call you a Thief: Criminal Tribes of India", *Economic and Political Weekly,* July 3, 1999, pp. 1751-53 and reviews of books by Rudolf C. Heredia in Seminar No. 508, pp. 59-61.
17. For details see "Notes on the Relation between Apa Tanis and Their Neighbours", NEFA Administration Branch, A File No. Tribal, pp. 155-144.
18. For details see A.K. Thakur, "Historiography of Arunachal Pradesh in the Context of Medieval India Historiography", *op. cit.*
19. For details see V. Elwin, *Philosophy for NEFA, op. cit.,* p. 9, and A.K. Thakur, *Slavery in Arunachal Pradesh, op. cit.*
20. *India's Culture: The State, the Art and Beyond,* Delhi, 2001, 1998, pp. 58-65.
21. A.K. Thakur, "Pattern of Pre-Colonial Trade and Polity Formation in Arunachal Pradesh: A Study of Their Relationship", *PNEIHA,* Imphal Session, 2000; item, "Pre-Colonial Trade in Arunachal Pradesh: A Reconstruction of Economic History" accepted for publication in the *RESARUN,* Vol. XXVII, (Directorate of Research, Government of Arunachal Pradesh, Itanagar), and item, "Trade Culture and State: Interaction and Impact in Pre-Colonial Arunachal Pradesh", paper presented during the Indian History Congress, 62nd Session, Bhopal, 2001.
22. R.M. Lahiri, *The Annexation of Assam,* Calcutta, 1994, 1954, pp. ix and 31.
23. L.N. Chakraborty, *Glimpses of the Early History of Arunachal Pradesh,* Itanagar, 1989, 1973, pp. 1, 36 and 53-54.
24. K.A.A. Raja, "Arunachal: The Evolution of Personality", *Arunachal News,* June 1975, p. 5.

5

The Sources of the History of Pre-Ahom Assam: A Survey

D.K. Ganguly

The historian, engaged in the reconstruction of the history of pre-Ahom Assam, handicapped as he is by the total absence of a historical chronicle, has to depend upon traditional sources like literary works, both indigenous and foreign, and archaeological materials, in the shape of inscriptions, finds, through exploration and excavation, and coins.

Indigenous Literary Works

Of the indigenous literary works mention may be made of *Śāṅkhāyana Gṛhyasaṅgraha*[1] which is supposed by some scholars[2] to refer to Kāmarūpa as the land of sunrise. It is, however, pointed out by competent authorities that the term 'Prāgjyotisa' as used in this text, does not signify a territorial unit but means "before the appearance of any light", and as such, it is difficult to find any reference to Assam in the text, in question. Similarly, the view of P.C. Choudhury, ascribing the origin of the name of Kāmarūpa to as early as the time of the *Gopatha Brāhmaṇa* is likely to be repudiated in the light of the fact that the mention of Kāmarūpa, as a territory, is conspicuous by its absence in this *Brāhmaṇa* work.

A well-known legend of the *Śatapatha Brāhmaṇa* tells us that king Videgha Māthava, along with his priest Gotama Rāhūgna passed from River Sarasvatī to the land of Videha, after having crossed the Sādanirā, Sāyana, while commenting on the relevant passage of this Vedic text, has identified the Sādanirā with the Karatoyā. The story of Videgha Māthava as recorded in the *Śatapatha Brāhmaṇa*, has accordingly been interpreted by some scholars as pointing to the spread of Aryan culture to the east of the Karatoyā which is known to have been the traditional boundary of ancient Kāmrūpa in the west. But *Śatapatha Brāhmaṇa* is explicit enough to suggest that the Sādanīrā from the western boundary of Videha, which has unanimously been located by scholars in North Bihar, and not of Kāmrūpa or Prāgjyotisa. River Sādanīrā is, in all probability, the same as the modern Gandak which rises in Nepal and joins the Ganges near Patna. The episode of Videgha Māthava as narrated in the *Śatapatha Brāhmaṇa* is not likely to shed any light upon the ancient history of Assam.

Bilhana's *Vikramāṅkadeva-carita*, dated about AD 1085, refers to the total annihilation of the prowess of the king of Kāmrūpa *(ūnmulita-Kāmrūpa-pati)* by Vikramāṅkadeva of the Cālukya dynasty during the reign of his father around the middle of 11th century AD. This king of Assam has been tentatively identified with Pala king Harsapāla.

The *Mahābhārata* mentions Bhagadatta as the king of Prāgjyotisa and associates him with the Cinas *(Cīnaiś-ca)*, the Kirātas *(Kiratāiś-ca)* and the dwellers of the sea-shore *(sāgar-ānūpa-vāsinath)* but is clear enough to suggest that besides Bhagadatta, there were other rulers *(mleccha-nrpatīn)* in this part of eastern India, to the other side of the River Lauhitya *(Lauhityam-agamat balī)* identified with the Brahmaputra.

The *Kiskindhyā Kānda* of the *Rāmāyaṇa* refers to Naraka's city of Prāgjyotisa as being situated on the Varaha mountain, and surrounded by the deep sea *(agadhe varun - alaye)*. The suggestion that the *Ādi Kānda* of the *Rāmāyaṇa* speaks of Amūrtarāja as the founder of the city of Prāgjyotisa is hardly compatible with the Bombay edition of the text where there is hardly any reference to Prāgjyotisa or to Amūrtarāja. But this and other account of the epics belong more to the domain of mythology than sober history.

The *Arthaśāstra* of Kautilya does not make any mention of Kāmarūpa and Prāgjyotisa but speaks of a variety of perfumes and articles that include Jongaka, Pārasamudraka, Grāmeruka, Suvarṇakudyaka, Pāurṇadvīpaka, Pāra-Lauhityaka and Āntarvātyaka, which as the commentator Bhattasvāmī would make us believe, were all manufactured in the places by the same names in Assam. Suvarnakudya has been identified with the village of Sonakudiha situated in Kamrupa district, Assam. Both Pāra-Lauhitya *(Pāra-Lauhityakam Kāmarūpe Lauhity-*

ākhya-nada-pāra-bhavam) and Āntarvatya *(Āntarvātyam Kāmarūpesu eva Antarvaty-ākhya-nadī-tīra-Jātam)* are supposed to be situated on the banks of the rivers Brahmaputra and Antarvati in Assam, respectively.

Kālidāsa, who is usually placed by scholars in 4th-5th centuries AD refers to both Prāgjyotisa and Kāmarūpa in his *Raghuvamsā*[16] where Raghu, in the course of his expedition *(digvi-jaya)*, is said to have crossed the river Lauhitya *(tīrna-Lauhitye)*, made the king *(Prāgjyotis-eśvarah)* tremble *(Cakampe)*, and induced the lord of Kāmarūpa *(Kāmarūp-eśvarah)* to pay him homage, and worship the shadow of his feet with flowers, made of jewels *(ratna-pusp opahārena Chāyām-ānarca pādayoh)*. B.S. Upadhyaya[17] and M.M. Sharma[18] have taken the term Kāmarūpa in the sense of the territory to the east of River Brahmaputra and the word Prāgjyotisa as the name of the capital city of the kingdom of Kāmarūpa. P.C. Choudhury[19] has interpreted the term Prāgjyotisa as signifying the same kingdom as Kāmarūpa. Since Prāgjyotisa is known to have been the name of both a capital city[20] (*tatah Prāgjyotisākhy-eyam pure Śakra-purī-samā*) and a kingdom[21] (*Prāgjyotisesu Durjyay-ākhyam puram-adyh-uvāsa*) it is extremely difficult to decide which of the two suggestions is preferable to the other. Kālidāsa's description, highlighting Raghu's conquest of the Brahmaputra Valley, does not help us at all in ascertaining the political condition of Kāmarūpa at about 4th- 5th centuries AD, although the light it sheds upon the historical geography of Assam of the period is interesting.

Casual references to Prāgjyotisa or Kāmarūpa may be encountered in a Puranic work. The *Vāyu Purāṇa*[22] mentions Prāgjyotisa as an eastern territory but refers to Lauhitya as a *tīrtha,* situated on the banks of River Vaitarani. The *Brahmānda Purāṇa*[23] mentions Prāgjyotisa as a kingdom. The *Markandeya Purāṇa*[24] mentions Prāgjyotisa and Lauhiutya as two territorial units *(Prāgjyotisa sa-Lauhiutyah)*, and describes the former as an eastern territory *(pracya-janapadah)*. Mention is made in the same Purāṇa of a city called Vijaya on a hill *(nag-opari)* in Kāmarūpa *(Kāmarūpe)* in the east *(prācya)*. There is, moreover, a reference to a forest called Guruvisāla in Kāmarūpa, and the forest is eulogised for its suitability for sun-worship. It is far from being clear from this short description on them, to be found in the *Mārkandeya Purāṇa,* whether Prāgjyotisa and Kāmarūpa denote two distinct regions or one and the same territory in eastern India. The *Garuda Purāṇa*[25] mentions Kāmarūpa as a great centre of pilgrimage, being presided over by Goddess Kāmākya *(Kāmarūpam mahātīrtham Kamakhya yatra tiathati)*. The *Skanda Purāṇa*[26] in its chapter entitled *Kumārikā Khanda,* refers to Prāgjyotisa. An objective analysis of these and other Purāṇic references to Prāgjyotisa, Kāmarūpa, Lauhitya, Kāmākhyā, etc is likely to reveal some interesting details about the historical geography and relations with the early history of Assam.

The *Bṛhatsaṁhitā* of Varāhamihira, assigned to about 5th century AD in the *Kūrma-vibhāga* section,[27] refers to Prāgjyotisa and Lauhitya as two contiguous territories, and the *Graha-Bhakti* section mentions Prāgjyotisa along with Magadha, Cīna and Kāmboja.

The *Harṣacarita*[28] of Bānabhatta, attributed to the early part of 7th century AD tells us how Bhāskaravarman's emissary Hamsavega visited the camp of Harsavardhana with varieties of gifts, described his master's lineage and disclosed his king's desire to form a perpetual alliance with the Pusyabhuti ruler who gladly accepted the proposal and expressed a desire to meet his new ally. Here, the description of the gifts serves as an invaluable evidence of the economic history of ancient Assam; the genealogy, as presented by Hamsavega, favourably compares with what is furnished in the epigraphic records of the Varmans, and the formation of the political alliance between the Pusyabhutis and the Varmans proved to be an event of great magnitude for the political history of North India.

Rajāśekhara, who flourished in 9th century AD, in his *Kāvyamīmamsā*[29] mentions Prāgjyotisa as a city and Kāmarūpa as a mountain. In his *Karpūramnjari*[30] he refers to Kāmarūpa as being conquered by the Pratihara monarch Mahendrapāla of Kanauj but this may be a panegyrical glorification by a court-poet, for the Pratihara invasion of Assam is not corroborated by any definite evidence.

Grouped under the category of the *Upa-Purāṇas*, the *Kālika Purāṇa*, composed in Assam in or around 10th century AD, contains invaluable materials about the religion, society, state-craft, historical geography, etc of Assam in particular, and India in general, and lays special emphasis on the worship of the Mother Goddess Kāmākhyā. It refers to Kāmarūpa as triangular in shape *(trikoman)*, 100 *yojanas* in length *(yojan-aika-śat-āyatam)*, and 30 *yojanas* in breadth *(trimśat-yojana-vist iranam)*, extending from River Karatoyā in the west (Karatoyā *-nadī -pūrabam*) to the *pītha* of Dikkaravāsini in the east *(yāagd-Dikkaravāsinīm)*. The *pītha* of Dikkaravāsinī is usually located at or near Sadiya in Upper Assam. The information that *Kālikā Purāna* supplies about the political history of ancient Assam can hardly be treated as authentic.

Bilhana's *Vikramānkadeva-Carita*, written in AD 1085, refers to the total annihilation of the prowess of the king of Kāmarūpa[31] *(ūnmulta-Kāmarūpa-nrpati)* by Prince Vikramāđitya VI of the Cālukya dynasty during the reign of his father, Someśvara I. As Someśvara I died before the return of his victorious son, the expedition, in all probability, occurred not long before AD 1068. The king of Assam has been tentatively identified with the Pāla king Harsapāla.[32]

An interesting sidelight into the topography of ancient Kāmarūpa is, likewise, shed by the *Yogin Tantra* which defines the land as extending from River Karatoyā in the west *(Karatoyā tu paścime)* to River Diksu, identified with a stream near the modern town of Sibsagar in the east (*tīrtha-śrestha-Diksunadī pūrvasyām*) and from the Kaṅja mountain in the north (*uttarasyām Kaṅjagiri*) to the confluence in the south (*sangamavadhih*). The identification of the Kaṅja mountain still baffles a definite solution, and the location of the 'confluence'[33] still remains uncertain. Far more important is, however, the account that it preserves in detail, as regards the cult of the Mother Goddess and numerous Tantric rites and practices that gained momentum in eastern India from about 8th century AD onwards.

Foreign Accounts

Of the foreign authors whose writings are supposed to throw light upon the history of ancient Assam, notice may be taken of the anonymous author of the *Periplus of the Erythraean Sea* (1st century AD) and the Greek geographer Ptolemy (2nd century AD) who have mentioned in their respective works numerous names of hills, rivers, places and peoples of eastern India in Greek terms which have not yet been satisfactorily identified with the local names. One such name is 'Kirrhadae', mentioned by the author of the *Periplus* and 'Ptolemy' as the name of a tribe which was engaged in the trade of gold and malabathrum. Attempts have been made to identify the Kirrhadae with the Kiratas of Assam, and it is held that in ancient times gold came chiefly from the river washings in Assam and North Myanmar, and that malabathrum was produced in the tracts, including the eastern coast of the Brahmaputra estuary. It is worth noticing in this context that the ancient Kirata people were not confined to Assam alone but were scattered over a large area in eastern India. Further, the account of the *Periplus* seem to imply that the Kirrhadae tribe lived in a tract to the west of the river Ganges. Similarly, the attempt to associate the gold coins, called Kaltis in the *Periplus* and the tribe called Colubae by pliny, with the so-called Kalitas of Assam, as has been done by P.C. Choudhury[34] is not likely to meet with the general acceptance in the community of scholars.

Of the Chinese works reflecting the condition of Assam, reference may be made to the account of a Chinese political agent named Chang K'ien who speaks of a trade route through eastern India, connecting Bactria in Afghanistan with South China in the 2nd century BC. It was through this route that silk and bamboo-flutes were exported from China for their markets in India and the western world.

The Shung-Shu[35] which covers the period from AD 420 – 479, record the dispatch of two embassies from India to China of which one was sent by Yu-chai in AD 428 from the Kapili Valley. The Kapili Valley corresponds to the present

Nowgong region of Assam and its king has been identified with Kalyānavarman[36] (AD 420-40) of the Varman dynasty. This account implies the existence of an overland route, connecting eastern India with South China through the hills of Assam and upper Myanmar, thus corroborating the testimony of Chang-k'ien who spoke of the same trade route about five centuries earlier.

Of the Chinese work, throwing light upon the history of Assam, the *Si-yu-ki,* compiled by the celebrated Chinese pilgrim Xuan Zang, stands out prominently, thanks to its rich contents on the multi-faceted condition of this part of the Indian subcontinent of 7th century AD. Reference to the land, its king and people, the Chinese pilgrim who came to Kāmarūpa (Ka-mo-p'o) after having crossed River Karatoyā (Ka-lo-ta) about AD 643 observes, "The country was low and moist; the crops were regular; the jack-fruit and coconut were in great esteem, though plentiful; there were continuous streams and tanks in the towns; the climate was genial. The people were of honest ways, small of stature; their speech differed a little from that of mid-India ... they worshipped the Devas and did not believe in Buddhism. So there had never been a Buddhist monastery in the land ... the Deva temples were some hundreds in number and the various systems had some myriads of professed adherents. The reigning king who was a Brahmin by caste and a descendant of Narayana Deva, was named Bhaskaravarman, his other name being Kumāra (youth) ... the sovereignty had been transmitted in the family and his subjects for 1000 generations. His Majesty was a lover of learning and his subjects followed his example; men of ability came from far-off lands to study here; though the king was not a Buddhist he treated accomplished Sramanas with respect."[37]

While evaluating the statements of Xuan Zang it is to be borne in mind what the Chinese pilgrim has said requires to be corroborated by other sources before it is accepted as authentic. However, his references to Bhaskaravarman's Brahmin lineage, an unbroken one thousand generations of kingship of the Varman family and non-existence of Buddhism in Assam of the period of his visit have unquestionably resulted from his mistaken conception of things that detracts, to some extent, the merit of his otherwise invaluable observation on the political, social, religious and economic condition of Assam of 7th century AD.

The *Life*[38] by Xuan Zang, compiled by the pilgrim's disciple Hwui-li, contains many interesting statements about Bhaskaravarman and his relations with his Pusyabhuti contemporary Harsavardhana, on the one hand, and the illustrious Chinese pilgrim, on the other. Bhaskaravarman's threat to reduce the Nalanda monastery to ashes if its patriarch Silabhadra would not send the Chinese pilgrim to his court, and the Kāmarūpa king's journey in the company of Zuen Zang, along the Ganges to meet the Pusyabhuti king at Kajangala near Rajmahal, as recorded in the *Life,* may be taken as a proof of Bhaskaravarman's political hold over parts of Bengal even during the lifetime of Harsavardhana, consequent upon Śaśaṅka's death, sometime after AD 620.

Interesting light upon the diplomatic alliance between Harsavardhana and Bhaskaravarman is, likewise, shed by the *She-Kia-fang-che,* composed by Tao-si-yan, a disciple of Zund Zang when it, while referring to King Harsa, states, "So the king with Kumārāja (ie Bhāskaravarman of Kāmarūpa) destroyed (subdued ?) the heretical King Śaśaṅka, his army and his followers."[39]

The works in Arabic and Persian have, likewise, proved to be useful to the reconstruction of early history of Assam. References to Kāmru ie Kāmarūpa, are sketchy in Alberuni's *India* which refers to the region as lying far to the east of Kanauj and containing mountains "which stretch away as far as the sea."[40]

The Persian text Tabaqāt-i-Nāsirī,[41] written by Minhajuddin Siraj, traces the history of the Muhammadan dynasties of Asia, in general, and India, in particular, from the beginning of the 9th to the middle of 13th century AD. The chief interest of the work, in the context of the history of Assam, centres round its account of the successive invasions of Bakhtiyar Khilji in AD 1205-06; Ghiasuddīn Iwaz in AD 1226; Nāsiruddīn, the son of Iltutmish, in AD 1228; and Malik Yazbak in AD 1256-57. The work further provides us with an interesting piece of information that horses in large numbers were imported to Assam and Bengal from Tibet through mountain passes.

Riyāz-us-salātīn,[42] compiled by Ghulam Hussain Salim in Persian, preserves an account of Bakhtiyar Khilji's unsuccessful expedition in Assam in AD 1205-06.

Of the Tibetan texts Lāmā Tāranātha's seventeenth century work on the history of Budhism is found to contain some stray references to the political and religious conditions of ancient Assam. Thus there are references to the Pāla king Dharmāpala's subjugation of Assam, Ditīka's introduction of Buddhism in this region, Aśvaghosa's triumph over some local Buddhist scholars in Kāmarūpa and the popularity of the solar cult in this part of the country prior to the spread of Buddhism. However, no corroborative evidence in support of these references has been found as yet.

Epigraphic Records

Far more important than the literary works are the inscriptions as a source of the early history of Assam. The inscriptions having relevance on the history of Assam may be said to comprise of outside epigraphs and also local epigraphs.

Of the numerous outside epigraphs mention may be made of the Aphsad stone inscription[43] of the Later Gupta monarch Adityasena (AD 672) which records that the mighty fame *(sphītam yaśo)* of Mahasenagupta *(Śrī-Mahāsenagupt-o'bhūt-tasmat-vīr-āgranīh sūtah ... yasya)* marked with the moment of victory over the illustrious Susthitavarman *(śrīmat-Susthitavarma-yuddha-vijaya-ślāghā-padāṅkam)* is constantly *(muhūh)* sung *(gīyate)* on the banks of the Lauhitya *(Lauhityasya tatesu)* till this day *(ady-āpi)*. The association of Susthitavarman with River Lauhitya indubitably shows his identity with the king of the same, mentioned in the Doobi and the Nidhanpur copper-plate grants as the father of the princes, Supratisthitavarman and Bhāskaravaman. Moreover, the mention of the *Siddhas*, as living in pairs *(Siddha-mithunaih)* on the banks of the River Lauhitya, dotted with the areca palm trees *(utphulla-Nāga-drūma-cchāyām)* may allude to the preponderance of the Tantric religion and practices in Assam at about the second-half of 7th century AD. The Aphsad stone inscription of Adityasena may thus be profitably utilised for ascertaining the political and religious condition of the Brahmaputra Valley of about the latter-half of 7th century AD.

Of the local epigraphs mention may be made of the Doobi copper-plate inscription[44] of Bhaskaravarman which records that early kings, usually identified with Bhutivarman, donated some land in favour of a group of Brahmans but the charter being worn out in course of time the land was regranted by Bhaskaravarman to the descendants of the original donees. Since one of the six plates, containing the description of the donated land is lost, the exact location of the land, gifted in favour of the Brāhmaṇa donees, is far from being known. But the real importance of the inscription lies in its rich content about the political history of Assam at the time of the Varman kings. Besides giving us a genealogy of the family of Bhaskaravarman, the inscription provides us with interesting details about Stiravarman's building up of a new city, presumably on the banks of River Brahmaputra *(punye nade s-o'tha purīm-akārsīt)*, and the discomfiture of Supratisthitavarman and Bhaskaravarman at the hands of a Gauda monarch immediately after the death of their father Susthitavarman. We are told that the two Varman princes were in their boyhood days *(prathame vayasy-api)* at the time of the Gauda invasion, became senseless *(mohaṅgatau)* while fighting with their enemies, were taken to the enemy's kingdom but were allowed to return to their own kingdom *(prāpya sva-rājyam-acirāt)* on being released by the captor. Opinions differ on the identification of the invader, some[45] equating him with the Later Gupta king Mahāsenagupta, others[46] identifying him with Śaśāṅka or his immediate successor. It may here be observed that the description of the invading army as *Gauda bala* in the inscription is hardly applicable to Mahāsenagupta, and the alleged identity of the invading king with him cannot explain Bhaskaravarman's alliance with Harsavardhana in AD 606 when the

Pusyabhuti king had embarked upon a campaign against Śaśāṅka, the king of Gauda.

The Nidhanpur copper-plates,[47] discovered from the Sylhet district in Bangladesh, record how Bhaskaravarman, probably in the later years of his reign, confirms from his camp at Karnasuvarna *(skandhavārāt Karnasuvarna—vāsakāt)*, in consequence to the loss of the original charter *(śāsana-dāhat)*, made by his great-great-grandfather Bhūtivarman about a century earlier, an endowment granting 166x 1/16 shares of land in *Mayūrasālmal-āgrahāra* in Candrapurī-*visaya*, on the principle of the rent-free enjoyment of land by one who brings it under cultivation for the first time *(bhūmi-cchidra - nyāya)*, for the enjoyment of the Brahmanas, no doubt, the rightful descendants of the original donees, and the maintenance of *bali* (worship), *caru* (oblation) and *satra* (hospitality) in a local shrine. Divergent views have been expressed on the location of the gifted land, K.L. Barua[48] locating it in the Purnea district in Bihar, P.N. Bhattacharyya[49] and P.C. Choudhury[50] identifying Mayūraśālmal-*āgrahāra* with a locality in North Bengal and N.K. Bhattasali,[51] J.C. Ghose[52] and R.G. Bhandrakar placing the site in the Sylhet district of Bangladesh. If the view, locating Mayūraśālmal-*āgrahāra* in Sylhet be accepted, and this seems to be the case, the inscription may be cited as a proof of the inclusion of the Sylhet-Cachar region in the Varman kingdom for at least a century till the latter half of 7th century AD when it passed into the hands of Lokanātha and his descendants.

The presence of Bhaskaravarman's victorious army in the city of Karnasuvarna has given rise to a series of controversies among scholars as regards the extent of the Assam King's political sway over Bengal, some suggesting Bhaskaravarman's control over the whole of Gauda, others restricting his paramountcy to the part of Bengal, lying to the east of the Ganges. More interestingly, the inscriptions preserve the names of Pusyavarman and his twelve successors who may be arranged in the following genealogical table:

Pusyavarman
1
Samudravarman = Dattadevī
Balavarman = Ramavatī (called Ratnadevī in the Doobi plates)
1
Kalyanavarman = Gandharvavatī
1
Ganapati (called = Yajñavatī (called Yajñavatī in the Doobi plates)

Ganendravarman in the Doobi plates
1
Mahendravarman = Suvratā
1
Narāyanvarman = Devavatī (called Devavatī in the Doobi plates)
1
Mahābhūtavarman = Vijnānavatī
(also called Bhūtivarman)
1
Candramukhavarman = Bhogavatī
1
Sthiavarman (= Nayanadevī
(called Sthiavarman in the Doobi plates)
1
Susthitavarman = Śyāmādevī
(called Dhruvalaksmī in the Doobi plates)
1

1	1
Supratisthitavarman	Bhaskaravarman

Archaeological Finds

As one turns to the archaeological finds, one is dismayed to see that no relics of the Palaeolithic Age, when men were hunters, food-gatherers and nomads, have as yet been discovered from Assam, although palaeolithic tools (tools including hand axes, choppers and snappers) have been reported from the neighbouring states of Meghalaya, Arunachal Pradesh and Manipur. The possibility of the discovery of such relics of the palaeolithic men from the hilly regions in Central and Southern Assam in future cannot be ruled out.

Any evidence of the habitation of the Mesolithic men is similarly conspicuous by its absence in Assam.

The tools of the Neolithic Age like blades, celts, hammers, adzes, etc have been recovered from several places of upper Assam, Daojali Handing in Cachar district and some places in Kamarup and Goalpara districts, showing affinity with the Mesolithic tools of South-west China and other East-Asiatic countries on the one hand, and those of South and Central India and the Gangetic Valley on the other. The paucity of materials hardly enables us to derive a comprehensive picture of the Neolithic Age which seems to have commenced in Assam at a date around 2000 BC.

Megaliths, which in general means structure or memorials, usually made of huge and rough stones, have mostly been found in Karbi Anglong and North Cachar in Assam which has earned world-wide fame for its wealth of megaliths. Megalithism has persisted in Assam since pre-historic times till this day among some of the local tribes like the Nagas, the Mikirs and the Khasis. Their chronological status is not definitely ascertained.

Historic Assam is rich in archaeological remains which consist of shrines, fortifications, sculptures and images, Buddhist, Brahmanical and Jain, dating back to 5th century AD, if not earlier. The places from where these remains have been recovered lie scattered throughout the state, the most notable among them being, among others, Dah Parvatia, Bamuni, Tezpur, Chariduar, Bishnath, Bihali, Guwahati, Kamakhya, Hajo, Goalpara, Gosaijuri, Akasiganga, Gachtal, Urdhaganga, Badganga, Sibsagar, Sadiya, Davaka, Holeswar and Surya Pahar. Since the process of the excavation of historical sites is yet to gain momentum in Assam, most of the ruins continue to be surface finds. The importance of these finds can hardly be undermined; they shed remarkable light upon the tribal-Brahmanical mosaic of the socio-religious life of the people of early history besides affording us interesting glimpses into Assam's contact with the main stream of Indian culture through ages, and the creative impulses and aesthetic experience of the local artists and masons who built up monuments and fashioned sculptures and images.[53]

Coins

The coins, which are few in number, have come from Dhulapadung in Sonitpur district, Tulip Tea Estate in Darrang district, Paglatek in Goalpara district, Bargaon in Kamrup district and a village in Nowgaon district. Paglatek has yielded Gupta imitation gold coins of about 7th century AD. The rest of the coins, all made of copper, with the exception of a couple of pieces, which were issued in the name of Tiyasiya (ie Tyāgasimha), show a letter each like *ha*, *ta*, *ba*, and *ga*. These are, no doubt, initial letters of the names of Harjaravarman, Tyāgasimha, Balavarman or Banamālavarman and an unknown king, respectively.

These coins may be cited as an evidence to corroborate the statement of the Silimpur copper-plate inscription[54] of King Jayapāla about the prevalence of a currency in Assam during the first-half of 12th century AD. A definite reference to cowries in the Tezpur rock inscription[55] of Harjaravarman, when studied against the backdrop of the discovery of coins and the testimony of the Silimpur copper-plate inscription, would point out, in no uncertain manner, to the simultaneous use of cowries and coins in ancient Assam.

Progress in the Utilisation of the Source-Materials

It may not be out of place here to put on record our gratitude to the galaxy of scholars who have rendered yeomen's service to the cause of the reconstruction of the early history of Assam. Gunabhiram Barua's *Asom Buranji*, published from Calcutta in 1884, seems to be the first systematic study of the history of Assam from the earliest times to AD 1874 when the region was given a chief commissionership. The author's treatment of the pre-Ahom period appears to be subjective and sketchy but his account of the geography, tribes and castes of Assam and his description of the social, economic and political condition of the region of the later period is fairly accurate. A notable contributor to the study of the Assamese history was Edward Gait whose *History of Assam,* published first in 1905 and subsequently in 1926, concentrates on the medieval period and takes scant notice of the early epoch.

In *Kāmarūpa-Śāsanāvalī,* published in 1926 in Bengali, Padma Nath Bhattacharyya edited as many as twelve inscriptions of the pre-Ahom period with critical notes and observations, and made in the introductory portion of the work through discussion of the dynastic history of ancient Assam. Notwithstanding the doubts that enshroud some of the suggestions and theories, as advanced in this text, the work still retains its importance as a source book of the history of ancient Assam. K.L. Barua's *The Early History of Kamarupa,* published in 1933, gives a comprehensive account of the history of Assam from the pre-historic times to the rise of the Koch power in 16th century AD. Based on all the available materials, till then, the work presents the political and cultural history of the state in a strict chronological sequence. His posthumous work entitled *Studies in the Early History of Assam,* published in 1973, incorporates a large number of articles on different aspects of the history and culture of the region.

Nagendra Nath Vasu's *The Social History of Kamarupa* is a painstaking study on some aspects of the social history of the region but his eagerness to prove the Bengali origin of the social institutions of Assam has considerably diminished the merit of the work. B.K. Barua's book, *A Cultural History of Assam,* Part I (1951) traces the political, and more significantly, the cultural history of Assam from the pre-historic days to the end of 12th century AD. The author's account of the pre-historic period is, however, sketchy, and his treatment of the historical period leaves ample scope for further improvement.

P.C. Choudhury's voluminous work, *History of the Civilisation of the People of Assam to the Twelfth Century AD,* based on all the available data – literary and archaeological – portrays a comprehensive picture of the multifaceted history and civilisation of the state from the Neolithic Age to the beginning of 13th century AD, which marks the rise of the Ahoms in upper Assam with such richness of details as are not met with in the earlier works, and though about four decades have passed since the time of its revision in 1966, it still continues to be a standard work on the subject. In spite of its comprehensiveness and some positive qualities, the work contains certain views which may not stand the test of a critical, objective scrutiny of the data, hitherto unearthed.

The relevant volume of *A Comprehensive History of Assam,* published under the supervision of H.K. Barpujari in 1990, is no doubt, a marked improvement upon the work of P.C. Choudhury. But notwithstanding the commendable efforts on the part of the contributors, the important issue of the periodisation of the Assam history has not been highlighted, the historical geography, has not been properly focused upon, the men and events, concerning the history of Assam have not been positioned in a broader Indian spectrum and above all, the existing gaps of our knowledge of the early history of Assam have not been adequately bridged. Planned, well-organised excavations on a large scale, discovery of fresh materials, a meaningful study of the survivals of the tribal customs, institutions and traditions and explorations of the remains of the material culture of the tribal population are likely to prove to be rewarding for a historian, engaged in the task of reconstructing the history of ancient Assam.

NOTES AND REFERENCES

1. Chapter II, 38 (Banaras Sanskrit Series).
2. P.C. Choudhury, *The History of Civilisation of the People of Assam to the Twelfth Century A.D.,* Gauhati, 1966, p. 9.
3. Mukunda Madheva Sharma, *Inscription of Ancient Assam,* Gauhati, 1978, pp. 2-3.
4. P.C. Choudhury, *op. cit.,* p. 9.
5. IV. I, 14-7.
6. E.J. Rapson (ed.), *The Cambridge History of India,* Vol. 1, New Delhi, 1955, p. 109.
7. III, 74.
8. M.M. Sharma, *op. cit.,* p. 12.
9. *Sabha Parvan,* XXVI, 9.
10. *Ibid.,* XXX, 26-7.
11. *Ibid.*
12. XLIII.
13. P.C. Choudhury, *op. cit.,* pp. 9-10.
14. M.M. Sharma, *op. cit.,* p. 5.

15. II, 11.
16. IV, pp. 81-84.
17. *India In Kālidāsa*, Delhi, 1968, p. 63.
18. *Op. cit.*, p. 12.
19. *Op. cit.*, p. 10.
20. *The Kālikā Purāna*, Chapter XXXVIII, pp. 124.
21. The Bargaon Inscription of Ratnapala (11th century AD).
22. Chapter LXXVII, 95.
23. Chapter XXVII.
24. LVIII, 13; LVII, 44; LXVI, 8; CIX, 57.
25. Chapter LXXXI.
26. Chapter LIX.
27. XIV, 6; XVI, I.
28. *Ucchvāsa* VII.
29. XVII.
30. Act I.
31. III, 74.
32. M.M. Sharma, *op. cit.*, p. 12.
33. The description of the confluence to be found in the *Yoginī Tantra* is confusing. At one place it is said to be the confluence of the River Brahmaputra *(Brahmaputrasya sangamam)* while elsewhere it states: *Brahmaputrasya Lāksāyāh saṅgam—āvdhih* (I, II).
34. *Op. cit.*, p. 29.
35. *Journal of the Royal Asiatic Society*, London, 1910, pp. 1187-1201.
36. P.C. Choudhury, *op. cit.*, p. 16.
37. T. Walters, *On Yuan Chwang's Travels in India*, Vol. II (1905), p. 186.
38. S. Beal, *Life of Hiuen Tsiang*, London, 1914, pp. 165 ff.
39. S. Chattopadhyaya, *Early History of North India* (Calcutta, 1968), p. 298.
40. B.C. Sachau, London, 1914, p. 201.
41. H.G. Raverty, *Tabaqāt-i-Nāsirī*, London, 1881.
42. Abdus Salam, *Riyāz -us- Salātīn*, Calcutta, 1902.
43. Fleet, *Corpus Inscriptionum Indicarum*, Vol. III, pp. 200-08.
44. *Journal of the Assam Research Society*, Vol. XI, pp. 33-38; *Ibid.*, Vol. XII, pp. 16-33; *Epigraphia Indica*, Vol. XXX, pp. 287 ff; *Indian Historical Quarterly*, Vol. XXVI, pp. 241-46.
45. This is precisely the view of P.C. Choudhury (*op. cit.*, p. 163). P.C. Choudhury is further loath to believe that Bhaskarvarman had ever sustained a reverse in his encounter with the Gauda king (*Ibid.*).

46. D.C. Sircar (*IHQ*, Vol. XXVI, pp. 241-46) holds this view. He is further of the opinion that the battle was a naval encounter, waged in the vicinity of Tezpur.
47. *Epigraphia Indica*, Vol. XII, pp. 65 ff; *Ibid.*, Vol. XIX, pp. 118ff, 245-50; P.N. Bhattacharyya, *Kāmarūpa - Śasanāvalī* (Banaras, 1931), pp. 1-43, M.M. Sharma, *op. cit.*, pp. 38-81.
48. *Early History of Kāmrupa*, Shillong, 1933, pp. 32-34.
49. *Op. cit.*, p. 64.
50. *Op. cit.*, pp. 145, 151.
51. Kamalakanta Gupta, *Copper-Plates of Sylhet*, Vol. I, p. 56.
52. *IHQ*, Vol. VI, p. 642.
53. For a vivid description of the archaeological finds, see P.C. Choudhury, *op. cit.*, pp. 431-80; T.C. Shrama's article 'Sources of the History of Assam - Ancient Period; N.R. Ray (ed.), *Sources of The History of India*, Vol. III, Calcutta, 1980, pp. 69-82.
54. *Epigraphia Indica*, Vol. XIII, pp. 289-95.
55. *Journal of the Bihar and Orissa Research Society*, 1917, pp. 508ff.

6

Graeco-Roman Sources for the Reconstruction of Assam History

P.C. Sarma

In exploring the sources for reconstructing the earliest phase of history of the Brahmaputra Valley, we have so far largely depended on myths and legends recorded by the epics and the *Purāṇas.* As these sources are not authenticated uptil now by any other direct evidences like epigraphy, coins, architectural remains and sculptural evidences, they have remained full of lacunae and ambiguity. In this background, authentic history of the region on the basis of reliable sources could be constructed only from mid of 14th century AD, when the Varman Dynasty started their rule in the kingdom of Kamarupa.

The Varmans have mentioned Naraka as thier progenitor. According to Kalikapuranam of 9th century AD,[1] Naraka was a prince from the kingdom of Videha in North India who had killed the last Kirata king Ghataka of the kingdom of Pragjyotisa and established the Bhauma Dynasty. He is also mentioned in the epics and some of the *Purāṇas* as a mighty king and is often depicted as a person of devilish character. But lack of historical sources including archaeological evidences have constricted the reconstruction of the chronological details of his dynasty. Thus, even though there are positive clues to prove the existence of a kingdom in the Brahmaputra Valley during the early centuries of the Christian era, we have not yet been able to compile the reliable history of this period.

The Periplus of the Erythian Sea and Ptolemy's Geography are two Greek sources primarily dealing with navigational accounts from the eastern coasts of Egypt and Arabia to the coasts of India and beyond. The first of these two accounts ends its eastern limit at the mouth of the Ganga while the second one crosses this limit to include South-east Asia and parts of Far East. As these two works include geographical accounts of the mouth of the Ganga and the regions to the east and north during the period of first-second centuries of the Christian era, we are sure to get some historical materials of eastern and North-Eastern India of that time if, however, they are studied in their proper perspectives.

The Periplus of the Erythrian Sea (hereafter, the *Periplus*) was written by an anonymous Greek trader; and its period of compilation is stated as AD 80-89.[2] The eastern limit of this travel, as stated above, was the mouth of the Ganga where existed a mart of the same name.[3] The writer has given some ideas of the areas beyond that point as also about commercial prospects in that region to some extent.

Describing the geography of the region, the writer has mentioned that the region towards the east of the mouth of Ganga was a vast expanse of sea and there existed a land known as *Khruse*, the meaning of which is said to be the 'Land of Gold'. The work has also mentioned that there existed a country known as *Thina* with the capital of the same name far beyond the northern limit of the sea that existed to the east of the mouth of Ganga. This clearly proves that the Bay of Bengal had extended in the first century of the Christian era far above the present coastal hills. This appears to be a possibility when we consider the following facts:

(*i*) While describing the country of *Thina*, the *Periplus* mentions that sacked Malabathrun from this land was traded by land route to India.

(*ii*) In another reference to this country, it has recorded that silk in raw state or woven into cloth out of yarns were exported by land to Bactria and beyond, or by the river route of the Ganga to the sea.

Why the Greek traders did not cross the mouth of the Ganga and sailed to the northern coast of the Bay of Bengal for reaching this commercially prospective area in the immediate north is not mentioned but we have points to speculate, which may be stated as follows:

(*i*) From Rennell's map of 1779, it is known that upto about 200 years back, both the Ganga and the Brahmaputra had separate courses with their independent embouchures.

(*ii*) While the Ganga maintained a more or less stable course throughout the best part of history with its flow through its branch river Hugly of the day, it can be surmised from the *Periplus* that the Brahmaputra ended its course somewhere near Jamalpur-Maimensing region, about 300 km north of the sea-coast of present Bangladesh or at least around Decca of the day. As the mouth of the Brahmaputra was heavily silted, similar to that of the mouth of the Sindhu, navigation in this part was impossible[4] and therefore the Greek traders must have treated the Brahmaputra Valley as the hinterland of the port of Ganga.[5]

(*iii*) That the Brahmaputra Valley experienced a deluge by about the first century AD or BC can be known from an episode mentioned in the garb of myths in the *Kalikapuranam* of circa 9th century AD. It was mentioned that all the scattered settlements of the valley which conducted Vedic rites making the region sacred, were washed away by a tidal wave coming down from the Parasuram Kunda in the eastern frontiers of this region.[6]

The *Periplus* has stated, as mentioned elsewhere, about a country *Thina* which was located far away from the northern limit of the sea contiguous to the east of Ganga. The source has also mentioned that the merchants from this country seldom came down to the port of Ganga because of its seclusion and severe cold climate. But silk in raw state or woven in fabrics were traded by land route to West Asia (Bactria), and by the Ganga to the Malabar coast (Limurike). This description seems to have indicated the Brahmaptura Valley and its adjoining mountainous region, which was untraversable for foreignness because of its topography and therefore was an unknown and mysterious land for them. Incidentally, the products which the *Periplus* has mentioned to be traded at the Ganga-mart, such as spikenard, Malabathrum muslin, etc (except probably pearls) and, of course, betel leaves, must have been exported from the Brahmaputra Valley as they were seen to be produced in this area throughout the historical past. Kautilya's *Arthasastra* of 3rd-4th century BC mentions that soft and best quality silk was produced in this region.[7] The tradition of producing fragrant objects in this region can be also known from the articles sent by the Kamarupa king, Kumar Bhaskara Varman (AD 594-650), to Emperor Harsavardhana as recorded in Banabhatta's *Harshacharitam.*[8]

The *Periplus* has listed betel and spikenard among the articles sold at the Ganga mart. Chewing betel leaf and arecanut has been a custom of all the indigenous people of this region. They have also been used traditionally in receiving guests and in rites and rituals. It is interesting to note that when the Mughal historian, Shihabuddin Talish, visited Assam in the mid of 17th century AD, he found that in the local market betel leaves were sold in large quantity.[9]

Further, as mentioned in the *Periplus* an interesting item which this region traded with other parts of India, was Malabathrum (Tejpaat), which was packed in sacks of three sizes made out of the fibres known as petroi. This fibre might have been *Maraapat* or jute, which grew naturally in this region. The petroi may also indicate the *Paatidoi,* a type of reed-like shrub from which very fine but strong and flexible strips can be made, which is used for making *Sitalpaati,* a type of mat. It may also indicate *Patrorna,* mentioned by Kautilya to indicate silk which is produced from cocoons of worms.[10]

The above facts recorded in the *Periplus* must have indicated existence of at least one kingdom worth the name to the east of the Ganga Valley which, though known to the Gangetic Hindus by the name of Pragjyotisa-Kamarupa, might have been known less to the marine traders from far west. That there was a commercial route across the Brahmaputra Valley from China to Bactria via North India can be known from a Chinese record of 126 BC.[11] But we do not have any other sources to confirm this fact. Probably, the western regions of Assam covering the district of Goalpara witnessed the prevalence of the Buddhist culture during the 1st century AD or BC, as suggested by the existence of some monolithic stupas at Suryapahar.[12]

Ptolemy's *Geography* was compiled[13] on the basis of his data collected from traders and seafarers and the author tried to give locations of each place through longitudes and latitudes. But, the locations of these places have already grown vague as,

> Many towns, marts, etc which had existed, and even flourished, at that period, and were recorded by our eminent geographer, have now disappeared from the face of the earth, as well as from the memory of man. While others have changed several times their names, each change being often into a different language, according to the race of people under whose sway they successively fell, and are now unrecognisable under their modern appellations.[14]

Therefore, the attempt of Gerini, who tried his utmost to justify his interpretations both philologically and from scriptural and chronicler point of view, may not be the last word. Particularly, his knowledge on the historical developments of this region makes his interpretations in relation to this region unacceptable in its face value.

Gerini, in analysing the location of the rivers and some places brought the Brahmaputra and the Borak valleys of Assam into his discussion. Despite his sincere attempts at exploring the possibility of linking them with Ptolemy's description, he had wrongly identified them as in within South-east Asia. Nevertheless, it may be suggested that Ptolemy had indeed referred to the areas presently covered by the state of Assam and its neighbourhood. Properly scrutinised, these references may serve as materials to identify the geographical areas of Assam during first-second century AD, some of which are noted as follows:

Regarding Ptolemy's description of the River Doanas, Gerini says that it is formed by two streams, one from the Southern Himalayas, "a little to the east of Tawang" and "the source of the eastern branch is from Damasa".[15] But the author rejects the possibility of existence of this river in Assam and identifies it with River Mekong. But this description exactly tallies with the River Brahmaputra, which may be justified on the following grounds.

Till a few hundred years back, the rivers Dihing and Lohit, the two major constituents of the Brahmaputra, flowed parallel to each other and joined near Chandrapur, only 25 km east of Guwahati. The main course of the Lohit was the Siang or Dihong River which originated from the Himalayas in the north. As regards the Dihing, it came down from the eastern mountains of the Indian frontier carrying the waters of perennial Dhansiri River from the Naga hills. It is possible that the region covering the basins of the Dihing, Dhansiri and Kapili, which are located in the southern side of the Brahmaputra, came under the Davaka kingdom which was in existence in the mid 4th century AD as a political power known to the Imperial Guptas.[16] Ptolemy, who collected his information from the Roman traders, got the impression of the river to have come from the eastern hills under Davaka, which he distorted as the Damassa range.

It is known without an iota of doubt from the *Kalikapuranam* of 9th century AD that the southern constituent of the two streams of the Brahmaputra was known as *Divya-Yamuna.* It is possible that the Roman traders knew the Brahmaputra by this name only and Ptolemy recordes it as Doanas. Obviously, the southern stream was more navigable compared to the other and might have linked the kingdom of Davaka (present Dhansiri and Kapili valleys) which offered prospects of trade more than the other. Even today, the Kapili and the Dhansiri are navigable throughout the year; but the northern tributaries of the Brahmaputra are heavily silted during winter.

In his pursuit to identify the Mekong as the Doanas, Gerini has brought the fact of presence of peculiar fishes and other aquatic creatures mentioned by another Roman author, Quintus Curtius. This author mentions the Dyardanes,

> flowing through the remotest part of India (evidently India-extra-Gangem) and breeding crocodiles and dolphins, besides various aquatic monsters unknown to other nations.

Discussing this reference, Gerini adds,

> And as the Dyardanes has been by several authorities connected with the Oidanes of Artemidoros, who, according to Strabo, described it as a river that bred the same creatures and flowed into the Ganges it has been concluded that both the Dyardanes and Oildance were one and the same stream with the Doanas and that such a stream was what is now termed the Brahmaputra.[17]

But Gerini, while accepting this identification to be logical geographically, finds it difficult to explain the sources of the two streams of the Doanas. The aquatic species which the Brahmaputra has bred to our living presence show variety of them, some of which are really big. This river is still famous for the river-dolphins. The river including its southern tributaries like Kapili and Kalang were known for large crocodiles, as large as 5 metres and above. It also contains big fishes like the *Garuwa* (Bargarius Yarrelli), *Kach* (Silundia gangetica), *Chital* (Natapterus Chitala) and *Baraali* (Wallaga attu). Smaller fishes are also in these rivers. Among aquatic quadrupeds, two smaller species locally called the *Woode* (otter) and *Utonuwa* (water mole) are still seen in tributaries of the Brahmaputra. Snake-like creatures of varied sizes and shapes and several snake-like fishes, big and small, locally called *Baami, Kuchiya, Tora,* etc are also seen. It is therefore logical to identify the river mentioned above as no other than the Brahmaputra.

In regard to some other names also, Gerini has implicity referred to the Brahmaputra Valley. But in spite of the similarity of words, he rejects the possibility of their applicability to this area and shows them as indentical to those in South-east Asia. But some of them can be logically identified as belonging to this region.

In describing the place-name, Pentapolis, he says that it may mean *Panca-Palli* or 'five cities' and had compared it with the Greek system of urban settlements such as Tripolis, Tetrapolis, etc. But *Polli* is a Sanskrit word and it means a small village. Thus, the Pentapolis or Panchapalli may mean five wards of a commercial establishment that was formed by the settlements of traders beside a port. In locating Pentapolis, with his geographical calculation, Gerini says it should be

> a little further up above the Chittagong inlet, either on the coast or on some of the islands at the embouchure of the old Brahmaputra.

But, it will be much logical to take this place as Pancharatna, about 40 km. upstream from the border-town of Dhubri which, along with its neighbouring areas show archaeological evidences since 1st century AD. Even the East India Company, because of its ideal geographical position, developed a well-planned township at Goalpara near Pancharatna in the later half of 18th century AD.

Gerini has identified Kirrhadia with "Silhet, Tipperah and Kachar".[18] He has quoted from Ptolemy that, "Beyond Kirrhadia, the Zamirai, a race of cannibals, is located near Mount Maiandros." As the Brahmaputra evidently served better as a passage for movement of people and, obviously information, Mount Maiandro may indicate the lofty Mairang hills, about 5 km away from Khanapara on the

Guwahati-Shillong road, which is traditionally said to be the abode of the earliest known king Mairang or Mahiranga of this region. Though we do not have evidence to prove the existence of cannibalism in this part, we cannot reject its prevalence either. As Ptolemy recorded these information from the mouths of Roman traders, it is also possible that all information recorded by him were either exaggerated or distorted.

Discussing the country of Dabasai, Gerini has said that this area was around the Patkai mountain.[19] He says that the word Dabasai was formed from the word *Daba* or *Data*. This, according to him, indicated the kingdom of Davaka of the mid 4th century AD which was also mentioned in the Allahabad *Prasasti* of Samudragupta. Historians are of the opinion that this kingdom was located in the Jamina-Kapili Valley of Assam and might have included the Dhansiri and Dhing valleys bordering the Patkai. The word "Daba" in Sanskrit also means wild-fire and "Kah" among others may mean Kamadeva,[20] the words which thus jointly keep parity with the background of the word Kamarupa born out of the Puranic episode of burning up of Kamadeva in the fire of Mahadeva's third eye.[21] Be that as it may, it is likely that Ptolemy's Dabasai may mean the kingdom of Davaka which as a political power came to all-India prominence by the mid 4th century AD, and which was brought to submission by the Gupta emperor Samudragupta.

Ptolemy has used some other place-names, such as Rhingiberi, Barrhai, etc which maintain phonetical similarity with some names of Assam. From the above analysis we are reasonably convinced that the Roman sources may supplement in reconstructing the history of Assam of the period beyond 4th century AD. Though the accounts of the traders were mainly concerned with the prospective areas for trade and the people connected with it, they indirectly throw a flood of light on the geography of the areas. Several scholars studying Greek and Roman sources, including Mc Crindle, Gerini, and Mazumdar, believe in the existence of a Roman trade route to East and South-east Asia along the Brahmaputra Valley.

It is to be noted in this context that the Ambari excavation in the seventies of the last century in the heart of Guwahati unearthed a few pieces of Roman and Chinese potteries which point towards the same conclusion.

In conclusion, it may be emphasised that Roman sources, backed by archaeological and other evidences, constitute invaluable materials for study and interpretation of the history of ancient Assam.

NOTES AND REFERENCES

1. There was some controversy in regard to the date of compilation of the *Kalikapuranam* and the Vivekananda Kendra Institute of Culture, Guwahati organised a talk to settle this controversy. The scholars like M.M. Sharma, D. Chutia, B.N. Shastri, etc were univocal in placing it in 9th century AD.
2. Mc Grindle, *Ancient India*, Patna, 1987, p. 5.
3. *The Periplus* has named the mart in the mouth of the Ganga as Ganga, which is used for our convenience as Ganga.
4. *The Periplus* has recorded in case of the mouth of the Sindhu that out of seven channels at its mouth, only one was navigable: *'The river has seven channels at its mouths, all shallow, marshy and unfit for navigation except only the middle stream, on which is Barbarikan, a trading sea-port'*. *The Perilpus*, p. 108.
5. The chronicler records that the Brahmaputra caused heavy floods and siltations during the last three hundred years resulting in its change of course. In points of turbidity, it is considered as the second-highest all over the world and next to the Hwang Ho of China. The annual suspended mud carried by this river since AD 1950 is said to be 403 million tons in an average, with 2.12 millions tons per day summer which, if counted in trucks arranged in a line will cover a length of 800 km; J. N. Sarma, *Asomor Nod-Nodi*, 1993, pp. 18-19.
6. *Kalikapuranam*, pp. 83-34.
7. The *Arthasastra* speaks of Suvarnakudya of the region east of the Mauryan Empire where golden coloured silk (Muga), very soft cloths were produced. Savarnakudya is identified as Sonkuriha, a village about 60 km north-west of Guwahati and within Nalbari district of Assam.
8. B.K. Barua, *A Cultrural History of Assam*, 1969, p. 104. The Mughal historian Shihabuddin Talish, who visited Assam in AD 1662, mentions abundance of spikenard, pepper, etc in Assam. E.A. Gait, *A History of Assam*, Guwahati, 1967, p. 146.
9. The 10th century AD copper-plate charter of the Kamarupi king Balavarman, records that the betel creepers were seen to coil round the areca nut trees in abundance in Pragijyotishpur, ie Guwahati. M.M. Sharma (ed.), *Inscriptions of Ancient Assam;* Guwahati, 1978, p. 133. X
10. *Arthasastra*, Ch. II canto, pp. 107-113.
11. The report of the Chinese Ambassador Chang-Kien of BC 126 shows existence of a trade-route by land between Eastern India and China via Assam and upper Burma P.C. Bagchi, *India and China*, Calcutta, 1981, pp. 21-2.
12. Prof. S.K. Saraswati placed these *stupas* in 1st century AD, *Prakash* (Assamese quarterly), Assam Publication Board, April, 1977, p. 45.
13. Ptolemy, p. 67.
14. Ptolemy, p. 3.

15. Ptolemy, p. 282. It may be noted that one of the earliest inhabitants of Assam who had lived in the Dhansiri-Kapili Valley were known as the Dimasa.
16. *Allahabad Prasasti of Samudragupta* (AD 340-380)
17. Ptolemy, pp. 281-282.
18. Ptolemy, p. 52.
19. Ptolemy, p. 54.
20. Sanskrit-English Dictionary; Apte, V.S., 1988, p. 247.
21. It is interesting to note that the Puranic Mahadeva-Kamdeva episode was popular in the early kingdom of Champa in the Tonkin Bay along the eastern cost of South-east Asia (ie Vietnam of the day).

7
Monoliths as a Source of Mizo History

J.V. Hluna

Pre-British Mizo history is yet to be fully explored. Mizoram is still a *terra incognita* as far as historical study is concerned. In this context, an attempt has been made to focus on the Monoliths of the early Mizos as a source material of Mizo history and culture. In the absence of proper source materials for the reconstruction of pre-British Mizo history, it is difficult to comprehend the different stages of historical developments and as such the usual periodizations into ancient, medieval and modern does not hold good in case of Mizo history. Overlapping is almost unavoidable when the reconstruction of the past has to be made from the scratches, and particularly so when we talk of the Monoliths as a source.

The memorial stone, in the ordinary sense of the word, is a memorial to the dead. It is also a custom of the Mizos to commemorate important events with a stone. Erection of gravestones, to mark the spot where the remains of the dead are buried, is an almost universal practice even among the western nations, and indeed among many ethnic groups of North-East India.

The memorial stones of Mizoram are similar in shape to monoliths, table stones or cromlechs in other parts of the world. These stones are menhirs on vertical stones, some are table stones or dolmens (a pre-historical monument formed by a large, flat stone laid across upright stones).

1. *Lungphunlian:* The village, Lungphunlian was named after the great monoliths erected there. They are six in number. The tallest one is 14 ft.

high, 6 ft. wide and 2 ft. thick. It is not known when and how these monoliths were erected and by whom. Romesh Buragohain is inclined to believe that they were erected by the Meiteis because another rock with Meitei script has been found nearby.[1] According to him, proper decipherment of the script, may throw new light on the Meitei-Mizo relations of the time. However, Darchhawna, who visited the spot, inclined to believe that these stones were planted by the Riangs (Tripuris), who migrated to Manipur from Tripura sometime in the later half of the 17th century. According to him, an evidence of their work is also seen at Rengdil (western part of Mizoram).[2] There, a buried house was unearthed by the Department of Art and Culture, Mizoram. But since continuation of the work was not possible without the permission of the Archaeological Survey of India, the excavation work had to be abandoned.

2. *Vangchhe Lungphun:* Several other monoliths were also found near Farkawn near the Tiau River (Myanmar and Mizoram boundary) which seems to be erected by Vangchhe people. The spot is called Mualbawk. Some monoliths were erected sometime in the middle of the 17th century. They were bulging inscriptions. The Vangchhe people moved North-East from Farkawn to Ruantlang and Zote, thence to Vapar and Lungphunlian leaving behind them monoliths and menhirs in all these places. So Darchhawna supposed that these monoliths at Lungphunlian were the work of the Vangchhe people.[3]
3. *Mangkhaia Lung:* A memorial stone found at the southern extremity of Champhai paddy field near Zote village is called Mangkhaia Lung. Mangkhaia who belonged to the Ralte clan was the son of Mangthawnga, the chief of Champhai. The stone was planted by Mangthawnga in memory of his son who was arrested and killed on his way back to Bawlte village by his enemy, Darkhawla, the chief of Zotlang. The rock is 5 m high with human figures and *mithun*-heads inscribed on it and it was a bulging engraved rock. A.G. Mc Call is of the opinion that it is a monolith of the PreLushai period.[4] This stone memorial suggests the beginning of interclan conflicts and contradictions relating to property and possession. Shakespeare, in his book *Lushai-Kuki,* has written the changing condition thus: "The picture has changed today. The Raltes have lost their separate identity by being fully assimilated in Major Lushai tribe, so much so indeed that they do not use their dialect even in their close inner circles. They have almost completely accepted Duhlian, the *lingua franca* of Mizoram in place of their own language. The uniqueness of this stone appears to repose not only in massive structures but also in engraving of a series of

human figures standing side by side with hands interlocked, giving nearly an impression of the large security their spirits offer collectively to the great Chief in his celestial above."[5]

4. *Sibuta Lung:* This stone was erected by the villagers of Tachhip to commemorate the cruel deed of Sibuta, son of a concubine of a powerful chief of Tachhip. Tachhip village is situated about 20 kms south of Aizawl. This stone is about 12 ft high. While other stones were erected to commemorate the great deeds of the chief or planted as a memorial stone of the dead, this stone reminds people of the cruelty of their chief. The former chief of Tachhip had a daughter named Darlalpuii who expressed her dislike for Anhuta by inflicting punishments often without any justification. Sibuta, being the son of a concubine, dared not resist his step-sister. But he often talked of his aspiration to became chief someday when he could retaliate. Indeed Darlalpuii in her vain glory, ignored these talks. Sibuta one day succeeded Darlalpuii's father as Chief since the latter left no male issue from his legal wife at the time of his death. Darlalpuii was taken away from the chief's house for fear of Sibuta when the latter became the chief. But Sibuta never forgot what had been done to him in the past. He then made up his mind to take retaliation on Darlalpuii.[6]

   One day, he performed the Khuangchawi ceremony. Instead of killing a gayal, Sibuta decided to kill Darlalpuii for sacrificial offering. The villagers were much shocked by this cruel decision but dared not raise any objection for fear of being killed by the cruel chief. Darlalpuii was brought and tieded up at "seluphan" (the sacrificial post). Sibuta then took vengeance on her by piercing her to death and hanging her head up at the top of the post.[7]

5. *Lalruanga Lung:* Five rocks/stones big enough to be carried by one man alone, were found in Suangpuilawn, situated at a distance of about 75 kms North-East of Aizawl. Lalruanga, who might have been the chief, is said to have pulled out these stones from River Tuivai which is about 7 kms from Suangpuilawn by tying them with a single hair of his person. The marks, which are still to be seen on the stones are said to be the impressions of his hair. It also contains very finely finished holes on it. In Mizo mythology, Lalrrunga was a very powerful sorcerer and he did so many other peculiar and strange things. Burgohain says, "wherever might be the river as the source of water, the big stones as the protective means and the heroic feat of the chief might have served as the nucleus of the early organised village settlements of the Mizos."[8]

6. *Lallula Lung:* The big stone that stands with a large inscription on it at Sialhawk village about 80 kms east of Aizawl was erected by the Sailo chiefs to commemorate Lallula's heroic deed of killing "Thlanrawn Pawi". It is said that the Paws in their glorious days would collect tax from the Lushais living in the villages near them. Such an act was strongly resented by the Lushais. In course of time, Lallula who was the father figure of Sailo chiefs mapped out a plan to liquidate the Pawi chiefs who were responsible for the imposition of excessive taxes. One day, he invited them to his village at Zopul promising them rewards and feast. The Pawi chiefs and their attendants then came to the Lushai village. However, Lallula had already worked out a plan for the massacre of not only the Pawi chiefs and their attendants but also the destruction of their village in their absence. The whole plan was carried out with precision and ruthless severity and harshness. Lallula was then acclaimed as the greatest of the Sailo chiefs. He and his friends jointly erected this big stone to commemorate their victory over their rivals.[9]
7. *Lungvando:* These stones are erected all in one line. They are roughly hewn and not tapered unlike those found in Khasi hills.[10] The one great stone located near Biate village about 90 kms southeast of Aizawl is called "hungundo". This is typical rock pillar in shape. It is very tall and beautifully chiseled pillar made of stone about 75 cms in diameter and 3 m in height. Given the roundness and fine finishing of the stone, it is believed to be the work of a master-craftsman. Darchhawna opined that this is a boundary pillar erected at the time of the Treaty of Yandaboo.[11] But there is no historical proof. But according to legends, in ancient times this stone pillar was very tall, almost touching the heavens, and no one could touch it without endangering life. Once a peacock landed on it and got crumbled into pieces. It appears that this probably was a very tall memorial stone of a chief of the Biate tribe who was a resident of the area before the Lushais came and defeated Biates who then settled in the plains of Cachar.
8. *Darthiangi Lung:* Not far from Farkawn village was a big stone erected jointly by Darthiangi and her husband, Chertuala, before they were physically separated. This stone was erected to commemorate their imperishable love for each other. It is known as Darthiangi Lung. Darthiangi, who belonged to Dulzawl village was an exceptionally beautiful maiden.[12] She was married to Chertuala, the then chief of Farkawn. But unfortunately, she failed to bear any child. One day the couple decided to separate in the interest of the continuity of the chief's

family. It is said that Darthiangi, while packing up to leave her husband's house, wept bitterly and sang a self-composed song.

9. *Lamsial Puk:* The cave Lamsial Puk is situated near the village Farkawn in the southeast of Aizawl. This cave carries evidence of a fight between two enemy camps in which many warriors were killed. In this cave a big heap of human skeletons was found. The skeletons appear to be of people who were taller than the Mizos and might have belonged to some other race inhabiting the area before the Mizos. The legend has it that these people belonged to a tribe called "Tlau".

   Long ago, they suffered from a severe famine. As the villages were independent under different chiefs, who were at war with each other, these people could not leave their village in search of food. This resulted in the death of many of them. The survivors decided to go elsewhere and entered the cave where all perished due to starvation. This is a pathetic story of famine which had frequently cast dreadful shadow in Mizoram. It also tells of the miseries of lonely villagers who dared not move out of the village for help as they were scared of their enemies.[13]

Buddha's Image near Mualcheng Village

Animesh Ray, former Deputy Commissioner of Mizo Hills District of undivided Assam, found an engraved image of Lord Buddha at a place 8 km away from Mualcheng village and 50 km from Lunglei town. According to him, on either side of the image, there are images of dancing girls. On another slab of stone there are engraving of footmarks and various articles like spear-head and dao.[14] It appears that these engravings were done by metal chisels. This indicates the "know how" for sharpening of metal implements. This place, being situated near the Chittagong hill tracts, was under Buddhist influence for a few centuries in the past. It is felt that perhaps these engravings were made by some Buddhists from those tracts before the Mizos came into the area.

Sikpui Lung: Sikpui Lung lies flat on the ground far on the hillside of Zote village. From the inscription on it, we know that the stone was planted by Zahuala Sailo. It reads as follows:

"Heng Lung Hi Hmanlai Ho Sikpui Lung a Ni Tin Keini Kum 28-2-1918 A Hian Kan Awh Ta Zahuala Sailo."

Times back, the Hmar settled here at Zote and lived in their exclusiveness with a fairly different cultural pattern from that of the Lushais. The Hmars had their own festivals, the most famous of which was known as Sikpui. During this festival, villagers enjoyed good health and harvest at least for some three consecutive years. It is the custom of the Hmars to erect stone in commemoration of their joy and happiness.

Unnamed stone erections: There is one unnamed stone erection with a script closely resembling the Shan-Burmese script. Unless deciphered, nothing could be said about this.

There is yet another stone erection with inscriptions in Assamese alphabet. But its language is Bengali.[15] A proper study of this inscription in a new light might reveal much about the history of Mizoram during the 14th and 15th centuries.

Chhura Farep: This is believed to have been erected by the chief, Chhura, to whom the Hmar clan of the Mizos claims their origin. There is an engraving of a human figure holding a spear, and the figure of a pig at its bottom.

The legends connected with this *Chhura Farep* suggest the beginning of the *Jhum* cultivation on a large scale and domestication of animals as the first stage of settled family life. *Chhura Farep* is found in the old village Tlaikhuang near the present Khawbung village.[16]

In conclusion, it can be said that megaliths were among the oldest socio-religious monuments of the world. In-depth study of these monoliths of Mizoram might unfold hitherto unknown facts on the life and culture of the Mizos.

NOTES AND REFERENCES

1. Romesh Buragohain, "Lungphun" in Romesh Buragohain (ed.), *Proceedings of International Seminar on "Studies on the Minority Nationalities of North East India: The Mizo"*, April 7-9, 1992.
2. Darchhowna, "Monoliths of Mizoram", *Historical Journal Mizoram,* Vol. VIII, December, 1998.
3. *Ibid.*
4. A.G. Mccall, *Lushai Chrysalis,* 1977 (reprint), cited in B. Lalthang-liana, *Mizo Chanchin,* p. 815.
5. John Shakespear, *The Lushai-Kuki Clan,* cited Darchhawna, n. 3.
6. Interview with a Mizo Historian, R. Vanlawma on 27-2-2002.
7. *Ibid.*
8. Romesh Buragohain, *op. cit.*
9. Interview with R. Vanlawma, a Mizo Historian on 27-2-2002.
10. Darchhawna, *op. cit.*
11. *Ibid.*
12. *Ibid.*
13. Interview with Lalthangpuia, a villager of Farkawn.
14. Animesh Ray, Mizoram, National Book Trust, India, 1993, p. 20.
15. Buragohain, *op. cit.*
16. B. Lalthangliana, *op. cit.,* p. 815.

8

Sculpture as a Source of Social Life

(with special reference to the sculptures of Guwahati)

Paromita Das

Art is a reflection of contemporary society. The art of sculpture is an important source of information of the society that created it. This paper focuses on certain aspects of social life in Assam in the period 5th-13th/14th century AD as revealed by a study of the sculptural remains, with special reference to those of Guwahati.

Religion played a dominant role in the life of the people. This is evident from the fact that the majority of the sculptured remains are religious in nature. The sculptures found in the city of Guwahati are mostly those of Brahmanical gods and goddesses. Sculptures of Jain and Buddhist deities have also been discovered. Sculptures of Shiva (icon as well as in the aniconic linga form) number more than 70; those of Gaṇeśa (free-standing as well as rock-cut) are more than 38 in number. Sculptures of *Visnu* number 63, those of Brahma 4, of *Devi* (including yonipithas) 163, Surya more than 12, and those of miscellaneous Brahmanical, Buddhist and Jain deities 57. Non-religious sculptures are in a minority. And the latter too have been generally found at sites of religious importance like the Nilachala hill, Ambari, etc. This category includes terracotta plaques, animal sculpture and other sculptural motifs and are 74 in number. (The figures take into account only those identified during field study and in published sources.)

Secondly, all the icons, whether Brahmanical, Jain or Buddhist, indicate that their creators were familiar with canonical norms and *Pauranic* lore. Thus the Sun-god Surya[1] is always depicted holding two lotus flowers, and often riding on a chariot drawn by seven horses, sometimes accompanied by his consorts. Brahma[2] is depicted with his usual *ayudhas* and upon his *vahana,* the swan. Vishnu,[3] Indra[4] and other gods and goddesses of the Brahmanical, Buddhist and Jain pantheon are all depicted in accordance with the norms laid down in the silpasastras.[5] A large number of Sakti[6] icons, especially those of *Mahisasuramardini* Durga[7] have been recovered from the site of the Ambari excavations. Other sculptures depict Shiva killing the demon Andhakasura, Vishnu as *Narasimha,*[8] killing the demon Hiranyakashipu, Vishnu as *Varaha, Kurmavatara, Vamana* and *Trivikrama,*[9] etc. Elsewhere, we find sculptures depicting the banishment of Rama, the escape of Yogamaya, Arjuna the archer, and other stories from the epics and Puranas.

The deification of rivers is indicated by the recovery of two sculptures from Ambari. They are the anthropomorphic representation of the rivers Ganga and Yamuna.[10] The former is depicted riding on a crocodile and has a three-hooded snake canopy over the head. The latter rides the tortoise and has a single-hooded snake canopy.

Music and dance appear to have played an important role in society, probably as a part of religious ritual. Portions of a broken pillar[11] recovered from Nilachala bear four sculptures on the four edges. The first is that of a male dancer, the second is of a female *vina* player, the third that of a male playing on the fltue while the fourth figure is that of a male playing the *dundubi* (kettle-drum). A terracotta plaque recovered from Kukurmuta[12] depicts three female figures dancing in gay abandon. Another plaque from the same site is that of a dancing skeletal figure,[13] probably a devotee of Shiva. A plaque from Uzānbazār depicts a female dancer with her *guru* (teacher). These terracotta plaques may have been attached to temple walls. Similar plaques have been recovered from Bhaitbari in the Garo Hills, and also from the Cotton College campus. Remains of a stone temple have also been discovered at the last site. Sculpture panels depicting some of the figures in a dancing posture, while others play on musical instruments, can also be seen on the walls of the stone temple at Madan Kamdev Parvat, near Baihata Chariali.

The sculptures also provide a glimpse into everyday life. Some sculptures on the Nilachala hill depict a mother, child, a householder engaged in prayers, a conch, a woman offering water to a tired man, etc. Sculptures of *maithuna* couples can be seen on the walls of the Shiva temple on Madan Kamdeb Parvat. Similar sculptures have also been recovered from different places in Guwahati.[14] It is quite probable that these erotic sculptures depict certain rites practiced by some sections of people as a part of the rituals of an obscure esoteric cult. Hunting and riding are portrayed in the sculptural remains.

Sculptures also provide valuable insights into contemporary mode of dress and ornaments. The icons are depicted according to canonical norms and their dress and ornaments cannot be taken as a reflection of contemporary society. But the sculptures that depict secular themes, though fewer in number, are very informative.

During the ancient period the men wore a *dhoti*-like lower garment. The drapery is often transparent. Some men also sported a conical headdress. The flute and conch blower depicted in niches on the eastern gateway of the Kāmākhayā temple both wear a *dhoti* and a headdress. The women wore a long *sari*-like garment as depicted in the terracotta plaques from Kukurmutā. They also wore a long flowing garment on the upper part of their body called *uttariyā,* as does the sculpture of the women worshipper at Kāmākhyā. The sculptures of the early period do not appear to depict any stitched garment, only long pieces of cloth wrapped around the body of both men and women. The icons are similarly clad. Many display an *upavita mālā.*

Ordinary men and women as well as the icons are adorned with a great variety of ornaments. While most icons invariably have a halo and the male ones a variety of crowns, they otherwise display the same type of ornaments as ordinary people. Thus the neck is adorned with kanthahāra, the ears with patrakundala and puspakundala. Women knotted their hair either at the top of their heads or a little to the side, while the men too knotted their hair or let it hang loose on either side of the head. Women also wore beautiful head-dresses adorned with beads as seen in a terracotta mutilated miniature sculpture recovered from the Āmbārī site. The sculptures are adorned with bangles, armlets, waistbands, anklets and bracelets as well as bead necklaces.

In the medieval period, however, the use of ornaments is far less, though not absent. Men are depicted with turbans, long flowing gowns or tunics, as well as with a trouser as lower garment. An 18th century terracotta plaque in the ASM shows a hunter wearing shoes with pointed toes. Women are sometimes shown wearing a long skirt and a blouse.

Various racial types inhabited the city in the historical period if the sculptures are taken to represent the physiognomic type of the contemporary population. Thus, we see sculptures with long and sharp noses as well as ones with a broad face, flat nose and thick lips. The sculptures to a large extent depict Mongoloid features, as for instance, the ones abutting on the river at Sukreśvar. The Vishnu image sitting on a lotus, protected by a nine-hooded snake, placed in the *bada* of the temple has a flat and broad nose. A 13th-14th century Kinkara image from Sukreśvar has a Negroid face and is stiff in attitude.[15] From this time onwards, the earlier slender and fluid sculptures give way to ones that display a heavy sensuousness in body posture. However, it is also possible that as a result of that break in artistic traditions, probably brought about by political uncertainty and lack of royal patronage, the earlier style died to be replaced by a new one. The creators of this new style, untutored in the old tradition, created solid figures which may not have been a reflection of the racial type of the contemporary society.

Sculptural remains are thus an important source of social history. They provide us glimpses into the daily life of the people. They tell us about the religious leanings, the dress, ornaments and social beliefs and practices of the society that created them.

NOTES AND REFERENCES

1. Assam State Museum (henceforth ASM) 6739.
2. ASM 1985.
3. ASM 7528, 7516, 6741.
4. ASM 1985/1.
5. R.S. Gupta, *Iconography of the Hindus, Buddhists and Jains,* Bombay, pp. 27-35; 49-52; 108-121; 174-175; H.K. Barpujari, (ed.), *Comprehensive History of Assam,* Vol. I, Guwahati, 1990, pp. 346-422.
6. M. Sonowal, "A Brief Note on the Sakti Icons Found at Ambari", *Journal of the Assam Research Society,* Vol XXXII, No. 1&2 Guwahati, 1992, pp. 42-53.
7. ASM 7468, 7527.
8. ASM 11, 2122.
9. ASM 6743, 6734.
10. ASM 6744, 6745.
11. ASM 2541.
12. ASM 2127/1.
13. ASM 2127/2.
14. ASM 45, 46.
15. M. Dutta, *Sculptures of Assam,* Delhi, 1990, p. 101.

9

Sculptures of Assam from Earliest Time to 12th Century AD

Nishipad Dev Choudhury

Sculptures as one of the archaeological sources has been considered important by itself apart from the other branches of archaeology, such as epigraphs, numismatics, art and architecture, iconography, pottery, etc. It is of higher illustrative value and greatly in assessing the power and magnificence of some of the ancient dynasties.[1]

The monuments which are scattered throughout Assam are eloquent testimony to the artistic skill achieved by ancient Assam, and testify to the wealth grandeur during different periods of the history of Assam. They also give us greater insight into the culture of the people.[2]

Indian sculpture is generally to serve architecture chiefly as an ornament of the latter.[3] The sculptures of Assam, which serve as the decorative parts of the temples, mainly walls, ceilings, pediments, doorways, lintels, etc do not exist in the original places as the ancient temples in their original forms do not survive now. The majority of the sculptures that have been found in this region represent various gods and goddesses and other semi-divine figures.[4]

As subject of historical study, the sculptures are useful not only for their artistic value but also for the light they throw on the religious conditions of the people. The extensive remains mostly associated with religion also testify to the devotional zeal of the rulers and the ruled. The temples and the icons of the various deities of different faiths provide us with information on the state of social and religious life of the people.[5]

The sculptures of Assam, other than the gods and goddesses, may be classified into the following groups :

1. Human figures
2. Animal figures
3. Ornamental designs

1. Human Figures

Representation of human figures other than deities is limited to a few examples. The earliest instances of this category are found in some terracotta plaques from Dah-Parbatia, which was discovered by R.D. Banerji.[6]

One human figure has been shown seated cross-legged, having a broad chest, proportionately thin waist and well-formed hands and legs. The head of the figure is missing. The moulding of the torso and the general technique of the plaque may be dated to 6th century AD. Similar types of figures have been found in Rongpur and Paharpur.[7]

A human figure shown in *sukhasana* posture, wearing *dhoti,* katibandha and turban on the head, has been noticed on a niche of a wall from Gachtal, now preserved in the Nagaon Park.[8]

A stone slab containing a human figure having a good physique is seen in the Assam State Museum (ASM). The figure is shown standing in a wrestling pose. The muscles of his hands and legs are shown prominently.[9]

Terracotta plaques representing human figures have been found at Na-Nath-than and Mayang. A few terracotta plaques bearing human figurines were collected from Bhismak Nagar, Sadiya and preserved in the ASM. The first one of the human figure has been depicted in a standing posture, the second one in walking attitude, the third one represents a warrior, the fourth one a soldier, holding shield and sword in his hands; and the fifth represents a couple in *sthanaka* attitude.[10]

Terracotta plaques from Kundil Nagar, representing human figures, have also been found. One plaque shows a soldier. A man with a conical cap on his head, holding a spear in his right and with a dagger fastened on his girdles, is shown in a running posture in this plaque. This piece of terracotta sculpture can be compared with one from Bhismak Nagar representing a soldier. The lining methods of both the figures are same.[11]

Terracotta plaques bearing human figures are also found in Jugijan, Kenduguri, Mornoi and other places. Human figures carved on stone blocks are found in the ruins of Assam.

Dancing Figures: Dancing figures are representions of the poses described in the *Natya Sāstras.* The earliest from Assam has been noticed in the left *dvārśākhā* of the door-frame of Dah-parbatia. A miniature female figure has been shown dancing.

Sculptures representing dancing figures as well as music party are noticed on stone slabs fixed on the walls, panels, door-jambs, lintels, door sills, etc which formed an integral part of the temple decoration.

A large stone slab representing a very interesting dance scene has been found at Cole Park, Tezpur. The slab is divided into seven panels by round pilasters and each panel contains two figures either of males or of females, or both. The first one shows a man fighting with a lion; the second shows a male playing on a flute and a female dancing; the third a male playing on a pipe and the female dancing; the fourth a male playing on a drum and a female dancing; the fifth a male playing on cymbals and the female dancing; the sixth a female playing on a lyre and another female dancing on her left; and seventh a male playing on a drum with another male dancing on his right. Stylistically this piece of sculpture may be dated AD 9th century.[12]

A dance scene is noticed on a door-jamb, lying near the D.C.'s bungalow, Tezpur. The central vertical band is divided into three panels. The bottom one is occupied by a female dancer, the middle one by a male drummer and the top one by a dancing female figure. All the figures are shown under canopies. Another pillar, lying in the campus of the D.C.'s residence, Tezpur, has four sunken panels. The panels depict a music party, one in each panel.[13]

A door-sill from Barganga depicts two lions flanked and a *ghata* in the centre; and on both the sides of the sill, there are four panels, each divided by pilasters. All the panels are occupied by music party; from the right, the first one has a male playing on a cymbal; the second one also playing on cymbal; the third, a dancing female; the fourth, a male playing on a drum; on the left side, the first and second are broken, the third male playing on a drum, and the fourth, a male playing on a cymbal.[14] A frieze from Deopani depicts a scene of music; it contains the figure of a horse, a man, a woman seated and singing and another figure playing on flute.[15]

A beautiful dancing scene is carved on an octagonal pillar kept in the ASM. It depicts in the alternate four human figures, two male and two female, playing and dancing. In the first one a female is shown dancing, which is followed by a male playing on the flute. This is followed in turn by a female shown playing on *vina* and the last one is a male figure playing on a drum. These type of dancing scenes in sculptures are not commonly met with. It appears to be one of the interesting dancing scene depicted in the sculpture of Assam belonging to the medieval period.[16]

One terracotta plaque collected from Kukurmuta (Hedayatpur), Guwahati, and preserved in the ASM, represents an interesting scene of dancing. Here, one male figure has been shown playing on drum, the female one is dancing, and another male figure is seated and coaching the dancer. It represents the *guru* or choreographic master, imparting lessons to the female dancer. The hands of the male figure are in *Vyākhyāna mudrā* and he is seated in *bhadrāsana,* the typical sitting posture of a *guru.* Stylistically this sculpture may be placed in 10th century AD. This type of coaching of dance scene portraits in sculpture is rare.[17]

Terracotta plaques bearing figurines are also found in Kundilnagar. In addition to the group of dancing or music party portrayed in the sculptures, individual dancing figures are also found in Assam. Such type of male or female figures shown in dancing posture are frequently met with in the ruins of Assam.

Scenes from the Epics: Friezes (Rupapattika) are by far the most interesting features of the edifice in as much as the show in a series of panels scenes either drawn from Hindu mythology of domestic life including a few of an erotic character.

Scenes from the *Rāmāyaṇa* and the *Mahābhārata* are also depicted in the sculptures from Assam. A frieze from Deopahar having five panels shows Rama and Laksmana seated, the latter behind the former, while Sugriva is kneeling before Rama in supplication and Hanuman and another monkey are watching the scene with reverence, as indicated by their hands in *anjali hasts mudrā.* The scene portrayed evidently relates to the scene from the *Rayamana* in which Hanuman succeeded in securing the friendship of Rama for the protection of Sugriva. Another frieze represents the *Mahābhārata* story of Pandu, who shot a deer couple in coition. The third frieze represents a scene from the *Mahābhārata,* namely *Garuda Garbabhanga* or the extermination of Garud's pride.[18]

Scenes from Contemporary Life: The depiction of scenes from contemporary life on the temple walls gives us some idea regarding the social and domestic life of those days. Such scenes are numerous, and a few of them are described here. A frieze from Singri shows six women seated with folded hands, three in each of the two panels; another scene from Deopahar depicted in a panel shows two ladies grinding corn in a ural (grinding urn) and a third lady is shown talking to one of them.[19]

A frieze from Deopahar consists of three panels. The first one shows a woman as a toiler, the second a man dragging a woman from the scene where another is about to thrash her, while a second woman is dissuading him; and the third a man advancing with raised mace. It can be inferred that the scene depicts a quarrel in the village life.[20] The second frieze, having four panels, depicts from left to right, an ascetic pushing a goat before him, another ascetic dancing with *suja* and *dhakka* in his hands and Kamandalu hanging from his right arm; and a seated woman in an ecstatic mood.[21] The third frieze having four panels, depicts worshipping by sitting, and the hands are shown in *anjali hasta mudra.*[22] The fourth frieze is divided into two panels, illustrating a combat between two warriors. The actual combat is shown in one panel, while in the others, one of the warriors marches off in triumph with the severed head of the other held in his hand, the headless trunk staggering behind.[23] Another shows a man protecting his family rested on an elephant's back against a man attacking.[24]

A stone slab bearing a beautiful scene of a mother and a child is noticed on a *prakara* of the western torana at Kamakhya.[25] In this scene the mother is seated putting her left leg vertically and the right horizontally, keeping her child on her lap. The baby is seen sucking the right breast of the mother, who turns her on the right shoulder out of affection for the child and satisfaction. The baby is shown raising its legs out of joy. The mother holds the baby with both the hands. Indeed, such a realistic sculpture of a mother and child is very rare, and is significant from the aesthetic point of view. Another similar sculpture of mother and child is also found in the *prakara* of the torana.

A stone slab from the same *prakara* of Kamakhya depicts a scene where a female devotee is shown kneeling and offering water to an animal by pouring it from her water pot into the mouth of the animal. She wears a long cloth on the upper part of her body. Another slab contains a man who is shown blowing a *sankha.* All these sculptures are of a rare type.[26] A frieze from Cole Park, having three panels, depicts a dual. The first one shows two wrestlers fighting; the second one shows them lying on the ground with one over-powering the other, and the third one represents both lying straight in opposite directions, the right one holding the legs of the other, who seems to have surrendered.[27]

A stone block (36 x 26 cms) from Tarabasa bearing a male basket carrier, is noticed. Here the man is shown carrying a loaded basket on his head; while lifting up the loaded basket his legs bend and are wide apart. By strengthening himself to lift up, his right hand is kept pressed on his right kneecap. On the other side of the stone block is shown a female figure carrying a pot in her left hand and a stick in the right hand.[28]

A stone slab bearing a female figure carrying a basket on her head and some monkeys attempting to take away fruits from the basket is noticed. Such type of secular thems are found in sculptures all over the ruins of Assam.

Amorous figures: Amorous figures are also found in the ruins of Assam. The occurrence of this type of figures, as suggested by Sir William Rothenstein, was a part of the Tantric attitude which was characteristic of Indian religious philosophy between AD 10th and 12th centuries.[29] These erotic sculptures have the support of the traditional practices of centuries of temple building, and have been enjoined by the sacred texts such as *Kāmasūtra.* The *Agni purāṇa* enjoins that the door-way of temples should be decorated with *Mithunas.*[30]

An erotic scene is noticed on a stone slab from Singri ruins. Two niches are divided by circular pilasters of the panel, and each of the niches contains four figures. From the right, two seated female figures raising their hands to their eyes shown to be hiding from the erotic scenes on their right side. A male and a female are shown seated; he has raised her left leg horizontally, keeping her left hand vertically on the ground for support, the male with his right hand has embraced the left breast of the female. The male figure is seen in a copulating pose over the female; the body of the male lying between the raised legs of the female. The second niche contains a male and a female in a similar pose, the two female attendants, one on each side, are apparently trying to shut out the scene by keeping their hands over their eyes.[31]

A scene depicted in another frieze shows a male copulating with a female in the same posture as described above. In this panel only one female attendant is shown.

Another interesting scene is depicted on a slab from Change-chaki (Kamrup), wherein the male and the female figures are seated on an easy chair. The right leg of the male is spread horizontally and the left is bent and spread to the opposite direction and parallel to his right leg; his body is supported on this left leg; his right hand is vertically spread over the chair for support and his left hand is embracing the female's left breast. The male is seated on the right thigh of the female. The female has kept her right leg in such a way that the male can sit on the thigh, and her left leg is kept on the chair for support; with her left hand she has embraced the shoulder of the male. Both are adorned with *mukta, kundala, hāra, valaya,* etc.[32]

The Assam State Museum preserves five stone blocks bearing erotic scenes.[33] The right side of the first block carries a male and a female figure in sitting posture. The male is seated stretching both the legs forward horizontally on the seat. The female is seated in *utkatikāsana* posture on the lap of the male facing the same direction as he does. Both the hands of the male are placed on the bosom of the female. Both of them are shown in embracing, kissing and copulating posture. This sculpture depicts a beautiful scene of love of a young couple, and the scene is depicted in relief as well as profile.

Another niche of the same block depicts a male seated cross-legged and a female seated on the lap of the male. They are facing each other. The female stretches her legs raised over the hands of the male and the male by his hands pushing the hips of the female towards his body so as to have a perfect completion. The female embraces the neck of the male with both her hands. They are shown kissing.

The next slab shows a couple in standing posture. The male is seen trying to bring the female closer to him. He embraces the breast of his lover by his right hand and holding his erect *linga* by the left hand. Here the female is shown to feel shy.

The fifth scene is depicted on another stone slab. This slab bears six different scenes. In the first scene, a female is shown leaning on a piece of flat wood (?) placing both the legs on both sides of the male who is kneeling down. Both the figures are facing each other. The male is touching the right leg of the female with his left hand, while his right hand embraces her neck. The female embraces the shoulder of the male with her left hand, and places her right hand on the left wood for support. Here, it seems, the preparation for a union is depicted. Both the figures are in profile. The next *Khattaka* depicts a squatting male figure. The male is shown holding the erected *linga* with both the hands. This type of scene is very rare in sculpture.

On the other side of the slab there are three *Khattakas.* In the middle one, a couple is shown in an erotic posture. The female is shown sitting and stretching her legs forward. The male is kneeling putting his knees outside the legs of the lady and the lady holds his *linga* by one hand and embraces him with the other. The male holds the left leg of the female with his right hand and embraces her with his left hand. Both the figures are depicted in profile. To the right in other *Khattaka* is shown a male figure seated in *mahārājaliāsana,* holding his *linga* with the right hand and supporting the leaning head by the left hand. It seems like the male is shown masturbating. This stone slab bears six scenes: three masturbating, one dancing and two copulating scenes. All the sculptures of this slab are small in size.[34]

Another slab shows two erotic scenes. The first represents a female human figure engaged in a sexual act with a bull. The lady is shown kneeling and the left hand carries the weight of the body. The bull is shown jumping over the lady from her back side. The bull raises its tail and seems to be full of passion. This type of union or bestiality is found sculptured also in some other sites of erotic sculptures in India.[35]

The ruins of Madan Kamdeva Parvat yielded quite a good number of erotic sculptures. A slab bears two erotic sculptures. The first represents a lady and a male figure in copulating posture. Here the lady is shown lying on the ground upwards placing her hands on the ground to support the upper part of the body. She raises her legs on either side of the male, who is squatting and embracing the prostrate partner.

The other scene shows a male sitting on the ground. A lady is shown squatting in his front and with both of her hands holding the *linga* of the male. This type of erotic scene is rare.

Another slab bears an interesting amorous scene between a man and a she-goat. The she-goat is shown standing and turning its head backward. From the backside of the goat is shown a man mounting on it for sexual union. The man while doing so is kissing the she-goat. This type of bestialily is very rare.

In Madan Kamdeva, on a niche is depicted an amorous scene between varāha and a woman.

In addition to these erotic sculptures, a few erotic sculptures are noticed in other places. A few pieces of erotic sculptures are found lying outside the Guptesvar temple, Singri. On the northern *prakara* wall of the *Hayagriva-Madhava* temple at Hajo, erotic scenes are also seen on stone slabs.

At Deulgovinda, North Guwahati, a few *mithuna* figures are noticed sculptured on two *pattakas.* All these sculptures belong, on stylistic ground, to AD 9th-10th centuries.

Pingalesvar ruins have yielded quite a few erotic scenes. A stone slab from a modern house near Deulgovinda contains two erotic scene. Here a man is shown to be applying force on a female figure to bring her closer. All these sculptures on stylistic ground may be placed around 9th century AD.

Besides human figures, animals and birds are noticed in coupling postures. Such a scene from Na-nath-than is depicted on a pillar. A male deer is seated upon the back of a female deer in an act of coition. A frieze from Deoparvat shows a royal archer shooting a deer couple while in coition. In Madan Kamdeva a large number of erotic scenes depicted on stone slabs have been noticed. In the ruins of Pingaleswar, erotic scenes depicted on friezes besides other sculptures are found.

The postures of the erotic sculptures from Assam, it is clear from our discussion, are not very common. In most of the scenes, the figures are in copulating posture in samāpti form ie culminating point for both the parties and not in an ordinary love-playing posture. The scenes of masturbation are again very uncommon. Likewise, the scenes of bestiality (union between man and animal), though found in other places in India, seem to be slightly peculiar in that the figures of men and animals are shown in the culminating point of their sexual desire. On stylistic consideration, all these sculptures may be placed in 9th-11th centuries AD.

2. Animal Figures

In the art of Assam, sculptures representing animals are quite numerous. These figures adorn the walls, ceilings, pillars, doorframe, etc of the temple.

Elephants are very common in the ancient art of Assam and the elephant bust was used as the royal insignia in early times. A row of *gajathara* appears as the moulding of the *adhisthāna* (base) of some temple. Elephants busts in the attitude of supporting the structures of a temple are found in the ruins of Deoparvat. A frieze of the plinth from Deoparvat containing elephant heads is preserved in the Assam State Museum. Another piece from Deoparvat representing a row of elephants also in the attitude of supporting the super structure is seen in the modern Shiva temple at Numaligar, very near to the Deoparvat site. A frienze from Guwahati shows two elephants with their trunks raised to pluck tree leaves from both sides of the tree. Depiction of rows of elephants on friezes are also used as spouted drain found in ruins. Every copper-plate inscription of the kings of Kāmarūpa bears the head of an elephant.

A row of elephants (*gajathara*) is found as the moulding of the *adhisthana* of a temple. On a moulding in the Hayagriva Madhava temple at Hajo, about 61 cms about the *adhisthana* a row of caparisoned elephants ie *gajathara* motif encircles the *Vimana* and supports the edifice. Here the trunks, tusks and the forelegs of the elephants are vividly shown. In a temple at Seessee, on its round *adhisthana,* similar figure of an the elephant has been noticed. The *gajathara* motif was quite commonly employed in the temples of Assam.

An elephant carved on a block of stone is found in the temple at Kawaimari. A *dvara sirāpatti* preserved in the ASM shows two elephants and in the middle a *kumbha* (pitcher). A block of stone depicts two figures of richly decorated elephants marching forward. Both the figures are shown with tusks and a cushion on the back and a bell hanging down by the side from a chain.

The lion is frequently found in the art of Assam. The conventional representation of the lion shows that the inhabitants of the Assam Valley were not familiar with the king of beasts. The lions are mostly found in lintel, door-sills and friezes of the walls.

A door-sill (267 x 60 x 77cms) from Singri contains two lions; and they are in two different panels depicted in same directions. A door-sill (143 x 32 cms) from Akasigaṅgg contains a *ghata* flanked by two lions standing with raised tails. This motif is noticed on a door-sill (118 x 28 x 36 cms) from Barganga and in another (124 x 30 cms) from Gachtal. The representation of a pair of lions shown running away from each other with their heads bent towards the *mangala kalasa* are a very common decorative motive in early Assamese art.

In some cases lions are also carved on the capitals of pillars. Sculptures depicting a lion on an elephant, sometimes two lions on two elephants (*gaja-simha*) are commonly found in the ruins of Assam. A *gajasimha* motif is found in the Sankha Devi temple in Jugijan. It measures 108 x 104 cms. *gajasimha* motif from Arabasa depicts two lions seated on two elephants. The lions are shown as two bodies but with a common head as in the case of the elephants.

A *gajasimha* motif from Kāwāimāri shows the trunks of elephants bound by chains. It measures 50 x 36 cms. Sculptures of *gajasimha* motif are found at Bamunipāhār, Chāngchoti, Diphu Park, Madan Kamdeva, Budā-gosain-thān and many other places. A large number of these motifs of big and small sizes have been found in the ruins of Madan Kamdeva. These have affinity with the relics of the Pala period of Bengal.

This type of representation is common to the Orissa temples, where they are used as an architectural device. The figure of a lion is usually displayed on each of the *sikhara*—a projection specially in the Lingaraja and Konark temples.

In Bamuni Pāhār ruins, two large slabs of stone bear the *gaja-sardula* motif, which seems to have stylistic relation with the Pala school of Bengal. A similar sculpture is found at Numaligarh. Stone slabs bearing lions standing on a couch and vanquished elephants are seen in the ruins of Assam.

In the Assam State Museum, few images representing *gaja-sardula* have been seen. In this motif the elephant is depicted smaller in size than the standing lion who keeps its rear legs on the back of the elephant and the other two front legs along with the body rising up. The *gaja-sardula* motif is also found on either side of the *silapatta* of the icons of gods and goddesses belonging to a period ranging from 9th-12th century AD in Assam as in Bengal. The independent image of *gaja-sardula* motif belongs to the same period of 9th-12th century AD as known from the existing sculptures.

The carving of a pair of lions shown running from each other with their heads bent towards the *mangal kalasa* is commonly met with in old Assamese art as a decorative motif. This type of decorative motif is found on door-sills in the ruins of Assam. A broken *dvara-dehali* representing the scene of the *mangala ghata* and a retreating lion on either side, is seen in the Assam State Museum, which was brought from Hahcara, Sibsagar. A slab of stone bearing a figure of dvāra-pālika and a lion is noticed in the residence of R.C. Choudhury of Uzan Bazar, Guwahati.

Like elephant, lion was also treated as an important animal in the past and it found places in icons and work of art in Assam. The lion is the *vahana* of goddess Durgā. The elephant is the *vahana* of Indra. A terracotta plaque from Kundilnagar shows a lion standing on the two rear legs as the front ones being uplifted.

Representation of bulls (Nandi) are frequently found in the ruins of Shiva temples of Assam. Figures of bulls were found especially in Shiva shrines as *vahana* of Shiva with Shiva images. A seated Nandi (54 x 93 cms) showing *'astaraka'* on the back is noticed in Budagosain *thān.* Another bull (48 x 67 cms) from Akasiganga, has an *astaraka* on the back and with a bull hanging from the neck. A bull (47 x 38 cms) from Numaligarh, adorned with *astaraka* on the back and wearing garland of bulls (*khudra ghantika*) is found in seated posture. Two bulls from Gachtal preserved in Nagaon Park are shown wearing *astaraka* at Akasiganga. The figures of a cow and a bull are sculptured on stone slabs. Figures of the horse generally found in the image of Surya. A terracotta plaque from Kundilnagar shows a horse with the saddle and bridle.

Animals, such as horse, deer, bear, *varaha* and tiger are also represented in the sculptures of Assam. Carved horse, deer and tiger are noticed on the pillars from Na-nath-than and Gachtal. The carving of a bear on the capital of a pillar occurs in Kawaimari. Sculptures of the horse and *varaha* (pig) are found in Mahamaya-thān.

Birds are also depicted as decorative motif in the ancient art of this region. Among the birds, geese, peacocks and owls are noticed. The flying geese with long necks occurring on the door-jambs of Daparbatia are remarkable. The birds are met with in the terracotta sculptures from Kundilnagar and Na-nath-than. A plaque from Kundilnagar shows a pair of peacocks with their bodies twisted around each other in graceful embrace. The second plaque shows a falcon carrying a heron. The third plaque represents a bird and the fourth plaque shows a bird with its open wings.

In addition to the independent representation of animals and birds, we notice them with different deities as their vehicles.

Grotesque or mythical figures : Among the grotesque or mythical figures, the *Kirttimukha* (lit. glory ace) is the most common throughout the region as a mere artistic device and as an architectural ornament.[36] As an important motif it occurs in Indian art as a sacred symbol, than as a mere artistic device and as an architectural ornament. As an important motif in Indian art and architecture this has received popular recognition in the Indian sculpture. Almost all the Chalukyan monuments exhibit this trait.[37] In Assam, it occurs either on the front pediment or throughout the walls and on the pillars and their shafts. It is found in the capitals of the pillars from Tezpur, now preserved in Cole Park.

The antiquitity of this motif in India goes back to the Gupta period where it looks more realistic. This is particularly evident from the specimens belonging to the temples of Assam. The ruins from Tezpur, ie Bamunipahar and Cole Park, depict the motif more elaborately compared to those of the Gupta period. But the later temple of Deopahar represents the figure more in the ferocious lion, thus marring its own reality and shape.[38]

In Assam, the motif had undergone various types of stylisation with a profusion of decorative elephants. In most of the figures, the lower jaw is absent. The *Kirttimukhas* occurring on the coping piece of Deopahar are remarkably akin to the Javanese figures and are provided like the latter, with eyes having horn-like sockets.

In the image of the period from 10th-12th century AD, *Kirttimukha* is an invariable motif, which is depicted at the top of the stele (*Śilāpatta*) flanked by two figures of *Vidyādharas.* The figures of *Kirttimukha* were commonly used in temple decoration in the medieval period of Assam.

Among the composite animal figures, the *Makara* (whose mouth is that of an alligator or crocodile with a tail resembling that of an animal, *Suparna,* the mythical deity, half-man and half-bird) and *Garuda* are found in the art of Assam. *Garuda* is the *vahana* of Vishnu, *Makara* and *Kurma* (tortoise) are the *vahanas* of the river goddesses Ganga and Yamuna respectively. The figures of *Makara, Kurma* and *Garuda* are noticed in the door-frame of Da-parbatia. *Makara* and *Kurma* are also noticed in the door-jambs of Majgaon. In another door-jamb lying in the ruins of Majgaon, *Makara* is seen. One of the incarnations of Vishnu is *Kurma* and the Kurmāvatara of Vishnu is found in the pillars and door-jambs in many places of Assam.

Vyāla (lion) is generally depicted as grotesque in the art of ancient Assam. In addition to these grotesque figures we notice some other grotesque motifs, such as the hybrid form of a woman and a horse with the face of a horse (?) and the body of a woman. Such figures are known as *Kinnaras* (centaurs). Sometimes we notice the hybrid form of human being and snakes, or human being and fish; the upper portion is human and the lower portion is of snake of fish in the door jambs from Da-parbatia, and the lintels from Sankha Devi temple and Changchoki (Kawaimari). Another is a massive capital with huge *Kirttimukha* facing the four cardinal points with a *nāgi* with folded hands (hybrid form of a woman and snake) shown on all the corners of the capital. Besides these, we notice snake associated with some deities, such as Manasā Cāmundā, etc. Snakes were also used as the decorative motif in the art of Assam, particularly in the door-jambs and lintels of the Shiva temples.[39]

Dwarfs: The depiction of dwarfs was not a feature in the art and architecture of Assam. The stunted pot-bellied figures are noticed in the ruins of Madan-Kamdeva and Deopahar. Such figures are noticed in terracotta plaques from Ganes Pahar (Mayang) and Bhaitbari-Phulbari, shown wearing lower garment *chhannavira* and heavy *kundalas.*

3. Ornamental Designs

These are divided into three classes:

(*a*) Architectural designs
(*b*) Geometric designs
(*c*) Floral designs

(a) *Architectural designs:* The *caitya* window ornament occurring almost invariably in all periods of Indian monuments may be called an architectural design.[40] The early form of this ornament "imitates the window-like hollow portion on the facade of the Caitya caves at Bhājā, Kondan Bedsa, Karle, Junar, Nasik, Pitalkhora and Ajanta".[41] *Caitya* window (*candrasala*) ornament is generally marked by the hollow portion of a temple wall and the imitated design marked on the lintels etc. Two different types of *caitya* window are seen on the door-lintel of Daparbatia. One is a trefoil where the three arches are depicted in equal size, and in the second variety, the upper area is larger than the two arcs on the sides.[42] The interior of the sunken panels is entirely covered with geometrical patterns with a half rosette in the centre.[43] The *gavaksa* design (circular window), perforated (*surise*) window, ornamental shrine designs, and the replica of sikhara designs are the most common, depicted in the ancient art of the region.[44] The dome-like *stupa* and pyramidal roof are other architectural motifs.[45]

(b) *Geometrical designs:* Geometrical designs are mostly found on ceilings and pillars. Purely geometric designs are the concentric circles of decreasing diameters placed in an octagon. Geometric designs are noticed on ceiling slabs containing floral designs on the outer circles, while the inner circle is covered with a full-bloomed lotus in three courses. On the pillars of Kachamari and Dimapur, various geometrical designs are seen.[46]

In the ruins of Akasiganga, a lintel shows some design of a miniature temple. Similar lintels representing the temple design are also found in Bamunipahar, Majgaon, Singri, Madan Kamdeva, Akasiganga and other places. Rock-cut temples as ornamental motif are also found in Kamakhya. In the ASM two lintels bear the design of temple; one of the lintels was found in the Judge's field, Guwahati. Outside the western Torana of the Kamakhya temple, some similar miniature temple designs are noticed, beautifully carved on rock.

A few terracotta sculptures from Bhaitabari depict the *śikhara* of temple over the head of the deities. Here *śikhara* with *āmalaka* is shown. Stylistically, they may be placed to 10th century AD. At Gosainjuri, a capital is shown with a *gavāksa* design. A door-jamb carved with *yavanika* design is noticed in the ruins of Gosainjuri. *Kundraksabatayan, amalakas,* moulded architraves reminiscent of the Chalukyan style of decoration are noticed at Akasiganga.

(c) *Floral designs*: Floral designs comprising leaf and flower, creeper and purely leaf demarcation are commonly found. Of the floral designs, lotus was the most common, which was carved in various forms ie bud, half-blown and full-blown flowers. The pedestals (*āsana*) of the deities are mostly found in the shape of full-blown multi-petalled lotuses, the ceilings of the shrines contain a full-blown lotus carved on them, quite large and circular in size, which is called *visvapadma*. The ceilings bearing *visvapadma* design are noticed at Cole Park, Mathajhar, Bamunipahar, Changchoki, Pschim Tarabasa, Deopahar, Singri and other places. A cluster of lotuses in full bloom occurs on a stone slab from Deopahar, now preserved in the ASM. On a lintel from Dewalkhanda, a big half-blown lotus is carved. "Most of the images of various deities belonging to 10th-12th century AD have lotus bud (*Padma kosa*) design below the *āsana* of the deity. These are depicted coiling."[47]

The pot and foliage (*ghata-pallava*) motif is discernible in the region. "The vase from which spring out flowers with leaves falling downwards, decorate usually the lower part of the pillar of the Gupta temple, known as *Purnakalsa,* the bowl of plenty, typifying a renewed faith, the water nourishing the plant trailing from its brim, an allegory which had produced the vase and flower motif one of the most graceful forms in the whole range of Indian architecture.[48] This motif may have descended from the floral motif on the medallions on the railings of Bharhut and Sanchi *stupas,* Sankali. The first instance of this motif is noticed on the door-jamb of Daparbatia and another from Deopahar. The flowers are more luxuriant in Deopahar than in the former.

Another design, which is named "string course", "scroll" or "creeper", is essentially floral. This floral design is commonly met with in the door-jambs, door-lintels, pillars and other architectural features of this region. Most of these are winding or undulating scrolls containing flowers and foliage of various kinds and cover the leading bands of lintels and door-jambs.

A frieze containing spirited human figures in high motion is one of the interesting designs noticed in Deopahar.[49] Another interesting design is found in a door-lintel from Domukhi Jaljuri, Howraghat, the scroll in its loops formed by the creeper enclosing bull and flower one by one.[50] One door-jamb from Cole-Park containg three vertical bands and the extreme right band, in its loop formed by the creeper, encloses animals and birds, such as horse, hog and swan. A similar door- jamb is also found at Sibsagar. At the *adhisathāna* of the Ghantakarana temple at Kamakhya, one stone slab is a beautifully carved frieze in which the band represents a series of garlands and the lower scroll work in which some very spirited representations of animals occur as observed by Dikshit. Only four animals, namely buffalo, tiger, lion and deer are seen and the others are mutilated. The quality of art manifested in them is unsurpassed in Assam. According to Banerji these carvings belong to 7th/8th century AD.

These are also depicted in the door-lintel as decorative motifs. A *Kalpabriksa* motif is found on a stone slab, probably a piece of *torana,* from Deopahar. The twisted serpents are seen as decorative motif in door-jambs and lintels which run vertically from the bottom of the jamb and sometimes continue in the door-lintel; and in some of the door-frames, it starts from the lintel and continues to the bottom of the door-jambs. Examples are found in the door-frames of Gachtal, Sankha Devi, Daparbatia and other places.

The sculptures of Assam exhibit various regional characteristics. The monuments of the region belong to the earliest to 6th century AD. It is noticed that several decorative motif architectural designs and temple sculptures are aimitated from Bengal, Orissa and Central India.

Terracotta: "Clay has been regarded as the primeval material not only because of its ready availability, but also on account of its easy capability." It satisfies the creative impulse of ordinary man, as much for aesthetic expression as for domestic and ritualistic needs.[51] It has served as an easy and convenient plastic material from times immemorial.[52] In later Indian art terracotta is contently employed in various ways either for decoration of buildings or for votive plaques.[53]

In Assam, terracotta constituted the common and popular medium of the artistic expression of people. But only a few terracotta figures have been discovered in Assam.

In Daparbatia, R.D. Banerji discovered a number of terracotta plaques representing human figurines which portray a very close connection between the medieval art of Bengal and Assam.[54] They are of the same type as the terracotta figurines discovered at Birat in Rangpur district and at Paharpur in Rajshahi district.[55]

T. Block has discovered some terracotta tiles representing figurines at Kundilnagar, Sadiya.[56] From the stylistic point of view, the terracotta figurines from both the places are different according to Dasgupta and they are placed in the same age.[57]

K.L. Barua discovered a terracotta figurine of the Buddha in Guwahati. It represented the Buddha seated in *bhumi-sparsa mudrā* under the trefoil arch surrounded by a *sikhara* or pinnacle. The miniature *stupas* are represented on two sides of the Buddha. In this plaque, the figurine of the Buddha is indicated inside the great temple at *Vajrasāna vihāra,* ie Bodh Gaya. The Buddhist creed is inscribed beneath the *asana.* In the script of 11th century AD similar terracotta figurines are reported from Raghurampur, Sabhar and Nalanda. A few terracotta broken rings representing the Buddha's figurines as seated in *bhumi-sparsa mudrā* under the trefoil arch surrounded by *sikhara* were discovered by the author of this paper and a team from State Archaeology Department from village Majarpara, Barbhita near Paglatek in Goalpara district. A terracotta plaque bearing the figure of *vyala* is also found at the site.

A terracotta plaque representing a male human figurine, seated on *asana* in *yogasana* posture, has come from Na-nath-than, Jogijan. The right hand is shown raised holding an indistinct object, while the left hand is placed on the left thigh.

Another terracotta figurine (30 x 22 cms) has been found at Ganes Pahar, Mayang, representing a pot-bellied, squatting human figure and both the raised hands hold objects. A similar terracotta figurine has been reported from Mahasthan.

The third terracotta figurine (38 x 26 cms) has been found at Ganes Pahar, Mayang. It represents a crude figure in dancing posture. It holds some object in the right hand. The figure is emaciated. It wears a short loin cloth. Similar dancing figures were also found in Chenikuthi, Guwahati, Siddheswar temple, Sualkuchi, which are preserved in the ASM. Two similar figures have been found at Bhaitbari in Garo hills.

Two terracotta plaques from Jogijan are preserved in the ASM. The first one contains a human figure in a half kneeling position with folded hands. He is shown in *alidha* posture. He carries a quiver with arrows on his back. The bow is shown behind the figure. The other plaque bears two human figures, one seated cross-legged keeping both the hands on his knees. The other figure is shown standing to the left of the former. Both the figures wear crowns on their heads. Three similar terracotta plaques are noticed at Kenduguri near Na-nath-than representing a human figure, a banana tree and a bird.

The terracotta figurines from Assam, belonging to the early medieval period, can be compared with their proto-types found in Bengal, U.P., Bihar and Kashmir. In modelling of the figurines, according to Dasgupta.[58] there are points of similarity as well as difference among them. From the analytical study of modelling of the terracotta figurines of the medieval period, Dasgupta divided them into seven district schools. They are:

1. The Assam school represented by Kundilnagar specimens;
2. The Eastern school, evolved out of the Gupta sculpture and represented by some terracotta specimens of Paharpur;
3. The school of hybrid compromise between the eastern school evolved of the Gupta sculpture and the school of the indigeneous eastern Indian sculptures represented by some terracotta speciments of Paharpur;
4. The school of indigeneous eastern Indian sculptures represented by some terracotta specimens of Paharpur and Mahasthan;
5. The eastern Indian medieval school represented by some specimens found at Da-parbatia, Sabhar, Raghurampur, Bangarh, Paharpur and Nalandsa;
6. Central Indian type represented by Saheth-Maheth specimens; and
7. North Indian type represented by Avantipur specimens.

The bird figurines from Kundilnagar are remarkable as one of the specimens gives plastic expression to the conjugal love of the birds which is rarely found in Indian plastic art. Here, a peacock and a pea-hen are shown in an amorous copulating attitude in a sensitive manner.

In the modelling of the figurines from Assam belonging to the medieval period, we find similarity as well as difference. The terracotta figurines so far found in Assam may be divided into different categories. The Kundilnagar variety belongs to the Assam school, while the figurines from Da-parbatia belong to the eastern Indian medieval school; and the third category supported by the specimen from Mayang, Guwahati, Bhaitbari shows traits of the indigenous eastern Indian sculptures.

NOTES AND REFERENCES

1. P.C. Choudhury, *The History of Civilization of the People of Assam to the Twelfth Century A.D.*, Guwahati, 1966.
2. *Ibid.*
3. H.D. Sankalia, *The Archaeology of Gujarat* (including Kathiawar), Bombay, 1941, p. 116.

4. N.D. Choudhury, *Historical Archaeology of Central Assam* (from earliest time to 12th century AD), Delhi, 1985, p. 186.
5. P.C. Choudhury, *op. cit.*
6. A.R.A.S.I., 1925-26, pp. 115-16.
7. *Ibid.*
8. N.D. Choudhury, *op. cit.*, p. 186.
9. R.D. Choudhury, *Archaeology of the Brahmaputra Valley of Assam*, Delhi, 1985.
10. N.D. Choudhury, *op. cit.*; R.D. Choudhury, *op. cit.*
11. *Ibid.*
12. *Ibid.*
13. *Ibid.*
14. *Ibid.*
15. *Ibid.*
16. *Ibid.*
17. R.D. Choudhury, *op. cit.*, p. 168; B.K. Barua, *A Cultural History of Assam.*
18. *Ibid.*
19. *Ibid.*, N.D. Choudhury, *op. cit.*, p. 191.
20. R.D. Choudhury, *op. cit.*, p. 179; ASASI, 1936-37, p. 59.
21. *Ibid.*
22. R.D. Choudhury, *op. cit.*, p. 186; ASASI, 1936-37, p. 59.
23. *Ibid.*, N.D. Choudhury, *op. cit.*, p. 191.
24. *Ibid.*
25. R.D. Choudhury, *op. cit.*, p. 179.
26. *Ibid.*
27. ASASI, 1936-37; N.D. Choudhury, *op. cit.*, pp.190-91; R.D. Choudhury, *op.* pp. 179-80.
28. R.D. Choudhury, *op. cit.*, pp.179-80; Sankalia, *op. cit.*, p. 172.
29. Sankalia, H.D., *op. cit.*, p. 121.
30. O.C. Ganguli, 'The Mithura in India Art', *Rupam*, No. 202-23, 1925, pp. 54-56.
31. N.D. Choudhury, *op. cit.*, pp. 189-90.
32. *Ibid.*
33. *Ibid.*
34. *Ibid.*
35. *Ibid.*
36. C. Gangali, 'A note on the Kirttimukha', *Rupam*, 1920, p. 11; N.D. Choudhury; *op. cit.*; R.D. Choudhury, *op. cit.*
37. Sankalia, H.D., *op. cit.*, p. 123.
38. N.D. Choudhury, *op. cit.*, pp. 194-95.

39. *Ibid.*
40. Sankalia, *op. cit.*, p. 126.
41. *Ibid.*
42. R.D. Banerji, *The Age of the Imperial Guptas*, p. 196; ARASI, 1924-25, p. 97.
43. B.K. Barua, *op. cit.*, p. 201.
44. ARASI, 1936-37, pp. 54ff.
45. R.D. Choudhury, *op. cit.*; N.D. Choudhury, *op. cit.*, p. 196.
46. N.D. Choudhury, *op. cit.*, p. 196.
47. R.D. Choudhury, *op. cit.*
48. Percy Brown, *Indian Architecture* (*Buddhist and Hindu*), Bombay, Vol. I, 1956, p. 59.
49. N.D. Choudhury, *op. cit.*, p. 197.
50. *Ibid.*
51. S.K. Saraswati, *Early Sculptures of Bengal*, Calcutta, 1962, p. 91.
52. *Ibid.*
53. A.K. Coomarswamy, *History of Indian and Indonesian Art*, 1927, p. 94; *Early Indian Terracotta*, B.M.F.A.B, Vol. XXV, 192 f.
54. R.D. Banerji, ARASI, 1925-26, p. 1. LIV; *Age of the Imperial Guptas*, 1933, pp. 207-8.
55. *Ibid.*, ARASI, 1928, p. 116.
56. T. Block, ARASI, 1906-7; 1909, p. 1. VIII.
57. C.C. Dasgupta, *Origin and Evolution of Indian Clay Sculpture*, p. 228.
58. *Ibid.*, R.D. Choudhury, *op. cit.*; N.D. Choudhury, *op. cit.*

10

Historical Significance of the Sculpture at Unakoti

R.D. Choudhury

Unakoti is located in a hilly region of Tripura near the Assam-Tripura border. The distance from Agartala to Kailasahar is about 175 km; Kailasahar to the site is about 10 km. The site of the rock-cut sculpture is at a little distance under, thick forest.

The site is associated with a local legend. According to the legendary tales Śiva along with other gods and goddesses was marching to Varanasi. The team divinity reached the place just before it got dark. They also felt tired. So they decided to spend the night in this locality. Thereupon, the local population came to pay their respect to these divinities. The Śiva devotees urged lord Śiva not to proceed to Varanasi but, to stay in that place permanently. Śiva did not like to disappoint his devotees. So he imposed a condition. He said, he would stay there provided his devotees could carve one sculpture on the rock at the site within that night. The local people started the work with great enthusiasm and risk under the leadership of one Kālākamār. But the work could not be completed before dawn. They could carve images numbering one crore less one. As the work was not completed before dawn, Śiva left the place along with other divinities for Varanasi. That is why, the place is known as Unakoti, ie one crore less one. Local people still treat the images of the deities with reverence. Yearly one *mela* is organized by the local communities who come here to take bath in the *Kundas,* ie *Astami Kunda, Sitā Kunda* and *Bhagirathi Kunda* created by water of the streamlet, to get rid of their sins. However, no written records about Unakoti is available. The Tripura Rajmala is also silent.

The sculptures of this place can be broadly divided into two groups. The first group of sculptures is rock-cut. To the right of the streamlet there are huge engravings on the rock, which looks like a natural wall depicting *Jatādāri* Śiva. It is a huge engraving depicting the face of Śiva. The *Jatā* on the head is vividly portrayed. Above the *Jatā* the crescent moon (?) is shown. The face of Śiva is shown with exposed teeth. Towards the left of the bust of Śiva another bust is carved on the same rock. The exposed teeth are depicted in the same way. Both the figures are carved in low relief. The third one is also a huge bust of Śiva measuring 13.43 meter in height, 9.33 metre in width. The sculpture is very interesting. It has a big *Jatā* on the head. The exposed teeth are very clear. To the right of the imposing *Jatā* is seen the miniature figure of Gangā standing on her vehicle, a *makara* (crocodile), while to the left stands the figure of Pārvatī. The teeth of the figure of Śiva is exposed very clearly. Just to the left of the image the streamlet flows down touching the figure.

To the right of the huge engraving of Śiva head is seen depicted a huge icon of Gaṇeśa in the usual posture.

In the front of this row of rock-cut sculptures at a lower level on the down stream of the flowing streamlet a seated figure of Gaṇeśa and two similar figures with elephant heads, but showing two horn-like objects above the big ear each, possibly the *gana* of Gaṇeśa, are seen standing in the same row. The figure is seen to the right of the figure of Gaṇeśa. To the extreme right of the row of the figures is seen a standing human figure. Possibly, this figure represents a human devotee of Gaṇeśa.

All these figures are carved just near the bridges over the streamlet. In the rainy season water must have been flown over these sculptures. There is a trace of some sculptures which are sadly broken due to the effect of the strong current of water. Our very close observation leads us to identify it is the smaller engraving of the head of Śiva, similar to the main sculpture of the group described above. It must have represented the head of Śiva with *Jāta;* to the right a miniature standing figure of Gangā must have stood, which is now broken and gone. But her vehicle, the *makara's* head portion is still visible. To the left of the *Jāta* of Śiva, there must have been the standing figure of Pārvatī. Had this rock-cut sculpture been not distorted due to earthquake or the effect of strong current of water, one would have readily said that it was sculptured in the imitation of the bigger Śiva head seen in the earth of the rock-cut sculptures to the little north of the present broken sculpture. The Archaeological Survey of India had constructed a small bridge standing on which the figure of Gaṇeśa and other three figures in the same row and the broken Śiva head slightly at a higher level to the north can be noticed. The rock-cut row of sculpture including the figures of Gaṇeśa must have been tribal trait, as the other sculptures on rock.

As we are told by the local people, there are two images, one representing Pārvatī and the other Śiva at the foot of the hill on the bank of the streamlet towards downstream. These two are also rock-cut sculptures.

From the row of the row-out sculptures one can climb up to the right and get some levelled land at the top. At this place under a shed 11 stone sculptures of medium size are seen lying horizontally. These must have been lying under jungles around the area. At the site, the shed under which the sculptures are kept, there must have existed a small brick built, as the brick-bats at the place show. Still there is small modern shrine at the site using the old carved or used stone.

The stone sculptures kept horizontally under the temporary shed by the Archaeological Survey of India are: Gaṇeśa-1, Umā-Maheśvar-2, Hanumān-1, Narasiṁha-1, Viṣṇu-2, broken image-1, standing mutilated figure with arrow (Rāma?)-1, and standing Śiva (?)-1.

On stylistic consideration, all these beautiful works of art belong to 10th-12th century, ie carved in Pala-Sena style. Some of the sculptures show detail ornamentation, while others do not have the details because of bad stone quality. A few of these have been corroded. If we climb down to the bridge of the streamlet, we can see a *chaturmukahalinga* of Śiva bearing decoration and ornamentation of Pala sculpture. One face of this *mukhalinga* appears to have had beard on the chin, like the face of Brahmā. But it is an excellent example of stone art-work of Pala style of 10th-11th century.

From the style of the stone sculpture preserved under the temporary shed on top of the hill, it is clearly understood that around 10th-11th century, the site was occupied by the people from the plains of undivided Bengal, now Bangladesh, which was very close from the site at Unakoti. Considering the style of the rock-cut sculptures, including the huge Śiva head with Gangā and Pārvatī at the site, we may conclude that these art-work bear clear tribal traits. "In spite of large and huge stature the images and statues here are without grace and naturality. Their limits are disproportionate and so they are ugly to look at. The said sculptures, though of Aryan-Hindu religion, seem not being inscribed by the architects of Pala age (9th-10th century) undoubtedly in view of facial appearance or mode of style adapted therein."[1] This is the opinion of the Archaeological Survey of

India. Our contention is that these rock-cut sculptures are the product of tribal artists. The tribal physiognomy in every face of the rock-cut sculptures is prominent. The style of this group of sculptures carved on the rocks on both the banks of the streamlet at the site have no relation in so far as the style is concerned, with the stone sculptures kept on the top of the hill at the site, which were developed following the Pala period and found the Aryan physiognomy. It is very clear that the present rock-cut sculptures bear testimony to the fact that the tribal population at the locality accepted Hinduism and they worshipped the Hindu gods and goddesses. The rock-cut sculptures represent Śiva and his family. We do not see any image of Viṣṇu or other Hindu gods and goddesses. These rock-cut group of sculptures have no relation with Buddhism or Jainism. It is proved that the local tribal population became the devotees of Śiva.

It may be mentioned that the Tripuri tribes of Tripura and the Bodos of Assam have some ethnic links. The Bodos worship Bāthau. Bāthau is the tribal name of Śiva. There are a large number of *thāns,* ie place of worship of Śiva under some trees without any icons of Śiva. These *thāns* are treated as the place of worship by Khasi, Garo and Bodo tribes of Assam who believe in Śiva. However, there are also images of Śiva made of wood in tribal style. The Kokrajhar District Museum, Assam, has preserved a wooden image of Bāthau. Kokrajhar region is heart of Bodo population of Bodoland of Assam. Since the Tripuris have some link with the Bodos who worship Śiva in tribal form, although now the new generation of the Bodos have started accepting Christianity as their religion, it is justified to believe that the Tripuris also worshipped Śiva in tribal form. Though these tribes had their own faith in the past, due to the constant contact with Hindu population of the plains and considering the popularity of the Hindu religion, it was but natural that they came under heavy influence of Hinduism and some tribals accepted Hinduism.

Now to determine the age of the rock-cut Śaiva sculptures at Unakoti, we are to carefully examine all the factors. It is clear that on stylistic consideration it is difficult to determine the age of the group of rock-cut art-work. As far as stone sculptures are concerned we have got a date.

Let us examine as to who occupied the site earlier. It is certain that the present site attracted the artisans or the two groups of people – tribal and non-tribal. The attraction for the site must be, in the first place, the streamlet. In the second place, the huge rock on either side of the streamlet became the source of attraction to express the artistic talent to leave a message to the future generation. The popular legend says that local people were the devotees of Śiva. This legend of Śiva coming to this place must be very old and we can infer that it had some connection with the Śaiva rock-cut images at the site on either side of the streamlet. Therefore, it will be justified to give an earlier date to the rock-cut sculpture on either side of the streamlet. Had this area not been covered with the artistic activities of the tribal artisans, the artisans of the Pala-Sena period must have occupied this area for their art-work, considering the advantage of the streamlet and the plain rocks instead of going to the hill-top to do their activities. Therefore, we can safely say that the Śaiva art-work at the site bearing tribal physiognomy are older than the stone art-work of the Pala-Sena period.

It is clear that on stylistic consideration, it is difficult to determine the age of the group of rock-cut sculptures, as these are not common. But we are sure that it has no stylistic affiliation to the Pala-Sena art of Bengal. Nor has it any affinity with the art that flourished in Tripura in the Manikaya period. As far as stone sculptures at the site are concerned we have a date – the Pala-Sena period. Therefore, it will be appropriate to place the rock-cut Śiva sculptures in the pre-Pala period, ie 7th-8th century.

The artist who selected the site was really great. The idea to use the streamlet and conceive the idea of depicting the huge head of Śiva with *Jatā* flanked by the miniature figures of Gangā and Pārvatī is undoubtedly superb. The artist adds Gangā to the streamlet ads Gangā - as if Gangā is flowing from up and touches the *Jatā* of Śiva. That is why the artist confined his work to the head of Śiva and not the body or other parts of the god. The exposed tooth god has stood as a big problem to the scholars. But there is also a solution. We know that Pārvatī, the consort of Śiva, did not like Śiva for giving Gangā a place on his head. She, for giving Gangā a place on his head, complained to Śiva. For giving a position higher than her position could not be tolerated by Pārvatī. She took it as a great offence and strongly protested before Śiva. Pārvatī is depicted always in the same level with her husband. How she can tolerate a much higher position to Gangā. So, to satisfy Pārvatī, Śiva settled the dispute by giving her the space to stand on the other side of his *Jatā*. This is how Śiva arrived at a compromising formula. When Pārvatī accepted this and was satisfied by putting an end to her complaint, Śiva became very pleased and so he smiled, thus exposing his teeth. So, the tribal artist, who was a genius, expressed the great pleasure of Śiva through the exposed teeth - a great smile. The artist must have huge sculpture depicting the head of Śiva which is being quoted by the flowing water of the streamlet. The other heads of the same god clearly showing the *Jatā* do not show the miniature figures of Gangā and Pārvatī, the reason being that the streamlet which was taken as Gangā, does not touch the *Jatā* or head of the God. So artist thought it was meaningless to depict Gangā and so the miniature figure of

Pārvatī as in the first case. But as we have already mentioned, traces of a head of Śiva about the standing figures of Gangā and his devotees in a row is found sculptured on a rock over which the water of the streamlet flows. From the remaining portion of the *makara* (crocodile), the vehicle of Gangā, one can be clear that there was the figure of Gangā, which is broken and gone. We can assume that the figure of Pārvatī along with the mount was also eroded by the strong current of water of the streamlet. This head of Śiva, smaller in size, was carved with the figures of Gangā and Pārvatī in the imitation of the bigger one, as described above. Here Gangā (and also Pārvatī) near the *Jatā* of Śiva must have been depicted because, like the other huge head of Śiva, the streamlet here also flows touching the sculpture. The imagination of the artist in both the cases are really praiseworthy. Unfortunately, the entire sculpture is washed away or eroded by the current of the water in such a way that unless one observed from the bridge very minutely, it is difficult to trace it as the quality of rock has deteriorated.

The rock-cut sculpture represented Śiva and his family, including Nandi, the bull vehicle of Śiva. But we did not notice the figure of Bhringi. It should have been there. There is not a Śākti or Vaiṣṇava image in the group. It appears that the tribal group who were responsible for the creation of these sculptures did not believe in other cults. Even a ditch of the streamlet has been known as *Bhagirath Kunda*. It is known to all that Bhagirath brought Gangā to earth.

But at the hill-top, where the stone sculptures belonging to Pala-Sena period have been collected, we get a different picture. Here we get the images of Viṣṇu Narasiṁha, Umā-Maheśvar, Gaṇeśa, Śiva (?), Rāma (?) and Hanumān as mentioned above. There are few images which are badly affected and so their identities are not clear. It shows that by that period, people who patronised this art did not necessarily stick to only Śaivism. They popularised other deities of Brahmanical faith too. It is clear that Unakoti was even associated with the story of Rāma. The image of Hanumān with a female figure below his body (between his legs) is very interesting. To our knowledge the image of Hanumān is extremely rare in eastern India or North-East India. We have not noticed the *Svayam Pradhāna* (carved independently) image of Hanumān in this region including Assam datable to 10th-12th century. Hanumān is, however, very popular in north India and also in some other parts of the country. It may be noted that a small portion of the streamlet which flows below is known as *Sitakunda* which may be associated with the figure of Hanumān and Rāma. It is also proved that Śaivism maintained its popularity even in the Pala-Sena peroid. The *Ramāyaṇa* story was also popular.

From the above study we can conclude that the rock-cut Śiva sculptures prove that the local tribal people in Tripura (Tripuri) accepted Hinduism in the

7th-8th century itself and they occupied the site earlier. The Hindu people did their art activities at the site in 10th-12th century. The Śiva sculptural evidence or the rock at the site tell us that those tribal people were Śaiva. Though the tribal had their own faith, under the influence of the majority Hindus in the Bengal plain, they accepted Śaivisim, as in some parts of Assam, as at that time there was no Christianity nor the Islamic culture in India. The vision of the art master who executed the rock-work by translating his ideas into reality is excellent and unparalleled. Though we know about the rock-cut scene of decadence of Gangā at Mahavalipuram, there is no real flow of a streamlet near the scene. Here the artist has utilised the flowing streamlet, which he meant it as the actual Gangā *Bhagirath Kunda*, of the streamlet at the site proves that local people also wanted to associate the streamlet coming from the hill with decadence of Gangā.

After the tribal people abandoned the site, the Hindu people of the plain occupied the top of the site in 10th-12th century. But after that we do not have any archaeological evidence that the site was occupied in the Manikya period. The Rajmala is also silent. On the whole, the site is unique in character and very important. The sculptures should be treated chemically and Archaeological Survey of India should also survey the adjoining hills.

NOTES AND REFERENCES

1. Leaflet issued by the Archaeological Survey of India, Guwahati Circle, Ambari Assam, translated by Chandra Kanta Sinha, Founder Chairman, Unakoti Academy, Tikakakpur, Kailasahar.

11

Folklore as a Source of History of North-East India

Anima Choudhury

In the absence of any reliable recorded historical material, folklore can be used for reconstructing the ancient cultural and social history of North-East India. Most historians have been generally skeptical about the value of oral sources in reconstructing the past. However, the importance of oral source for correcting other perspectives as well as being corrected by the other perspectives has been realized by the professional historians now. Folklore is capable of tackling major historical and political questions in a distinctive way. It can help in retrieving the voices of the voiceless and can construct the history of history-less people whose views are generally disenfranchised by 'history from above'. Some scholars, including Romilla Thapar, have started thinking and describing myth as unrecorded history of the pre-historical times. The German scholar, J.J. Bachofen, also explained that,

> since the beginning of all development lies in myth, myth must form the starting point for any serious investigation of ancient history. Myth contains the origin... without knowledge of the origins, the science of history can come to no conclusion.[1]

Oral literature reflects the social cultural likes of the people and has a close relation with the history of civilization. The simple illiterate people express their feelings of love, happiness, sorrow, etc through folk literature only. Myths and legends lie in the borderline of the past evidences for construction or reconstruction of history and archaeology. History and myths, tradition and tales, fact and fiction are curiously intermingled.

> The study of the language of folklore material has been extensively utilised earlier for an interpretation of the material, particularly of myths. But modern linguistics have made great strides and developed such specialised branches as ethnolinguistics, sociolinguistics and psycholinguistics, which have considerable relevance for folkloristics. Studies of the languages of this region with the modern techniques could yield a wealth of information about the traditional cultures and cultural contacts.[2]

The Vedic tradition, which is transmitted orally, can furnish ample evidences of political, social, cultural and economic histories. The *Rāmāyaṇa*, the *Mahābhārata* and the *Puranas* were originally transmitted orally and be considered in the domain of oral epic. Albert B Lord said,

> Oral epic reflect the realities of a historical period, if not its details set in chronological relationship to one another. Oral epic presents a composite vision of the past.[3]

According to Dorson, tradition has historical validity.[4] The lives and activities of Lord Krishna, Lord Rama, the Kauravas and Pandavas who are considered as historical characters are known from the *Rāmāyaṇa*, the *Mahābhārata* and the *Puranas* only. The history of the period of Mahavira and the Buddha was reconstructed based on materials received from the *Jatakas* and the *Tripitakas* and other myths and legends connected with Mahavira and Buddha. Some historical references to Assam are interwoven with legends. The earliest history of Assam is associated with the earliest legend of the land. In Assam historical characters like Naraka, Bana, Bhishmaka of Kundilnagar are known from the *Rāmāyaṇa*, the *Mahābhārata* and the *Puranas*. All the historical dynasties of medieval Assam claim their common progeny to Naraka of the epical fame. We have a variety of legends on Narakasura. There are a number of myths and legends on Mother Goddess Kamakhya. The legend linking Narakasura with Kamakhya, and the Koch king, Naranarayana with Kamakhya, legends that associated with Ugratara, Vasisthashram, Ashwaklanta, Pandunath temple, Umananda, etc have helped in reconstructing the history of early Assam. Legends pertaining to Kamarupnagar, Bakhtiyar's invasion, Pratapghar, etc may lead us to the discovery of a lot of fresh material, important for the reconstruction or enlargement of the history of this region. There is no historical record in support of the Buddha's visit to Assam. But according to tradition, Buddha's *parinirvana* occurred at Hajo. The Bhutiyas believe that the image of Hayagriva-Madhava is that of the Mahamuni. Buddhist association with the shrines and temples of Assam may indicate an unknown historical link between Assam and Bhutan.

Historical ballads serve as an important source for the reconstruction of history of every nation. Many of the characters of heroic poetry have historical origin. Livy, a celebrated historian, collected materials for his history from heroic songs. Even the serious historians of Germany used heroic poetry as primary material for their studies. In Assam a number of ballads possess considerable elements of history which may cast new light on the accepted history of Assam. *Barphukanar Geet* relates the story of Burmese invasion of Assam; *Maniram Dewanar Geet,* relates to the events centring round Maniram Dewan who was hanged by the British in 1858. The song goes thus:

Sonar dhuakhowat khali o Maniram
Rupar dhuakhowat khali
Kino rajar gharat droh asarili
Dingit sipjari loli

(You smoked a gold hookah, Oh Maniram, you smoked a silver hookah, what treason did you commit to Royalty, that you got a noose round your neck.)

From the historical ballad of *Barphukanar Geet* it can be known that noblemen rewarded the minstrels for their performances :

Let my lord pay five quarter-rupees,
I sing the ballad of the Barphukan.
It's my good luck
That I have met my lord[5]

The songs of *Phulagurir dhawa* narrate the rebellion of the people of Phulaguri against the British administration. 'Dali Puran' describes the famous peasant uprising in protest against enhancement of taxes by the British administration in the year 1894. There are some ballads like *Haradatta Biradatta Geet, Nagarar Geet* and *Chikan Sariyahar Geet* which have a historical background. In *Haradatta Biradatta Geet,* the song goes like this:

Haradatta Jiyari Padma Kumari
Dhanarat nakhali bhat
Kumedan bangale hatat dhari nile
Padma bichari gol

(Padmakumari, the daughter of Haradatta did not take meal at *Dhanara,* as Kumedan the Sikh Commandant abdirected her. Her lover, Padma went in search of her.)

Rajam writes in her preface that "ballads should be utilized in the proper manner to reconstruct the past. The ballads reflect the view-point of the people and throw light on different aspects of history that cannot be studied otherwise."[6] In some folk-songs such as *biyageet, zikir, ojapali, lokageet,* some historical elements can be found. Some examples are given below:

1. *Patit Bahi Rukminiye matit mangal sai*
   Ketiya ahiba Krishna sonar bangshi bai (biya geet)

(Rukmini sitting on the floor is contemplating, when Krishna would come playing on his gold flute.)

2. *Patite bahihe Usha murcha gole*
   Oi ram, Anirudhak saponat dekhihe (biya geet)
   (Usha fell faint seeing Anirudha in her dream.)
3. *Urigoiya Kalinaga merate parila*
   Bau batah nai kene ghar dakhine halila (ojapali)

(Kalinaga reached the roof of the *merghar* and the *merghar* bent towards left without any storm.)

4. *Kundilate Rukminiye kare jor hat*
   Kenemote Jaiba bapu sai mahar bat (Kamrupi folk song)

(Rukmini worried, how the priest would be able to cover the distance in one day which generally requires six months.)

Folk songs, especially *bihu* songs, provide material for social history. The dresses, the ornaments, the vehicles used by the king or the officials of the Ahom period, construction of temples, roads, new capital, and the digging of tanks are often mentioned in some *bihu* songs. In *bihu* songs fresh compositions often reflect contemporary events. The opening of the tea-gardens, the coming of outsiders to Assam, the introduction of modern transport and communication, and the import of westernization have been noticed in some *bihu* songs, which provide some material for the construction social history.

1. *Sargadeo olale batcharar muraloi*
   Duliai patile dola
   Kanat jilikile makare kundale
   Gatgomsengar chola

(The king has come out and the *dola* is ready, he is wearing beautiful earrings and a shirt made of *gomseng.)*

2. *Sahab ahi pale bagicha khulile*
   Murat saruhen tupi
   Kulir choalik memoni karile
   Mukhate seleudal hupi

(The British came and opened up gardens. On their heads are small hats. With cigars on their lips they convert labour (coolie) girls to British women.)

3. Aliens have come into the land of Assam
   I have observed their vanity,
   Do not go, O dear, to an alien,
   There is no knowing what his love is (Datta 1994:62)
4. Brahmaputre ahile company r jahaj oi
   Prithibi talebalai...

(Ships of the Company have come through the River Brahmaputra creating vibration in the earth.)

Again folktales may serve as oral history, since this genre of oral folklore is regarded as the ethnography of a particular tribe or community. "The incidents depicted in the various genres of folklore can mirror the life of the people and their occupations and social life may in part be reconstructed from these tales."[7]

Traditional sites and spots bearing remains having historical significance can play a significant role in the history of North-East India. The stone ruins of Chandar Merghar found near Chhaygaon, 45 km from Guwahati, are supposed to be the remains from the snake-proof building of Chando as mentioned in the *Beula Lakhinder* legend. An area fortified with massive earthen ramparts near Odalguri in Darrang district is believed to have been the capital of Sahe Raja, the father of Beula. As per another popular legend, Kamala Kuwari was the queen of the all-female kingdom of Kadali. Goraksanath, the great disciple Mysyendranath, alias Minanath came to the east in search of his *guru* and rescued Minanath from the grip of Kamala Kuwari after cursing the entire womanfolk of the kingdom including the queen, to became bats. In his book *Kadali, Rajijen,* R.M. Nath has traced the route by which Gorakhnath undertook his search for the *guru* and identified the kingdom of Kadali as the village Kandali in the Nagaon district. In this context it may be mentioned that old ruins are seen at the Chapanola waterfall lying in the vicinity of Kandali and the place also contains a cave infested with millions of bats.

Many tribal groups of North-East India have no written text, or written history. They possess no written evidences except some official records of colonial period. But the region has ample folklore material. Most of the legends are either mere fantasy or an inflated and exaggerated form of some facts or experiences. In this situation, oral history is an important area where we could look for further data. Proverbs, songs, tales and myth can be highly useful in tracing the history of tribal people, provided the underlying symbolism is deciphered and interpreted accurately. But we must remember that tribal systems should be measured by tribal standard. Malinowski had pointed out that the folklorist should not be solely concerned with literary content of folklore material but must also study the total culture environment surrounding an event of folklore communication. Structural and comparative studies of the music, dance and drama could also provide an interesting insight into certain aspects of the traditional culture of the region.

In the historical study of society where there is no dearth of written data, oral history provides additional access to unofficial and alternative viewpoints. Oral sources reflect on the problems, needs and aspirations of the masses at various point of time. Oral tradition of an ethnic group or community can be potent source of history as they can fill the gap in historical records. With a scientific and systematic study, folklore can be a great source for writing the socio-cultural history of North-East India.

NOTES AND REFERENCES

1. J.J. Bachofen & Ralph Manheim, *Bollingen Foundation,* New York, 1967, p. 75.
2. B. Datta, *A Handbook of Folklore Material of North-East India,* Assam, 1994, p. 23.
3. A.B. Lord, 'Homer, The Trojan War and History' in *Folklore and Traditional History,* R.M. Dorson (ed.), The Hague, Paris, 1973, p. 19.
4. R.M. Dorson (ed.), *Folklore and Traditional History,* The Hague, Paris, 1973, p. 111.
5. P. Goswami, *Ballads and Tales of Assam,* Guwahati, 1960.
6. S.M.P. Rajam, *Vengalarajan Kataippadal - A Study,* M.Phil dessertation, Madurai Kamaraj University, 1989.
7. Franz Boas (ed.), *General Anthropology,* New York, 1938, p. 622.

12

Oral Sources of Mizo History

Sangkima

INTRODUCTION

History is made and it is made out of the raw materials otherwise known as 'sources'. There are two different sources of history: historical and traditional.[1] The historical sources may be of different types such as records, numismatics, archaeological, inscriptions, etc. The traditional sources may, likewise, consist of oral literatures, folklore, oral records, etc and therefore, they are indispensable materials where historical sources are not available. Hence, a historian who attempts to write about the early history of the Mizos has to rely solely on traditional sources because no historical evidence has so far been established.

However, oral traditions are now accepted all over the world as one of the complementary sources for reconstructing the past. In 1948-49, Prof. Allien Nevins of the Colombia University, started the first oral history project. In India, the Nehru Museum Memorial Library, New Delhi, started an oral history archives in 1966.[2]

With this background in view, an attempt has been made in this paper to unearth new light on early Mizos based on oral sources of information as explained in the following pages.

CHHINLUNG TRADITION

Traditionally, the Mizos believe that they came out of a very big stone cave called Chhinlung which is said to be located somewhere in China. Hence, the early

Mizo may have been cave-dwellers. The tradition is supported by folk songs and legends that have been handed down to generations. One such Hmar folk song is sung as:

"Ka siengna Sinlung ram hmingthang,
Ka nu ram, ka pa ram ngai.
Chawngzil ang kokir theih chang sien,
Ka nu ram, ka pa ram ngai."[3]

The meaning of the song is:
My motherland, famous Sinlung,
Home of my own ancestors.
Could it be called back like Chawngzil,
Home of my own ancestors.

Though we do not know how old the folk song is, the song expresses the sentimental feelings of the people towards Chhinlung. The song also expresses that the Mizos had their origin in Chhinlung. It also reveals that the people had a deep nostalgic attachment for the place of their origin where they wished to go back.

The people left Chhinlung in haste. They left it like a *mithun* jumping out of a cage. This is clearly narrated by the song. The relevant stanza goes like this:

"Khaw Sinlungah kot siel ang ka zuang suak a,
Mi le nello tam e,
Hriemi hraaih."[4]
The song means:
Out of the city Sinlung,
I jumped out like a siel.
Innumerable were the encounters
With the children of men.

The Mizos had to leave Chhinlung for three reasons. First, the people were compelled to leave Chhinlung due to their inability to repulse their enemies who were perhaps stronger than them. So, they had to move in search of new settlements. Secondly, they left the abode to avoid severe punishments from their cruel ruler Cheng better known in history as *Shih Hwang Ti* (249 -210 BC) who constructed a part of the Great Wall of China, the total length of which is about 2500 miles.[5] Tradition has it that the people were forced to leave the habitat when they were subjected to rigorous work. So, those who survived fled. Thirdly, the Mizos left Chhinlung on account of the growing conflicts between their leader, Prince Chhinlung and his father who was supported by his other sons. As a result, those who were loyal and faithful to Prince Chhinlung followed their leader out of their homeland.[6]

Chhinlung may, therefore, be identified in three different forms. First, Chhinlung is seen by some as a place where the Mizos are said to have originated. Secondly, Chhinlung suggested to be a derivative of Chin Dynasty in which Shih Hwang Ti (249-210 BC) was the first unified emperor of China. Thirdly, some even identify Chhinlung as a prince. So far as Chinese history is concerned, two princes, viz, Prince Chhinlung of Ngai-Loa and Prince Chien -Lung of Ch'ng (Manchu) Dynasty may be identified as Prince Chhinlung of the Mizo tradition. The former founded the principality of Yunnan in the beginning of Christian era.[7] The latter prince was Ch'ing rule who restored the Manchu ruler in Tibet after suppressing the Lasha uprising in 1751.[8] Whatever may have been the case, the places or names like Chinnlung, Kui-Lung, Tsin-Lung, Sinlong, Xinlong, etc which may perhaps be connected with *Chhinlung* or *Sinlung* of the Mizo tradition are basically found in Szechwan province of China. This, therefore, gives the Mizos strong sentimental grounds to believe Szechwan province to be an early habitat of the Mizos.

Kingship Tradition

It is historically true that kingship was first introduced among the Mizos in Burma. The chronology is, however, based on tradition because till now no historical evidence has been established. Yet, the system is an indispensable source for those who attempt to write about the early history of the Mizos.

Chronologically, Paihte and Sailo of the Lusei tribe have the same origin. The story goes like this: Chhinlung had two sons, Chawngthua and Chawngzova. Chawngthua had two sons named Chawngvawma and Ralhloha. Chawngvawma had two sons, viz, Dongula and Thahdova. Dongula had illicit sex with his own sister named Lalnemi who then conceived an illegitimate son whose name was Niguite.[9]

There is also another version of the tale. According to this version, there was one Paihte gentleman called Nova (not the man found in the Bible). Nova begot a son named Dongula who later had a son named Niguite.[10] Both the Paihte and the Sailo family claim common ancestry from Niguite.

The birth of Niguite is narrated in the form of a folktale as given below:

Dongula had illicit sex with his sister who later conceived a child. When the child was born he was named Niguite. Dongula insisted that his subjects should know nothing about the pregnancy of Lalnemi, his sister. To cover up the affairs Dongula then wisely deviced a trick by putting an egg inside a tree-trunk nearby his house. Then he told the people about the possibility of a child being conceived from the egg. One day a child was born to Lalnemi. Soon after birth, the child was placed inside the tree-trunk. Pretending that the child was born of an egg, Dongula then broke the egg and informed the people about the birth of the child. However, the name of the mother was concealed. He then asked all the unmarried women in the village to tend the child by turn. Unfortunately, no one could nurse the child to sleep because none had a breast to feed on. Then the turn came to the real mother. As the child could then be fed on the breast-milk of his mother, he had sound sleep and he was no longer a problem at night. Then, she was appointed as a foster mother.[11]

The child was named Niguite. He was so-called because the child was born on account of the rays coming from the sun. It was said so because Dongula knew very well that to hatch eggs a temperature of certain degree is needed. Hence, literally, *Ni* means 'sun' and *guite* may mean 'to born' or 'to scorch'. Niguite had two male issues, Ngeknguka and Bawklua, the progenitors of the Paihte tribe and the Sailo family, respectively. Now, we will trace only the descendants of Bawklua from whom the Sailo claim lineage.

According to tradition, Bawklua married Lawileri and a son named Sihsinga was born to them.[12] Once Sihsinga had a dream in which his penis was cut-off and then chopped into pieces. Then the pieces were strewn over every hill.[13] He told about the dream to his parents.

Sihsinga had one male issue named Ralna who later begot Chhuahlawma who was captured and then adopted by Lusei during the wars with Paihte tribe. Chhuahlawma got married and a son named Zahmuaka was born to him. Zahmuaka and his wife, Lawileri had seven sons but one died at infancy.[14] The sons, according to seniority, were Zadenga, Paliana, Thangluaha, Thangura, Rivunga and Rokhuma who are said to have started the tribes which were known after them. For example, the present day Zadeng clan was named after Zadenga and so on and so forth.

Zahmuaka, after repeated invitations from the Hnamte tribe, became the Chief by succeeding Chhanpiala, a Hnamte Chief who ruled over Khawrua and Tlangkhua villages. Chhanpiala died during the inter-clan feuds which were common among the tribes in those early days. After Zahmuaka was installed as successor to Chhanpiala, his sons were also made rulers over the scattered villages. Thus, kingship or chieftainship had firmly been established in Burma before the Mizos moved down to the present Mizoram. Thangura, the fourth son of Zahmuaka, had two sons, Chawnglula and Thangmanga, and the latter begot one Sailova from whom the present Sailo family originated.

Thangura is believed to have been born in the second-half of the 16th century, or in the beginning of 17th century AD. The former date is derived from the information given by Lalsanga, Chief of Ngur village, at the *Durbar* convened by A.G. McCall, then superintendent of Lushai Hills, in 1934. At the *Durbar* every chief present was asked to give his genealogical tree. Lalsanga could recall his lineage as far as Niguite, himself being the 17th generation.[15] Thus, on the basis of this information, taken 30 years as a generation, Thangura is believed to have exsisted about AD 1574. The latter date is, however, surmised by John Shakespeare, then superintendent of Lushai Hills. According to him, there were thirteen generations upto Thangura, the founder of the family and grandfather of Sailova.[16] On the basis of this information Thangura lived about AD 1604. Whatever the case might be, it will not be far from truth if we say that Thangura could have lived about AD 1850.[17]

Thus, the emergence of the kingship system among the Sailo clan on the scene may serve a very important purpose in searching for sources of information on the early Mizos. In this connection, it may further be suggested that the Lushais, now the Mizos, under the nomenclature of the Sailo clan began to appear in the present habitat sometime in the beginning of the 17th century and continued till the second-half of the 19th century.

Khampat Tradition

A section of scholars are trying to link the origin of the Mizos with that of the Khampat tradition. According to tradition, Khampat was the oldest town ever built by the Mizos in Myanmar. It was built before they migrated to Mizoram. The town is said to be a very big one which was perhaps divided into more than ten sectors. The central block was called 'Nun Yar' or 'Palace Site' wherein the ruler resided. The ruler is said to be one of the nine chief vassals of the Burmese king.[18]

The Mizos had to leave the town due to the pressures of the enemies or due to the ongoing process of migration to the west. But before they scattered, the people planted a banyan tree at the Palace site with a firm belief that they would return to the place when one of the branches of the tree reached the ground. The tradition, therefore, had a great and sentimental influence upon the Mizos to believe that one day the legend would come true. Therefore, by the time when some sections of the Mizos returned to Myanmar and settled in the areas around the Khampat site in the beginning of 20th century AD, the branches of the tree had already reached the ground.[19] Thus, many considered this as a fulfillment of the prophecy.

The Lost Tribe Tradition

Some sections of the Mizos claim that they are the descendants of a tribe of Israel in the House of Ephraim, the tenth tribe.[20] The Karen of Burma also have the same story which is considered true even by some Christian missionaries.[21] Therefore, we cannot simply ignore the claim made by the Mizos as totally baseless because it has a historical as well as biblical backing.

According to the old Testament of the Bible, the leader of the first Hebrews was Abraham who lived in Ur. His grandson, Jacob had twelve sons who are said to have started the twelve tribes of Israel which were named after them. During the time of Jacob, famine struck Cannan, and he led his people to safety in Egypt where they became slaves for centuries. Moses led them out of Egypt and took them back to Cannan around 1200 BC.[22] About this time, God established a *Covenant* (an agreement) with the people of Israel.[23] But the people were unfaithful by drifting themselves into idol worship. Then God sent prophet after prophet to bring them back to him but they did not succeed. God then told the people of Israel: "And the Lord will scatter you among all people from one end of the earth to the other; and there you shall serve other gods of wood and stone, which neither you nor your fathers have known."[24]

God then fulfilled his words by dispersing them by means of the Assurians who captured them in 701 BC. Many of them were carried away to Assuria as slaves again in 587 BC. Nabuchadnezzar, king of Babylon, crushed them and most of them were taken away as slaves. This was the beginning of the *diaspora,* the dispersion of the Jews, to different parts of the world which lasted into the 20th century.[25] They also came to the East in ancient times.[26]

Thus, tradition has it that those who came to the East arrived in the Himalayan Mountains where they were barred from farther advance. As they could not cross the mountains they were forced to sojourn for a while at the foothills of the Himalayas. Then the sojourners moved on saying, "Himaloi, Himaloi" which means "he lamah i kal ang" (let's go to this way). Hence, the Himalayas got its name from 'Himaloi'.[27] By following the routes at the foothills of the Himalayas the lost tribe then reached China.[28] Therefore, when Israel attained self-rule in 1948, about 5000 Jews migrated back to Israel from China. Jews in Cochin (India) also migrated back to Israel and settled in the Kibbutz.[29]

Chhinlung theory of origin and the lost tribe theory of origin are traditionally connected. Before he dispersed them, God cursed the Israelites to say to a tree, "You are my father", and to a stone, "You gave me birth".[30] Hence, Chhinlung believed to be a very big stone-cave which might be the birth-place of Mizo.

The origin of The Luseis or Lushais also has an oral tradition. According to one tradition, there were ten tribes in Burma and *Luse or Lushai* were the tenth. The word *Luse* or *Lushai* is rendered as *Lu* meaning 'people' and 'se' meaning 'tenth'. Hence, the tenth people. This 'tenth' is so significant because Ephraim, one of the sons of Joseph was considered as the 'tenth' of the twelve tribes of Israel.[31] Ephraim and his followers are said to have come to the East.

The Mizos were animist before the coming of the Christian Missionaries. During their long history of wanderings there was no evidence to believe that the Mizos worshipped gods other than the wood and stone. Neither Hinduism nor Buddhism had any influence upon them. Even Confucianism had no impact on the religious belief of the early Mizos. They did not form themselves as an organized religious group either. They remained animist.

Meanwhile, Joseph, son of Jacob, had two sons by his Egyptian wife. They were Ephraim and Manasseh. The latter's name was always chanted when sacrifices were offered. We may now cite some instances:

1. When one was coming home sick from Jhum, the sickness was believed to be caused by an evil spirit. Bawlpu (the priest) then had to perform an offering. The chant goes like this:

   "If tied, untie him,
   If manacled, unlock him,
   We are taking Manase home."[32]

2. In the act of epilepsy the priest had to chant as:

   "Release him, we are above your power,
   We are children of Manase."[33]

3. It is a custom of the Mizos to make a selection for a Jhum site. After making the selection, he has to go for *ram en* (to verify the site). In the past, if they found anything suspected to be taboo, they would shout saying "Go away, go away, we are bringing Manase here."[34]

4. Mizo religion was individualistic in nature because it was performed only when one family found it necessary to do so. *Kawngpui Siam,* a sacrifice for success in hunting, was the only sacrifice worshipped in the community. When it was performed, the priest, followed by his party, recited the following chant:

"Those above and those below, go away, flee, we, the children of Manasia are coming."[35]

These are only few examples wherein the name of Manase was mentioned. As a matter of fact, in this development, the role of Christian Missionaries had a part to play because the idea was developed only when the Mizos first heard about the Israelites. According to Myer Samra, "A significant link in the development was the custom of animal sacrifice evoking the sacrifices prescribed in the Bible."[36] However, in the idea of Samra,[37] the development was only a by-product of Christianity. Anyway, this section needs further investigation before making any definite conclusions.

Buddhism as Source of Information

While focusing our attention on sources of early history of the Mizos, a brief review on the Buddhist faith in China and Burma may help us to gather more information on the Mizos. Hence, the importance of the study.

The faith came from India via Central Asia. As regards Burma, the faith came about 5th century AD.[38] If we look at the faith in a wider perspective, it is surprising to note that almost the whole of South-East Asia professes Buddhism. The Mughs and the Chakmas of Tripura and Mizoram till today are Buddhists. In the same way, the Shans and other tribes lying between China and Burma embrace Buddhism.[39] The same faith entered the Chittagong proper, the adjoining hill tracts, and Tippera during 10th and 13th centuries AD. It was directly introduced from the Magadha Empire by the Bengali Buddhists.[40] Soppitt writing in 1893, therefore, fairly presumed that eight or ten centuries ago the doctrines of the faith were firmly rooted throughout China and Burma.[41] On the basis of this argument, it may further be said that any Mizo living between the two centuries would have embraced the doctrine. On the contrary, the Mizos, who are said to have come all the way from southern China through Burma to the present habitat, were not influenced by the faith.

From this proposition, it may, perhaps, be inferred that the tribes occupying the watershed lying between Burma and Assam crossed from China before the introduction of the Buddhist faith more than eight or ten centuries ago, that is to say, about AD 887 to AD 1087. Therefore, it is probable that the Mizos had left China and Burma before the introduction of the Buddhist faith because the Mizos, like some other tribes of present day Arunachal Pradesh, failed to adopt the faith. Hence, the exodus might have taken place prior to 887 AD and 1087 AD.

Interview

Interview, covering every part of history, forms an important aspect of source-material for the reconstruction of history and culture of every people. With the help of interviews with elderly and knowledgeable persons in locality, new light can be shed on every aspect of history. Thus, oral records in the form of interviews have an added advantage as source-material in areas where historical evidences are not available.

From this point of view, the role of interview as a source of information on the Mizos is immense and indispensable because till now no historical sources have been established. Here lies the importance of interview in constructing and reconstructing the past history of the Mizos.

Concluding Remarks

We may now conclude our discussion by giving emphasis on the need to rely on oral sources for writing the early history of the Mizos. The history has, however, a peculiar nature that unlike the others, it is almost impossible to divide the period of ancient and medieval into a separate entity because there can be no clearly marked periods between these two periods. As to the modern, we can begin the period from the coming of the British. And for this period there is no dearth of source-materials for we can collect them from archives. But for other periods of history, even if any, oral sources are indispensable.

Meanwhile, with the emergence of more historical writings, more books based on research are also being published. With the help of these published works, investigations are being done to bring out more light on the *Chhinlung* theory of origin and the findings are so far very encouraging. In the same way, researches are on to find out more evidences on the idea of having link with the Israelites. Hence, we cannot ignore it right now as unsound unless and until we have proof that Mizos are not Israelites. The same can be said of the kingship system which emerged at the same time.

Above all, all the conclusions being reached with the help of oral sources, they will remain open to modifications if more facts are established. Till now we are to depend on oral traditions as recorded in literature.

NOTES AND REFERENCES

1. Romila Thapar, *A History of India*, Vol. 1, New Delhi, 1990 (Reprint), p. 29.
2. Nikunja Behari Biswas, "Historical Research in Arunachal Pradesh: Oral Source and Method", *Proceedings of North-East India History Association (PNEIHA)*, Shillong, 1993, p. 55.
3. Rochunga Pudaite, *The Education of the Hmar People*, Indo-Burma Pioneer Misson, Silelmat, 1963, p. 21.
4. H. Hranglien Songate, *Hmar Chanchin* (Hmar History), Churachandpur, 1977, p. 11.
5. Kenneth Scott Lataurette, *The Chinese -Their History And Culture*, New York, 1947, p. 95.

6. Rev. Liangkhaia, *Mizo Chanchin,* Aizawl, 1983, p. 1.
7. Padmeswar Gogoi, *The Tai and the Tai Kingdoms,* Guwahati, 1968, p. 1.
8. Kenneth Scott Lataurette, *op. cit.,* pp. 321-323.
9. Zatluanga, *Mizo Chanchin;* 1996, pp. 11-12.
10. K. Zawla, *Mizo Pipute leh An Thlahte Chanchin,* Aizawl, 1993 (6th edition), p. 179.
11. Zatluanga, *op. cit.,* p. 12
12. K. Zawla, *op. cit.,* p. 179.
13. *Ibid.*
14. Sangkima, *Mizos, Society And Social Change,* Guwahati, 1992, p. 25.
15. Zatluanga, *op. cit.,* p. 89.
16. J. Shekespear, "Lushai or Duhlien", *Linguistic Survey of India,* Vol.-III, Part-III, Delhi (Reprint), 1967, p. 1.
17. Sangkima, *Some Sources of Early Mizo History: A Chronological Study,* PNEIHA, Jorhat, 1993, p. 92.
18. B. Lalthangliana, *History of Mizo in Burma,* Aizawl, 1977, p. 87.
19. "The Coming and Settlement of Myanmarese in Mizoram", paper presented at the Seminar organised by *Maulana Abul Kalam Azad Institute of Asian Studies,* Kolkata, 25 April 2002 at Aizawl.
20. Lalpa Zawnchhuah, *Mizoram,* Aizawl, 1979, p. 11.
21. H.I. Marshall, *The Karen People of Burma,* Ohio, 1992, p. 10.
22. *History Encyclopedia,* London, 1999, p. 24.
23. *The Holy Bible* (Rsv) Leviticus: 26:12.
24. *Ibid.,* Deuteronomy: 4:27-28 & 28:64.
25. *History Encyclopedia, op. cit.,* p. 25.
26. H.I. Marshal, *op. cit.,* p. 10.
27. Lalpa Zawnchhuah, *Mizoram, op. cit.,* p. 12.
28. *Ibid.*
29. Zaithanchhungi, *Israel - Mizo Identity,* 1990, p. 11.
30. *The Holy Bible* (Rsv), Jeremiah 2:26-27.
31. Lalpa Zawnchhuah, *Mizoram, op. cit.,* p. 13.
32. Zaithanchhungi, *op. cit.,* p. 34.
33. *Ibid.,* p. 35.
34. *Ibid.*
35. *Ibid.*
36. Myer Samra, "Judaism in Manipur and Mizoram, Byproduct of Christian Mission": Paper presented at the "International Seminar" organised by the Department of Higher & Technical Education, Government of Mizoram, 7th-8th April 1992.

37. Also see Myer Samra, n 36; B.B. Goswami, *The Mizo Unrest -A Study of Politisation of Culture,* Jaipur, 1979; Zaithanchhungi, *op. cit.*
38. F.S.V. Donnision, *Burma,* New York, 1970, p. 49.
39. C.A. Soppitt, *A Short Account of the Kuki-Lushai Tribes of the North-East Frontier,* Aizawl, 1976 (Reprint), p. vii.
40. *Eastern Bengali District Gazetteer,* Bengal Sectt. Book Depot, Calcutta, 1908, p. 68.
41. C.A. Soppitt, *op. cit.,* p. vii.

13

The Saga of Chao-Lung Siu-Ka-Pha as Depicted in DHAS Manuscripts Nos. 2 & 34

Romesh Buragohain

INTRODUCTION

There are innumerable Tai-Ahom[1] language manuscripts. Some are being collected by institutions and some still lying in the hearths and homes of individuals. These cannot be claimed as the original manuscripts and were copied from one to another and from time to time throughout the Ahom rule. The manuscripts that we are dealing with, may be attributed to the late 17th century.

The two manuscripts are MS. No. 2 & 34 preserved in the Directorate of Historical and Antiquarian Studies, Guwahati. These give us a lot of information about Chao-Lung Siu-Ka-Pha's[2] original home, his early state of the Mao-Shan empire[3] of the times, his long arduous journey through the hills and vales, his religion, socio-political aspects of the Tai people and about the Tai diaspora in the 13th century Assam. Recently, these manuscripts have been translated into both English and Assamese languages[4] but as source-materials, these are still to be used by scholars.

We are, in this paper, using Folios 2 (R) to (V) of Manuscript No. 2, and 8 (R) to 10 (V) of Manuscript No. 34. We are attempting here to make some new interpretations from the data rather than merely narrating them. These sources record the activities of Chao-Lung Siu-Ka-Pha in Assam; his role in founding a new kingdom elsewhere other than in his own place of birth; his armed adventures, nature of the conquests[5] and the king of the state-system that he brought with which became the backbone of his cherished kingdom striking deep roots in an alien soil. The economic system generating surplus, the military combining defence and productions were his unique and novel innovations. This system, as such, continued till the end of the Ahom rule.

The manuscripts clearly mention in detail, about the number of chiefs who joined him from time to time and place in his arduous march to Assam; the number of people accompanying him, the number of years which took him to reach upper Assam from Mong Mao-Lung, the number of adversaries he met on the way; the manner in which he dealt with the defying and turbulent opponents; his religious performances; the details of the commissariat, etc.

The political situation as stated in the two manuscripts do not speak of any major political turmoil. Siu-Ka-Pha was in Mong-Mao for nineteen years as the heir apparent to the king of Mong Mao-Lung. But the birth of Siu-Khan-Pha, the would-be successor to the reigning king, Pa-Meo-Pung, led him to decide to leave Mong-Mao in his own volition.

The records very clearly mention about the route followed by Siu-Ka-Pha with the names of places and the number of years he stayed in each one of them.

The records contain minute details about the number of horses brought, the names of the elephants, the names of the caretakers, the names of officers and the number of people accompanying him. The names of the tribes defeated on the way, the areas brought under control are also recorded. With each occupation, orderly administration was installed giving the charge to high officer who was left to govern there.

The documents indicate that it was in the nature of a joint conquest[6] and it had large bearing upon the administrative system that Chao-Lung Siu-Ka-Pha organized. The system gives an impression of a combined monarchy with military aristocracy. The sacred status of the sovereign with hereditary succession is fairly stated from the very beginning.

Parentage of Chao-Lung Siu-Ka-Pha

Pa-Meo-Pung was the ruler of Mong Mao-Lung belonging to the Tai race. His younger sister was Nang Mong Blok-Kham-Sen. She was given in marriage to Chao Chang-Nyeu, the prince of Mong-Ri Mong-Ram. Out of this wedlock, Chao-Lung Siu-Ka-Pha was born. He was brought up in Mong Mao-Lung by his grandmother. Pa-Meo-Pung had no male issue. Hence, Siu-Ka-Pha was the designated the Crown Prince of Mong Mao-Lung. He was in this capacity for 19 years. But later on, Nang Nam-Ap, the queen of Pa-Meo-Pung, gave birth to a son. His name was Siu-Khan-Pha. Siu-Ka-Pha decided to leave Mao-Lung in search of a new home. This resulted in a Tai diaspora under his leadership. This was of immense significance as far as the medieval history of Assam was concerned.

Mong Mao-Lung (The original homeland of Chao-Lung Siu-Ka-Pha)

Where was this Mong Mao-Lung which the *Buranjis* (Ahom and Assamese language chronicles) mention so much? In India, Assam in particular, the general conception is that the Tais of 13th century Assam (later came to be known as the Ahoms) came from Thailand. It is simply because of the two names *Tai* and *Thai*.

However, scholars now agree that Siu-Ka-Pha and his tribe had their homeland somewhere at the conjuncture of extreme northern-most Myanmar and extreme southern-most China. There are some substansive evidence that the state of Mong Mao-Lung was in extreme southern China than in upper Myanmar where no such name could be found. A Tai state, Mong Mao-Lung by name existed in south-western Yunnan till it was abolished by the Chinese Government in 1952. The Chinese have now named it as Ruili, located in Dehong Dai-Singpho Autonomous Prefecture. Otherwise also, scholars believe that Siu-Ka-Pha and his followers belonged to the Pai-I (Tai Yai) of the Chinese border-groups of people who were not Buddhists.[7] Besides, there is another positive testimony that the Dai language alphabets of this area are strikingly similar with that of the Tai-Ahom language alphabets of Assam as found in the Ahom language chronicles.

It may be noted that the 13th century Tai world in upper Myanmar and southern China might not have been regular and fixed political delimitations at that time. It might have been somewhat loose. We may say that different Tai kingdoms did exist and flourished, known as the Mao-Shan states. We also get a glimpse of the different Tai-Shan principalities from the route followed by Chao-Lung Siu-Ka-Pha in his westward march towards North-East India. Some such principalities were Mong-Na Mong-Ti, Khawk-Chang Ving-Mien; then crossing the Namkiu (Irrawady River), Chak-Chang-Khai Mong-ke, Mong-ke, Mong-Kong, Mong-Mi Che-Khao, Mong-Khao Mong-Kan, Pha-Ke-Che-Rin; then crossing the Pa-Tu-Lung hill ranges, Rin-Pen Mong-Nen, Nam-Ti-Lik Kang-Tai, Mong-Kha, Mong-Ja, etc.

The Nucleus of the Emerging Kingdom

Siu-Ka-Pha was a shrewd observer of the new environment. He could see that staying merely at Tipam would not give him a new kingdom he cherished. So he undertook an extensive survey of land after staying three years at Tipam. It took him almost twenty-one years to finally settle down at Che-rai-doi (Charaideo).[8] He moved from place to place in search of good cultivable land. His main purpose was to study the reactions of the local people to his occupations lest there should be violent protests. He was thus calculating and cautious. All these surveyed lands were within the river valleys of present Buridihing (Nam-Khan) and Dikhow (Nam-Sao) rivers, the tributaries of the Brahmaputra. These three river valleys became the nucleus around which Chao-Lung Siu-Ka-Pha founded his new kingdom.

Siu-Ka-Pha's move was slow and silent. He generally moved into the low-lying areas lying fallow and uninhabited. He did not disturb the local population either by evictions or forcible occupations or by exterminations. He gave them full opportunity to observe him closely. When no harm appeared from him, they began to trust him. For further confirmation of this fact, Siu-Ka-Pha did not stay at a place for more than three to six years. He asked his followers to carry on the wet rice cultivation there. The sources do not indicate that Siu-Ka-Pha resorted to wanton aggressions which could have been an impolitical act at that moment. Of course and at the same time, Siu-Ka-Pha and his followers could establish themselves as a cohesive ruling group.

It appears that Siu-Ka-Pha was satisfied with mere subjugations. He avoided unnecessary wars and aggressions, conquests and annexations as far as practicable. With his tact and political prudence, he aimed at political subjugations and laid stress on socializations. On the whole, Siu-Ka-Pha's attitude towards the subjugated people was one of equanimity.

Siu-Ka-Pha's departure from Mong Mao-Lung was not an event of sudden occurrence. It was fully planned.[9] So he could say, 'I go to the Mong Pa-Kan country in the west to rule over there.'[10] The manuscripts mention that a host nobles and chiefs[11] accompanied him with nine thousand strong[12] armed of men. This shows that the people who accompanied Siu-Ka-Pha in his adventurous armed march, had full faith in him and in his leadership. In short, a state was moving with Chao-Lung Siu-Ka-Pha *sans* territory. As such it can be noted that Siu-Ka-Pha's prime concern was to establish good and orderly administration in the areas that came under his control. This was the key to his success and so he had unstinted support from his followers without any dissension among them. On the other hand, the subjugated people also began to rely upon him for guaranteeing perfect economic security, peace and protection from within and without. It reveals the fact that Siu-Ka-Pha was an excellent organizer in peace and war alike.

Religion of Chao-Lung Siu-Ka-Pha

Very often a question is raised as to what religion did Siu-Ka-Pha bring with him when he first landed in upper Assam? The two manuscripts in our discussion throw a good light on this.

Both the manuscripts record about the observance of certain religious ceremonies. Thus, *Rik-Khawn*[13] religious rites were performed before he finally settled down at Che-rai-doi (Charaideo).[14] Entombing has also been mentioned. Then a tree (*Tunpang*) was worshipped by coiling round gold thread and by putting a pot of silver there. Then *Me-Mong Me-Ban*[15] religious ceremony was performed.

Two other manuscripts[16] mention about ancestor worship, worshipping of the jungle god *Phi-Chao* and other gods and spirits. Incidentally, there is no mention of worshipping of the *Chun-Pha rung seng mong* or *Somdeo*[17] in these manuscripts as found in some other Tai-Ahom and Assamese language chronicles. Hence, it is difficult to say as to what religion Chao-Lung Siu-Ka-Pha had when he landed first in upper Assam. Be that as it may, the spirit of his religion from such records could be easily followed. His religion was basically the concern for the welfare of the state as the term *Me-Mong Me-Ban* would suggest. Again the term *Rik-Khawn* invariably means to keep the people ever alert to protect the country from external aggressions. For all these, the blessings of the forefathers (*Me-Dam Me-Phi*)[18] were a must in the interest of the nation. One can say at best, this was a religion of loving one's country ungrudgingly and with dedicated service and sacrifice. In other words, a sense of patriotism marks the religious outlook of Chao-Lung Siu-Ka-Pha.

Siu-Ka-Pha – The Man

Chao-Lung Siu-Ka-Pha, as can be seen from his life and activities, was a man of outstanding personality, indefatigable in his pursuits, an excellent organizer in setting up orderly administration. He was singularly persuasive, and provenly ruthless[19] where necessary. He was equally sagacious while dealing with the subjugated people. He knew the art of turning hostility into solid support as exhibited in his relations with the subjugated Moran and Borahi people. The followers of Siu-Ka-Pha had full faith in him. They took him as their undisputed leader in the pursuit of a new home.

CONCLUSION

Amongst all the Tai princes of 13th century, South East Asia, Chao-Lung Siu-Ka-Pha alone had a very significant role in the Tai diaspora to the far west, up to the North-East region of India. The records suggest his sagacity, magnanimity, his extraordinary capacity for organization and his administrative acumen. These are not only remarkable but inspiring too for any statesman *per se.* His successes in laying the foundations of a strong Tai kingdom sustaining some six hundred years after him by a single dynasty in an unknown land, still baffle many a thinkers, intellectuals and historians as well.

Yet, the historians, particularly of Assam and of the South East Asian region, have paid very little attention in the study of this uncommon historical figure. The Tai political culture as epitomised by Chao-Lung Siu-Ka-Pha is not generally noticed elsewhere. We believe, studies on the medieval history of Assam in particular and that of India in general will remain incomplete without any reference to Chao-Lung Siu-Ka-Pha's unusual achievements.

NOTES AND REFERENCES

1. Here our translation is based on the exact pronunciation according to the Tai-Ahom language as recorded in the manuscripts.
2. The name of Siu-Ka-Pha is written in diferent ways, such as 'Sukapha', 'Sue-Ka-Pha', 'Chukapha', 'Hso-Ka-Hpa', etc.
3. For details on the Mao-Shan Empire, see, P Gogoi, *The Tai and the Tai Kingdoms,* Gauhati, 1968, pp. 102-208.
4. J.N. Phukan, *et al., Chao-Lung Siu-Ka-Pha*, Documentary History of the Ahom, Vol. 1, Celebration Committee, 770th Anniversary Year (1997-98), Guwahati, 1998, pp. 11-41.
5. The nature of conquest here means that the conquerors do not resort to wanton aggressions, the vanquished are neither exterminated nor driven out but made partners of peace and progress along with the ruling group.
6. The tribe of Siu-Ka-Pha, after they came to be known as the 'Ahoms', always considered that Assam was their joint consequest and not by single individual alone. It resulted in the formation of a sort of military democracy where the king's power mostly depended upon the support of the military aristocracy. Later, the emergence of the *Satgharia* Ahom clan (seven ruling clans) monopolising the offical bureaucracy was out of this notion of joint conquest.
7. H.K. Barpujari (ed.), *The Comprehensive History of Assam*, Vol. II, Guwahati, 1998, p. 50.
8. In the manuscript, it is mentioned as *Che-tam-doi Che-lung Che-Kham.*
9. It appears that Siu-Ka-Pha might have had some knowledge of eastern Assam from the conquest of Sam-Lung-Pha, the famous Mao-Shan General, who according to

Ney Elias preceded the arrival of Cha-Lung Siu-Ka-Pha in upper Assam. While the Tai-Ahom language manuscripts do not corroborate it, Gait argues that this is not necessarily incompatible. Likewise, Gogoi also states that Siu-Ka-Pha's entry into Assam through the Patkai hill ranges remains historically unexplained. For us, the problem is to fix the date of Sam-Lung-Pha's conquest of the Chutiya kingdom since the time sequence and the chronology of the two events are quite unclear and are at variance. See Ney Elias, *Introductory Sketch of the History of the Shans*, Calcutta, 1876, p. 9; Guwahati, p. 76, P. Gogoi, *op. cit.*, p. 268.

10. Phukan, *op. cit.*, pp. 20 and 39.
11. For the names of the host of nobles and chiefs, see Phukan, *op. cit.*, p. 37.
12. The Tai-Ahom language words for this are, *sam ring ding mao khoo sam kin le sam khun.* When computed, it becomes nine thousand. See Phukans, *op. cit.*, p. 21.
13. Rik-Khawn means 'call to life'. It was a state-level ritualistic religious celebration to give life force to the people and the state.
14. Che-rai-doi is situated to the south-east of Simluguri town in the Sibsagar district of Assam. It still encapsulates the glory of the teeming millions in the constructives in terms of roads, ramparts, dykes and tanks and eye-catching burial mounds (Moidams) of the Ahom monarchs. Recently, it has come to limelight due to the excavations carried on by the Archaeological Survey of India in one of the biggest burial mounds. The materials unearthed have revealed the superb technology of constructing burial mounds.
15. *Me-Mong Me-Ban* is also a state-level religious celebration, meaning oblations offered to the country and the villages.
17. DHAS Ms. No. 6 (A) & 10 (A). See Phukan *op. cit.*, pp. 44 and 48.
18. Said to be an icon given by the progenitor Lengdon. Only the king had the privilege to worship it alone once in a year. This said to have been in the possession of the last king of the Ahoms, Purandar Singha.
19. *Me-Dam Me-Phi* was a state-level public religious ceremony, offering oblations to the forefathers and invoking them for blessings to achieve successes in the life of the country. It was celebrated before and after defeats and victories.
19. To terrorise the turbulent, undaunted and defiant opponents, the flesh of the elder brother was cooked and the younger brother was forced to eat. See Phukan, *op. cit.*, pp. 23 and 39.

14

Hagiographies as Historical Sources: The *Carita-Puthis* of Assam

Radha Das

The *carita-puthis,* the vast corpus of hagiographic literature of Assam are important sources for the study of pre-colonial history of the region. They are of particular importance and indeed, have been extensively used in the past to study the nature of medieval *Vaishnavism* in Assam.

Hagiographies are texts which contain the life-stories of saints/*sants* and claim to recount the events of the life/lives of a particular saint or a number of saintly personalities. The *carita-puthis,* which belong to this category of literature, were compiled in the 17th and 18th centuries. They formed part of the vast body of vernacular *Vaishnava* literature which sprang up around this time and were designed to spread the message of *bhakti* among the people.

The Assam variant of medieval *Vaishavism,* popularly known as the *eka-saran-nama-dharma* or the *mahapurusiya dharma,* was formulated by Sri Sri Sankaradeva around the late 15th century and carried forth by succeeding generations of saintly personalities. The most prominent of these were his two principal disciples, Madhavadeva and Damodaradeva. *Caritas* of this and other saints abound, and have played a significant role in popularising *bhakti* in the region. In fact, the *nama dharma* has since dominated the process of Assam's cultural formation and still continues to be a common mode of expressing one's relationship with the divine.

TOWARDS A 'SOCIAL-CULTURAL' HISTORY

It is emphasised here that while utilising the *carita* texts as sources, there is a need for a shift of focus from the religio-philosophical aspects of *bhakti,* or a reconstruction of biographical sketches of saintly personalities, to a broader socio-cultural analysis, keeping in mind the particularities of the region. Medieval Assam comprised of the three states of Kamarupa, Assam and Kamata, broadly corresponding to the modern state of Assam, parts of North Bengal and the neighbouring state of Arunachal Pradesh. Together they form a distinct geographical unit, having markedly uneven levels of topographical and socio-cultural formation. This includes fertile river valleys inhabited by settled agricultural communities having a caste-divided society, and tribal settlements outside the realm of brahmanism in close proximity to one another. The continuous interactions between these groups have played a crucial role in shaping the historical developments in this region. Hence, the imperative to locate *bhakti* within this wider cultural setting. Therefore, the socio-economic structure of Assam (which showed a much greater flexibility in relation to North India) needs to be situated in the backdrop of a loosely-knit political system which witnessed gradual emergence of a rudimentary state under the Ahoms and their subsequent attempts at centralisation. The emergence, sustenance and spread of *bhakti* have to been seen in this context.

Hitherto, most studies have been based upon a literal interpretation of the *caritas* and hence represent an inadequate exploration of these texts. Even when the 'history of the faith' or the institutional base of the 'movement' have been the subjects of researches,[1] the 'processes' and 'dynamics' of *bhakti* in the region have not really been explored. The problem primarily derives from the treatment of the sources. An understanding of the peculiar characteristics of this genre of literature demands that they be subjected to rigorous critical scrutiny and do not lend themselves favourably to literal interpretation. The concerns of numerous recent studies centring on saints and their cults, especially in Europe, arising out of an increasing interest in the study of popular cultural forms and the perceptions and world view of the lower strata of society appear particularly germane. Most works have emphasised the need to locate these 'saints' and their 'cults' in their broad socio-cultural setting. In a recent compilation of essays on the subject, Pierre Delooz in his sociological study of canonised sainthood in the Catholic church, has explored notions of sanctity among the people for an understanding of the 'social construction of sainthood'.[2] Robert Hertz's research on the cult of St. Besse in a remote Alpine region in Italy, emphasised the significance of the physical environment and the folklore and legendary tales existing among the mountainous inhabitants of the region, which, according to him, provides the vital clues for an understanding of the pattern of diffusion of the cult and the consciousness of these remote people.[3]

INTERPRETING HAGIOGRAPHIES

To function as meaningful historical sources there are two dimensions to be looked into in relation to the texts. The first is the problem of 'popular culture' and how it should be viewed. The second relates to the treatment of these texts which are replete with myths, legends and eulogistic exaggerations.

Historians are finding it increasingly difficult to justify the existence of 'low' or 'popular' culture as an exclusive category, opposed to the 'high' or elite', and instead stress their mutual interactions, as these categories are not always clearly demarcated. Denying their 'pure form' it has been emphasised that these can be seen only in an interlacing in a complex and contradictory synthesis.[4]

This is important in the present context, as *carita* texts are viewed as works meant for the common people and hence their 'popular' content is often taken to be self-evident. Based on this view, most works formulate certain generalisations relating to the attitudes of the *Vaishnavas* towards crucial issues, such as caste, position of women, etc which may be open to question. The problem of homogeneity in the conceptualisation of popular culture has also led to inadequate attention to the factor of internal differentiation of groups within the 'popular'.[5] This point relating to the internal group dynamics is particularly important, because a blanket category 'popular' often leads to the invisibility of certain groups such as women and tribals in studies of movements involving collective action.

Generally speaking, hagiographies have remained in the periphery of historical research. Historians have tended to question their validity because these contain a liberal smattering of fantastic, mythical and legendary episodes relating to the saints' lives. The problem, however, stems from the tendency among historians to view these myths, legends, etc as static entities which make them miss out the reality which produced these particular fantasies. The need, therefore, is to locate such texts within the historical and cultural context in which they developed, as well as to take note of their socio-cultural function so as to obtain an objective picture of existing social realities.

Another factor is the importance of oral tradition in a largely illiterate society and its influence on the written texts which grew out of it. The co-existence of the oral and the written even after its codification also need to be considered.[6]

By emphasising the study of hagiographical works against the background of underlying socio-cultural structures, it may be pointed out that these works reflect not only the socio-religious processes or modes of religious perception but being rooted in the very society where they occurred, these also throw light on other aspects such as social relations and the world-view of the common people. Legends, eulogies and fantastic tales are extremely important as they allow us access into the underlying structures of consciousness of a particular society. These offer historical explanation of the emergence of 'socio-cultural' movements and the ways in which their traditions were preserved over a sustained period of time. The legends take the form of stories related by members of a society about and for themselves. More significantly, these often serve to legitimise or protest assymetrical relation of power that prevail in the large societies of which the communities that tell the legends form a greater or lesser part. This may be noticed in the stories relating to Sankaradeva and other *Vaishnava* saints of Assam. The earlier biographies, however, are generally more sober and there is matter of fact in their accounts while the later texts came to be embellished with more and more legendary and miraculous episodes.

Again, these texts are more relevant as source-materials for the period of their composition, ie the 17th and 18th centuries than the earlier times they claim to represent.[7] By necessarily requiring the saint to be placed within a particular setting, the narrators inevitably drew their own contemporary experience, which was a period later than the person whose life they relate. This is particularly evident in the later *caritas.* Nevertheless, the *caritas* developed from an existing body of oral traditions carried over from an earlier period, and themes were repeated in the later works along with the incorporation of newer elements, in the course of their evolution.

The *Cairta-puthis* of Assam

To place them in their context, the *carita-puthis* were rendered into the written form in the period following Sankaradeva (1449-1568) from the existing oral tradition, within the precincts of the *sattras* or *Vaishnava* monastic institutions. These had become the principal organisational base for the dissemination of *Vaishnava bhakti* ideals of the *eka-sarana-nama-dharma.* Reciting the saints' lives had, in fact, come to be regarded as an essential part of the daily congregational prayers or *namkirtanas* conducted in the *sattras.* Any study of these texts, therefore, necessitates locating them in their proper context.

A few of the biographies will be considered here to illustrate this point. These are Daityari Thakur's *Sri Sankardeva-Madhavdeva Carita,* Bhusana Dvija's *Sri Sri Sankardeva,* Ramananda Dvija's *Guru Carita,* Ramacarana Thakur's *Guru Carita* and another by an anonymous writer, *Guru Carita Katha.*[8] The first three have been ascribed a date around the early 17th century while the latter two are said to belong to the late 17th and 18th centuries.[9]

Daityari Thakur, the earliest of the biographers, was the son of Ramacarana Thakur and belonged to the *Kayastha* caste of the Bhuyan community. His father was the nephew of Madhavadeva and spent most of his life with the latter, who initiated him into *Vaishnava* fold. Daityari mentions that his work was compiled through discussions with several learned persons including his father.[10] This may help in understanding the reason why Daityari dealt at length with the life of Madhavadeva and restricted his work to a brief account of Sankaradeva. His father's allegiance to Madhavadeva might explain the ways in which the latter differed from his *guru* Sankaradeva, and the changes he introduced. Bhusana Dvija's grandfather was Cakrapani, a *brahmana* who had been initiated into the fold by Sankaradeva. It is significant that Bhusana Dvija does not mention any differences of opinion between Madhavadeva and Damodaradeva, and instead describes the latter as the undisputed and principal *mahanta.*[11] Ramananda Dvija was the son of Sriramadeva who was a disciple of Bhavanipuriya Gopala Ata of the *Kala samhati.* His account includes a very detailed genealogy of Sankaradeva's predecessors, tracing their origin from Gujarat through Kanauj, Bengal, and finally Kamarupa. This was possibly done to forge a connection between the *bhakti* cult in Assam and those in different parts of North India. Situating the texts in their proper context – the social background and religious inclinations of their authors – helps us to explain and resolve certain discrepancies that sometimes occur regarding the same event in these texts. By the time of the latter *caritas* were compiled, the *Vaishnava* order had undergone various divisions, resulting in the emergence of *sampradayas* or sub-sects, which accounts for the changing practices and beliefs and new forms of adjustments, within the order.

This also led to increased contact with areas outside Assam. All the later *caritas* consider Sankaradeva, Caitanya of Bengal, Harivyasa (probably of the Nimbarka sect) and Ramananda of North India as quadruple incarnations of Vishnu. The tendency to trace the origin of *bhakti* from Adi Sankaracarya is a feature of this group of *caritas.* Further, these, including the *Guru Carita Katha,* mention a number of disciples of Sankaradeva from outside Assam.[12] There is also an attempt to include various holy places all over the country in the itinerary of Sankaradeva's pilgrimage. The *Guru Carita Katha,* which was probably compiled in the 18th century, clearly reflects the wide expansion of *Vaishnava* order. Consequently, the *Gurulore* also escalated, coloured by the schisms of the order and interests of the multiplying *sattras.* It gives an account of twenty-five *Vaishnava* saints of Assam.[13]

In the context of medieval *Vaishnavism* in Assam the *carita-puthis* contain many details which indicate the interaction between different sections and groups of the society and reflect the existing contradictions and ambiguities. The *bhakti* ideals developed by Sankaradeva were often critical of the brahmanical practices and were meant for the common people. Thus, he drew heavily on various elements of the existing local traditions. The movement, however, also had to adjust with brahmanism and this process of interaction transformed both. The *caritas* show that there emerged within the same movement various conflicting strains as the *Brahma, Purusha* and *Nika samhatis,* practising various brahmanical rituals and practices while the *Kala Samhati* strictly and totally forbade them.

Hagiographies fulfilled a variety of functions. Statements were made to stimulate devotion and provide examples of piety, boost particular cults and further the interests of different groups of institutions. This was done through the use of symbols familiar to the society at which they were aimed. For example, *Guru Carita Katha* tells us how the celebration of the *guru's* lifestory *(gurujana caritra-kirtana)* came into being as a part of the prayer services in the *sattras,* following the stylistic form of the lores of the Lord (*Sriramar Krsnabalabhadrar carita*), when Madhavadeva became the head of the faith.[14] The saint's articulation of religion, society, and everyday aspect of life, developed a language which was lived among the people of the region.

The writers of the *caritas* used the vernacular language. The pattern of composition of these texts was also designed keeping the needs of the illiterate common people in mind. These works were mainly anecdotal and episodal in form. The narrative style was ideal for holding the attention on lay listeners. The *carita-puthis* truly represent the consciousness of the people as they formed a part of the mechanism developed for the transmission of *bhakti* ideals among the people. The subject-matter was derived from popular themes of the existing society. In a predominantly agrarian society where a large section of the population was illiterate, it was easier for the people to *identify* with or grasp the concrete rather than abstract philosophical speculations—the legendary episodes and miraculous acts of saints included in the prayer services, therefore, caught the imagination of the people.

In the *caritas,* therefore, frequent comparisons are drawn between *bhakti* and the agricultural process - "just as sowing and cultivation earns people food, the place to earn *hari bhakti* is the *guru bhumi* through *sarana* and *sanga*-why don't you cultivate this (*bhakti*)....[15] Similarly, imageries related to trade and traders also occur in the *Guru Carita Katha* making our minds the guide of our boat, sell it at the feet of the *Paramatma Sadagar*... put all our wealth at the feet of Hari."[16]

The person of the saint represented for the people a concrete object of veneration who also fulfilled many of their practical and emotional needs. Sankaradeva performed miracles which were closely related to day-to-day experiences of the people. Instances of curing people from pain, disease and snake-bite with a mere touch of the hand is a common occurrence in the *caritas*.[17] References to deaths due to illnesses also occur. Sankaradeva forbade the propitiation of gods like Durga, for curing illnesses. *Vaidyas* or physicians were often portrayed as ineffective. Diseases were dreaded by the people and the miraculous acts of saints gave them assurances. All sections of people were drawn by these episodes which closely related to the insecurities of their existence. Thus, the theme of the healing touch narrated by the *caritas* was a popular one. The *guru*-lore thus gained popularity and the *caritas* of many local *gurus* also came to be written, which perhaps enjoyed a certain influence within particular communities/ localities.

It is clear that being rooted in the local folk tradition and incorporating images of everyday life, the *caritas* played a significant role in the popularisation of *bhakti* in the region. It is in this light, therefore, that they need to be viewed – as carriers of the message of *bhakti* and as an important source for the socio-cultural history of pre-colonial Assam.

NOTES AND REFERENCES

1. See M. Neog, *Sankaradeva and His Times: Early History of the Vaisnava Faith and Movement in Assam*, Gauhati, 1965; S.N. Sarma, *The Neo-Vaisnavite Movement and the Satra Institution of Assam*, Gauhati, 1966.
2. P. Delooz, "Towards a Sociological Study of Canonised Sainthood" in S. Wilson (ed.), *Saints and Their Cults*, Cambridge, 1983, pp. 189-212.
3. R. Hertz, "St. Besse: The Study of an Alpine Cult" in S. Wilson (ed.), *op. cit.*, pp. 55-89.
4. A.J. Gurevich, AJ, *Medieval Popular Culture: Problems of Belief and Perception*, Cambridge, 1990, pp. xviii, 15.
5. S. Desan, "Crowds, Community and Ritual in the Work of E.P. Thompson and Natalie Z. Davis" in L. Hunt (ed.), *The New Cultural History*, California, 1989, pp. 47-71.
6. A.J. Gurevich, *op. cit.*, pp. 1-20.
7. W.H. Mcleod, *Early Sikh Tradition: A Study of the Janam Sakhis*, Oxford, 1980, p. 257.
8. R.M. Nath (ed.), *Sri Sri Sankaradeva - Madhavadeva Carita* by Daityari Thakur, Sylet, 1969 Saka; D. Borkotoki (ed.), *Sri Sri Sankaradeva* by Bhusana Dvija, Jorhat, 1986;

M. Neog (ed.), *Guru Carita* by Ramananda Dvija, Gauhati, 1957; B.K. Bhattacharya (ed.), *Guru Carita* by Ramacarana Thakur, Nalbari, 1985; M. Neog (ed.), *Guru Carita Katha*, Anonymous, Gauhati, 1987.

9. M. Neog, *Sankaradeva and His Times*, pp. 2-15.
10. *Ibid.*, pp. 5-7.
11. D. Borkotoki (ed.), *op. cit.*, Preface, p. 5.
12. M. Neog (ed.), *Guru Carita Katha*, *op. cit.*, Introduction, p. 138.
13. *Ibid.*, p. 2.
14. *Ibid.*, p. 1.
15. *Ibid.*, p. 222.
16. *Ibid.*, p. 114.
17. *Ibid.*, pp. 20-21, 44.

15

Tripura Buranji – A Source of Historical Geography of North-East India

I.S. Mumtaza

Tripura Buranji, or 'a chronicle of Tipperah in Bengal', written by Ratna Kandali and Arjun Das in the early part of the 18th century is unique among the Ahom chronicles. It explains the pan-Indian interest of the Ahom king, Rudra Singha (AD 1696-1714) and gives information about the land route, history, topography, resources and the customs of the people of Tripura. The authors visited the Tripura kingdom as well as its royal court between the years 1709 and 1715 as the envoys of the Ahom king on three different occasions. In AD 1709, Rudra Singha sent two persons in the name of Barbarua to Tripura in company of Anandiram Medhi, who visited the Ahom royal court and received rich presents from him.[1] They were received by the Tripura king, Rama Manikya, who in AD 1710 sent his envoys, named Rameswar Bhattacharyya Nyayalankar and Udaynaryan Biswas with the two Ahom persons with two letters, one for the Ahom king and the other for Barbarua. The Tripura envoys were warmly received at the Ahom court and in AD 1710 they were sent back. With them also went two Ahom envoys with letters to the Tripura court. The Ahom envoys were received by Ratna Manikya in 1712, but soon the Tripura king was killed, and his step-brother, Ghanashyam Thakur proclaimed himself king under the style of Mahendra Manikya. The new king sent the Ahom envoys back in 1713 along with his own envoy named Aribhinarayan. The Tripura envoy was received by Rudra Singha towards the end of 1713, and in 1714 he was sent back, accompanied by Ahom envoys to Tripura. A few months later, before the Ahom envoys reached the Tripura capital, Rudra Singha died at Guwahati, and in the beginning of 1715 Mahendra Manikya, too, passed away. He was succeeded by Dharma Manikya. The Ahom envoys were sent back by Dharma Manikya with letters but without his envoys. After this no diplomatic exchange between the Ahom court and that of Tripura was recorded. In 1724, the Ahom envoys wrote an account of their missions to Tripura under the title *Tripura Desar Kathar Lekha*, which was published in 1938 as *Tripura Buranji.* In the following pages an attempt is made to study the *Buranji* as a source of historical geography of North-East India.

The Ahom envoys sent to the Tripura court in AD 1711, went by the rivers and where rivers were impossible to navigate they took the land route. Parts of the route passed through the Kachari kingdom and its capital Khaspur, a place in the southern part of North Cachar Hill district. The chronicle, however, is silent about the route taken by Anandiram Medhi accompanying Ratna Kandali and Arjun Das to the Tripura capital.[2] On their return journey, unaccompanied by Medhi, they, with the envoys of Ratna Manikya, passed through Kailash Pargana, a place in the North-Eastern part of Tripura in North Tripura district, now known as Kailashahar, and Khaspur to reach Raha.[3]

The chronicle gives a detailed description of the route from the Ahom kingdom to the Tripura capital, Udaypur and beyond. The envoys of the Ahom kingdom sailed from Raha up the Kapili River for five days and arrived at Demera, a place on the bank of Diyung, not far east from the confluence of Diyang, from there they followed the land route for eleven days to reach Khaspur. Geographically, this area was covered by the Barail plateau and had sharp ups and downs; the watersheds under this physiography were impossible to navigate. Then they proceeded to Udarban, a place in Cachar at the North Cachar foothills, by land from where they sailed down the Makhura, a tributary of the Barak, now known as Madhura River, and arrived at its confluence into the Barak and then continued to sail down the Barak for four more days to reach Lakhipur, the southern frontier province of the Kachari kingdom. It took them another five days through the Barak to reach the frontier of the Tripura kingdom.

Sailing down the Barak for five days the envoys arrived at the confluence of the Rupini River into the Barak. This place was marked as the boundary between the Kachari and Tripura kingdoms. This area was covered by the branches of the Patkai ranges with no human habitation. They continued their journey for three days and reached Rangrung, a place in the North-Eastern part of Tripura bordering the present Karimganj district. From Rangrung they proceeded by land for four days to reach Rupinipada, a place on the left bank of the Rupini River and then Tailajpada, a place in North Tripura district, west of Sakhanlang range. From here they walked for four more days and arrived at a place called Kumjang, on the Charthang River, a tributary of the Kusiara. Leaving Kumjang, after six days, they arrived at Chairangsuk, a place in North Tripura district, west of Sakhanlang range. The inhabitants of this place were mostly Kukis. They used to supply annually methon (the Indian Bison), ivory, cotton, black pepper and *china cloth* (a type of cloth) to the Tripura king. From here they sailed down the Aevagang on a bamboo raft, and then sailed up the Manugang, and reached Kerpa, a place not far from Udaypur to its east. From here they marched for two days, passed through Chotamarichari and then reached the village of Baramarichrai. Both the places are in South Tripura district, perhaps near Nagribari. Leaving the place they marched for four days to reach a place near the Khakrai River, a tributary of River Gomti. The place was very near to the capital, at a distance of about one and half hour journey only.

It may be noted here that during their stay in the Tripura capital the envoys were kept in camps at different places. The camps were either within the administrative centres, or adjacent to them, and geographically these places were situated on a higher ground.

In addition to the detailed narration of the route the chronicle gives description of places visited by the envoys, the resources of the country and the customs of the people of Rangrung, the frontier province of the Tripura kingdom, and of Udaypur, the capital city. Rangrung[4] was bounded on the north by the Kachari kingdom and Manipur. Physiography of the area was hilly and the hills were populated by some three hundred hill people known as the Kukis, who were similar to the Nagas and the Daflas (Nishi) of the Brahmaputra Valley. The chief of the province was selected by the Tripura king from among these people and was called Halmacha. In his administration he was assisted by a band of officers called Galim, Gabon, Chapiya, and the Daloi. An officer sent by the Tripura king also resided here. The people used bows and arrows, shield and spear as their weapons. Their food habits and dresses were the same as those of the Nagas. The Rangrungiyas, the inhabitants of Rangrung, supplied annually to the Tripura king horse, methon, ivory, gold, dishes of bell metal, *china cloth,* cotton and black pepper. They had trade relations with the Kacharis and for this purpose they sent annually one methon to the Kachari king. The products of the province were paddy, black pepper, areca nut, betel leaves, *tarbuj* (watermelon), *kanidhan* (a kind of small grain), ash ground, colocasia, ginger, *chinal* (a kind of melon), *karela* (a bitter vegetable), brinjal, cotton, etc. The forest of the area was teemed with methon and elephants. The headquarter, also called Rangrung, was not only a political centre but also a trading place, where the traders of the Kachari and the Manipur king doms were seen in large numbers. To these markets the Tripura traders used to bring bronze, salt, oil, molasses, tobacco, dried fish, and *tatar guwa* (dried (?) areca nut); the Kachari traders brought with them goats, ducks, fowls, dried fish, rice, salt, oil, molasses, tobacco and *tatar guwa* while the Manipuri traders used to bring gold, dishes of bell metal, *dhakdhaki* (a kind of narrow-necked water vessel), and *china cloth.* The Manipuri traders also brought horses for supply to the Tripura king.

The region from Rangrung to the capital was hilly and the products of this area were the same as those of Rangrung except areca nut and betel leaves. Like Rungrung the people of this place were also Kukis. Their chief apponited by the Tripura king from among these people, was called Munshi.[5]

The capital city[6] was surrounded by an earth rampart of six cubic feet (about 2.75 metres) high. The main gate *Rupar Duar* (silver gate) was guarded by about forty persons with weapons like bows, arrows, cannon, shield, and swords. There were four temples on both sides of the road. After these temples there was another gate, *Sonar* Durga (golden gate) and inside the gate there were courts, of the Crown Prince of Barthakur and other officers like Uzir, Nazir, Karkone, Dewan and so on, and then the royal stable for horses and elephants. Next to the royal stable there was the capital complex. The king's offical residence was again surrounded by a brick rampart of six cubic feet (about 2.75 metres) high. Within this complex, there were several buildings – the royal court, king's household, temple, a few sleeping chambers for king and his wives, the royal treasury and so on.

The *Buranji* indicates that the capital city was well connected with other administrative headquarters as there were references to a few *Rajpaths* (highways).[7] Outside the city on these highways there were several markets, where the traders brought commodities like copper, bronze, cloth cotton, salt, sugar, bataca (a kind of sweet made of sugar), milk, ghee, etc for transaction.

Geographically, the whole kingdom was hilly, and was inhabited mainly by the people called Tripura or Tripuri. They used to drink alcohol, eat pork and burn the dead bodies and observe a month mourning. The priest was called Somtaya. The chief products of the region were paddy, mango, jackfruit, coconut, areca nut and betel leaves.[8]

The chronicle also gives an account of the shrines and forts of Tripura as well as of the residences of the principal nobles, pointing out in many instances the similarities with the corresponding ones in the Ahom capital, Rangpur.[9]

Through study of the historical geography we find a clear picture of the boundary, particularly the northern and western boundary of the Tripura kingdom in the early part of the 18th century. The Barak River was the northern boundary of the Tripura kingdom and on the north of the River was the Kackari kingdom. The confluence of the Rupini River and the Barak was the northern-most point of the Tripura kingdom. The western boundary of the kingdom can be determined from the list of (frontier) *parganas* (administrative units). They were: Meherkul, Khandal, Mandal, Bakasai, Lohagarh, Tisina, Tili, Lonnagar, Mirzapur, Bhusna, Bisgaon, Kailashpur and Dharmmanagar (some of these areas are, at present, in Bangladesh, bordering Tripura).[10]

The above discussion shows that the *Tripura Burani* is an important source-material for the study of the historical geography of North-East India.

NOTES AND REFERENCES

1. After the victories over the Kacharis and the Jayantiyas, Rudra Singha wanted to occupy Bengal ousting the Mughals from there. With this intention he organised a confederacy of the Hindu chiefs of eastern India who had been subordinate to the Mughals. He not only cultivated friendship with them, but also, to obtain good-will and support of the inhabitants of Bengal, invited leading Brahmin scholars, musicians to his court. Anandiram was one such visitor to the Ahom court and had intimacy with the Tripura king, Ratna Manikya. Rudra Singha utilised this opportunity to establish friendly relations with one more Hindu ruler, Ratna Manikya against the Mughals.
2. Anandiram Medhi first went back to his native place and then visited the Tripura court. Hence, his route was different from that of later visits. Most probably he went through the plains of present-day Meghalaya.
3. S.K. Bhuyan (ed.), *Tripura Buranji*, Gauhati, 1983, p. 6.
4. *Ibid.*, pp. 21-22.
5. *Ibid.*, pp. 21-33.
6. *Ibid.*, pp. 27-29.
7. *Ibid.*, pp. 22-23.
8. *Ibid.*, pp. 23-32.
9. *Ibid.*, pp. 25-32.
10. *Ibid.*, p. 33.

16

A Brief Note on the Manipuri Historical and Cultural Materials available in Some British Museums

N. Lokendra

A number of British frontier officials and anthropologists who worked in Manipur at different periods of time and in different capacities donated a large number of their collections to some museums of England, ie Pitt-Rivers Museum, Oxford; British Museum, London; and the Horniman Museum, London. There are also a few other collections available in the Victoria and Albert Museum, Kensington; University of Cambridge Museum; and Archaeology and Anthropology and the British Library, London. A preliminary list prepared by Dr. John Parrat of the University of Birmingham on the Manipuri ethnographic materials available in England and also a brief catalogue of these holdings available in Manipuri State Archives provide interesting information on the nature of these source-materials.

Pitt-Rivers Museum

Many rare Manipuri ethnographic materials taken out of the state by the British officers during the 19th and 20th centuries are lodged in this Museum. Col. Shakespeare (1905-8; 1909-14), who once served as the political agent in this native state, had taken with him a number of local artifacts and these ethnographic materials certainly are indispensable sources for the reconstruction of the economic history of 18th and 19th centuries Manipur. In 1919, two years after he returned to England, Shakespeare donated to Pitt-Rivers Museum, two sets of dice from deer antler and the background information provided with the holding states that the specimens were confiscated from a gambling prosecution.[1] Indeed *Cheitharol Kumbaba,* the royal chronicle, is replete with many entries regarding gambling as a serious social menace during the first half of the 20th century. After three years, in 1922, the former political agent again deposited a few oval[2]-shaped ivory, wooden and deer antler disks used in the traditional game of *Kang* (the name is derived from the seed of a creeper). A *circular ivory disk* was supposed to have been used by women whereas a *wooden* disc was meant for the children. Another disc made o*f deer antler bond* was used normally by the male members of the royal family.[3] W. Moccullock noted that the *Kang* was a traditional game played on a polished and well-levelled mud-floored court with an approximate size of 15′ x 30′. Two teams mostly of women and girls with sprinkling of men on each side tried to hit the *Kang* (a circular seed of a creeper having an average diameter of about 1½" and ¾" thickness) with the help of ivory disks. The side, which hits the creeper seed most, wins the game.[4]

In 1923 again, Col. Shakespeare donated a pair of cast brass models of *Kanglasha*[5] (horned animal, symbol of Manipuri sovereignty). 'Cheitharol Kumbaba' recorded that the original *Kanglasha* statues, which were standing inside the 'Kangla' (traditional place) was blasted when the colonial military occupied Kangla on 27 April 1891.[6] These statues were also smeared with blood, symbolising the British military victory over Manipur.

The museum has also acquired a valuable collection of forty-six *sels* (native coins). These *sels* are undated and small in size, being only about 16 grains.[7] *Sels* are in fact, traditional bell metal coins minted at the Raja's *karkhana*. The metal was obtained chiefly from Burma although some of it was also procured from British-India.[8] During the 19th century these coins widely circulated at Manipur Valley. E.W. Dun recorded that during the last quarter of the 19th century, one British or Burmese rupee used to have a value fluctuating from 420 to 450 *sels* and in 1873, one British rupee was having an exchange rate of, 428 *sels*.[9] A precise dating as well as an examination of the exact metal content of these coins would be crucial for a proper reconstruction of the contemporary social and economic history of the state.

J.H. Hutton, an eminent anthropologist as well as a colonial political officer who served in the Naga Hills as Deputy Commissioner for a number of years during the 1920s also donated in 1918 *two Penas* (traditional musical instrument).[10]

During the 18th and 19th centuries, *Penas* were the only musical instruments which used to accompany all forms of local folk music. It was, in fact, a sort of fiddle with two parts; one part known as *Maru* was formed of the shell of a coconut whereas the bow of the fiddle known as *Cheijing* had rows of little bells which jingled in harmony with the musical notes.[11] In 1919 during his short visit to England, the former Deputy Commissioner handed over to the authorities of the museum an *Iron* share and a plough used by the Tangkhuls and Manipuris along with an indigenous comb (Shamjet) made of bamboo splits.[12] In 1931, Hutton again donated a pair of brass cymbals,[13] some pieces of jewellery, including a necklace.[14] These specimens along with an animal *trap*[15] donated in 1939 by Ursula Graham Bawer, a lady anthropologist who studied extensively the Zemi Nagas of North Cachar Hills, provide interesting insights into the knowledge of agricultural as well as hunting technologies of the Manipuris during the 19th century.

J. Dalton Woodthrope, a British political officer based at Cachar (Assam) also donated a rich collection of horse equipments to Pitt-Rivers Museum. Some of the more important items are – a few elaborate saddles, girths, stirrup, well decorated hand stalls and tail ornaments. J. Johnstone (1877-1886) also donated to the same museum a polo saddle and mallets.[16] It may be relevant to point out that during the 18th and 19th centuries the British political officers were extremely impressed by the efficiency and capability of the Manipuri cavalry in their fight against the intruding Burmese forces. J.C. Higgins, who also worked in Manipur in different capacities as Vice-President, Manipur State Durbar, as well as a political agent between 1910 and 1924, gave a collection *of* twenty *Arambais* (traditional darts) with hollow shafts of peacock feathers and iron points. Each *Arambai* has a length of 840 mm and is displayed along with quivers. The *Arambais* used to be a very important weapon for the Manipuri cavalryman during their fight against the Burmese forces (1819-26). The former colonial officer also donated in 1932 a few *Kaoshels* (ornamented brass-ware which were probably used as a *Pan box*).[17] It may be relevant to point out that since *Pan*-chewing was an extremely popular practice among the Manipur aristrocacy as well as the masses during the 19th century, 'Supari' (betel nut) used to be one of the important items of Manipur during the 19th century.[18]

The British Museum

Some of the rare artifacts crucial for the reconstruction of the social and cultural history of 18th and 19th centuries Manipur are also available in the British Museum. About 50 gold coins, most of which are undated but of different shapes and sizes, ie hexagonal, round and square, are also displayed in this museum.[19] It may be relevant to point out in this context that in the 1763 treaty between King Gourshyam of Manipur and the East India Company, the Manipuri king agreed to pay 500 *Mekle gold rupees* along with many other local products amounting to Rs. 70,800 to the Britishers in return for the Company's assistance in fighting against the invading Burmese forces.[20] The use of *Sana Tanga* (gold coins) and *Loopa Tanga* (silver coins) are frequently mentioned in many of the local chronicles (Puyas) but none of these coins are at present available in any of the museums at Manipur and other parts of the countries.

Some other important Manipuri holdings available in this museum are the exquisitely engraved *Nine stone panels* given by Mrs Moyses, the daughter of Col. Maxwell[21] who worked as Superintendent of the state during 1892-1905 with three/four years of interruptions. Col. Maxwell, in fact, is known to the Manipuris for his close relationship with Princes Sanatombi. While panel 1 and 3 show figures, probably of gods, sitting beneath a snake, panel 2 reflect the dance of Radha and Krishna. Panel 9 also shows figures seated on a variety of animals in war-like poses. It may be important to point out in this context that since 1710 when King Garibaniwas had declared Hinduism as the state religion there had been a strong process of forcible imposition of Hinduism from above in Manipur. Hindu religious ideas and philosophy were also popularised through numerous paintings and sketches in the temples spread over different localities in the state.

Another significant collection available in this museum includes *four firearms* donated by J.C. Higgins. Three of the four arms are rifles with iron flint-lock mechanism with engraving on some of the metal parts. The other fire-arm is a pistol, also engraved, with a cap-firing mechanism.[22] It may be interesting to point out that the Kukis had for long been provided with arms and were settled in different strategic areas of Manipur hills ostensibly on grounds of protecting themselves from wild animals and other aggressors but with an ulterior motive of countering any form of anti-British moves in the hill areas. The Kukis, however, revolted against the British authority in 1917 to protest against imposition of house tax, ban on the formation of new villages and also recruitment of labourers for the First World War. Since then, the British administrator confiscated many of the guns which were earlier issued to them. Tour diaries of the political agents as well as the President, Manipur State Darbar, particularly those of J.C. Higgins, W.A. Cosgrave and L.O. Clark, are replete with such information.

Horniman Museum

In addition to the above items there are also a large collection of paintings lodged at the repositories of Horniman Museum at Forest Hill, London. Professor

Coddrington handed over as many as sixteen small-sized but framed paintings, depicting boat racing and court scenes.[23] E.W. Dun wrote that during the 19th century, boat race (Hiyang) was one of the biggest festivals of the state. The festival was celebrated for five days and it took place on the boat which surrounded the Raja's enclosure. Two boats of great length which could accommodate at least seventy persons each used to compete in the race.[24] Although these paintings are undated and of unknown origin, a careful scrutiny of these paintings would be crucial for the reconstruction of the art history of 19th and 20th centuries Manipur. There are also a few undated and untitled *Manipuri manuscripts* (Puyas) available at the British Library, Oriental and India Office Collection. A sanchi bark manuscript of 26 leaves which is decorated and lacquered, seems to be an astrological text. Another manuscript with 69, paper-leaves provides significant information on the religious themes related to Radha and Krishna. A third palm leave manuscript of 67 leaves between wooden boards contains Ram legends.[25] The Victoria and Albert Museum has also a few Manipuri dress items, including an elaborate costume for the *Ras lila* (a Manipuri classical dance form representing a combination of traditional Manipuri movement pattern and Hindu religious theme). A few personal ornaments, including, necklaces of Naga origin, are also in the custody of this museum.

Thus, the historical and other ethnographic sources available in the museums of England are of prime importance for the reconstruction of the 18th, 19th and 20th centuries social and cultural history of Manipur. These artifacts have not, however, been properly dated and catalogued. It is, therefore, suggested that some immediate steps be taken up towards preparing a comprehensive catalogue and background information with reference to the Cheitharol Kumbaba, Ningthoral Lambuba and other local sources, otherwise the importance of these source materials will go unnoticed and wasted.

NOTES AND REFERENCES

1. Manipuri State Archives, *Pitt Rivers Museum, Manipur item*, p. 22.
2. *Ibid.*, p. 29.
3. J. Parratt, *A Note on Manipuri Ethnographic Materials Held in Museums in England.*
4. W. McCulloch, *Account of the Valley of Manipur* Delhi, 1980, p. 26.
5. Manipuri State Archives, *op. cit.*, p. 29.
6. N. Khelchandra and L. Ibungohal (eds.), *Cheitharol Kumbaba*, 1967, p. 493.
7. E.W. Dun, *Gazetteer of Manipur*, Delhi 1981, p. 66.
8. *Ibid.*
9. *Ibid.*

10. Manipuri State Archives, *op. cit.*, p. 18.
11. E.W. Dun, *op. cit.*, p. 66.
12. Manipuri State Archives, *op. cit.*, p. 21.
13. *Ibid.*
14. *Ibid.*, p. 20.
15. *Ibid.*, p. 27.
16. J. Parratt., *op. cit.*, *Ibid.*, pp. 9-10.
17. Manipuri State Archives, *op. cit.*, p. 19.
18. W. McCulloch, *op. cit.*, p. 27.
19. J. Parratt, *op. cit.*
20. E.W. Dun, *op. cit.*, p. 40.
21. J. Parratt, *op. cit.*
22. *Ibid.*
23. *Ibid.*
24. E.W. Dun, *op. cit.*, pp. 23-24.
25. J. Parratt, *op. cit.*

17
The Manipur Puyas

Rena Laisram

The major source of history of Manipur of the pre-Hindu period (1st century-18th century AD) is the mass of manuscripts called *Puyas. Puyas* may be defined as written records handed down to posterity by the forefathers of the Meiteis. Like the *Puranas* which form a definite class in Sanskrit literature, the *Puyas* are a particular kind of old narratives of Meitei literature.

To be able to produce written literature, people must have a certain level of economic, political and cultural development. It may be mentioned here that the people of Manipur were in close contact with a branch of the Shans of Upper Burma called the Pong. It is widely believed that the Meiteis learnt the art of record-keeping from the Pongs with whom they had a close contact over the centuries. S.K. Chatterjee is of the view that among the Tibeto-Burman languages, the most important and in literature certainly of much greater importance than the others is the Meitei or Manipuri language.[1]

This paper attempts to study the *Puyas* as a source for the reconstruction of the history of Manipur of the pre-Hindu period. In presenting a background of this source-material it deals-aspects like script, language, dating and authorship. A survey and an analysis of some *Puyas* have also been attempted to ascertain the extent to which these texts can be reliable records of the past. The reign of King Kyamba is a watershed in the cultural history of Manipur. The first reliable record of *brahmaṇa* migration begins from 15th century AD during the reign of Kyamba. We, however, cannot rule out the migration of *brahmanas* to Manipur from an early period. But from the time of Kyamba regular inflow started. They intermarried with local women and were allotted clan names and finally, finding a place in the local population.[2] By the time of King Khagemba, there seems to have developed among the people a keen sense of writing. The royal chronicle, *Cheitharol Kumbaba,* records of the king's endeavour for the spread of education. It also records that manuscripts came to be produced from the year AD 1616.[3]

It is possible that the *brahmanas* who came and settled in Manipur from the 15th century onwards began writing in their own scripts. Those *brahmanas* from Nadia and Sylhet must have used Bengali script while those from Gujarat and Kanpur used Devnagari script or some other local script. Keeping in mind the Shans, Burmese, Tibetans and perhaps Chinese influence, it must have created a chaos. This necessitated the need for inventing a script for scholars and common men alike.

Before the 19th century, Manipuri was written in a script called Meitei *mayek.* When exactly this script came into use has been a matter of controversy. The earliest reference to writing is that recorded in Ningthourol Lambuba where King Irengba (AD 084-1074) is described as a person who was very fond of reading and writing even in his old age.[4] A study of the epigraphical sources reveal that the *Phayeng Copper Plate,* written in Meitei *mayek* has been assigned to AD 799 by W. Yumjao Singh, a pioneer in the field of archaeology in Manipur. The plate, now available in English translation, refers to Shiva, Ganesha, Durga and Hari.[5] The mention of these deiteis, leads one to doubt regarding the validity of the dating. S.N. Parratt believes that the use of non-Manipuri and Sanskrit words would place the date not earlier than the first-half of the 19th century.[6] The earliest recorded inscription in Meitei *mayek* is the inscription assigned to 15th century AD during the reign of King Kyamba.[7]

Manipuri manuscripts were originally written on small, thin, rectangular boards of the sapwood of a tree called *agaru* or *agar (aquilaria agallocha).* The ink used was made of lampblack and gall and the pen was made of fully matured and seasoned bamboo.[8] Modern Manipuri is written in Bengali script which was introduced after the introduction of *Vaishnavism* as late as 18th century AD. The majority of the manuscripts in archaic Manipuri are now rendered into modern Manipuri.

The main task of manuscript writing was done by learned *Maichous* (Pandits) who were employed by the royal court. Most of the manuscripts were in the possession of the kings and writing was done under their guidance. These manuscripts were preserved, sandwiched between wood and sometimes wrapped by a thin piece of cloth, tied securely by a string. Manuscripts were also kept inside a *lobak* (bamboo basket) and kept on a *lap* (bamboo rack) to prevent exposure to moisture. The *lap* was made high up on the *phungga* (hearth).

The *Puyas* are in the possession of various individuals and organisations. The State Kala Academy Library itself has collected more than a thousand such manuscripts covering various aspects of Manipuri culture.[9] *A Catalogue of Manipuri Manuscripts* published by Manipuri Sahitya Parishad shows that the *Puyas* covered a number of human disciplines.[10] The list is as follows:

Subjects	Number of *Puyas*
Administration	48
Arts and Culture	42
Charms and Mantras	94
Creation Stories	03
Fine Arts	01
Geography	31
Geology	03
Health and Hygiene	06
Genealogy	90
Poetry	40
Prediction	11
Prose	29
Religious Philosophy	72
Scripts	02
Supernatural Stories	08
Yek, Salai	42
Miscellaneous	64

The *Puyas* are treated as sacred texts and for this reason they were kept at a place in the home where they could be kept untouched, except on auspicious days when they were brought out. The *Puyas* itself mention that only a sincere and upright individual after bath, change into fresh clothes and burning of incense lamp, can read the *Puyas*. This superstitious belief has resulted in the difficulty in the collection of these texts. More than that, the infamous *'Purana Meithaba'* or the burning of the *Puyas* had altogether destroyed many of them. The royal chronicle records thus: "On the 17th day, Sunday, in the year 1654 saka (AD 1732) at the instigation of the Guru Santidas, King Garibniwaz after sending message on horseback to all the corners of the kingdom, collected the old manuscripts in front of Kangla Uttra of the royal palace and destroyed by burning them."[11] Another reason for the disappearance of the *Puyas* is the consequence of the seven wars fought between 1741 and 1747 saka (AD 1819-1825). These wars with the Burmese resulted in the taking away of many Meitei captives to Burma who were later absorbed into the Burmese community. They took away the *Puyas* which had been worshipped reverently by them. The fear of oppression by Meitei kings must have led the custodians of the *Puyas* to keep these texts in secret places for a very long time.

Ch. Manihar believes that all the manuscripts, except a few like those of astrology, medicine and genealogy, were meant to be sung or recited.[12] The codification of the *Puyas* must have started from about the 15th century AD when initial influence of Hinduism is seen. The coming of the institutional religion must have a role in the codification process.

The *Puyas* today may be classified into five groups. In the first category are included the *Puyas* which are written in Meitei *mayek,* viz, *Khununglon.* The original *Puyas* in Meitei *mayek* are transliterated in Bengali script and in this category is included *Sanggai Phammang.* Those which are translated into the spoken language of today and written in Bengali script form a good section, viz, *Leithak Leikharon Puya.* Another group of *Puyas* are the compiled and edited manuscripts written in Bengali script in transliterated form, viz, *Sanamahi Puya.* The last group includes those which are extracts of the original *Puyas* written in Bengali script, viz, *Parishadki Ariba Manipuri Wareng Lairik.*

The five forms in which the *Puyas* are available and the subjects covered have been already dealt with. It is important to briefly analyse the *Puyas* in order to examine their historical value.

The ancestor cult of the Meiteis must have necessitated the recording of lineage and descent of each clan. There has been a tradition of recording the pedigree of each *sagei* (sub-clan) by the head of each *sagei. Langthabalon* is a *Puya* which is classified strictly under the group genealogy. *Leithak Leikharon Puya* is a text which deals with creation and cosmology in general as the central theme. It is also a compendium of historical accounts on the origins of clans in Manipur. Often referred to as a Manipur *Purana,* it has parallels with the classical *Purana* in content such as creation of the universe, re-creation after destruction of the universe, genealogy, mythical periods of time, etc. Of course, the local materials were used within the larger framework of a *Purana. The East Thounirol Puya* deals with various details of rituals which form a very significant aspect of religious expression of the Meiteis. Some *Puranas* such as *Sanamahi Puya* are dedicated to particular deities. They help gather information on the with the deities, myths associated, names by which the deities were known, rituals to be performed for them, items of food and flowers to be offered to them, etc.

By far the most important source for the study of Meitei history is the royal chronicle *Cheitharol Kumbaba.* This State chronicle was recorded in Meitei *mayek* in the court by the learned *Maichous.* It records the historical events of nearby two thousand years covering the reign of seventy-eight kings from Nongda Lairen Pakhangba (AD 33-154) to Bodh Chandra Singh (AD 1941-1955). The chronicle which runs to about eight hundred pages is a voluminous one. When exactly this chronicle came to be recorded has been debated by many scholars. The chronicle itself mentions that it was King Kyamba who introduced the system of *cheithaba* or counting of years in AD 1485.[13] The chronicle is said to have been re-compiled in AD 1780 on the orders of King Bhagyachandra. The language and style of the text make scholars to believe that the chronicle must have started recording historical events from 15th century AD.[14] The contents of the chronicle are varied and all-embracing. Taking at random, it records the accession of rulers on the throne, military expeditions, royal excursions, pleasure trips to lakes, pilgrimage to the abode of deities, major social and religious events, visits of holy men to Manipur, migrations of *brahmanas* and Muslims to Manipur, religious conversions, natural calamities and a host of other information. The significance of this chronicle lies in the fact that this is the only *Puya* which records dates, days and year of the historical events.

An other chronicle is *Ningthourol Lambuba* and the focus here is the recording of royal tours and explaining the place names connected with military expeditions.[15] However, the years in which the events took place are not mentioned although the events are recorded according to the reign of each king. Read alongside *Cheitharol Kumbaba,* it is possible to find out the time of most of the events which took place between 1st century and the 18th century AD. This chronicle is believed to have been written towards the end of 17th century AD.

The Meitei philosophy and thoughts are dealt with in the *Sakok Lamlen Ahanba Puya.* It tells the reader about the gods to be worshipped, the ways to worship them, certain myths associated with them and the codes to be followed in order to attain salvation, etc. It also contains information on the social customs of the Meiteis of early Manipur.

Manipur history witnessed migrations of various people from different directions from early times. *Nongpok Haram* describes the inflow of various people like the Burmese, from the eastern direction. The account of the migration of people from the west is recorded in *Nongchup Haram.* Another *Puya* on migration is *Poireiton Khunthokpa*. This text gives an account of the long journey undertaken by Poireiton and a horde of men on their coming to Manipur. Although, initially the book seems like mythology, it contains historical facts of people and place names. Further, Nongda Lairen Pakhangba, the first historical king is said to have married Laisna, the sister of Poireiton. This *Puya* also finds mention in the *Cheitharol Kumbaba*. The migrations of the *brahmanas* to Manipur is recorded in the *Bamon Khunthoklon Puya*. This historical evidence is important in understanding the gradual transformation of the religious history of the Meiteis from ancestor worship to Hinduism.

The central issue is whether the *Puyas* can be treated as historical records of the past. In order to initiate the discussion, we have examined two major forms of the *Puyas*, viz, genealogy and myths. Of the *Puyas* under the category of genealogy are the royal chronicles and those *Puyas* recording the lineage and descent of *sageis* (sub-clans) and *salais* (clans). Genealogies have played a noticeably important part in the Indian historical tradition, even when they are known to be fabricated.[16] The continuation of the lineage system also required the continuation of the records of such *Puyas* relating to genealogy. It was also important for the usual search for legitimacy, especially in the case of State chronicles. The genealogical material was central to the tracing of genealogical relationships irrespective of whether they were real or fictional and these relationships were indicators of power. The traditions as recorded in the *Puyas* show a clear attempt at systematisation of the different *salais* or clans, ie the principalities at a point of time when they were moving towards the formation of the Meitei confederacy under the Ningthouja *salai*. The keeping of genealogies became important with the emergence of property, for right to ownership links. Even right to women, in the form of marriage alliances between lineages are closely linked to this need to maintain genealogical records. These records also help in identifying the *piba* or the head of a social group who is also the keeper of the *sagei Puya*. The *Chada Leihui Puya*[17]which traces the lineage of the kings through the mother's side has revealed the possibility of the Meitei society being a matrilineal one at some point of Meitei history. Keeping these aspects of genealogical records in mind, this class of *Puyas* are a very important source of Meitei history and can largely be treated as historical documents.

The historical value of the *Puyas* is limited by the fact that they were consciously and deliberately re-written at a particular period subsequent to the events. Majority of the *Puyas* classified under religious philosophy, charms and mantras, supernatural stories, creation stories, etc contain historical narratives along with myths. What is important is to try and understand why certain myths were regarded as relevant to the narration of events. The *Poireiton Khunthokpa Puya*[18] which deals with the migration of a man named Poireiton, reads like mythology. However, a careful study reveals that it is a mine of information on aspects of the geography of Manipur, origin of the names of some hill-tribes and the contact of the Meiteis with the Shans, the Tripuris, etc.

Taken in totality, the *Puyas* can be included certainly in the category of historical literature. Within this categorisation, the records available in the royal chronicles and the *Puyas* on genealogy for the period after 15th century AD may be taken as fairly reliable. From the above study, we may conclude that the *Puyas* contain invaluable historical information on almost all aspects of Meitei history establishing the community's roots in the past.

NOTES AND REFERENCES

1. S.K. Chatterjee, *Kirata-Jana-Kriti: The Indo-Mongoleids and their Contribution to the History and Culture of India,* Calcutta, pp.157, 179.
2. L. Iboongohal Singh and N. Khelchandra Singh (eds.), *Cheitharol Kumbaba,* Imphal, 1989, p. 18.
3. *Ibid.,* p. 36.
4. Ningthourol Lambuba, p. 73, cited in R.K. Jhalajit Singh, *A History of Manipuri Literature,* Imphal, 1987, p. 9.
5. W. Yumjao Singh, *Report on the Archaeological Studies of Manipur,* Bulletin No. 1, Manipur State Library, 1935.
6. S.N. Parratt, *The Religion of Manipur,* Calcutta, 1980, pp. 107-109.
7. M. Bahadur and P. Gunindra Singh, *Epigraphical Records of Manipur,* Imphal, 1986, pp. 1-3.
8. R.K. Jhalajit Singh, *op. cit.,* p. 7.
9. *Exhibitions of Old Manuscripts and Academic Publications,* Manipur State Kala Academy, Imphal, 1989.
10. N. Khelchandra Singh (ed.), *A Catalogue of Manipuri Manuscripts,* Manipuri Sahitya Parishad, Imphal, 1984.
11. L. Iboongohal Singh and N. Khelchandra Singh (eds.), Cheitharol Kumbaba, *op. cit.,* p. 93.
12. Ch. Manihar Singh (ed. and tr.), *Naothingkhong Phambal Kaba,* Imphal, 1983, p. 5.
13. L. Iboongohal Singh and N. Khelchandra Singh (eds.), *Cheitharol Kumbaba, op. cit.,* p. 20.
14. *Ibid.,* p. (iii).
15. O. Bhogeswar Singh (ed.), *Ningthourol Lambuba,* Imphal, 1967.
16. Romila Thapar, *Ancient India Social History: Some Interpretations,* New Delhi, 1996, p. 198.
17. N. Khelchandrsa Singh (ed.), *Chada Leihui,* Imphal, 1966.
18. Kh. Yaima Singh (ed.), *Poireiton Khunthokpa,* Imphal, 1971.

18

Indigenous Literacy Sources of the History of Manipur

N. Joykumar Singh

History is the creation of historians. But historians cannot write history without any basis; the reconstruction, interpretation and perspective of historians are the basis of the creation of history. Therefore, the informations and evidences are the basic sources and foundation of the writing of history.

The history of Manipur is an outcome of the reconstruction of the past based on indigenous literacy sources, archaeological evidences, and archival materials and foreign accounts. In the reconstruction of the early history of Manipur, the indigenous literary sources play a vital role. The chronicles, clan genealogies, religious literature, etc are the main literary sources of the history of Manipur. These literary sources are known as place 'Puyas'. It is observed that this word may be a corrupted version and short form of 'Puwari' (story of forefathers). An attempt has been made in this paper to analyse the importance of these literary sources in the reconstruction of the history of Manipur.

CHRONICLES

The chronicles are the most important sources of information for the writing of the history of any country. Rather, it may be treated as an authentic source of information in the writing of history. Therefore, every country had maintained the chronicles with great care and attention. In the case of Manipur there are two important chronicles, ie *'Cheitharol Kumbaba'* and *'Ningthourol Lambuba'*. There is a slight difference in the approach of the style of writing between these two chronicles. But both of them rendered maximum valuable contribution in the process of writing the history of Manipur.

Cheitharol Kumbaba

The Cheitharol Kumbaba is an important source of the history of Manipur. It records the historical events of nearly two thousand years from the period of Meidingu Nongda Lairen Pakhangba (AD 33) who was the first historical king of Manipur, to Meidigu Bodhachandra Singh (1941-1955). The name 'Cheitharol' comes from the institution of 'Cheithaba' (Chei—stick, Thaba—to leave). So, 'Cheitharol' means a study of the institution of 'Cheithaba'. According to the practice of this institution, at the end of every Manipuri year a ceremony was held in the presence of the king. A previously selected man predicted all the misfortunes which would befall the king in the coming year. And the coming year was also named after him. The man was called 'Cheithaba'. The 'khumbaba' is also another corrupted version of 'Khumpaba' (khum = year, Paba = to count), ie the count of the year. So, Cheitharol Kumbaba is a chronological diary book maintained in the 'Pandit Loishang' by the learned royal scribes. It was written in the archaic Manipuri script. Then with the coming of Hinduism it was written in Bengali script and edited by Pandit Thongam Madhob Singh. During the period of Meidingu Churchand Singh, with his permission, the Cheitharol Kumbaba was again edited. It was published only in 1967.

According to records, the first 'Cheithaba' was in the year AD 1484 and his name was Hiyangloi. So, the practice of record keeping perhaps started from this year. On the basis of this information the 'Cheitharol Kumbaba' may be classified into three parts, ie AD 33 to 1484, AD 1484 to 1780 and post AD 1780 period.

The period from AD 33 to 1484 may be treated as the early phase. The information provided by the chronicles of this period is very sketchy. The first Cheithabab was during the reign of Meidingu Kyamba. So, the chronicles of the pre-Kyamba period may be reconstructed out of the available sources of scattered informations. However, the events and records of this period mentioned in the Cheitharol Kumbaba are quite historical. They are also corroborated by other literary sources. So, the information of this period, though it may be a later interpolation and reconstruction out of the available sources by the writers of the chronicles, has contributed immensely in the writing of the history of Manipur.

The period from 1484 to 1780 may be regarded as the middle phase. This is from Meidingu Kyamba to Meidingu Bheigyachandra. The events of this period were properly written. The years, months, even the dates of events are properly mentioned. However, there are some irregularities in the entries of record, particularly of the birth of the princes, death of kings and their accessions to the throne, etc. Inability to manitain regular records, as a consequence of repeated invasions by the neighouring countries was one of the reasons behind this. It is mentioned that due to the repeated Burmese invasions records could not be maintained properly; indeed, they were re-written in 1780 by Chirom Shyamaram and Oinam Anandaram under the supervision of Ananta Shai.

The post-1780 period may be taken as the later phase of the 'Cheitharol Kumbaba' and from this period the entries were properly recorded. However, during this period also some disturbances occurred due to the invasion by Burma in the year 1819. There was a long gap in the process of the entry of records. It is mentioned that the writing of 'Kumbaba' was started in 1844 during the reign of Meidings Nara Singh. The writing of 'Cheitharol Kumbaba' was started at the initiative of Mr. Maxwell in the wake of the British occupation of Manipur in 1891. The major portion of the records was confined mainly to the post-sixteen century period.

The chronicles record the king's birth, death and accession to the throne, events of war, name of heroes, prisoners of wars, description of weapons, animals, kind of tribes, creation of departments, appointments of nobles, etc. There was no aspect which the Cheitharol Kumbaba left untouched. It recorded the tribal dance, the relationship between hill people and valley people, rituals of different types and even the religious functions. The type of punishment given to the criminals was also clearly recorded. The history of the foreign policy of Manipur and nature of relationship with other countries can be easily reconstructed from the record of 'Cheitharol Kumbaba'. Another noteworthy aspect of the chronicle was its proper record of the visits of Lord Curzon and Lord Irwin to Manipur. Apart from this, the proper recording of the phenomena of nature, like flood, earthquake, etc are also another significant aspect of 'Cheitharol Kumbaba'. The first appearances of a comet recorded in the chronicle was in 1664 and the first recorded lunar eclipse was in 1666. Thus 'Cheitharol Kumbaba' recorded all the aspects of life of the people.

However, some reservations were expressed by some local scholars about the authenticity of 'Cheitharol Kumbaba'. They were of the view that since the maintenance of record was started from the year AD 1484, ie from Chithaba Hiyangloi, the records of the pre-Kyamba period cannot be established as an authentic one. On the other hand, they also agree that the records from 13th century is highly reliable. But their observation was not accepted by other scholars.

L.M. Ibungohal Singh, a pioneer writer, described 'Cheitharol Kumbaba' as the most authentic manuscript. Rajkumar Jhallajit, another writer said, "Indeed, Manipur is fortunate in having such a reliable chronicle at such a comparatively early period. It is not possible to write a good history of Manipur without the help 'Cheitharol Kumbaba'. W Yumjao said that 'Cheitharol Kumbaba' simply records the changes of rulers suppressing the historically important movements and information. Despite its limitations, however, the 'Cheitharol Kumbaba' is the most comprehensive chronicles and one of the most important sources for the reconstruction of the history of Manipur.

Ningthourol Lambuba

The 'Ningthourol Lambuba' is another important chronicle next in importance only to Cheitharol Kumbaba. The 'Ningthourol Lambuba' means the 'account of the tour of the kings'. Like 'Cheitharol Kumbaba', the writings and recordings of this chronicle started from the reign of Nongda Lairen Pakhangba, ie AD 33 to Bodhachandra. It is published in two parts. The first part, ie from Nongda Lairen Pakhangba to Garibniwaz was published by Oinam Bhogeshore Singh and the second part from Maramba to Bodhchandra was published by Dr. Bilashini Devi.

The nature of the 'Ningthourol Lambuba' is slightly different from that of the Cheitharol Kumbaba. The account of the tours of the kings and queens are the principal subjects of this chronicle.

The 'Ningthourol Lambuba' give a detailed account of the activities and characters of the kings and queens, information of events, etc which is not found in any other chronicle. Secondly, it gives detailed information about the origins of the place-name of Manipur and the Kabaw Valley. While recording the tour of a king or a queens the 'Ningthourol Lambuba' also explains the origin of the names of different places. It helps in understanding the ecology of then Manipur state.

A major drawback of the 'Ningthourol Lambuba' is the absence of dates of the events mentioned there. This, however, can be remedied by reading events with the entries in Cheitharol Kumbaba.

Apart from this, there are also other chronicles of this type, ie Moirang Ningthourol Lambuba (chronicle of Moirang principality), Khuman Ningthourol Lambuba (chronicle of Moirang principality), etc. These chronicles are also indespensable sources for the reconstruction of the history of Manipur.

On Immigration of People

Some important literary sources are throw lights on the migration of people. They are :

Poireiton Khunthok (the immigration of Poireiton)

The Poireiton Khunthok gives a very good account of the process of immigration of Poireiton. It informs us about his background, the purpose of his coming to the valley and his attempt at the throne of Kangla. He was a contemporary of Nongda Lairen Pakhangba. From this book, apart from his activities, we can reconstruct the socio-economic history of this place before the coming of Nongda Lairen Pakhangba, the ruler of Kangla.

Bamon Khunthok (the immigartion of Brahmins)

The emerging influence of 'Hinduism' is a very important part of the history of Manipur. Indeed 'Hinduism' played a major role in the social, political and cultural transformation of the people of Manipur from the middle of 17th century. In this respect, the 'Brahmin' groups played a major role. This literary work gives detailied information of the coming of different groups of 'Brahmin' people to Manipur and the places their origins. It also gives a detailed account of their religious activities and their relations with the king.

Nongpok Haran (the arrival of people from the East)

The Nongpok Haran deals with the arrival of people from the eastern side of Manipur. People from the East means people mainly from different places of upper Burma. It is recorded that people from the east arrived in Manipur in the year 1467. It is also mentioned that as a token of good relationship with the king of Manipur, the king of Shan kingdom sent a group of people belonging to different professions, including one scribe. They were allowed to settle in different places of the valley and they also actively participated in every social, cultural and economic activities of the country. Thus, this piece of literature gives a very good account of the contribution of these people in the development of the country.

Other literary sources like (*a*) Kaherilon (the immigration of Kshetriyum), (*b*) Lairikyengbam Ion (the immigration of Lairikyengbam), (*c*) Nongchup Haran (the immigration of people from the West), give valuable information on immigration of people.

The following works are also important sources for the reconstruction of the history of Manipur:

(*a*) *Pakhangba Phambal* (accession of Pakhangba to the throne): It gives a detailed account of the socio-political condition of the country before the emergence of Nongda Lairen Pakhangba and his struggle for the throne of Kangla.

(*b*) *Pakhangba Nongkarol* (death of Nongda Lairen Pakhangba): This book gives a good account of the conflict among the different communities of Manipur.

(*c*) *Takhel Ngamba* (the conquest of Tripura): This book gives a very good account of the relationship between the king of Manipur and Tripura which in Manipuri is known as 'Takhel'. The story about the conquest of Tripura by Manipur was clearly written in this piece of literature.

(*d*) *Awa Ngamba* (the conquest of Burma): Like 'Takhel Ngamba' this book gives a very good account of the military conflict between Manipur and Burma (Awa).

(*e*) *Khaki Ngamba* (the conquest of China): This is another important literary work on about the relationship between of Manipur and China (Khaki).

The literary sources mentioned above, together with other sources, if properly used, can be of immense value for the reconstruction of the social, cultural, economic and political history of Manipur.

19

Sources of the History of Precolonial Tripura

Mahadev Chakravarti

The early history of the erstwhile princely state of Tripura, in the North-Eastern part of India, is shrouded in the mists of myths, legends, curious tales and traditions because of the dearth of dependable sources. To trace the early history of the people of Tripura, we may take the help of linguistics. For example, it is pointed out that the word Tripura is apparently a Sanskritised form of two 'kok-barak' (tribal language) words, viz., 'tui' (meaning 'water') and 'pra' (meaning 'near' or very close) – 'Tui-pra' meaning a land adjoining the water. Thus we can have an idea about the location of the ancient kingdom. It is also pointed out by the linguists that in almost all tribal languages of North-East India and the Sino-Tibetan or Tibeto-Burmese group of languages 'Tui' is mostly a common word meaning 'water' with slight variations here and there. Again, the linguists have proved the great antiquity of the so-called non-Aryan word 'Tui'. In Sanskrit, we have a similar word 'Teya' (meaning 'water') which emerged later on and it might be a 'loanword' from the Sino-Tibetan or Mongoloid group of languages. Thus through scanning language, we may delve deep into the hoary past and mutual relations between different groups of people. This may offer good insight into the problem and may be treated as a background note.

The rulers of Tripura were at first 'Pha' and then became 'Manikya'. The Ahom kings also used the suffix 'Pha' at the initial stage. The replacement of the tribal word 'Pha' by the Sanskritised title 'Manikya' by the kings of Tripura indicates how the process of Sanskritisation or Hinduisation was taking firm roots in the soil of Tripura. Like many other royal dynasties of India, the tribal rulers of Tripura claimed *Kshatriya* status as the scion of the Lunar dynasty of epic fame. This may also be treated as another indicator of the process of Sanskritisation. It is said that 184 kings ruled Tripura since the legendary period. Unfortunately, our only source in this regard is the *Rajamala* (chronicle of the royal family of Tripura) which is sometimes compared with Kalhana's *Rajatarangini.* But most of the details of the *Rajamala* about the early period require verification from other sources which are yet to be done.

Literary Sources

Historicity of Rajamala

In the 15th century, the appointment of Bengali Brahmin scholars like Pandit Sukreswar and Baneswar by Dharma of Tripura to record in Sanskrit the past glories of the royal house as *Raj-ratnakar* on the basis of the stories as narrated by the *Chantai* (tribal priest of the presiding royal pantheon of fourteen gods) Durlabhendra forms the nucleus of the *Rajamala* in Bengali. It is also claimed that there is a *Kok-Barak* version of the same, but unfortunately the manuscript is yet to be traced. However, there are various versions of the *Rajamala* in Bengali, the court language of Tripura, by various authors, like Kaliprasanna Sen Vidyabhusan and Kailash Chandra Singha. Despite the fascinating style of the *Rajamala,* the historical value of this chronicles, in the words of Suniti Kumar Chatterjee, 'is not much for the period prior to the 15th century.'[1] D.C. Sircar, another reputed Indologist, similarly expressed his doubts about the *Rajamala* in the following words:

> ... the details furnished by the earlier part of the present *Rajamala* regarding the history of the Tripura Royal Family down to the 18th century require verification from other sources.[2]

Like the *Rajamala,* other literary texts of Tripura too were just eulogies of the respective Manikyas of Tripura. Thus we have: *Champaka-Vijaya* (anecdotes of Prince Champaka, grandson of Kalyan Manikya) by Saikh Mahaddi; the *Gaji-Nama* (biography of Samser Gaji who usurped the throne of Tripura with the help of the Nawab of Bengal) by Manohar Shaikh; the *Krishnamala* (life of Krishna Manikya as told by Chantai Jayantain in presence of Rajdhar Manikya) by Pandit Ramganga Sharma; the *Srenimala* (the genealogical tables of the kings and their matrimonial relations) by Durgamani Ujir; the *Tripura-Vangshabali* (important names of Tripura Royal dynasty) by Dwiji Bangachandra; the *Pancha-Manikya* (life of the five Manikya kings: Dharma, Dhanya, Vijay, Krishna and

Bir-Chandra) by Kaliprasanna Sengupta. How all the above literary documents, without proper verification, can be used as genuine sources of history may be debated. However, the value of all these old literary documents in Bengali, though simply eulogies of respective rulers, cannot be underestimated.

ARCHAEOLOGICAL SOURCES

Numismatics

The shape, type, metal, era, script, legend, etc of the coins of Tripura throw welcome light on many unknown chapters of the history of Tripura. Rama Manikya I (15th century) was perhaps the first coin-issuing king of Tripura, as no coin prior to his has so far been found. Coins were issued by the Manikya rulers of Tripura on various occasions, eg coronation, marriage, pilgrimage, holy festivals, conquest, etc. These were commemorative in nature and not issued as mediums of exchange for the subjects. What then were the mediums of exchange? Was it simply the barter system or the use of cowrie? Why other than gold and silver, no other metal was used in the coins? In spite of having their own calendar *Tripurabda*, why did the Manikya rulers upto Ishan Chandra Manikya (AD 1850-62) use only *Sakabda* or the Saka era in their coins? Why was it only in the period of Birchandra Manikya (AD 1862-97) that *Tripurabda* was used in the coins? Why did the Manikya coins contain the names of the queens along with the kings? Does it indicate the superior status of women in Tripura society? Why did Birchandra Manikya replace the traditional 'lion-type' coins by the 'court of arms'? Was their any mint in Tripura? What were the similarities and dissimilarities of Manikya coins with the neighbouring coins of contemporary times? These and many such queries may make the history of the Manikya coins as well as the source-materials both interesting as well as informative.

Epigraphic

Inscriptions are also very important source-materials for the reconstruction of the history of Tripura. They are, however, yet to be seriously examined by epigraphists. The copper-plate land grants of the early Manikyas, the inscribed stone and terracotta slabs and bricks as used in various old temples and structures still await the attention of serious epigraphists. However, Chandradaya Vidyabinode in his *Silalipi-Sangraha* has drawn the attention[3] of scholars to some temple inscriptions. They include the inscriptions of Tripura-Sundari, Mahadev-Bari, Rajbari temple, Jagannath-Bari, Chaturdas-Devata or Radha Madhav temples, etc. Although the inscriptions of Tripura were written in Bengali script, the language was not always Bengali. Sometimes it was in Sanskrit and Assamese. The Manikyas of Tripura were deeply influenced by Brahmanical culture. Most of them were Shaivas, Saktas or Vaishnavas. They wanted to follow a 'superior type of culture', and in the process neglected the tribal language (*Kok-Barak*) and culture. The inscriptions, no doubt, are important sources of history, although utmost care and caution may be needed to utilise epigraphic materials of eulogistic nature.

Monuments etc., Art and Architecture

There are many sites, mounds in the hills and valleys, ruined houses or temples or mosques from where a lot of images, figurines, seals and variety of art and sculptural specimens are already found and many more still await the attention of the Archaeological Survey of India. Udaipur, once the capital of princely Tripura, was a temple-town. In temple architecture, Tripura style (also called *'Tribeg'* style) not only combined Brahmanical *chala* (hut) with Buddhist votive *stupa,* but also accepted Islamic buttress[4] (*minar* type) to enrich it aesthetically. The ruined or nearly-ruined structures may furnish abundant source-materials to reconstruct the history of Tripura. Again, head-worship, instead of full image of the deity, is something unique in Hindu ritual; but this is to be found in Tripura in the case of the fourteen god-heads of the Tripura or the god-heads at Unakoti.

Unakoti (one less than a crore) in North Tripura, is regarded as the most important site of religious sculptures of the early medieval period. *Shiva* is carved here in his theriomorphic, anthropomorphic and phallic forms. The rock-cut figures of colossal *Shiva*-head and a host of other deities and figurines carved on the rocks convey the artistic ability of the sculptors. Striking resemblance is reported to have been noticed between this colossal rock-cut sculpture in bold relief at Unakoti and the Bhuban *tirtha* of Cachar in Assam. Unfortunately, this rich work of art is now on the verge of ruins.

It is interesting to note that though the rulers of Tripura did not profess Buddhism, still Buddhist art, in various forms, flourished in the southern parts of Tripura, particularly at Pilak. Colossal stone images of Avalokiteswara, Gaṇeśa, Narasingha, etc, and a number of terracotta temple plaques and sealings with depiction of both Buddhist and Brahmanical creeds, are stylistically very closely related to the Mainamati art of Comilla (now in Bangladesh), not very far from Pilak. The mounds of Pilak are yet to be fully excavated; and if it is done, it may reveal art of multi-religious sects belonging to different periods. This task is very important for the reconstruction of the history of Tripura.

Though crude in concept, the rock-cut figurines of the Deotamura hill, South Tripura, are mentioned in some old texts. But this big panel of rock-cut images, particularly the *Mahisasura-Mardini* figure, are so worn-out today that it is difficult to identify these.

In a word, the art, architecture and sculpture of Tripura still demand attention of the scholarly world, because the importance of archaeology for the reconstruction of early history needs no elaboration. To have a people's history, emphasis may also be given on the terracotta art, as it was the art of the common people without having any patronage from the dominant of the society. Tripura terracotta, so far unearthed, reflect both flora and fauna, both religious and secular specimens, both plaques for temple decoration or simple toys which are of 'ageless' character. Unfortunately, no outstanding work on Tripura terracotta has seen day-light till today.

Travellers' Accounts

Travellers had visited Tripura in different periods and some of them had recorded their experience of the contemporary times. They constitute an importance source of history. For example, Raja Swargadeva Rudra Singha of Assam sent two envoys, Rama Kandali Sharma and Arjundas Bairagi to the court of Rama Manikya II (AD 1685-1772) with a mission to form a confederation against the Muslim rulers of Bengal. The two envoys left an account of Tripura entitled *Tripura Desera-Katha Lekha* which was later on edited and translated in English by S.K. Bhuyan as *Tripura Buranji.*

The account of some other travellers, particularly the French traveller Tavernier who visited during the reign of Chhatra Manikya in the 17th century, contain some interesting information about contemporary Tripura.

Some Non-Conventional Sources for the History of the People

The non-literate tribal people, who once constituted the majority in Tripura, have virtually no written record or document. Ethnological and craft objects – items of daily use by the tribal people in the past, be it pottery, textiles, utensils, tools, weapons, basketry, musical instruments, etc– might throw lights on their socio-economic history. Thus, the anthropological, ethnological and sociological antiques may be searched and scrutinised. However, without an inter-disciplinary approach the entire task is impossible.

NOTES AND REFERENCES

1. Suniti Kumar Chatterjee, *Kirata-Janakriti,* Calcutta, 1974, p. 131.
2. *Journal of the Asiatic Society of Bengal,* 1951, Vol. XVIII, No. 21, p. 76.
3. Chandrodaya Vidyabinode Bhattacharyya (ed.), *Silalipi-Sangraha in Bengali,* Agartala, 1904.
4. Adris Banerjee, *Temples of Tripura,* Varanasi, 1968.

20

Medieval Persian Sources of the History of North-East India: A Brief Survey

F.A. Qadri

The Muslims first set foot in North-East India during the period of rapid expansion of the Turkish power. The expedition of Malik Iz-al-Din Muhammad bin Bakhtiyar Khalji was an effort in this direction. This expedition, however, proved to be the *Achilles Heel* of the otherwise most successful, daring and adventurous personality of medieval India. The disastrous failure of Muhammad bin Bakhtiyar inaugurated an era lasting over five centuries during which parts of North-East was, temporarily though, dominated and ruled by Muslim invaders. During this period of over five centuries numerous historical sources developed which provide invaluable information helpful in reconstructing history of the region. The political chronicles supply not only the details of political or military history, but also provide important facts of political and economic geography, social and cultural history and fix the chronology of their rulers. There are non-political literature of different types: Sufi hagiographies, travelogues, collection of conversation of the Sufis *(Malfuzāt)*, royal decrees *(Farāmīn)* and news-letters *(Waqai)* and hence the vastness and variety of source-material for the history of medieval North-East India be easily acknowledged.

Tabaqāt-i-Nāsiri[1] of Maulana Minhāj al-Din Abul Ulmar Usmān Bin Siraj al-Dīn Jurjānī is the principal source of information about the expedition of Muhammad Bin Bakhtiyar Khalji in the region. Minhāj's account is the only connected and coherent narration of the political and military activity of the period. He supplies an eye-witness account of the stage through which one of the greatest empires of the medieval period had to pass in order to take shape. Tabaqāt-i-Nāsirī is a general history of Muslim dynasties of Asia, including Hindustan between 810 to 1260. Starting from the patriarchs and prophets he brought the story down to his own day.

More than a mere political chronicler, Minhāj Siraj was a great scholar, well-versed in religious sciences, inspiring as an orator, calculating and shrewd as a politician, connected with the ruling house of Ghur, impressive as a theologian and possessing statesman-like qualities. Along with Sultan Shams al-Dīn Iltutmish and his Prime Minister Nizām al-Mulk Junaidi, Minhāj Siraj appears to be one of the founding fathers of the Delhi Sultanate. It is perhaps due to these qualities that eminent successor Zia al-Dīn Barani remarks that, "in the compilation of Tabaqāt-i-Nāsirī Sadr i-Jahan Minhāj ul-Dīn Sirāj Jurjānī has shown miraculous powers."[2]

After Iltutmish, like many religious men of the period, Minhāj Siraj also plunged headlong into politics. During the next three decades, till rise of Ghiyath al-Dīn Balban, he was one of the most active politicians of Delhi. In 1241, during the reign of Muiz al-DīnBahrām, he was made Qazi of Delhi. But he was so active in politics that the Wazīr, Khwaja Muhazzab al-Dīn, hired some villains for his assassination. He was actually attacked in the Jama Masjid but somehow escaped unhurt. When Alā al-Dīn Masud Shah reappointed Khwaja Muhazzab al-Dīn as Wazir in 1242, Minhāj resigned from his post and left for Lakhnauti. He remained there for two years.

It was during his sojourn at Lakhnauti in Bengal somewhere in 1243-44 that Minhāj was told about the dramatic events that had taken place forty years ago. Here Minhāj met one Samsām al-Dīn entitled Mu'tamad al-Daulah who had been in the service of Muhammad Bin Bakhtiyar, and from him he gathered information about Bakhtiyār's exploits in Bihar and Bengal and tragic circumstances of his death.[3] Minhāj talks about the tribes of Koch, Mech and Tharu. Interestingly, Minhāj provides earliest reference to the conversion of a Mech Chief, Ali by Muhammad Bin Bakhtiyar during his march. Ali conducted Bakhtiyar in the hills of the region.[4] He also provided interesting information about people, language, religion, land, population, flourishing villages, forts, valour, weapons and methods of warfare of the people and hence, he stands out pre-eminently as a very systematic and discerning chronicler of the time. More than that, being a pioneer, he bequeathed to posterity of historians the heritage of an all-India view in their compilations. Notwithstanding his shortcomings, Minhāj remains our principal source of information. What a blank our knowledge would have remained about the most significant event in North-East India before the coming of the Ahoms, had not Minhāj endeavoured and supplied these informations to us.

References to the North-East in the early Mughal political chronicles are incidental and fragmentary. Abul Fadl in *Akbar Nama*[5] mentions the establishment of a defensive alliance with Koch Behar, the break-up of Koch kingdom, the events of the Koch-Mughal war, imprisonment of Raja Parikshit Narayan and Mukarram Khan's expedition to Assam. Medieval Persian accounts are replete with the amazing description of the region. The fatigue and dangers of various expeditions coupled with the climatic conditions and environmental tensions of the pestilential country. The amazing accounts of magic, sorcery and witchcraft was so impressive that even the medieval doyen like Abdul Fadl while talking of the prosperous silk industry of the region never forgets to mention that the people of Kamarupa are good-looking and addicted to the practice of magic.[6] Jahangir refers to the hostilities between Lakshmi Narayan, king of Koch Bihar and Parikshit Narayan, king of Koch Hajo (Kamarupa) leading to the Mughal-Ahom conflict and conquest of Kamarupa.[7]

Seventeenth century is a period of crucial significance in so far Persian writings on North-East India is concerned. There is a definite shift-perception of the Mughal writers and that seems to be the result of direct contact of the writers with the land and people of the region. The first writer Alā al-Dīn Isfahanī alias Mirza Nathan was an important military officer in Mughal Kamarupa and his father Ihtimān Khan was *Mir-i-Bahr* or in-charge of Mughal naval fleet in Bengal. Mirza Nathan took a leading part in all the campaigns in Bengal and Assam during the region of Jahangir and hence records the history of Bihar, Bengal and the kingdoms of Koch Bihar and Kamarupa for sixteen years from 1608 to 1624 in his work *Baharistan-i-Ghaybi.*

The original *manuscript* of this work belongs to the *Bibliotheque Nationale Paris.* It was first brought into public notice by Sir Jadunath Sarkar, who published some articles on it in the Bengali bi-monthly journal *Prabasi.* Later, he wrote an article in the journal of Bihar and Orissa Research Society, 1921, giving an account of its discovery and a full table of contents. Sarkar also found that the description of the relevant Persian manuscript in *Bibliotheque Nationale,* Paris, was wrong. The discoverer gave the title of the work as *Baharistan-i-Ghaybi* and the translator Dr. M.I. Borah has accepted the same.[8] It's a matter of great surprise that the author Mirza Nathan nowhere calls it by the name of *Baharistan-i-Ghaybi.* Curiously enough in the course of narration he record at one place[9] and the author of this *Iqbal Namaī-Ghaybi* that tantamount to suggest that the real title of the work is *Iqbal Nama-i-Ghaybi* and not *Baharistan-i-Ghaybi.*

But the work since its discovery in 1919 and translation into English in 1936 has been in vogue with the title *Baharistan-i-Ghaybi.* The work is not exactly a work of history, rather a memoirs of Mirza Nathan and its discovery had no doubt immensely contributed towards the reconstruction of the history of North-East India.[10] It is undoubtedly a work of rare historical value. All the events and details however revolve round the personality and activities of Mirza Nathan.[11] Regrettably, almost all the scholars have seen *Baharistan* only as a source of information for Mughal-Koch or Mughal-Ahom conflicts. The *Baharistan* is a mine of information for the history of both north and south banks of the Brahmaputra and equally about some of the hill and plain tribes of this region. It still awaits a more close and careful scrutiny. The present author has made some move in this direction.[12]

The shift is gradual among the Mughal writers in their understanding of North-East India and there is ample literary proof from 17th century onwards which can be put forward with evident pride:

> Its trees are fully loaded [and fruits that they prefer; Al-Qurān (VI-20)] and its streams [where from they get no aching of the head nor any madness; Al-Qurān (VI-19)] are redundant in savour. Its openness provides the sight of the people with un-burnt collyrium. It's extensiveness gives the delicate ones dammed by sorrow a pleasing delight. Its meadow are just like the splendours of paradise and promotes one's comfort. Its greenery as if a heaven on earth.[13]

That is how a Mughal observer writes about North-East India in the early 1660s. An accomplished writer and a keen observer of men and environment, Shihab *al-Dīn nom* de plume Talish accompanied Mir Jumla as a news writer *(Wāqia Nawis)* during the former's Assam campaign in 1662-63. He was in constant attendance of the Mughal General and was not only an eyewitness but actually shared all the fatigues and dangers of the expedition. Talish wrote accurate and detailed account of the expedition and description of not only Assam but of the major part of present North-East – its geography, landscape, people, their customs manner, weapons, methods of warfare, bravery, prowess, their hardiness, enterprising nature and their skills. The authors named the work *Fathiyah Ibriyah*, ie victory and admonition, as the Mughals gained victory and also learnt lessons from their expedition.[14]

Fathiyah Ibriyah is a unique work of its kind.[15] The approach of Shihab al-Dīn Talish is literary and one event leads to another. All the aspects covered in the work have been given equal treatment. Never before and after any of the medieval Persian chronicles provided so clear and categorical accounts of the region than *Fathiyah Ibriyah's.* It provides a rare insight into the history and culture of the region and unfolds the panorama of socio-political activities hitherto unexplored by the modern scholars of medieval North-East India.

Muhammad Kazim's *Alamgir Nama,*[16] gjves accounts of Koch Bihar and Assam, largely based on *Fathiyah Ibriyah.* Since Shihab al-Dīn Talish was a news writer and Muhammad Kazim a royal chronicler, the latter being in advantageous position incorporated the informations on North-East in Verbatim from Talish's writings which a careful reader of *Alamgir Namah* and *Fathiyah Ibriyah* could easily make out. Whereas Muhammad Kazim portrays a big canvas, Shihab al-Dīn Talish concentrates on North-East India.

Riyaz al-Salātīn of Ghulam Hussain Salim is the only work on medieval Bengal which provides the fullest account of the province of Bengal.[17] While describing the boundaries and environs of Bengal, Salim provides detailed informations about Koch Bihar, Kamarupa, Assam and other parts of North-East during the medieval period. But like Muhammad Kazim, the author of *Riyaz al-Salātin,* he also largely depends on *Fathiyah Ibriyah.* Salim, during the course of narration, often quotes a book shown to him by Hāji Ārif Qandhārī. The *Fathiyah Ibriyah* also mentions about Háji Ārif Qandhári who was with Talish during the Assam campaign.[18]

Medieval Sufi literature, particularly collection of conversation of Muslim Saints *(Malfuzāf)* and their hagiographies, are the best corrective, corroborative and confirmatory source available from 13th century onwards.

There is a general confusion whether Ghiyath al-Dīn Bahadur Shah conquered Kamarupa around 1321-22.[19] But the collection of conversation of the celebrated 14th century Saint of Bihar, Shaykh Sharaf al-Dīn Yahya Manerī (1298-1381) entitled *Munis al-Murīdīn*[20] refers to a discussion between Sultan Shams al-Dīn Firoz Shah of Bengal and his *Wazīr* Arsalan Khan where the Sultan wanted *Wazir's* counselling on the choice of next Sultan among his two sons, Hatīm, the *Hākim* of Bihar and Ghiyath-al-Dīn, *Hakim* of Kamru.[21] That means to suggest that Kamarupa was conquered by Shams al-Dīn Firoz Shah of Bengal and was placed under the Governorship of his son.

Malfuz literature of medieval period is very useful in reconstructing the socio-cultural history of the region. One of the collections of the great Indo-Islamic Saint, Shaykh Nizam al-Dīn Auliya of Delhi (d. 1325), compiled by his favourite disciple Amir Khusro refers to the spiritual territory of Shaykh Jala al-Dīn Tabrezi in a region where human sacrifice was common.[22] This Saint came from Delhi to Kamarupa via Bengal and was peripatetic by nature.[23] He is credited to have done away with the sacrifice.[24] This is again corroborated by another collection of the same genre, Jawami 'al-Kalim of Shaykh Bandanawāz

Gesudarāz of Gulbarga.[25] We know that human sacrfice was offered by the Chutiyas, Tippers, Kacharis, Koches and some other North-East people to a deity called Kesaāi Khati.[26] The conversation of the *Sants* also testify that the group of people who were relieved from such ghastly acts were converted to Islam by Shaykh Jalāl al-Dīn Tabrezi.[27] It happened in the first-half of the 13th century and was probably the first instance of group conversion to Islam.

An interesting feature of spiritual history of medieval North-East India is the presence of warrior Saints *(Ghāzī Auliya);* and Shah Jalāl of Sylhet is the classical example. He is credited to have helped the military commander of Bengal, Sikandar Khan Ghazi against the Raja of Sylhet, Gaur Gobinda and the region was annexed to the Muslim kingdom of Bengal.[28] Muhammad Ghauthī Shattarī author of *Gulzār-i Abrār,* is the only oldest serving hagiographic worker to reconstruct the life of Shah Jalal of Sylhet.[29] Written during the reign of Jahangīr in AD 1613, Ghauthī Shattārī had extensive knowledge of Sufi literature of the medieval period and was a disciple of Shaykh Muhammad Ghauth of Gwalior (d. 1563). The Shattārī Saints were well-connected in the Sufi circles of Bengal and the Shattari traditions about Sufi activities in the region can be relied upon.[30]

The oft-quoted work regarding Shah Jalal of Sylhet is Nasir al-Dīn Haider's *Suhayl-i yeman* (Star of Yemen) written in 1857.[31] As the title suggests, Nasir al-Dīn Haider Halis Shah Jalal was a native of Yemen. Ghauthi Shattārī, however, says, "he was of Turkish origin but born in Bengal".[32] *Suhayl-i Yeman* is based on two other compositions, *Raudat al-Salehin,* 1124AH/AD 1712, and *Risalah* by Mu 'in al-Dīn (1134 AH/AD 1721). There is a much later work in Urdu named *Tarīkh-i Jalālī* still in manuscript form in *Al-Islāh* library, Sylhet.[33] Though a mixture of fiction and fact, these hagiographies of medieval Saints, active in parts of North-East India are interesting sources of information about cultural integration and also social and polity formations. This is more evident from the case of Shah Isma'īl Ghāzī, a commander under Sultan of Bengal (1459-73), who was beheaded by the Sultan on charges of being in collusion with a Hindu Raja. Earlier Shāh Isma'īl had helped the Sultan in the expedition against the Raja of Kamarupa. He lies buried at Kamta Duar, from where the famous Risalal al-Shada was discovered during the 19th century.[34]

NOTES AND REFERENCES

1. Text edited by Nassau Lees, Khadim Hussain and Abd al-Hayy, *Bib. Indica* Series, Calcutta, 1864. English translation: H.G. Raverty, *Asiatic Society of Bengal,* New Delhi, (reprint), 1970.

2. *Tārikh-i Firoz Shāhī*, edited by Sir Syed Ahmed Khan, *Bib. Indica* Series, 1890, p. 21.
3. *Tabāqut-i Nāsrī, op. cit.*, Vol. I, pp. 557-558.
4. *Ibid.*
5. Text edited by Abd al-Rahim, *Bib. Indica,* Calcutta, 1837-87; English translation: Henry Beveridge, 3 Vols., *Bib. Indica,* New Delhi, (reprint) 1979.
6. *Ain-i Akbari,* Vol. II, English Translation: H. Blochmen New Delhi, (reprint), 1977-78, pp. 130-31.
7. *Tizuk-i Jahangiri,* or *Memoir of Jahangir,* English Translation: Alexander Rogers, edited by Henry Beveridge, 2 Vols. in 1, 2nd edn., New Delhi, 1968.
8. English translation published by the Department of Historical and Antiquarian Studies, Government of Assam, 1963, Guwahati, (reprint), 1992.
9. Book II, Chapter I of the English Translation of *Baharistan-i Ghaybi, op. cit.,* p. 264.
10. M.I. Bora, *op. cit.,* Introduction, xxi.
11. Q. Ahmed, *Mirza Nathān, Historians of Medieval India,* Muhibbul Hasan (ed.), Meerut-New Delhi, 1968, p. 75.
12. F.A. Qadri, "Garo Factor in Mughal North-East Frontier Policy", *Milton S Sangma Felicitation Volume,* Shillong (forthcoming).
13. Shihīb al-Dīn Tālish, *Fathiyah Ibriyah,* edited text, unpublished M.Phil, dissertation by Md. Abd-ur-Rahaman, Manipur University, Imphal, 1990.
14. F.A. Qadri, "Fathiyah Ibriyah: Manifestation of the Mughal Interest in North-East India", *Proceedings of North East History Association,* Imphal Session 1990, pp. 46-57; "Mediaeval Perception of North-East India", *Proceedings of North East History Association,* Imphal Session 1990, pp. 62-69.
15. An analysis of the work was published by H. Blochman, *Journal of Asiatic Society of Bengal,* Part I, 1872, pp. 63-96. Sir Jadunath Sarkar published its summary in the same journal in 1906, pp. 257-267 and 1907, pp. 405-425. Sarkar also translated 19 folios as, "Assam and the Ahoms in AD 1660", *Journal of Bihar and Orissa Research Society,* Patna, Vol. I, Part II, 1915, pp.179-195.
16. Edited by Khadim Hussain and Abd al-hay, *Bib. Indica,* Calcutta, 1865-73.
17. English translation by Abdus Salam, Delhi, reprint, 1975.
18. *Fathiyah Ibriyah, op. cit.*
19. H.K. Barpujari (ed.), *The Comprehensive History of Assam,* Vol. 11, Guwahati, 1992, p. 40.
20. Ms. Khuda Baksh, Patna, n.d.
21. *Ibid.*, ff. 17b-18a.
22. *Afdal al-Fuad,* Delhi, 1305 A.H., p. 132.
23. F.A. Qadri, "Shaykh Jalāl al-Dīn tabrezī: Is He the Saint of Hajo?", Paper presented at 22nd Session of North-East India History Association, Tezpur, *Proceedings of North East History Association,* Imphal Session (forthcoming).
24. *Ibid.*

25. *Jawamī al-Kalim,* Hyderabad, n.d., p. 157.
26. E.A. Gait, *A History of Assam,* Calcutta, 1963, p. 43.
27. *Jawamī 'al-Kalim, op. cit.*
28. J.B. Bhattacharjee, "Pre-Colonial Political Structure of Bearak Valley" in Milton S Sangma (ed.), *Essays on North-East India,* Milton S. Sangma, Delhi, 1994, p. 70.
29. MS. No. 24, *Asiatic Society of Bengal,* Calcutta, Urdu translation as *Adhkar-i Abrar,* Lahore, n.d., pp.124-25.
30. F.A. Qadri, "Abu Yazīd Bistīmi and Shattari Suli Thought", *Islamic Culture,* Hyderabad, Vol. LXXV, No. 4, pp. 79-95.
31. Published from Calcutta, 1894.
32. *Gulzar-i Abrīr, op. cit.*
33. Shaykh Muhammad Ikrīm, *Aab-i Kauthar,* Delhi (Reprint), n.d., p. 303.
34. Authored by Pir Muhammad Shattarī, it was discovered by G.H. Damant who published its English translation in his "Notes on Shīh Isma'īl Ghāzī", *Journal of Asiatic Society of Bengal,* Vol. XLIII, No. 1, 1874.

21

Pemberton's Report: Trade and Trade-Routes between Assam and its Neighbourhood

Priyam Goswami

Captain R.B. Pemberton's *Report on the Eastern Frontier of British India,* first published in 1835, is one of the pioneering works and therefore provides invaluable source- material for the study of the Eastern Frontier of British India. The description of the territory from Assam to Arracan was the result of Pemberton's 'personal examination'. This has added to the authenticity and credibility of the report. What adds additional importance to the report is the author's insertion of a list of documents and works consulted in its preparation for he rightly believed that they would be of immense help to those engaged in research on the subject in future.

The Anglo-Burmese War of 1824-26 had revealed a glaring ignorance of the British about the geography of the region which had, in fact, impeded operations on several occasions. The subsequent occupation of the region following the Treaty of Yandabo, made it imperative that a detailed study be made. With this objective in mind, Captain Pemberton, Joint Commissioner of Manipur, was instructed to compile a report on the Eastern Frontier. The report covers a wide range of subjects relating to the physical, anthropological, economic and political conditions of the people inhabiting a large area including Assam, Manipur, Arracan, Ava and a few other places in Burma. However, Pemberton laid considerable emphasis on providing information on the following: (i) a general description of the great chain of mountains from the southern borders of Assam to the southern borders of Arracan; (ii) the nature of the passes and countries by which these mountains have been penetrated; (iii) a description of the countries beyond the mountains extending to the frontiers of China; (iv) an estimate of the comparative value of the different passes from British territories into Ava and to offer such suggestions as may appear likely to render them either lines of commercial intercourse or military operations; and (v) a general description of the Khasi hills and the kingdoms of Cachar and Jaintiya. The report also incorporates valuable data on the trade and commercial routes between Assam and Burma and on the passes between Assam and Bhutan.

The occupation of Assam by the British and their gradual penetration into the entire region had opened up immense prospects. In the initial stages of colonial penetration the importance of Assam and the Eastern Himalayas was not only for its resources but also for its strategic location, the region having a common frontier with Tibet and Burma. The British were haunted by fears of a renewed Burmese invasion and so it was strategically important for them to ensure that the region did not relapse into anarchy. However, soon this apprehension faded into the background and the prospect of increased trade and commerce became the dominant factor that influenced British policies in this region. The British search for overseas market has to be seen in the context of the general economic condition of Europe. As European trade diminished, the vacuum was sought to be filled by development of trade with these countries. Trade with Tibet, moreover, had an added importance as it imported more than it exported and the balance was made up in gold and silver.[1] As long as the chiefs of the Newar dynasty ruled over the petty kingdoms of Kathmandu, Patan and Bhatgaon, a flourishing trade had existed between India and Tibet,[2] but the Gurkha conquest of the Newar state disrupted the traditional trade between India and Tibet and an alternative route to Tibet became an urgent necessity. In this backdrop, several of the Company's servants were employed for extending the Company's geographical knowledge and information on the economic potentials of the frontier and beyond.[3] Pemberton's project was a result of this general policy of the government. In his report, Pemberton writes that David Scott was averse to any attempt being made to acquire any such knowledge 'under a most mistaken and exaggerated opinion of the unhealthy nature of tract of the country through which the exploring parties must pass' and that it was only after Jenkins took over charge of the province that the matter was taken up in right earnest.[4] The fond hope of extension of commerce to Tibet and China found expression in the following words of Jenkins:

> There is every prospect of our bringing all the races of hill-men bordering on this province under the same control as our Assamese subjects and at no distant period of opening out, through them, a direct trade with the Tibetan and Chinese province from which we are divided by narrow ranges of hills but from which we are absolutely shut out by the intractable rudeness of the intervening tribes.[5]

British commercial enterprises were excited at the prospect of getting thousands of new customers for their industrial products. It was also believed that ,

> as Sadiya would have to be a forwarding agency between India and China, it would become a station of considerable importance and by its commerce attract enterprise and thus materially assist in opening out Upper Assam.[6]

The frontier trade of Assam had been fairly extensive since the time of the Ahoms who, for reasons of political expediency, had maintained commercial relations with the tribes of the neighbouring hills. In fact, this trade had been the basis of the plains-hills contact in the entire area.[7] This was accomplished through an organised market system in the adjoining plains and foothills to the mutual benefit of the people on both sides as the surplus generated in an area balanced the deficit in the other. The entire volume of trade with the frontier tribes passed through the *Duars* or passes in the North-Eastern and North-Western borders of the Brahmaputra Valley. The hill-tribes also provided the routes for commercial transactions with Bhutan, Tibet, China and Burma.

Pemberton, commenting on the 'extraordinary fertility of the soil', the 'former affluence, abundant population and varied products of Assam', was convinced that the province would prove a 'highly valuable acquisition to the British Government' and that with renewed communications with the various hill-tribes on the border, new channels of commerce would be obtained 'that cannot fail to enrich the country through which they pass, and give a stimulus to its own agricultural and manufacturing industry.' He also pointed out that 'the opening of lines of communication, and facilitating thereby the merchants with their goods, is the object of primary importance for the effectual development of the resources of that country, and those bordering it'.[8] It can, therefore, be safely assumed that Pemberton's very positive views on the subject played a vital role in the Company's decision to annex Upper Assam three years later.

Routes to Cachar

Around 1833 attempts were made to explore and ascertain the nature of the tract which separated southern Cachar from central Assam, when a route extending from Bikrampur Pass (in Cachar) to Raha Chokey was visited by

Jenkins and Fisher. On exploration, they came across three other routes. The first extended from Kartigora, on the north bank of the Surma, through the central ridge of the Dowsang Pass, across the Jatinga *nullah* , through the Kopili Valley to Raha. The length of this route was estimated at around 150 miles. The second route, west of the first route, passed from Sylhet across the boundary of the Khasi hills, through the Jaintiya kingdom to Raha Chokey and covered a distance of 130 miles. Apparently this line of communication was taken by Captain Horsburgh in 1824 and was subsequently surveyed by Captain Jones in 1828. The western-most route, covering a distance of 126 miles, was the one which led from Sylhet to Guwahati via Cherrapunjee. Of all the above-mentioned routes, the last was the one through which almost all communication between Assam and Cachar was carried on. The other routes were rarely frequented because of the nature of the terrain through which they passed and also because of objections raised by the Jaintiya king against its use by foreigners.[9]

The importance of better communication facilities between Assam and Cachar grew after the annexation of the latter kingdom in view of the increasing prospects of trade. Rice, being the principal article of food, was extensively cultivated in Cachar. Pemberton observed that as sugarcane also grew luxuriantly, it held tremendous potential as a possible plantation crop. He further reported that at a time when the British were exploring all possible sources of acquiring cotton, 'the northern acclivities of the dividing range are peculiarly favourable to the cultivation of cotton'. But most important of all, it was believed that a timber trade too could flourish.[10] The three main varieties of timber, *Gundah, Dum* and *Kari,*[11] were principally used for boats, beams and posts. At a time when rivers formed the principal routes of communication, boat-building was an important industry and with the development of trade and commerce, the demand for good timber, suitable for boat-building, was likely to grow. Pemberton's report was, in fact, the first official document which provided the much-needed information on a region about which little had been known hitherto.

Routes to Manipur

Manipur was another neighbouring kingdom on which Pemberton made elaborate comments. Jai Singh, while fleeing to Assam after his defeat by the Burmese in 1774, was said to have crossed the great western range of Manipur to the village of Thonglang, and from there travelled in a north-westerly direction across the hills until he reached River Dhansiri, following the banks of which he arrived at Jorhat. This appears to have been the only route known to the British for a long time. Twenty years later, when Captain Welsh came to Assam, he met emissaries of Raja Jai Singh at Jorhat who also traversed the same route. After the Burmese

War, efforts were made by Pemberton and Jenkins to explore new avenues of communication between Assam and Manipur. This resulted in the exploration of a second route, east of the one which already existed, by Lieutenant Gordon and Raja Gambhir Singh in 1833. Both the routes were very similar. Pemberton records:

They both leave the Manipur Valley by defiles, which stretch for many miles among the hills; they then cross the Barak River, ascend at different points of the same great chain, round the eastern borders of Assam, stretch along its whole southern frontier, and terminate 500 miles distant at the western bend of the Brahmaputra... there is very little more than 20 miles difference in length of the two routes.[12]

Gambhir Singh was anxious to extend his western frontier. His intention, in fact, was to bring all the tribes inhabiting the territory through which the routes passed under his subjugation with a view ultimately to facilitate communication with Assam.[13] This was necessary not only for military purposes but for economic reasons as well.

Trade with Assam was important for the economic development of the kingdom. Pemberton records that Manipur was extremely rich in forest products. Apart from *Keo,* from which the celebrated Burmese varnish was obtained, the availability of timber was extensive and varied. But trade in these products was practically non-existent because of difficulties in transportation and communication.

The possibility of trade in salt was also considerable. The valley was particularly rich in salt which, Pemberton recorded, was of a very superior quality and could be a profitable article of trade. The quantity of salt, obtained by artificial evaporation, was about 1/19th of the weight of water and if subjected to further purification, the proportion was likely to be reduced to l/20th, which was nearly double the quantity obtained from Newcastle. He also described the process by which the salt was extracted.[14] All the wells were considered the property of the Raja who levied a tax of l/5th upon the quantity of water drawn; from the remainder, the wages of the manufacturers were paid at the rate of 12 seers per month equivalent to between Rs.3/- and Rs.4/-. Considering the fact that Assam had to import almost the entire quantity of her requirement of salt, Pemberton believed that a profitable trade could be set up in that direction. Pemberton had gathered reports of a brisk trade having flourished between Burma and Manipur via the Kabo Valley prior to the Burmese invasion. Chinese merchants from Yunan also visited the kingdom to sell gongs, Chinese silk and boxes, in exchange for wax, ivory, clothes, cotton and ponies. Apart from the existing articles, Pemberton saw great possibilities of transforming other products such as tobacco, sugarcane, indigo, mustard, pulses and opium, which were cultivated in considerable quantities in Manipur, into valuable articles of trade with proper management. Manipuri silk, 'remarkable for its strength and brilliancy of colours,' was also identified as a potential article for export.

TRANS-PATKAI ROUTES

Pemberton records that between the 94th and 96th degrees longitude and 25th and to 27th degrees latitude, was an extensive, unexplored mountainous tract. However, on the eastern confines of this unexplored region, were traces of communication, between the Assamese and the Shans, who migrated to the territory through a pass in the Patkai hills. It was through the same pass that the Ahoms first entered Assam and through which the Burmese subsequently invaded the land. Being the most accessible and well-known route, Pemberton was of the opinion that through this route alone could the British hope to 'establish a commercial intercourse with the populous and wealthy cities of Mogaung and Bhamo, and the country around them'.[15] As early as 1828, Lt. Burnett had been deputed by David Scott to explore and report on this pass and to proceed to Mogaung, with the object of exploring the possibilities of establishing a commercial intercourse. However, owing to the opposition of the Singphos, who occupied the intermediate space between the summit of the pass and Mogaung, the party could not proceed beyond the summit. The total distance between Sadiya and this point was about 80 miles while the remaining distance to Mogaung, another 40 miles or so. It was essential to open this route to regular traffic because Mogaung served as a nerve- centre of the trade in the region with routes connecting it with Yunan, Bhamo and Ava. Chinese caravans normally visited the town annually during a specific time of the year while many Chinese merchants even resided at this place permanently.

> Whether we obtain their merchandise direct from the Chinese themselves, or through the Shans, the result in either case must be to create an equivalent demand for British products, and to disseminate them generally among the numerous tribes with whom we have at present little or no intercourse.[16]

It was, therefore, extremely important to keep the Singphos under subjugation as they practically controlled the route to Mogaung. Troubles at the Sadiya frontier arising out of internal feuds among the Singphos in the 1830s caused serious anxiety to the British Government. When peace missions under Captain S.F. Hannay and G.T. Bayfield failed, Jenkins proposed to set up an advanced outpost under a European officer.[17] Although the Governor-General-in-Council initially expressed serious doubts as to the expediency of the project,[18] in 'view of the emergency and the growing deterioration in relation with Ava', it was decided to establish a frontier military outpost on the Buridihing.[19] By the beginning of the following decade, military control over these tracts proceeded at a faster rate. The security afforded by the presence of British troops in the region had generated so much confidence among the trading community that there is even a reference to four enterprising Marwari merchants from Western India residing at Sadiya who carried on a lucrative trade with the neighbouring hill-tribes and across the mountains in the Hukong Valley.[20] This route from Assam through the Hukong Valley to Upper Burma and then on to China passed through Bisa, south of Sadiya, and Old Bisa in the Hukong Valley.

Pemberton had anticipated that the functioning of trade through this route would not be smooth because of the constant inter-tribal feuds. John F. Mitchell, confirming this fear, observed in his report in 1883, that this was indeed true,[21] and that an additional obstacle was the attitude of the Burmese officers in-charge of the commercial outposts who indulged in heavy extortions from the traders in direct contravention of the Commercial Treaty signed between the British and the Burmese in 1826.[22] Hence, it was believed that if a more direct line of communication higher up the Irrawaddy, through the country of the Khakoo Singphos to Bisa, could be established, the intercourse between Yunan, Sechuen and Assam would not only be easier but more profitable as well. Pemberton had, in fact, suggested the exploration of such a route as certain trade marts already existed in this region. This was perhaps the route taken by Captain Wilcox a few years later. Robinson writes:

> Tracking the Noa Dihing which enters the Lohit, the great eastern branch of the Brahmaputra, a few miles above Sadiya, Wilcox was able to proceed by water conveyance within 9 days march of Munlung on the Irrawady, and this journey he accomplished without any difficulty.[23]

The importance of the Hukong Valley route was stressed from time to time. As late as 1896, possibilities for the construction of a railway from Makum to Mogaung was surveyed. The projected cost of Rs. 3,83,00,000 for the 284 miles of 3' 3/8"gauge railway line was considered too high by the government who felt that the line did not hold out adequate prospects of being commercially successful.[24] Hence the project fell through.

The Burmese Government was, meanwhile, beginning to appreciate the value of commerce and the king of Ava himself was said to have remarked, on several occasions, on the extension of trade and commerce resulting from the growing confidence of the merchants subsequent to the permanent residence of a British officer at Ava.[25] This was, no doubt, an important indicator of the willingness of the Burmese Government to encourage foreign traders and to assist in the opening up of new commercial routes. In the context of trade with Assam, this was of special significance because it held out prospects of extending commercial intercourse to Bhutan and Tibet.

The tract of country separating British territory from the Bhutan hills was a narrow strip extending along the foot of the lower ranges from the Dhansiri in the east to the Teesta in the west. Within this area there were 18 *Duars* or passes, either wholly or partially dependent on Bhutan. Of these passes, 11 touched the northern borders of Bengal, and 7 that of Assam, and it was through these passes that the plains-hills contact was maintained. Two of the passes in Assam, viz, *Buriguma* and *Kulling Duars*, were situated in Darrang while the *Ghurkola, Baksha, Chapagur, Chapakhamar* and *Bijni Duars* were situated in Kamrup.[26] The jurisdiction of the *Duars* in Darrang was held alternately by the British and the Bhutias — the former retaining jurisdiction from July to November and the latter for the remaining eight months. The *Duars* adjoining Kamrup were held exclusively by the Bhutias. Through these passes, the Bhutias held their sway over the border and established their *de facto* right on the entire belt of border territory although theoretically they were expected to pay the British a certain amount of money as tribute.[27] The loose control of the British over the Bhutias can be easily perceived from Pemberton. Each *Duar* was under the authority of a *Jongpen* (a local Bhutia magistrate) who was also in-charge of the district to which the *Duar* was attached.[28] Enjoying no fixed salaries and deriving little advantage from the barren lands in which they resided, the *Jongpens* looked to the *Duars* as their only source of income. Hence, almost every article of consumption was taken from the plains in the name of tribute. This inevitably led to continuous friction on the frontier, hindering trade and blocking routes. As early as 1833, T.C. Robertson, Agent to the Governor- General for the North-Eastern frontier, had written to the Government of India of the necessity of entering into some definite treaty with the Government of Bhutan as past experience had shown that the frontier officials not only intercepted all communications to the Raja complaining of their conduct but also misrepresented facts so as to make each incident appear as an act of British aggression.[29] The British Government, in an effort to secure peace, occupied all the Assam *Duars* in 1841.

The interest of the British in Bhutan was, however, not merely political. Apart from the inconvenience and political danger arising out of turmoil on the frontier, Robertson believed that 'there would also be an indirect loss sustained by the cessation of that commercial intercourse, whence there is every reason to hope that great benefits may soon accrue to Assam.'[30]

An important trade route between Bhutan and Asam was by the valley of the River Manas via Tassagong and Dewangiri to Hajo.[31] The groups of Bhutias were usually accompanied by 'very beautiful assets', all of which were laden with coloured blankets, gold dust, silver, salt, chauries (tails of the Tibetan yaks), musk, bees wax and munjeet. They took back with them raw and manufactured silk, cotton, dried fish and tobacco.[32]

From early times an extensive trade was known to have existed between Bhutan and Tibet, and in the context of the British occupation of Assam, this was of tremendous significance. Pemberton pointed out that if a line of communication could be opened up into Tibet through Bhutan, a trade 'to an extent never before attained' would flourish and 'be the means of widely disseminating British manufactures through the vast regions of the Tibet and Bhootan'[33] into China. West of the *Buriguma Duar* was the *Kuriapara Duar* which had been the main channel of trade between Tibet and Assam. Pemberton believed, on the basis of earlier reports of Turner and Hamilton,[34] that a line of communication did exist between Assam and China during the time of the Ahoms and that this ought to be immediately revived. Quoting Hamilton, he writes,

> At a place called Chouna, two months' journey from Lassa, on the confines of the two states, there is a mart established, and on the Assam side, there is a similar mart at Geegunshur, distant four miles from Chouna. An annual caravan repairs from Lassa to Chouna, conducted by about 20 persons, carrying silver bullion to the amount of about a lakh of rupees and a considerable quantity of rock-salt, for sale to Assamese merchants at Geegunshur, to which place the latter bring rice, which is imported into Tibet from Assam in large quantities; tussa cloth manufactured by the native women in Assam, from queen downwards: iron and lac, skins, buffalo horns; and pearls and corals first imported from Bengal.[35]

There were two principal routes from Lhasa to Peiking. The first and the shorter one through which the post was carried, took around 20 days, while the second route, and the more convenient one for the conveyance of baggage, was the one generally used by merchants although it took almost eight months.[36]

The discovery of the tea plant in Assam was intimately connected to the opening up of commercial intercourse with Bhutan, Tibet and the neighbouring regions. Pemberton noted in his report that he anticipated a huge market 'with the view of rendering it a staple article of trade with the regions in which it is so extensively consumed, and where the peculiar mode of preparing it for use, less skill in its culture would be necessary than in those varieties which were intended for European markets.'[37] He also observed that the tea plant grew naturally on the hills between Manipur and the Kabo Valley and that, therefore, 'it would flourish on all the inferior heights and in the sheltered nooks'.[38] In the light of subsequent events relating to the annexation of Upper Assam,[39] it may be assumed that Pemberton's observations on the subject must have influenced British policy in this region to a considerable extent, considering that he laid considerable stress on the trade and commercial aspects while conducting his investigations.

While the report was prepared to meet the East India Company's immediate strategic and commercial needs, it has stood as an invaluable and monumental document for historians and researchers. Pemberton has not only succeeded in giving vivid details of the variety of topics that he has dealt with but has also been able to provide authentic information on a region about which little was known earlier. Indeed, it can be rightly regarded as a first step in an extensive field of interesting inquiry. But apart from recording the existing state of things, Pemberton has thrown enormous light on the mind-set of the colonialists under the banner of the East India Company. Read in isolation, the report is a narrative of a virtual *terra incognita;* read and interpreted in a contextual framework with the help of other materials, it is a blue print for the East India Company's penetration into North-East India and beyond.

NOTES AND REFERENCES

1. A. Lamb, *Britain and Chinese Central Asia - A Road to Lhasa,* London, 1962, p. 5.
2. *Foreign Defence (Secret F),* May 1885, No. 752. Memorandum on relations with Tibet by Col. Macaulay, Secy. to the Government of Bengal.
3. P. Goswami, *Assam in the Nineteenth Century: Industrialisation and Colonial Penetration,* New Delhi, 1999, p. 8.
4. R.B. Pemberton, *Report on the Eastern Frontier of British India* (henceforth REFBI), Guwahati (reprint), 1966, p. 61.
5. *Assam Secretariat Records,* General Department, Feb. 1944, No. 12.
6. *Ibid.,* File No. 167 J of 1878.
7. J.B. Bhattacharjee, 'The Eastern Himalayan Trade of Assam in the Colonial Period', *Proceedings of NEIHA,* 1980, pp. 174-189.
8. *REFBI,* p. 76.
9. *Ibid.,* pp. 76-78.
10. *REFBI,* p. 213.
11. Captain Fisher, *Journal of the Asiatic Society,* 1832, cited in Pemberton, *REFBI,* p 213.
12. *REFBI,* p. 65.
13. H.K. Barpujari (ed.), *The Comprehensive History of Assam,* Vol. IV, Guwahati, 1992, pp. 61-63.
14. "The spots containing these springs are said to be discovered by a very subtle vapour;... as soon as the fact is clearly ascertained, a shaft is sunk down to the spring, and cylinders, formed of the hollowed trunks of large trees, let perpendicularly into the opening, are preserved in an erect position, by ramming earth between them and the sides of the well. The diametre of the cylinders is seldom more than 6 feet, and the depth varies from 40 to 60 feet." *REFBI,* pp. 30-31.
15. *REFBI,* p. 67.
16. *Ibid.,* p. 149.
17. *Foreign Political Consultations,* 1836, 2 August, No. 81.
18. *Ibid.*

19. *Ibid.*, 1837, 15 May, No. 12.
20. They imported broad cloths, muslins, long cloths, various crockery items, salt, opium, liquor, glass, betel-nuts, tobacco and rice for the troops. These articles they bartered to the neighbouring hill-tribes for gold-dust, ivory, silver, musk and Chinese boxes. *REFBI*, p. 74.
21. Mitchell, J.F., *The North-East Frontier of India,* Calcutta 1883 (reprint, Delhi 1973), p. 125.
22. C.U. Aitchison, *A Collection of Treaties, Engagements and Sanads Relating to India and Neighbouring Countries* (reprint), Delhi, 1983, p. 234.
23. William Robinson, *A Descriptive Account of Assam,* 1841 (reprint 1975), p. 248.
24. *Administrative Report on Railways in India, 1907,* Simla, 1908.
25. G.T. Bayfield, *Historical Review of the Political Relations between the British Government in India and the Empire of Ava,* Ava, 15 December, 1834, LLII-LLIX.
26. R.B. Pemberton, 'Report on Bhutan', 1838, *Indian Studies Past and Present,* Calcutta 1839, p. 15.
27. At the time of the British annexation of Assam, the total amount of tribute did not exceed Rs.4,785-4 annas, although the total amount of revenue realised by the Government of Bhutan from these *Duars* was around Rs.39,000 per annum.
28. B.C. Chakravorty, *British Relations with the Hill Tribes of Assam since 1858,* Calcutta, 1981 (reprint), p. 17.
29. Robertson to Government of India, letter dated 6 December, 1833, cited in R.B. Pemberton, 'Report on Bhutan', *Indian Studies, Past and Present,* Calcutta, 1838, pp. 27-28.
30. *Ibid.*
31. The Bhutias flocked to Hajo to visit the temple of Maha Muni situated on top of a hill. According to Bhutia tradition the image in the temple was carried off surreptitiously by a Brahmin from a monastery at Lhasa.
32. *r.* p. 79.
33. *REFBI,* p. 84.
34. Hamilton, *Hindusthan,* and Turner, *Embassy to Bhootan and Thibet,* in Pemberton, *REFBI,* p. 181.
35. *Ibid.*, pp. 181-82.
36. *Ibid.*
37. *Ibid.*, p. 184.
38. *Ibid.*
39. H.L. Gupta, 'An Unknown Factor in the Annexation of Assam', *Proceedings of the Historical Records Commission,* Vol. XXXIV, Pt. II.

22

Reconstructing the History of the Nepalis in Assam: A Look into the Sources

Lopita Nath

Assam, the pivotal state of North-East India, located at the base of the eastern Himalayas, also lay on the path of various migratory groups, who at some time or the other in regional history, made it their home. These migrant groups assimilated into the host society, though not without the occasional checks, giving Assam its pluralistic, multi-cultural ethos. One group that entered Assam since the pre-colonial days and more so during the colonial period were the Nepalis from Nepal. The term 'Nepali' needs some clarification. While Nepalis living in Assam and other parts of India define themselves as an 'ethnic community', the so-called Nepali migrants in India and Bhutan actually belong to the tribal ethnic communities (non-Bahun) and from the Newar community in the Kathmandu Valley in Nepal. While in Nepal they assert their own ethnic identities, in the North-East and elsewhere in India, the Nepali migrants tend to identify themselves as a single Nepali (Gorkhali in Darjeeling) community. In Assam the earlier generations of migrant Nepalis have so assimilated with the Asamiya[1] nationality that they prefer to identify themselves as the 'Nepali Asamiya'. Assam's relations with Nepal rooted in its matrimonial alliances in the 8th century and in the 16th century, and ethnic ties,[2] fostered pre-colonial migrations into the North-East Assam. These early migrations were, however, not so large, and the early migration merged imperceptible into the host community. Large-scale Nepali migrations with serious socio-political ramifications took place only in the colonial period. The colonial vision of Assam as the last land frontier of British India turned into reality, when the economic transformation that began with tea plantation, set off economic forces that gave an impetus to immigration. The active policies pursued by the colonialists opened up the valley to the Nepali highlanders.

One of the early sources of Nepali migrations to the North-East Assam in the colonial period was the 'Gorkha' soldiers in the Indian army many of whom were encouraged to settle in the foothills, forest fringes and other strategic points of Nepali settlements in Arunachal Pradesh, Assam, etc.

The colonials required a pliant labour force to help open up forest lands for lumbering, settlement and plantations and the Nepali migrant provided the perfect fit (K. Dixit: *Lowly Labour in the Lowlands*). Besides granting wastelands on favourable terms and giving pecuniary assistance for their journey to Upper Assam, the Nepalis were encouraged to settle in the districts of Sibsagar, Lakhimpur, Darrang and Kamrup. In course of time, compact Nepali settlements emerged in parts of eastern and Upper Assam (Lakhimpur, Digboi, Dibrugarh, Sadiya) and in western Assam (Darrang, Tezpur, Bongaigaon and Kokrajhar districts).

In the early decades of the twentieth century, these settlers along with providing the man-power to the colonial expanding economy, laid the foundations of their own economic base as graziers, marginal farmers, ex-soldiers, combining in him the qualities of a good peasant, military discipline, in addition to artisans and semi-skilled professionals. Their availability – for any kind of chore from an agricultural labourer and dairy farmer to a potter, carpenter, blacksmith or worker in roads – much in demand in the urban and rural areas, made them easily acceptable to both the ruler and the local communities. These provided the pull factors on the Assam side, which desperately needed labour and enterprise. On the Nepal side, usurious conditions in Nepali village, created by taxation imposed by the Rana rule, ecological crisis through deforestation, expanding population without cultivable land, fragmentation of land holdings and the chronic deficit of foodgrains accelerated migration across borders to ensure survival.

In the post-colonial period, after 1950, the earlier trends of migration found formal manifestation in the Indo-Nepal Friendship Treaty of 1950. Article 7 of the treaty ensured equal rights and privileges on a reciprocal basis for both nationals of Nepal and India, in terms of residence, ownership of property, employment, occupation, movement and other privileges. This, followed by the

Tripartite Delhi Agreement of 1951 and the revised Indo-Nepal Agreement of 1956, increased the volume of migration to Assam. The non-reqirement of a visa or passport made movement across borders easy.

In the 1960s and 1970s, the eradication of malaria and the official encouragement to colonise the Terai forests provided an outlet for migratory pressure, but the continuing need for sustenance and survival, the peasantry spilled through the porous Indo-Nepal border to take advantage of the work opportunities available in the modernising economy of independent India. Industries, development of roads, public infrastructure etc., encouraged Nepali migration into the province. This was facilitated by the growth of the Indian middle class, who needed household help. Higher income levels, better educational facilities and the continuing matrimonial alliances were at the base of the continuing Nepali exodus to the Brahmaputra Valley.

In the present times the Nepalis are spread out and well-settled in different parts of Assam.

The Nepalese, who thus, migrated, found the social climate congenial in the host society. Ethnically belonging to the Kirata stock, migration to the east was just an extension of their eastern habitat. They thus merged imperceptibly first, into the tribal milieu and then as they descended into the plains with the Assamese community. With their labour and cattle, they found employment in the farms and soon came to occupy agricultural land. They settled in the Assamese villages, started learning the language, their children went to Assamese vernacular schools, they adapted to the lifestyle and even celebrated festivals like Bihu as a part of the community. The assimilation of the Nepalis was reflected in their contributions to Assamese language and literature. Writers like Hari Prasad Gorkha Rai, Agni Bahadur Chetri, Man Bahadur Chetri, etc. with their writings enriched the language. This strengthened their roots in Assam and gave them an inner confidence. The Assamese society, which had hosted various migratory groups earlier, absorbed the Nepali migrants into its fold. A mutual and reciprocal response was noticed in their adjustment to each other.

Being accepted, the Nepalis began to move to the urban centres, to take advantage of the better educational facilities and employment opportunities there. The versatility of the Nepalis as an agricultural labourer, grazier or pastoralist, be it as a porter, watchman, gardener, driver, mechanic, cleaner, carpenter, etc. made him easily available to any private or corporate agency for any Sunday work on modest payment. This increased their acceptability.

This, however, did not last long. The present Assam is neither land abundant nor thinly populated. The presence of the Nepalis, well-integrated into the

Asamiya community and the continuing immigration, began to evoke feelings of doubt in the Asamiya mind, given vent to the real or imaginary injury to the Asamiya nationality caused by the fear of losing their identity in their own homeland. The first found expression in the Assam Movement in the 1970s, when along with the immigrants of East Bengal origin, Nepali immigration into Assam and their presence here was questioned. The leadership of the movement deliberately ignored the Indo-Nepal Treaty of 1950 and also their long (pre-1951) presence in Assam, which had made them eligible to vote. The Nepalis throughout Assam became apprehensive about the movement. The demand for removing the names of the Nepalis from the electoral rolls, deporting them from Assam and categorising them indiscriminately as foreigners profoundly affected them. The question of Nepali identity came into focus. The immediate crisis, however, soon passed with the signing of the 1985 Assam Accord, where it was agreed that only post-1971 illegal migrants were to be detected and deported. The Nepalis here pleaded that the cut-off date for the Nepalis be 30th July, 1976, the date of the imposition of the RAP – Restricted Area Permit.

The Bodo Movement for a separate homeland followed the end of the Assam Movement. The Nepali presence in the Bodo Autonomous Council Area (BAC) made them victims of an ethnic cleansing campaign. Subir Bhumik writes,

> Groups that had grown to think of the land as historically theirs resented the influx of (newer) migrants ... what began as ethnic strife between 'indigenous' and 'foreign' groups ... turned into ethnic between populations that had essentially become local to the area (Bhumik IDP Project, February 2000: 22-24).

Since 1985, the immigrants were asked to move out of the BAC area or face consequences. Beginning 1993, violence occurred in the Bodo areas of Kokrajhar, Bongaigaon and Gossaigaon. Attacks followed in 1994, 1995, 1996 and again in 1998. These attacks, though directed mostly against the Santhals, also affected the Nepalis living in these areas. These attacks displaced the Nepalis from their homes and they had to take relief in camps or move elsewhere.

Today in the aftermath of these two movements, a feeling of fear, insecurity and deprivation, afflicts the community. The Nepali community in Assam today suffers from the twin issues of being 'Foreigners' and 'Displacement' both needing an immediate solution and both eluded by the government. There is a resurgence of Nepali identity under various organisations. Their demands include legal and constitutional protection, to be recognised as 'Special Protected Class', representations of the Nepali-speaking people in the Parliament, State Assemblies, proposed Legislative Council of Assam, autonomous districts and regional councils and effective implementation of Nepali language as the official language and as a constitutionally recognised language and Nepali vernacular in schools.

PRIMARY PRE-COLONIAL PERIOD

The above accounts are the history of the Nepalis in Assam in a nutshell. To reconstruct the history of the community in Assam, a look into their origins in Nepal is important. The early history of Nepal, shrouded in legends and myths, has left a legacy of temples, shrines and inscriptions, which is perhaps unsurpassed in the east. These had attracted the attention of leading orientalists and Sanskrit students, including the patent researches of a succession of British officers such as Brian Houghton, Hodgson, Doctor Wright, Doctor Oldfield, Sir William Hunter, Sir Clements Markhom, Vansittart and the scientific investigations of one of the world's greatest Sanskrit scholars, M. Sylvain Levi. But these works have failed to evolve a really coherent history before the middle of the 14th century. However, many of the temples and shrines comparatively unscathed by any invasions and Muhammaden encroachments serve as a link between the India of the 7th and 8th centuries and that of the 20th century. To the scientists, the monuments of Nepal have proved be of value in tracing the relationship of Buddhism and Brahmanism. Nepal, one of the cradles of Buddhism, has now reached the stage of transformation in which Buddhism and Brahmanism have been mingled. The greater part of the treasures of art and architecture as also the writings relating to these early periods are in all probability centred in the valley of Kathmandu. These constitute the only sources for the early period and Nepal's links with India.

Assam's relations with Nepal can be dated to the early times. Suniti Kumar Chatterjee, in his *Place of Assam in the History and Civilization of India,* and in *Kirata Janakriti,*[3] writes that the Limbu, Tamang, Lepcha, Magar, Gurung and Sherpa belong to the Kirata group and they live in the eastern parts of Nepal. In Assam, the Bodos, Kacharis, Rabhas and the Mishings also belong to the Kirata group.[4] Ancient works like the *Vajasenaya Samhita,* the *Atharva Veda* and the great epic *Mahābhārata* mentions the Kiratas as people living along the Himalayan borders.[5] Assamese historians, Kanaklal Barua in his *Early History of Kamrupa* has traced the early matrimonial alliances between Assam and Nepal. He writes that Rajyamati, the daughter of Sri Harsha Deva of the Salastambha dynasty, who ruled from AD 730 to about AD 750 was married to Jayadeva King of Nepal. It is stated in the Nepal inscription that Jayadeva wedded, as if she were a fortune, Rajyamati possessed of virtues befitting her race, the noble descendent of Bhagadatt's royal line and daughter of Harsha Deva, Lord of Gauda, Odra, Kalinga, Koshala and other lands....[6]

The Nepal inscription was recorded in the year 153 of an era, pointed out by Sylvian Levi as the Tibetan era, 11 years earlier than Sri Harsha era. The year

153 roughly corresponds to AD 784, fixing the date of Harsha's reign from AD 730 to 750.[7] The extent of his empire as referred to by Barua and accepted as correct by historians and scholars of Bengal and elsewhere, was over nearly half of northern India from Sadiya in the east to Ayodhya in the west and from Himalayans in the north as far as Bay of Bengal and Ganjam in the south.[8] The Nepali connection can be traced to the Himalayan limits of his empire.

Various historical accounts also refer to Assam's relation with Nepal from the 14th century onwards. D.R. Regmi in his *Modern Nepal*, Vol. I, has remarked that several ruling families were mixed up in blood with royal dynasties, which originated from Mongoloid Kiratas or Semi-Aryan Khasas. Such royal families might be those, who ruled in eastern Terai and Koch Bihar. Similarly, K.L. Barua in his *My Reminiscences*, ed. by Maheswar Neog, has remarked that the process of assimilation going on in Assam since time immemorial 'explains the complete fusion of Gaudiya, Utkal, Dravidi, Kamrupi, Maithile, Kanaujia, Marwari and Nepali Brahmins in the Assamese Brahmin society of the present days'. Assam's relations with Mithila (North Bihar) has also been mentioned by various historians and writers, Important works include *Studies in the Early History of Assam;*[9] and in *Stray Notes on Buchanan's Account of Purnea*.[10] Buchanan in his account refers to Purnea and Mithila as the same place and denotes this place as a portion of the dominion of Gorkha. Further at one time the racial, linguistic and cultural affinities between Mithila and Kamrupa were very close. Accounts also refer to matrimonial alliances between the Koch king, Biswa Singha and Ratnakantidevi of Nepal in the 16th century. Again in the 17th century, the Nepali king, Pratap Malla is said to have married two girls from Bihar.[11] In addition to the above WW Hunter's *Statistical Account of Assam*[12] and Robinson's *A Descriptive Account of Assam*, have referred to Assam's early relations with Nepal. These writings on the early links with Assam have proved valuable sources in reconstructing the pre-colonial history of Assam. Those writings can be taken as primary source-materials, since information on the pre-colonial history is scattered and fragmentary.

Colonial Period

History of the Nepalis in Assam becomes much more coherent in the colonial period. In Nepal, the rise of the Gurkhas under Prithvi Narain Shah from 1750 (he occupied the valley of Kathmandu in 1769), and the expansion of the Gurkha kingdom in both east and west, brought them into contact with the British colonial empire in India. This extension of empire led to a war with China concluded by a treaty in 1972. During the war with China, the Nepal Government sought the aid of the EIC and Lord Cornwallis, the then Governor-General, sent

Colonel Kirkpatrick as commissioner. He spent only a month in Nepal, but his reports forms, the basis of nearly all the known history of Nepal.[13] Two other accounts written by colonial officers, one, *Nepal* by Lieut. Colonel Terence Keyes, C.S.I, C.MG., C.I.E., written from Kathmandu in 1928,[14] and another one, *Memorandum on Nepal* (Part I) and *Who's Who in Nepal* (Part II) by Lieut. Colonel C.T. Daukes, C.I.E., 1933,[15] Although based on the history of the Gorkha rule and Nepal's relations with the EIC, these two booklets marked 'Confidential' and preserved in the State Archives, Dispur, can be used in combination with other sources. They make references to the Nepali migration to Assam following the Treaty of Sagauli in 1816.

Since the history of the Nepalis in Assam in the colonial period is the history of their migration, government files and reports available at the State Archives provide important information. The *Annual Reports on Immigration in Assam*, 1876-91 as well as the *Agricultural and Revenue Proceedings of Eastern Bengal and Assam*, since 1850 and especially the section on *Immigration*, give us information on Nepali immigrants and the graziers. Similarly, the *Reports on Labour Immigration into Assam* for the post, 1826 period and the *Assam Labour Committee Reports*, 1906, 1921-22 deal with the labourers imported for employment in tea gardens, in coal mines in upper Assam and in a few saw-mills. Information is available here on the labour immigrants from Nepal, The *Annual Land Revenue Administration Report* of 1930-31 to 1950-51 are also important sources. Although these reports sometimes appear one-sided and fragmentary, they at least provide us with a basis on which we can build our accounts. In addition to the above, a few government files, both in the Political Branch[16] and Confidential A,[17] supply information on the government dealings with the Nepalis in Assam.

For the data on the Nepalis population, etc. in Assam, we are largely dependent on the Census Reports. The 19th century data provided by Hunter (1879)[18] based on the first *Census Reports of India* (1872) indicates a very small number of Nepali population (total 983) in the Brahmaputra Valley, exclusive of the soldiers in the colonial army. It shows the larger concentration of Nepali population in the districts of Sibsagar (476), Lakhimpur (260), and Kamrupa (125). The *Census Reports from 1901-1931*, trace the growth of Nepal's population in these years, from 9.35% (21,347) in 1901 to 1.02% (88,306) in 1931. C.S. Mullan's *Census of India 1937*, Vol. II, Assam, Part I, is also a valuable source as far as population growth is concerned.

Post-Colonial Period

For the post-colonial period, the *Census of India Reports* from 1950-1991 can be consulted for the data on the growth of the Nepali population in Assam. According to the Census Reports of 1950, one in every 10 Nepalis had immigrated. According to the 1971 Census Reports, there were 1.3 million Nepalis living in India. Further, during the period from 1951-1971, the growth of Nepali population in Assam was also very high. Numerically, they rose from 1,01,338 in 1951 to 3,49,116 in 1971, indicating a nearly 3.5 times growth within a span of 20 years. The percentage of growth, which was 1.26% in 1951 increased to 2.38% in 1971. It is, however, interesting to note that in the 1991 reports, although there was an increase in the growth numerically, the percentage decreased to 1.93%. This may be due to the troubled times of the 1970s-80s (Assam and Bodo Movements), when many Nepalis had either left Assam or returned their mother tongue as Assamese during the census surveys. Another probable reason that can be attributed to the decrease in the percentage is the formation of the states of Meghalaya, Nagaland, etc. which redistributed the Nepali population in these parts.

The *1991 Census, Language Reports* shows the district-wise break-up of the number and percentage of Nepali population in Assam. This report has shown that the Nepali population is now spread out all over Assam with the highest concentration in the district of Tinsukia (7.91%) followed by N.C. hills (7.90%), Karbi Anglong (5.74%) and Sonitpur (6.43%). There is a sizeable population in Dhemaji (4.74%), with Kokrajhar, Darrang, North Lakhimpur and Golaghat having only a population of 2.5% on an average. This in contrast to the earlier settlements in Sibsagar, Darrang, Lakhimpur and Kamrup, also shows the movement of the people over the whole of Assam. The development of Tinsukia as a business centre has probably led to the high Nepali population there. These census reports, no doubt valuable as primary source-materials, have to be used carefully, as there are instances that often miscalculations and discrepancies occur. Moreover, there are also reports that surveyors have not visited the remote areas, where the Nepalis in search of grazing lands are living.

For the post-colonial period other primary sources are the Government of Assam correspondences and official files. The *Gazeteers* of the State Government also provide information on the Nepalis.

The Government of Assam, *Reports of the Committee on Welfare of Scheduled Caste and Scheduled Tribes Relating to Land and Revenue*, 1979 and the 1974 *Draft Outline: Fifth Five Year Plan Sub-plan for Scheduled Tribes (Plains), Scheduled Caste and other Backward Classes*, Dept. of Planning and Development, Guwahati, offer valuable information on the present status of the Nepalis in Assam.

The Minutes of the Nepalis in Assam and reports of the various Nepali organisations like the A.A.N.S.U., etc. are valuable source-materials.[19]

SECONDARY

Writing on the Nepalis in Assam are very few and far between. Srikant Dutt's, *Migration and Development: The Nepalese in North East*, EPW, Vol. XVL, 24, 13 June (1981) was perhaps one of the earliest writings on the community in Assam. He was followed by A.C. Sinha in 1982 and in 1990.[20] But these writings were not very much accessible to readers. Yet, they remain the pioneering works on the Nepalese in Assam. Sumanraj Timsina's work (1992) *Nepali Community in India'*,[21] devotes some pages on the North-Eastern Nepalis, but his main objective was to trace the evolution of the Gorkhaland in West Bengal. Leo Rose's *The Nepali ethnic community in the North East of the sub-continent*[22] is an important source.

Nepali writers in Assam, thought very few, have made considerable contributions towards the development of their history. *Itihasar Adharat Asomor Nepali,*[23] writen by Shyamraj Jaisi and translated by Agnibahadur Chetri, is an important historical writing up to the 20th century, tracing the growth of the community from its early days. Man Bahadir Chetri's work[24] published by the Assam Sahitya Sabha (1983) is an account of the society and culture of the Nepalis in Assam. Rudraman Thapa's work based on his Ph.D. thesis, traces the growth of political consciousness among the Nepalis in Assam.[25] Besides these, there are a number of articles and books written by Nepali authors, published and unpublished, which give an insight into the community in Assam.[26]

Monirum Hussain's *The Assam Movement - Class, Ideology and Identity*, 1993,[27] throw light on the situation of the Nepalis in Assam during the movement. Two other recent publications – H.K. Baypujari's *North-East India: Problems, Policies and Prospects* (1998)[28] and Sanjib Barua's *India against Itself* (2001)[29] – have discussed at length the problems faced by the Nepalis against the backdrop of the larger North-Eastern context. Amalendu Guha's *Planter Raj to Swaraj...*[30] and also a few articles in magazines and journals deal with the Nepalis in Assam.

In addition, several unpublished, theses of the Tribhuban University, Nepal, deal with different aspects of Nepali migration.[31] Various articles, published occasionally in the local and national dailies, both in English and Assamese, also provide information on the Nepalis in Assam.[32] Further, the Assam Sahitya Sabha proceedings do contain information on the Nepalis in Assam.

We cannot rule out the importance of the internet websites, specially those on issues of migration, refugees, internal displacement and human rights. Few websites like the *www.hrdc.net,*[33] *www.refugees.org,*[34] *www.idpproiect.org* and also on *EPW* and *Contemporary South Asia,* supplement information on the Nepalis and their present problems.

Field Study

Field study in social sciences, a research genre often labelled 'ethnography', 'case study' or 'qualitative field study' by different disciplines are all alike, featuring direct, qualitative observation of natural situation or setting, using mainly the techniques of participant observation or intensive interviewing or both. In the study of the Nepalis in Assam, field study forms an important source of information. Since writings on the present Nepali situation are scarce, the field has been used to generate primary data. Also in the understanding of their culture-customs, religion, language, extent of assimilation, etc., importance of participant observation and intensive interviewing could not be minimised.

Field study allows us a glimpse into the lifestyle of the Nepalis in different parts of Assam. However, oral sources have to be used carefully to avoid being sympathetic towards the respondents. This might distort the final reporting.

Conclusion

Reconstructing the history of a community is not an easy task. More so, as with growth of ideas on history, there has been a radical change in the technique of writing history. Historical methods as developed, tried to present past events in their correct perspective by the diligent collection of all relevant data, by the critical examination of that data to derive the truth, by the intelligent interpretation of data to explain its significance, and by the lucid presentation of the shifted and tested data. The writing of the history of a community requires the reconstruction of the past as nearly as it had really happened. For this, the material has to be dealt with great care and a number of mental operations have to be performed, for the element of subjectivity is very great. A historian has to be constantly on guard, lest he slips into fiction. In reconstructing the history of the 'Nepalis in Assam', similar care had to be adopted. The lack of recorded events and scattered and fragmentary information, hints at the danger of the connecting stream between one event and the other being lost. One thus, has to be extremely careful in the available material so as to maintain connectivity and also correctly interpret the events. Another major problem faced is the overlapping of vital issues like that of 'citizenship' and 'nationality' (Indo-Nepal Treaty 1950), which many Nepalis themselves are confused about. The element of subjectivity is also very strong during the fieldwork, where the sympathetic feelings might override proper interpretation of data.

Yet, we have to admit that despite the great drawbacks, enough material and data are available to at least make a beginning in the writing of a well-documented history of the 'Nepalis in Assam'. Assam today is at a crucial juncture of her history, when social and political forces are sharply divided in their approaches to the ethnic identities and development. In such a situation, a written history of a marginal group like the Nepalis will go a long way in addressing the genuine needs of a community, who had contributed immensely to the development of Assam in the past two centuries.

NOTES AND REFERENCES

1. Throughout the paper the term 'Asamiya' instead of 'Assamese' has been used to specifically mean those people, who have accepted/adopted the Asamiya language as their mother tongue. Including those domiciled in the state of Assam, the term also includes the Na-Asamiya Muslims, the Nepalis and many other tribal groups, who speak the Asamiya language.
2. Assam and Nepal had matrimonial alliances in the 8th century and in the 16th century, when the Koch king, Biswa Singha married Ratna Kanti Devi of Kathmandu, followed by Niladhvaj and Naranarayana. As a consequence, a number of Nepali Brahmin priests, a group of Pandas to the temple of Kamakhya, Chetri warriors, farmers, artisans and herdsmen were brought from Nepal to Assam.
3. Suniti Kumar Chatterjee, *Kirata Jana-Kriti,* Asiatic Society of Bengal, Calcutta, 1951; Idem, *Place of Assam in the History and Civilisation of India,* Gauhati, 1970.
4. R.M. Nath, *The Background of Assam Culture*, 1948, Shillong, p. 13-15, writes according to the Nagarjuni Kunda Inscription (1st & 2nd century AD), Greek writers of the period, silk traders from central Asia, Tibet and China were known as 'Kiratas'.
5. *Ibid.*
6. K.L., Barua, *Early History of Kamrup*, Shillong, 1933, p. 111. Odra is Orissa, Kalinga-Ganjam on the South and Koshala – North Bihar in the West. The Nepal inscription states that he was *Gaudodradi-Kalinga-Koshala pati.*
7. *Ibid.*, p. 112.
8. *Ibid.*, p. 113.
9. Maheswar Neog (ed.), *Studies in the Early History of Assam*, pp. 312-313, Guwahati, 1973, p. 26 (JARS, Vol. I, No. 2, July 1933, pp. 44-46).
10. *Ibid.*, p. 5 (JARS, Vol. I, No. 2, July 193, pp. 44-46).
11. Netra B. Thapa, *A Short History of Nepal*, Nepal, 2001, p. 69.
12. W.W., Hunter, *A Statistical Account of Assam*, Vol. I & II, 1975, Delhi (Reprint) , 1879.
13. Kirkpatric, *An Account of the Kingdom of Nepal*, Shimla, 1793.
14. Govt. File No. 26C. of 1929, Confidential B, March 1929, Nos. 269-271, Serial No. 287, 'Treatise on Nepal' by Lieut-Colonel Terence Keyes, Simla, Govt.of India Press, 1928.
15. Govt. File No. 382, Confidential B, Sept. 1934, Nos. 7-14, *Memorandum on Nepal* (Part I), *Who's in Nepal* (Part II), by Lieut Colonel C.T. Daukes, C.I.E., Simla, Govt. of India Press, 1933.

16. S. No. 157, Political Branch, Proceedings B, Dec. 1911, No. 61 - 'Supply of Khukris for the Nepali Coolies for the Miri Mission'.
17. Confidential A, Sept. 1932, Nos. 10-27, 'Scheme to Settle Gurkhas from India in the Nepal Terai'.
18. W.W. Hunter, *A Statistical Account of Assam*, Vol. I & II, 1975, Delhi (Reprint).
19. Manik, Handique, Sisyanuragi Samajkarmai Babudhan Thapa Debar Suwaranat (in Assamese) in B. Chetri (ed.), *Souvenir, All Assam Nepali Students Union*, Barpathar, 1998.
20. A.C., Sinha, 'The Nepalese in North-East India: Ethnicity and Resource Appropriation' in J.B. Bhattacharjee (ed.), *Social Tension in North-East India*, Shillong, 1982; 'The Indian Northeast Frontier and the Nepalese Immigrants' in *Himalayan Environment and Culture*, Shimla, Indian Institute of Advanced Study, 1990.
21. Suman Raj Timsina, *Nepali Community in India*, Delhi, 1992.
22. Leo E. Rose, "The Nepali Ethnic Community in the North-East of the Sub-continent", *Ethnic Studies Report*, 12 January, 1994.
23. Jaisi Shyamraj (Trans Agni Bahadur Chettri), 'Itihasar Asomor Nepali', n.p., n.d.
24. Man Bahadur, Chetri, *Asamiya Nepali Samaj aru Sanskritir Ruprekha* (in Asamiya), Jorhat, 1983.
25. Rudraman, Thapa, 'Asamat Nepali Janagusthir Rajnaitik Jagaranar Patbhumi', Sadin, September 21, 2001.
26. Gita, Upadhyay 'Asamiya Sahitya-Sanskritiley Nepali Sakalar Abadan' (in Assamese), Sreemayi, 1994; Kripa, Upadhyaya, 'The Nepalese in Assam: A Sociological Enquiry', Digboi, 1998.
27. Monirul, Hussain, 'The Assam Movement — Class, Ideology and Identity', Delhi, 1993; 'State, Identity Movements and Internal Displacement in the North-east' *Economic and Political Weekly*, December 16, 2000.
28. H.K. Barpujari, *Northeast India-Problems, Policies and Prospects*, Guwahati, 1998.
29. Sanjib, Baruah, *India against Itself: Assam and the Politics of Nationality*, New Delhi, 1999.
30. Amalendu, Guha, *Planter Raj to Swaraj: Freedom Struggle and Electoral Politics in Assam 1826-1947*, New Delhi, 1977.
31. Kedar Prasad, Neupane, 'Migration in Nepal: A Concise Study', Kathmandu, 1975; Tiwari, Hari Babu, 'Migration in Nepal: A Case Study of the Kabhre Palanchok District', Kathmandu, 1983.
32. *The Assam Tribune*, Nepalese demand and review of Indo-Nepal Treaty, May 26, 1998; Introduction of passport system between India-Nepal demanded, May 15, 1999; Special status of Gorkhas demanded, June 20, 2000.
33. Human Rights Features, No Refugee: The Plight of Conflict-Induced Internally Displaced Persons in India Embargoed for 16 March (www.hrdc.net), 2001.
34. USSR: Country Reports: India (www.refugees.org), 1999.

23

Anandaram Dhekial Phukan's 'Observations on the Administration of the Province of Assam' – A Classic Document for Rewriting the Social History of Modern Assam

S.D. Goswami

Anandaram Dhekial Phukan's 'Observations on the Administration of the Province of Assam' is a very useful and reliable account of the socio-economic situation of early 19th century Assam. Originally written in 1853 as a memorandum presented to A.J.M. Mills, 'this lengthy memorial was subsequently published in 1854 as Appendix-J of Mills' *Report on the Province of Assam.* Based on personal knowledge and experience, this treatise gives an in depth insight into the various aspects of British administration in Assam. While highlighting the chief evils and weaknesses of the British rule, it also advocated 'reforming measures' like reducing of the tax burden, increase in the number of *mofussil* courts, appointment of more judges from among the native population and giving them more powers, improvement in agriculture, revision of the complicated procedure in the law courts, opening technical schools for imparting technical knowledge, supervision of the religious and charitable institutions by government officers, establishment of English schools for providing knowledge of 'European science and literature', restoration of Assamese language as the vernacular language of the province and stoppage of the supply of *abkaree* (excise) opium from outside the province.

Born at Guwahati on 24 September 1829, A.D. Phukan was the son of Haliram Dhekial Phukan, a historian and social reformer. Anandaram had his collegiate education in Calcutta where he came into contact with the contemporary Bengal renaissance. Ill-health and other domestic problems cut his collegiate career short. Returning to Assam he joined government service and became a Munsif in 1849; sub-assistant of Nowgaon in 1852 and officiating junior assistant in 1854. An admirer of British rule and deeply concerned for his countrymen, Dhekial Phukan, while submitting his observation in the form of a descriptive account, explained in clear terms that the purpose of presenting his views, which were also shared by his countrymen, was not merely to single out the 'imperfections' of the government, but to 'give a succinct view of the present state of the country, and to point out the defects in the revenue and judicial administration, as well as improvements which is now in the power of government to effect'.[1] Such a step was, in his opinion, necessitated by the fact that,

> The heads of the government have never taken occasion to inquire into the state of the country; and although twenty-eight years have elapsed since the annexation of Assam to the British Empire, little perceptible change had been effected in the condition of the people and good governance of the province.[2]

The first point that Dhekial Phukan raised in his memorandum was the revenue system introduced by the British which he described as 'far from being much favourable to the advancement of cultivation and the general improvement of the country'. It may be mentioned here that the change from *khelwaree* to *rayatwaree*[3] was originally effected through a series of administrative measures. The province was partitioned into small fiscal divisions called *mouzas*. The task of collecting the revenue was left in the hands of a number of native officers, styled chaudhury, patgiri, bisaya, etc. Though called by different names these officers possessed more or less equal power. These officers enjoyed no judicial or magisterial power; their duties were confined to collection of revenue. The officers were appointed by the government and were remunerated with a commission varying from 10 to 17 per cent of the gross collection. They were permitted to appropriate any increase in the assessment arising from extended cultivation during the term for which the collections were made.[4] At the end of the period a fresh survey of the land was made and the revenue fixed for the next period.

From his own experience Dhekial Phukan observed that the persons to whose care the government had entrusted the responsibility of improvement of the country have had very little interest in such a cause since they were least concerned whether cultivation advanced or decreased as 'they are certain that their exertions will in the ensuing year serve only to swell the public treasury, without adding to their own gain'. To remove this possibility he conceived a plan which was likely to bring about necessary modification by making the fiscal officers to have a 'more lasting interest in their charges, subject to the restriction necessary to guard against abuse'.[5] He was of the opinion that while granting leases, which should be done on the basis of an assessment to be fixed on accurate survey and measurement of lands the farmers be allowed to 'appropriate to their own use any increase of the revenue which they may be able to effect during the period of their lease, holding them at the same time responsible for any deficiency caused by other than accidental natural causes'.[6]

He further suggested that at the expiration of the lease the assessment be fixed on a re-measurement and survey of the farms; the lease continued to the original farmer; and the farms be allowed to let out all the unoccupied and waste lands within their farms such terms as they may deem best conducive to their interests.[7]

Bearing full testimony of the various anomalies associated with land survey and assessment, he pointed out that in Assam assessments were mostly made without any particular distinction being observed as to the quality and productivity of the soil; the low *rupit* (arable) lands yielding fifty *maunds* of corn per *poora* (approximately one and half acre) were assessed at the same rate as high *rupit* lands producing only fifteen to twenty *maunds*. This, according to him, made the burden of taxation light upon some but heavy upon others.[8] Dhekial Phukan suggested,

> Justice seems to require that the *rupit* or rice lands be levied into two or three classes according to the quality and capabilities of the soil, and that they be proportionately taxed, the assessment on the poorest quality of the *rupit* being moderately reduced.[9]

Regarding the burden of land revenue on the people, he regretted that the current rate of taxation had far exceeded the limit that had been observed by the former rulers of Assam and opined that,

> an enhancement of the rates under the present circumstances of the province, without any marked improvement in agriculture and commerce, would be to over-burden the people with taxes which they should but ill afford to bear.[10]

He, therefore, fervently appealed that before any enhancement of revenue was decided upon in future, the government must ensure a corresponding improvement in the paying capacity of the people. He cautioned, unless the government provides the people with better and improved means of cultivating their lands, an increase of assessment will inevitably lead to an increase of the unhappiness of the people.[11]

Later, history proved that Dhekial Phukan was very correct in his assessment of the situation.

Even though Dhekial Phukan expressed great concern at the tendency of revising the rates of assessment every now and then, he understood that the lot of the peasantry and the common people could not be improved by merely suspending an enhancement of revenue for long time to come. He was well aware of the need of increasing production by an improved means of cultivation. For this purpose he urged the government to take the lead in bringing agriculture experts from outside to teach the people to raise varieties of very valuable crops, improved methods of irrigation, drainage and embankments and all other things connected with agriculture. He asked the government to furnish every cultivator with machines, ploughs and harrows, improved breed of cattle and supply of good quality seeds, etc. He was hopeful about the long-term benefits of these measures when he said:

It cannot be denied that the ignorance of the Assamese, from their proneness of follow the footsteps of their ancestors, and their profound veneration for the customs of their forefathers, may at the outset be unable duly to appreciate the value of the importance of measures now suggested, and consider these innovations little likely to terminate in any beneficial results. The experience of a single season, however, will at once convince them of their intrinsic value, and induce them eagerly and cheerfully to co-operate in the happy fulfillment of this all-round object.[12]

For improvement of agriculture Dhekial Phukan advocated importation of foreign technical know-how and improved implements for the time being. His ultimate objective was to make people self-reliant and entirely relieved of the necessity of relying on foreigners for the supply of their tools of agriculture.

No nation can secure to itself the blessings and comforts of civilised life until it has manufactures of its own; and in short, a country can rise to wealth or importance that is deficient or imperfectly versed in the art of manufacture.[13]

He, therefore, pleaded for the establishment of a number of technical schools to impart training in useful branches of manufacture, including implements and machines of husbandry and other works of utility. In fact, Dhekial Phukan was the first Assamese who realised the importance of such studies. His views were undoubtedly very advanced and progressive.

A strong supporter of English education, Dhekial Phukan thought it necessary to raise the standard of the two existing English schools by the recruitment of adequate number of teachers qualified for the job. At the same time he believed that vernacular schools should be given the care they deserved. Though well-versed in Bengali, he had no scruple to raise his voice against the imposition of Bengali as the medium of instruction in the schools of Assam and urged upon the government to replace it by Assamese. He pointed out very aptly that even if it be argued that Bengali bears an affinity with the Assamese, he saw no reason why the latter be sacrificed for the sake of the former. He boldly declared:

> We beg to point out that the Bengali bears no closer resemblance to the Assamese than it does to the Uria language, and if the courts of Orissa be allowed the privilege of using the language of the country, we are unable to understand why the same benefit should have been withheld to the Assamese.

He further wrote:

> By the substitution of the Assamese, we do not mean to suggest that Bengali should be altogether abolished from the schools. On the contrary, we are of the opinion that it should be cultivated as a language indispensable to complete the course of vernacular education, and that the standard Bengali works should likewise be introduced in the higher classes. We are only opposed to its exclusive adoption as the medium of instructing the people in literature, science, and other useful branches of knowledge. We feel certain that the outlay of a few thousand rupees will enable the government to supply the schools with a complete series of elementary educational works in the Assamese language, in every useful department of learning, literature, history, science and art.[14]

Expressing shock and anguish at the slow progress of vernacular education in the province, he was constrained to remark that the continuation of the foreign language was the most formidable barrier in the progress of education. He, therefore, suggested the publication of a series of 'popular works on the different branches of native and European knowledge in the Assamese languages, the establishment of a normal school to train up the body of teachers and the creation of a separate department for the study of Sanskrit in the several vernacular schools.' A country frequently ravaged by disease and sickness like cholera, Dhekial Phukan lamented, had neither any facilities of treatment, nor the adequate number of doctors well-versed in the treatment of such dreaded diseases. Consequently, in most parts of the country, 'incantations, charms and amulets are substituted in the place of medicines, and the number of deaths caused by ignorant and opposite treatment is prodigiously great'. In view of this, he suggested the establishment of a few district medical schools and supply of appliances and apparatus to fight the diseases. Such a step would not only make modern medical sciences much more popular among the masses, but would also motivate many among them to 'study medicine as a profession – a practice which already has been adopted in the neighbourhood of Calcutta'.

Another subject to which Dhekial Phukan's attention was drawn was the widespread use of opium by the Assamese people. It is needless to say that in the 13th century opium had been a commodity of daily consumption for a vast majority of people. There was initially no restriction in its cultivation and consumption, and people 'being burdened by no governmental restrictions' began to be engaged in a considerable extent of its cultivation.[15] To limit the immoderate use of this vile drug, the government decided to introduce excise on opium in Assam from 1850, thereby 'placing it beyond the means of all but the most wealthy'. Unfortunately, by this policy of 'putting down Assam opium with one hand and offering Bihar opium with the other', consumption could not be reduced. Statistics showed that abkaree (excise) opium supplied by the government could neither drive the indigenous *kanee* (opium) out of the market nor was there any appreciable fall in its consumption.[16] The enlightened Assamese class was alarmed by this state of affairs and demanded that as a preliminary step the supply of excise opium be discontinued forthwith, in order to make the article 'less abundant and more scarce'. Anandaram Dhekial Phukan who shared the anxiety of his contemporaries made no secret of his apprehension when he argued:

Whether, by interdicting the culture of the drug by the people, the government contemplates to expel the general use of opium from the country, or whether the government proposes to substitute its own in lieu of the Native opium, we are alike ignorant. The extensive introduction of government opium, however, leads us to conclude that the measure will be productive of consequences other than the extirpation of the drug from the country. If it be advanced, that by abolishing the production of opium in the country, and rendering it dearer to the people, the use will be rendered less universal, we would beg to submit that the people will never shrink from the use of the drug as long as they continue to obtain supplies of it; and that whatever may be the price put upon it they would seldom consider themselves too poor to purchase it .... We conceive that no other remedy than the gradual diminution of the supply of opium can produce the desired effect. The tree will grow so long as the root is not destroyed.[17]

Commenting on the judicial system of the province where the Principal Assistant (later redesigned Deputy Commissioner) acted as a Judge, Magistrate and Collector, Dhekial Phukan observed that such a system had 'utterly failed to afford any satisfaction to the people'. He was of the opinion that the public courts of justice were exclusively for the benefit of the rich and the powerful and therefore it was imprudent and foolish for men of humble means to resort to them for relief. In most cases the procedure followed in the courts being 'defective, tedious, dilatory (and) expensive, he called for immediate removal of such handicaps as inefficiency of the policy, paucity in the number of courts and large-scale corruption among ministerial officers attached to the courts of justice.[18]

A product of the Hindu College and inspired by the Bengal renaissance, Phukan was constrained to notice the degrading socio-economic situation of the province where the bulk of the people, despite having 'entertained sanguine expectations of peace and happiness from the rule of Britain', had not actually lived in comfort. A true spokesman of his people and one who had intense love and respect for them, Dhekial Phukan thought it prudent to take advantage of the opportunity created by Mills' visit, to draw the attention of the government to the scores of evils associated with the British administration with the hope that prompt and remedial steps would be taken to remove them. Unfortunately, he did not live long to see the fulfillment of his dream. His untimely death in 1859 at the young age of thirty deprived Assam of the services of a man of vision and far sight.

Writing on the basis of his personal experience and observation, this classic document 'couched in most polite but forceful language'[19] demonstrated Dhekial Phukan's vast knowledge of the history and culture of the people of Assam and the various intricacies of the British administration, even though, at the time of its submission, he was only twenty-five years of age. His observations were impartial, free from bias or malice and based on facts. Similarly, the suggestions he made were pragmatic and reformative. It is a pity that despite being a very useful and authentic source-material, this descriptive account or memorandum has not been used by the historians the way it should have been used to study and understand the true nature of British rule and its impact on the people. It is hoped that future historians and others will pay more attention to this document in order to explore its usefulness as source-material for rewriting the social history or modern Assam.

NOTES AND REFERENCES

1. Anandaram Dhekial Phukan, 'Observations on the Administration of the Province of Assam' in A.J.M. Mills, *Report on the Province of Assam,* Calcutta, 1854, p. xxxii.
2. *Ibid.*
3. The ordinary land tenure in the Brahmaputra Valley was called *rayatwaree.* Under this system the tenant was held to have the right of occupancy as long as he paid his revenue, though the government had full right of resumption of his land whenever required for public purposes.
4. For details of the working of this system see Amalendu Guha, 'Assamese Agrarian Society in the Late Nineteenth Century: Roots, Structures and Trends' in *The Indian*

Economic and Social History Review, Vol. xvii, No. 1 (January-March 1980), pp. 37-38, 47-50.

5. Anandaram Dhekial Phukan, *op. cit.*, p. xxxiii.
6. *Ibid.*, p. xxxiv.
7. *Ibid.*
8. *Ibid.*, p. xxxviii.
9. *Ibid.*
10. *Ibid.*, p. xxxii.
11. *Ibid.*, p. xxxviii.
12. *Ibid.*, p. xxxix.
13. *Ibid.*, p. xi.
14. *Ibid.*, p. xii.
15. For details see Shrutidev Goswami, 'The Opium Evil in Nineteenth Century Assam', *The Indian Economic and Social History Review*, Vol. xix, Nos. 3 & 4, 1982, pp. 365-376.
16. The quantity of *abkaree* opium consumed in the Assam Valley was 301 mds. 32 srs. in 1851-52; 320 mds. 5 srs. in 1855-56 and 387 mds. 24 srs. in 1857-58. Board of Revenue Proceedings, February 1860, No. 39, Statement of *abkaree* opium sales in Assam.
17. Anandaram Dhekial Phukan, *op. cit.*, p. xliv.
18. *Ibid.*, p. xlvi.
19. H.K. Barpujari, *Assam: In the Days of the Company*, Gauhati, 2nd Edn., 1980, p. 317.

24

Sources of the History of the Khasi-Jaintias in Libraries and Archives in the United Kingdom

David R. Syiemlieh

INTRODUCTION

The Khasi-Jaintia connection with the British goes back to the late 18th century. The East India Company's rule over Bengal brought it into restrained control over the Khasi-Jaintias living in the foot-hill of the plateau adjoining Sylhet. The Company's rule was not extended over the hill people till the third decade of the 19th century. Their initial interest in trade and commerce later broadened into political interference, which by 1830-1835 had taken shape in the annexation of the Jaintia hills into the British dominion and a political control over the 25 Khasi states. Other forms of interaction were to come in the wake of the opening of hills with the interest of a number of mission societies in spreading Christianity among these hill people. Meanwhile, the Khasi resistance to 'British rule being suppressed by 1833-1834, experiments were conducted by the Company to establish a sanatorium and a cantonment for European troops in these hills'. By early 1834, the experiment had shown a lack of interest in Cherrapunji in preference for Darjeeling, but the station's importance continued with it becoming the headquarters of the Khasi Hill Political Agency in 1835. While the Khasis apparently had come to accept their fate, either directly under British rule, as in the case of 31 British villages, or indirectly in the case of the 25 Khasi states, the Jaintias, who had little semblance of British authority over them, reacted to the alien rule. Over two phases in resistance between 1860-1863, the Jaintias conducted the 'Little War of North-East India' as an expression of their resentment against British rule in the hills.

After years of resistance and adjustment, the Khasi-Jaintias seem to have accepted British imperial rule and government. The later decades of the 19th century upto the end of colonial rule witnessed a comfortable adjustment—least resistance and little interference from the government.

Location, Content and Use of Sources

Much of the material used in reconstructing the history of the Khasi-Jaintias over the period of their interaction with the British have hitherto been drawn from local sources in the form of oral tradition, and a variety of written materials in Bengali, Khasi and English located in libraries and archives at Shillong, Guwahati, and New Delhi. Few historians have so far been able to use the impressive collection and variety of records, memories, private correspondence and accounts left by British administrators, soldiers, botanists, missionaries, traders and even the casual visitors to the Khasi-Jaintia hills which are available in libraries and archives in the United Kingdom. The purpose of this paper, therefore, is to provide information on the location of the material in the United Kingdom, their content and the use of the material for reconstructing the history of the Khasi-Jaintias under colonial rule.

The India Office Library and Records, now the Oriental and India Office Collection at St. Pancras, London, has the largest collection of manuscripts, books and records on India. Its records comprise the archives of the East India Company (1600-1858) the Board of Control (1784-1858) and the India Office (1858-1947). These voluminous records have numerous references to the Khasi-Jaintias. Some of these records are available for consultation in the West Bengal Archives, Kolkata, and the National Archives, New Delhi. However, for a more complete understanding of the operation of British rule, the consultation of records in the Indian Office is invaluable.

Among the private collection in this Library many relate to the Khasi-Jaintia hills. Those of John Colpoys Haughton (1817-1887) who was Civil Commissioner in these hills when the Jaintia resistance raged, has a number of correspondences between the Commissioner and others on the suppression of the disturbances. The collection comprises the *Letters Books* of J.C. Haughton in two volumes (MSS. Eur. D. 529) and the letters of J.C. Haughton (MSS. Eur. D.

530). Book 1 of the *Letter Books* has his correspondence with L (ionel) Inglis[1] whom he advised 'to be vigilant to prevent strong parties of plunderers from going down towards Assam'. A number of letters are also addressed to B.W.D. Morton, the district's Deputy Commissioner.[2] In one of these he advised that 'when any rebel is caught and brought before you, you should at once regularly try and sentence him, the substance of all the proceedings being recorded in your own hand.' This letter continues, 'I would say the traitors caught may well be hanged but surrendering persons, unless guilty of actual murder, might be guaranteed their lives but no more'. Haughton regularly kept Cecil Beadon in Calcutta informed of the developments in the hills and gave suggestions for a speedy return to peace.[3] One letter is addressed to Major Thelwall, in-charge of a section of the British forces engaged in the Jaintia campaign.[4]

The letters to J.C. Haughton are all private correspondences with his father. There is an interesting letter he writes in which he mentions:

> he had the satisfaction of sentencing the very last of the rebels to transportation. He was a most desperate ruffian and it is believed had committed many murders in cold blood. Yet I find one of the papers actually censoring me for not pardoning him!

(Of the Jaintias who were tried) Haughton informs that, three were sentenced to transportation, two to death and about twenty to short periods of imprisonment by the Military Commissioners with special powers appointed by the government 'and with whom I could not interfere if I desired to do so'.[5]

Another large collection with the O.I.O.C. are the papers of Sir Robert N. Reid who was the Governor of Assam between 1937-1942. His diaries, notes, letters, photographs and collection of articles covering two boxes of many volumes were deposited with the Library by Lady Reid and Mr. E.D. Reid in 1965 and 1980. A very informative source is his unpublished manuscript 'Assam and the North East Frontier of India',[6] written in 1946 when he was home on retirement. It has many references to the Khasi and Jaintia hills, their administrative and constitutional positions and the plans he had for these and other hill areas in India's North-East. In his collection is also a copy of a document he wrote while in Assam. 'A Note on the Future of the Present Excluded and Partially Excluded and Tribal areas of Assam',[7] as the title suggests was meant to examine the position of these three areas in the last years of British rule. Researchers may also draw useful material from his speeches[8] and his articles which he wrote following retirement for a number of journals.

Still other collections that have some references to the Khasi-Jaintias are the Charles Wood Collection (MSS Eur. F. 78/89/Bundle 3), which has something on the aftermath of the Jaintia resistance;[9] the J.C. Hutton papers (on microfilm 2406 B) on the reforms proposed in the 1930s preceding the Government of India

Act 1935; the V. Linlithgow collection, (MSS. Eur. F./125) that has a correspondence between the Governor and the Governor-General; and the political department collection, (particularly files L/P & J/6787, 6789 and 10635) on developments in the North-East hills just prior to the transfer of power and after. The ardent researcher will still find much more material in this great storehouse of information. The India Office Library and Records' *Select List of Private Collections in the European Manuscripts* only gives an indication of some of the more important collections.

The private and some official letters and correspondence of Lord William Bentinck deposited in the University of Nottingham, Manuscript Department is a useful source for studying the early years of British control over Assam and the Khasi Hills.[10] The Bentinck papers form part of the Portland Collection deposited by the Duke of Portland with the University in 1949. While Bentinck's personal correspondence on the Cherrapunji experiments are few, the letters he received from George Swinton, the Chief Secretary of the Bengal Government, R. Benson, his Military Secretary, David Scott, agent to the Governor-General, North East Frontier, and military, medical and other officers involved in the Cherrapunji sanatorium, are impressive in terms of information they provide in size and content.

The collections relevant to our study has been catalogued as follows:

PWJF 2781 (1829-1833) Letters and Enclosures from George Swinton.

PWJF 2791 (1830) Correspondence concerned with North East Frontier.

PWJF 2811 (1831) Correspondence with George Swinton.

PWJF 2820 (1831) Correspondence with George Swinton.

PWJF 2857 (1832-1833) Miscellaneous (including letters) from George Swinton.

Surprisingly, these papers do not provide much information on the Khasi Uprising (1829-1833) other than a reference or two of the 'bow and arrow insurrection'.[11] Nor is there anything on the developments prior to the incorporation of the Jaintia Raj into the British dominion. The collection, however, has to offer much material on the official view of the British connection with Khasi hills from 1829 to 1834. The private letters also make very interesting reading, particularly the concern David Scott's friends had for his health, details of his death,[12] Scott's own interest in the economic development of the Khasi hills, the construction of the road, survey operations by Capt. Fisher, the discovery of coal in Cherrapunji and the plans to set up a cantonment at Cherrapunji and the beginning of problems and the eventual collapse of the Cherrapunji Cantonment plans in 1834.[13]

The Nottingham University muniments comes to significance when read with the material found in the papers of the 9th Earl of Dalhousie on deposit in the Scottish Records Office, Edinburgh. The Earl (father of the more renowned Governor-General), was Commander-in-Chief in India between 1829-1832, and the papers listed in GD 45/5 relate to his service. An interesting deposit is GD/45/48. It is a letter from George Swinton at Calcutta with two enclosures, one a map of the 'Cossya independent estates' and the other an extract of a letter from Scott to Swinton dated 27 October 1830. The map referred to was the first to be made of the Khasi states and is dated 1829. It illustrates the territories of some of the large states that the British had come to know. It indicates the line of the road that was to be built between Jaintiapur and Raha.

Scott's letter to George Swinton, his Fort William College friend and then Chief Secretary, Government of India, throw light on a variety of subjects such as the life of European troops stationed in India, the advantages of Cherrapunji, the drinking habits of soldiers, etc. He wrote:[14]

> I am more than ever convinced of the immense advantage that the European force would derive from being cantoned in this quarter. If the recruits were at once brought up here they have no opportunity of acquiring idle, dissolute habits and they would remain vastly superior as soldiers.

Scott had other worries of the men stationed at Cherrapunji. He informed Swinton:[15]

> They have all behaved exceedingly well... the Cossyas being ready in all other matters to be hale fellows well met and having no objection to give any of them a glass of grog in the very penetratia of their houses. The carpenters, platers, etc are, all men that cannot be trusted out of sight and I do not therefore like taking any of them over to Myrong.

Other materials useful for the history of early British administration in Eastern India are dealt with in the administration of justice in the Non-Regulation Provinces (GD 45/6/137); papers relating to the Ghoorka Corps (GD 45/5/26); Memorandum on the relations between civil and military authorities (GD 45/5/50); Letters and copies of letters to and from Lord William Bentinck (GD 45/5/60); and finally Bengal Army List (1831), (GD 45/5/84).

Many British families had traditions of keeping their members' private and official correspondence, notes, memoirs as the Bentinck and Dalhousie records indicate. For their safe custody and (restricted) use many of these eventually have found their ways into Universities, libraries and archives, though some continue to be in smaller private holdings. Another collection that has become useful for studies on Eastern Bengal, particularly Sylhet and Cachar and the Khasi and Jaintia hills, is the Robert Lindsay Muniments. Lindsay arrived in

Calcutta in the autumn of 1772 as an eighteen year old writer. After occupying various subordinate posts under the Calcutta Presidency, he was transferred on promotion to Dacca in 1776. In August, the following year, he was appointed as Superintendent of the frontier district of Sylhet. He remained there as its Collector for twelve years. Apart from his official duties, which ranged from revenue collection, judicial and executive administration, Lindsay, like 'Sylhet' Thackeray before him, engaged himself in a variety of trading activities ranging from limestone (*chunam*) trade with the Khasis, elephant hunting, construction of ships, grain export, collection of cowries on a commission, and sale of jute from lower Assam to Bengal. From a combination of all those enterprises he amassed a considerable fortune and enough to see him through early retirement. In 1822 he wrote, 'Mr. Robert Lindsay: Memoir of His Life'.

Lindsay kept a meticulous account of all his private and official correspondence. These muniments were brought back with Lindsay following his resignation and today forms part of the much larger Crawford and Balcarres papers. In 1946, the entire collection was transferred from the family archive to the John Rylands University Library of Manchester. There they remained till 1988 when they were shifted to the National Library of Scotland in Edinburgh.

The papers of Robert Lindsay are listed: 9769/30/5. Of the manuscript volumes those with numbers 9769/30/5/1 to 9 and 18 relate to his Indian experience. Volumes 10 to 20, excluding 18, gives an account of his business transactions, and ledgers and correspondence on his return home till his death (1836). Indian Baggage Book 1784 is a slim volume which lists the baggage Lindsay sent home, possibly on one of his own ships. What is of interest to us are the contents he lists in Box 4, 5 and 6. Here were packed 2 hill dresses containing five pieces each; 3 ivory quivers mounted on brass and silver; bundles of arrows; a rhinoceros head and 3 horns; a tiger's head, swords, bows and hill shields. Lindsay presumably had made frequent visits into the hills. Indeed, he just might have been the first European to have gone beyond the limestone foothills.[16]

The most important volumes for information on Lindsay's commercial activities are 9769/30/5/4, 5 and 9. Here he writes in detail of how he got interested in the limestone trade, the names of his employees, the patronage he gave to William Raitt, his brother Henry and other European and Greek traders who were taking an interest in the *chunam* and salt trade. 9769/30/5/8 are the three volumes 'John Shaw and George Reid: Estate Accounts 1782-92'. In Volume II he notes his worry that the defence of Sylhet was insufficient.[17]

From its vicinity to the mountains we are surrounded on three sides by troublesome neighbours. Acting offensively against them we have found from long experience ineffectual and the only mode of ensuring their good behaviour and of preventing their incursions is by supporting armed boats upon the lakes and several forts and passes leading towards the hills.

Lindsay found that 'the hill people are most troublesome (at) the beginning of harvest.' In a letter to Lt. James Davidson, he suggested to him to 'prevent the hill people from cutting crop and carrying the rice to the mountains'. Ten years' experience had taught him,[18]

> that there is no other mode of preserving their peaceable behaviour and of enforcing them to our accommodation than by stopping their usual supply of grain – this I have always found had the desired effect in the course of two or three months.

In Volume II of Linday's 'India Letter Books' is to be found, possibly, the first report of information on the Khasis written in the English language.[19] Lindsay was then in Calcutta and had tendered his resignation as Superintendent of Sylhet. The Board of Revenue's letter to the Scotsman informed him that his resignation had been accepted and directed him to 'furnish a particular description of the life of the Cosseahs, the nature of the country they inhabit and their particular habit of life.' Lindsay promptly replied for he was eager to sail for home. This very short account[20] has no details of the Khasis, but some insights are there. For instance, he refers to their eating habits; the cremation of their dead; the independence of each of the small Khasi states and the reaction to those who do them wrong. Even two hundred years ago this observer could say that the Khasi women were industrious.

The only part of Lindsay's papers that have been read, other than the reference mentioned above, is his memoir.[21] It was written in 1822 and entitled 'Mr Robert Lindsay: Memoir of His Life'. It was published with a new title 'Anecdotes of an Indian Life' in *Lives of the Lindsays* or *A Memoir of the House of Crawford and Balcarres,* Vol. III, London, 1849. The 77 pages memoir has become an important source on the early British trade with the Khasis; it has references to the trade in iron and jute; has descriptions of the Khasi men and women and their habits. Lindsay recollects a hunting expedition he made into the hills accompanied by the Jaintia Raja.[22]

Much of the material located and used and referred to above, could not have been possible without M.D. Wainwright and Noel Mathews' authoritative guide as a starting point.[23] The editors have produced a very useful reference after an extensive study of the nature and contents of the 'private' sources.[24] One very interesting manuscript was followed from a reference in the guide. Lt. Edward H. Steel's 'Account of the Khasiah Tribe on the Bordrss of Eastern Bengal and Assam' in the *Nightingale Collection*[25] is located in the Western Manuscripts section of the British Library attached to the British Museum. The 24-page account, and presumably its accompanying photographs, sketches and artefacts were purchased by the Museum from Major Golding and Lawrence in January 1877.

Lt. Steel of the Royal Artillery may have been stationed in the Khasi-Jaintia hills long enough for him to write the account with some academic interest. In all probability he may have seen service in the Jaintia campaign and the transfer of the district headquarters from Cherrapunji to Shillong. The manuscript starts with a description, in the first few pages, of the Khasi hills, the neighbouring plains areas, the climate and so on. From page 5 onwards, he describes the Khasi physique, their dress, the status of their women, their customs at birth, marriage and death, Khasi dances, their basketry, the erection of megaliths and their economic activities, including iron smelting, agriculture, their defence mechanism and finally, fishing.[26] Though Steel does not go into any detail, his account is useful for the observations he makes. This early account on the Khasis has not been published. It has not been used by scholars. Its more extensive use of it promises to open up hitherto unknown details of the Khasis. Should the photographs, sketches and artefacts accompanying this manuscript be located and used, it will provide different and useful material for understanding the Khasis of that period. Indeed if his photographs are traced, they could be the first photographs of the Khasis. On pages 14 he writes thus after witnessing a Khasi dance: 'The demure looks of the girls, some pretty enough, and the ardent glances of the youth as they pass round and peep shyly at their lovers is amusing enough and makes a pretty picture.' This picture, together with those of the monoliths and his Khasi servant need to be located and preserved for their value in capturing time in photographs.

Much of the material on the Welsh connection with the Khasi-Jaintias has been utilised by missionaries in their historian of the mission.[27] However, the histories in the Welsh, and English languages published in the U.K. are largly drawn from material available there, and those published recently in India on the Welsh Mission in the Khasi-Jaintia hills has drawn from sources here. The only person to have used a wider choice of materials has been Nigel Jenhin. In an article[28] in a popular Welsh journal and more recently a book[29] he has indicated that there is so much more to locate and use. Nigel Jenkins has translated with notes Welsh into English, a number of books and reports on this connection from what is available in Swansea and Aberystwyth. Their use in the church histories would be enriched when used judiciously.[30]

Of late there has been a 'Raj' nostalgia. A smaller version of it may be called the 'mission' nostalgia. Missionaries who served in these hills continue to inspire their childern or descendants to put to writing their life works. One such is Alum Irfonwy Bannister's translation from Welsh into English of letters of his great-

great-grandfather Rev. William Pryse, who was one among the earliest of the Welsh Missionaries to serve the Khasi hills and Sylhet (1849-1866).[31] The foreword, 2 maps, 6 letters, extracts from two articles in Welsh make the 48 pages delightful reading and significant as a source for the study of the Khasis. There could be still more of such writing, only to be brought out in time.

The Cambridge (University) South Asian Archive is another fine repository which has not been sufficiently gone through for material on the Khasis. Even a cursory glance through its *Principal Collection of Papers,* edited by Lionel Carter and Dusha Bateson indicates a variety of material deposited in the Archives. Similarly, the Public Records Office and the Royal Botanical Gardens, both in Kew, Richmond would have sources not yet utilised. In the Botanical Garden's library are the diary and notes of the botanist, William Griffiths who stayed for some months in the Khasi-Jaintia hills in the 1830s. Useful material may also be with the London Missionary Society whose missionary Jacob Tomlin came to the Khasi hills in 1837-1838.

The material sources in the libraries and archives mentioned above (and there could be many more) is an indication of their volume and usefulness. They are well-preserved and easily available for research. The British past with India and these hills in particular may be difficult to appreciate but as one Welshman wrote: 'the past need not be passed'.[32]

NOTES AND REFERENCES

1. Letter dated Cherrapunji, 10 November 1862.
2. Letter dated Cherrapunji, 11 November 1862, 18 December 1862, 19 December 1862, 14 January 1863, and Maflong 24 April 1863.
3. Letter dated Cherrapunji, 14 November 1862, 8 January 1863, 15 April 1863.
4. Letter dated Cherrapunji, 11 January 1863.
5. MSS. Eur. D. 530/214, letter dated 31 January 1864.
6. MSS. Eur. E. 278/19.
7. MSS. Eur. E. 278/4.
8. MSS. Eur. E. 278/11.
9. Cited in D.R. Syiemlieh, *British Administration in Meghalaya: Policy and Pattern,* New Delhi, 1989, p. 95.
10. See *ibid.,* and N.K. Barooah, *David Scott in North-East India,* New Delhi, 1970.
11. C.H. Phillips, *The Correspondence of Lord William Convendish Bentick,* Vol. I, Oxford, 1977, No. 130, p. 265; No. 175, p. 381.
12. D.R. Syiemlieh, "The Last Days of David Scott", *Proceedings of the North East India History Association,* Fifth Session, Aizawl, 1984, pp. 107-113.
13. D.R. Syiemlieh, "The Cherrapunji Experiment (1829-1834)", *Proceedings of the North East India History Association,* Fourth Session, Barapani, 1983, pp. 116-123.

"Cherrapunji Versus Darjeeling: The Search for a Sanatorium for Lower Provinces", *Proceedings of the NEIHA*, Sixth Session, Agartala, 1985, pp. 219-225.

14. Dalhousie Muniments GD 45/5/48 No. 1.
15. *Ibid.*
16. Robert Lindsay, "Anecdotes of an Indian Life" in *Lives of the Lindsays or a Memoir of the House of Crawford and Balcarres*, Vol. III, London, 1849, pp. 176-185.
17. Lindsay Papers 9769/30/5/9 Volume 2, letter dated 29 October 1786.
18. *Ibid.*, letter dated 3 November 1786.
19. *Ibid.*, 9767/30/5/9 Volume 2, letter from Lindsay to Sir John Shore, President of the Board of Revenue, Calcutta, 14 December 1787. The letter is also printed in W. Firminger (ed.), *Sylhet District Records*, Vol. II, Shillong, 1917, No. 301, p. 204.
20. An introduction to this manuscript and its entire text may be read in D.R. Syiemlieh, "Leaves from the Past: An Early Account on the Khasis", *Khasi Studies*, Vol. V, October-December 1991, No. 3, pp. 86-90.
21. Refer to E.A. Gait, *A History of Assam*.
22. The Memoir has been reprinted with an elaborate introduction by the present author. See D.R. Syiemlieh (ed.), *Anecdotes of an Indian Life*, North Eastern Hill University Publications, Shillong, 1997.
23. M.D. Wainwright and Noel Mathews (eds.), *A Guide to Western Manuscripts and Documents in the British Isles Relating to South and South East Asia*, Oxford University Press, London, 1965.
24. Here a distinction is made between 'official' government records which are not included in the guide and 'private', covering a variety of records which the *Guide* provides information on.
25. Addl. 30240 B. It is yet to be established whether this manuscript was published as E.U. Steel, "On the Khasia Tribe", *Transaction of the Ethnological Society of London*, Vol. VII, n.s. 1869, pp. 305-312.
26. For details of this account read D.R. Syiemlieh, "Leaves from the Past: A Soldier Account on the Khasis", *Khasi Studies*, Vol. V, July-September 1991, No. 2, pp. 36-40.
27. Read John Huge Morris, *The History of the Welsh Calvinistic Methods' Foreign Mission*, Carnavor, 1990; J. Fortis Jyrwa, *The Wonderous Works of God*, Shillong, 1980.
28. Nigle Jenkins, "Thomas Jones and the Lost Book of the Khasis", *The New Welsh Review*, No. 21, 1993, pp. 56-64.
29. Nigle Jenkins, Gwalia in Khasis, Dyfed, 1995, An Indian edition is entitled *Through the Green Doors: Travels Among the Khasis*, Penguin, India, 2001.
30. Some of the translations are of Griffith Ellis, *William Lewis, Khasia*, Gwrecsam, 1903, Griffith Hughes, *Bryniau Cassia*, Caernarfon, (n.d.); "An Account of the 1897 Earthquake", by Rev. Robert Evans, and J. Herbert Roberts, *Ymweliadd A Bryniau Khasi*, Liverpool, 1988.
31. Bannister A.I., "A Past Aquaintance", typescript, Bishopston, February 1993, The author is the grandson of William Pryse, missionary to the Khasis and the people of Cachar-Sylhet, 1850s-1860s.
32. *Ibid.*, Dedication page.

25

Sources of Labour History of North-East India

Dipankar Banerjee

The foundation of some modern industries in India was laid during the second-half of the 19th century. Plantation of tea, jute and cotton manufacturing, coal mining and petroleum exploration got the real boost during the period, though all these industries were essentially aimed at serving the British capitalist interest. Through a new systematic policy which was actuated by the intense desire of the British manufacturing interest to turn India into an agricultural farmland of England, necessary steps were taken to acquire land by the British to set up plantations in India.

In North-East India, tea, oil and a limited quantity of coal were explored during the period. Plantation was the first capitalist industry that was set up in India under purely European ownership. Labour, being an important factor of production, a new labour-force came into existence in the region during the period. Particularly there was greater degree of concentration of labour in the plantations. This labour-force was characteristically different from the traditional work-force. As factors of production labour contributed much towards the economy and they were important component of social history. If we agree that 'social history is a study of social aggregates and groups in their institutional organisation, of institutes and their organisations and of the causes and consequences of changes in institutions and social organisations', then the importance of the study of labour history cannot be over-estimated. The 19th century Indian labour experienced recurring period of hardship—soil desertion, desertion from land, a decline of self-sufficiency, growth of capitalist enterprises and a number of other factors were responsible for the same. All these made the labour-force restive which led their frustration snowball into anger. The labour began to show their anger through occasional outbursts after they began to organise themselves. The history of the working class movement in India is the record of the struggles of the working class in modern factories, plantations, mills and mines for betterment of their wages as well as working conditions. Labour immigration, their socio-economic life, their struggle against the capitalist exploitation and their effective organisation into trade unions are essential components of labour history. It was a historical eventuality that the labour movements in India originated in the plantations. In Assam it originated in the tea gardens.

Unfortunately, labour history of the North-East India has remained an unexplored field of research till now. Considering the fact that plantations in Assam has the largest concentration of working-class population among the Indian industries during the pre-independence era, there is immense scope of research in the field. Further, all the main industries in Assam—tea, oil, coal and match—mostly remained under the ownership of the Europeans till 1950s. The working-class movement of the region during the British period, though fought on economic grounds, was an anti-imperialist struggle as well. Not much serious study in these aspects have been undertaken till now.

One of the greatest handicaps in the field of labour research is the lack of availability of primary source-materials. Consequent to the shifting of the Assam State Archives from Shillong to Guwahati more than a quarter of a century has passed. But the Archives in Guwahati is still to be properly organised and therefore accessibility to archival records inside the state still remains a difficult task. However, there are materials available elsewhere for undertaking serious study in the unexplored field of labour research of the region.

The collection of the manuscripts, private papers and other materials at the Oriental and Indian Office in London is a gold-mine for the students who want to undertake historical research in the related field. This largest collection on India include diaries of plantation managers, correspondences of Governor of Assam to the Viceroy of India on labour issues and vice-versa, memories left by the planters, civil servants and other British officers stationed in the region. Private letters of some British planters, army officers and civil service officials are also there in the Oriental and Indian Office collections.

In relation to Assam, the papers related to the period 1860-1947, are particularly important as very little of these materials have been used. The records generated by the East India Company and later by the officials under the crown[1] and the manuscripts collected at the India Office Library and records on the National and different State archives of India—are the primary sources to reconstruct the facts and facets of British India and construction of the institutions of colonial rule. To quote Prof. Bernard S. Cohn, "These archival publications are a tribute to the extraordinary labours of thousands of employees of the company who produced this seemingly endless store of information.[2]" The collection of different papers and annual reports of the Indian Tea Association which are preserved at the erstwhile ITA headquarters at London are also very valuable documents of research in the related field.

Among the indigenous sources the Assam Administrative Reports, Board of Revenue Papers, Assam Police Abstract of Intelligence, Home Political Files, Confidential Reports on vernacular publications, Home Department's Review of Native Newspapers, quarterly review of intelligence, Home Secret correspondences, Files on Labour Immigration, etc. are important source-materials for labour history.

This paper attempts to make a sweeping survey of some of the above-mentioned source-materials for research on labour history of the North-East India. The list is obviously not complete and exhaustive—it only includes those materials to which the author had access for personal consultation.[3]

FOREIGN SOURCES

Collections at the Oriental and Indian Office, London.[4]

Manuscript No. MSS. Eur. F. 3059

This manuscript titled "Correspondence from the Government of Assam to the Viceroy of India, 1939" contains some invaluable letters and semi-official and official letters from H.J. Twynam, the Governor of Assam. The correspondences basically centre round workers' strike at the Assam Oil Company, Digboi. The correspondences do not deal only with the incident of police firing on the striking workers and the Governor's defence of police but also reflect the British Government's stand towards labour-related issues in Assam. Some papers also deal the handling of the labour situation by the Premier, Gopinath Bardoloi and the provincial Governor's personal assessment of the Ministry in respect of labour issues. The papers also reflect Governor's partisan attitude towards the planters as well as the AOC management. The manuscript contains a good number of files.

Photo-Manuscript Section. File No. Photo. Eur. 53

This file is a photocopy of diaries and papers of Henry Joseph Twynam who served as the Governor of Assam for some time. These personal papers and diaries contain his personal views and assessment of the labour scenario in Assam. Of particular interest is the difference of official and personal observation on some contemporary labour-related issues, particularly in relation to labour unrest in the oil and plantation industries.

Manuscript Section. File No. L/P and J/7/2580

This file, a part of OIOC, titled "Assam: Strike at Digboi", contains valuable documents related to Assam Oil Company strike at Digboi in 1939. The documents include different press clippings of English newspapers from India, Burma and Great Britain which carried out reports related to the working-class agitation in Assam, particularly, the labour strike at Digboi. The file also include the Assam Chief Secretary's correspondences and notes on contemporary labour issues, report on Premier Gopinath Bardoloi's visit to Digboi, observation of the red-shirt or communist influence on the workers and also the reaction/observation of the Governor of Assam regarding the British MP's queries on the safety of the European employees at Digboi.

Manuscript No. MSS. Eur. F. 125/32

This manuscript consists of letters and other correspondences of Viceroy, Lord Linlithgow. Some of the letters are related to Assam labour situations in the oil industry and the plantations. Of particular interest is the Viceroy's deep concern to protect the interest of the planters and AOC management in the face of threat from the working-class. Some observations regarding the functioning of the Assam Ministry and the role of the Congress also make interesting reading. In one of the letters to the provincial Governor, the Viceroy promised "full backing" to the Governor in the event of Premier Bardoloi raising any difficulty to the Governor's initiative to resolve labour dispute.

Manuscript No. Mss. Eur. F. 286/5

This manuscript basically contains papers of the Indian Tea Association; some confidential documents related to labour unrest in the tea gardens of Assam; some file contains minutes of discussion of 49 Annual General Meeting of ITA held at Calcutta where the planters from different gardens of Assam assembled. The file also contains valuable documents regarding strategy and policy of the tea industry to tackle the labour strike in the gardens of Assam.

Manuscript No. MSS. Eur. F. 174/630

This important manuscript contains files in which correspondences of Tea Estate Managers with the officers of the Indian Tea Association Managers and their replies have been stored. The collection also includes Annual Reports of different Tea Estates, including labour recruitment and labour relations strategies, labour welfare measures, production statistics, etc. The files also include some garden manager's statements/observations regarding strike, desertions, trade union activities in their respective gardens, etc. In some cases impact of the "Gandhian" and "Red Cap" volunteers in the gardens have also been discussed.

Manuscript No. MSS. Eur. E. 278/5

This manuscript contains the personal papers, letters, official notes and drafts of speeches and also some personal photographs of Robert N. Reid who served as Governor of Assam during 1937-42. The manuscript contains interesting account of AOC administrative chief Lingeman's discussion with Rajendra Prasad and the Governor's comment of the same. The file also contains "Secret Reports" from the acting Governor of Assam to Lord Linlithgow incorporating some strategies that the Governor had taken in connection with the labour strike. It also includes documents containing the public demand to appoint a Court of Enquiry in respect of Digboi firing. The file also contains interesting documents related to externing of Sudhindra Pramanik and other leaders of the Assam Oil Company from Digboi.

There are two other manuscript collections of Robert N. Reid under Manuscripts No. MSS Eur. E. 278/19 and MSS. Eur. E. 278/4 which contain valuable documents on the hill district of Assam. In one of these contains a long draft of an unpublished manuscript written by Robert N. Reid titled "Assam and the North East Frontier of India", which is a very valuable document for research on the British frontier policy.

Manuscript No. Mss. Eur.F. 174/2055

This manuscript contains a file titled "Labour and Trade Union in Tea Estates". It contains correspondences between ITA officials of Calcutta and London. In some papers working of Tea Estate Emigration Act, statement regarding total remittances from the tea districts of Assam to the eleven chief recruiting districts, etc. have been mentioned. The papers also include interesting accounts on how the Assam Oil Company workers' strike had profoundly influenced the neighbouring tea estate workers and the resultant anxiety that had caused to the powerful planters of the Brahmaputra Valley.

Manuscript No. Mss. Eur.F. 174/2055

This manuscript titled "South Indian Association in London: Labour and Trade Union in Tea Estates" contains valuable information on meeting of the Assam Premier Gopinath Bordoloi (and his senior colleagues in the Ministry, including Finance Minister Fakhruddin Ali Ahmed, Labour Minister Ramnath Das) with D.C. Hudson, Chairman, Emergency Committee of ABITA, H.F. Clark, Secretary SVBITA, R.B. Lagden and others regarding the repercussions of Digboi Oil Strike on the gardens of India. The manuscript also contains records of the meeting of the Governor of Assam with R.B. Lagden, Chairman, ITA and others regarding the labour agitation in the tea estates. The Governor expressed the view that these strikes were political, anti-British and not related to economic issues.

Other Collections at OIOC and ITA, London

In addition to the above, there are some other manuscripts at Oriental and Indian Office collections which contain valuable source-materials for labour history research of the North-East India. Among those are included Salvia Bowlby Collection (Manuscript No. MSS. Eur. C. 300); Memoirs of Robert Percy and Benzamin Percy (Manuscripts No. MSS. Eur. C. 345); Sir Robert Graham Collection; (Manuscript No. MSS. Eur. F. 174/2070), etc.

The Indian Tea Association headquarters at London also has a very good collection of papers. These ITA papers contain the correspondences of Indian Tea Estate managers with ITA, Calcutta and London offices on almost all issues related to labour (recruitment, wages, strikes), Annual General Meeting Proceedings, annual ITA dinner lectures, and ITA collection of press clippings, etc.

All these foreign collections are great storehouse of information for the students and research scholars of labour history. In addition, some very old ex-tea estate managers, senior superintendents and engineers of Assam, Darjeeling and Dooars who left India permanently in the 1950s and 1960s are still living in different parts of the United Kingdom. Their interviews may bring to light some interesting facts which may serve as important source of labour history.[5]

Indigenous Sources

Materials for reconstructing the political history of North-East India have so long been drawn mainly from archival records. H.K. Barpujari, Amalendu Guha, J.B. Bhattacharjee and others who have done pioneering works on the modern history of the region have extensively used archival materials in their works.

They have also used private collections of prominent persons in their work. There still remains some impressive collection of private and official papers which may help the students immensely in the field of labour history research. There is an urgent need to collect these materials immediately, otherwise these will be permanently lost to the posterity. Appended herewith a list of some of these private papers/collections:

PRIVATE COLLECTIONS[6]

Apurba Kumar Ghose Collection

A file and some correspondence regarding AMCO strike of 1936, including the minutes of discussion of AMCO management with the workers' union in possession of late Apurba Kumar Ghose, a provincial Director of AMCO, Dhubri.

Assam Match Co. Dhubri Files and Papers

These official papers are available at the AMCO office at Dhubri. The papers include labour recruitment and wage statistics related to the years 1925-39. Some isolated papers in relation to 1936 strike could also be located in the office. There is also a separate file marked "Skilled Office and Factory Employees in WIMCO and AMCO".

Assam Oil Company Workers' Union Collection

Some papers related to Digboi strike, souvenirs and photographys of 1939 AOC workers' strike are preserved in AOC workers' Union Office at Digboi. The collection also includes press clippings in relation to felicitation of Sarajubala Chakravarty, wife of Satyendranath Chakravarty who died in police firing at Digboi during 1939 worker strike.

Bipin Chandra Chakravarty Papers

A bunch of papers, leaflets, press clippings, pamphlets and posters in relation to Assam Match Company workers' strike at Dhubri in 1936 were in possession of late Bipin Chandra Chakravarty, veteran trade union activist of Assam. Some correspondences with the Bengal Labour Party was also in his possession which were invaluable in relation to early trade union movements in the province.

Bijay Chandra Bhagaboti Collection

Some papers, including letters exchanged among congress leaders like F.A. Ahmed, Kedar Nath Goswami, and Bijay Chandra Bhagaboti on labour-related issues, and press clippings, are included in this collection.

Lakhyadhar Chowdhury Collections

Lakhyadhar Chowdhury, writer, political and social activist, was teaching in a school when Digboi strike of 1939 broke out. Chowdhury, then 25, maintained a diary. This reflects an Assamese youth's reaction to the developments at Digboi. Chowdhury also collected some money from the public and took part in a number of meetings organised at Guwahati to express solidarity with the striking workers of Digboi.

Mohan Deka Collection

Photographs and some press clippings in relation to AOC workers' strike of 1939 are in possession of Mohan Deka, president (1998-99) of Assam Oil Company workers' union.

Sriman Prafulla Goswami Collection

The collection includes interesting accounts of the activities of Congress Socialist Party in the labour front. Particularly, its activities during 1939-40 are incorporated in this collection.

Prafulla Misra/Chinmohan Sehanavis Collection

This is essentially a collection of papers related to the Left Movement and growth and activities of the Communist Party of India in the Surma valley which includes comments from social activist Jyotirmay Nandy. Amalendu Guha informs that these were compiled by Prafulla Misra of Shillong for years, beginning in 1930s, which was made available to him through Chinmohan Sehanavis of Calcutta in whose custody the file is preserved.

Sarajubala Chakravarty Collection

Copies of condolence resolution, felicitation addresses, some press clippings in relation to AOC strike, papers related to final wage settlement of Satyendranath Chakravarty (the Assam Oil Company worker who was killed in the police firing at Digboi strike in 1939), are in possession of Sarajubala Chakravarty, octogenarian wife of Satyendranath Chakravarty, who is presently (1998) residing at Ramnagar Road, Bongaon, West Bengal.

In addition to the above, All India Congress Committee papers and files of 1886 onwards (preserved at the Nehru Memorial Museum and Library, New Delhi), Assam Pradesh Congress Committee papers (1936 onwards) and Bengal Pradesh Congress Committee papers also contain some important information regarding the Congress labour policy and its response to the working-class movement.[7]

Official records, reports and proceedings

- *Assam Administrative Reports.*
- *Assam Gazette.*
- Assam Police abstract of intelligence.
- Board of Revenue papers, Govt. of Bengal, select revenue files for the years 1854 and 1876.
- Confidential report on native newspapers, Govt. of Bengal, 1936-47.
- Confidential report on native newspapers report in Bengal.
- F.R. Mallet's *Report on Geological Survey of Assam*, published in GSI Survey Report, Vol. XII, Calcutta, 1876.
- Home Political Files, Fortnightly Reports, 1921-40, Govt. of Assam.
- Home Political File, Quarterly Review of Intelligence and Select Files, Govt. of Assam [in addition two reports, one related to tea garden labour 1936 and Archives along with some other reports, without any file number and undated].
- Home Political Proceedings, Govt. of Bengal, relevant papers on labour unrest and confidential report on the vigil on workers of the Bengal Labour Party, 1926, 1939.
- Home secret correspondence, File No. B.SB-316 of 1939 (related to Bengal).
- Immigration Branch, (Files marked Immigration B), Govt. of Assam, select issues related to 1939.
- India in 1921-22, A report prepared for presentation in the Parliament, Calcutta, 1922.
- *Parliamentary Proceedings, House of Commons, 1939*, select portions of 1939, London.
- *Proceedings of the Assam Legislative Assembly*, Shillong, 1936-1939.
- *Proceedings of the Assam Legislative Council*, 1921, 1926, 1936, 1939 and 1940.
- *Proceedings of General and Judicial Dept*. (Files marked Gen & J), Govt. of Assam, select issues.
- *Reports on an enquiry into the conditions of labour in Mineral Oil Industry in India.* (D.V. Rege, ICS), Delhi, 1945.

— *Reports of the Assam Labour Enquiry Committee*, 1921-22, Govt. of Assam, Shillong, 1922.
— *Reports on the Board of Conciliation for Assam Oil Company, Digboi*, (K.K. Hazra, 8 August 1939), Govt. of Assam. Shillong, 1939.
— *Report of the Court of Enquiry into the affairs of Digboi*, (J.C. Higgins, Chairman, 7 January 1939), Govt. of Assam, Shillong, 1939.
— *Report of the Committee of Enquiry into the affairs of Digboi*, (M.N. Mukherjee, 25 November 1939), Shillong, 1939.
— *Report of the Imperial Geological Survey in India*, Calcutta, select issues.
— "Annual Govt. Resolutions on Immigrant Labour in the Assam Districts of East Bengal and Assam" in the *Proceedings of Eastern Bengal and Assam Legislative Council, 1906-1921.*

Newspapers and Periodicals

Contemporary newspapers and periodicals also constitute important source-material of labour history. During the pre-independence era, some newspapers occasionally carried out reports on Assam labour problems and plantation-related news which might provide good inputs to the students engaged in labour history research. Some such English newspapers include *Advance* (Calcutta), *Amrita Bazar Patrika*, (Calcutta), *The Assam Herald* (Dibrugarh), *The Daily Mail* (London), *Forward* (Calcutta), *The Hindusthan Standard* (Calcutta), *The Light of Burma Herald* (Delhi), *The Statesman* (Calcutta), *The Times* (London), and *The Times of Assam* (Dibrugarh). Among the vernacular (Assamese and Bengali) newspapers *Abakan* (Calcutta), *Anada Bazar Patrika* (Calcutta), *Asamiya* (weekly from Dibrugarh), *Banhi* (Calcutta), *Gana Chabuk* (Dhubri), *Bharat Sramajibi* (Calcutta), *Tinidinya Asamiya* (Dibrugarh) and *Yugantar* (Calcutta) published news items related to labour issues in Assam.

Some other Publications

Two other publications, namely *Report on Labour Conditions in India* (report presented by J. Hallsworth and A.A. Purcell after their visit to India),[8] published by Trade Union Congress General Council, London, in 1928 and *The Assam Directory and Tea Areas Handbook* (annual publication), Calcutta also contain important observations, facts and figures related to the labour history of the region. Some issues of the *Journal of International Labour Movement*, published from London, also carried some articles on the labour problem of Assam. *Indian Quarterly Register* and *Indian Annual Register* which were edited by N.N. Mitra during 1921-39, also provide important information on labour-related issues.

BRAHMO LITERARY SOURCES

Another, rather unconventional, source for the labour history of Assam is the good amount of Brahmo literature which came into existence during the last part of the 19th century.[9] Being sympathetic to the tea garden's condition of virtual serfdom, the Brahmo Samajists decided to mobilise public opinion against the most crude capitalist exploitation of the Planter Raj.

Ramkumar Bhattacharjee (Vidyaratna) came to Assam as an emissary of Brahmo Samaj during 1879-80 and wrote a book named *Udasin Satyasrabar Assam Brahman* in which he gave a vivid description of the tea garden life of Assam.[10] In 1888, Ramkumar's famous book *Coolie Kahini* was published, which is very touchy but a faithful portrayal of the life in the tea gardens of Assam as it was in the last quarter of the twentieth century. *Tatwabodhini Patrika, Tarwakaumudi Patrika, Brahmo Public Opinion and Sanjibanee* – these four papers were published by the Brahmos at Calcutta. *Brahmo Public Opinion and Sanjibanee* carried a series of articles on Assam labour problems and their hardships. Brahmo activists like Dwaraka Nath Ganguly wrote as many as thirteen articles in the *Bengalee* on the Assam coolie problem.[11] Ramkumar Vidyaratna wrote a series of articles in the *Sanjibanee*. How valuable these articles were could be judged from the reaction of the British planters. When some of these articles were translated into English and published in the journal *Rice and Ryots*, the planters declared openly that 'the contributors to *Sanjibanee* will be the first victims of the planters' guns.'[12]

NOTES AND REFERENCES

1. Some of these records are now available in the published form. For example, *The Letters Received from its Servants in the East, Plain Tales from the Raj.*
2. The Fort William India House Correspondence.
3. Webster's Collegiate Dictionary, 1948.
4. While preparing for his Doctoral dissertation on "Working Class Movement in Assam: Assam Oil Company Workers' Strike of 1939" (submitted at Gauhati University in 2000) the author has partially consulted these files at India Office Library at St. Pancras, London. Its collections are now known as "Oriental and India Office Collections". This list is not exhaustive. There are definitely much more materials on labour history of the North Eastern Region at OIO collections. The author has consulted part of the huge collection.
5. Some such interviews with ex-tea garden managers of Assam were conducted by the author in 1992 in UK. Those interviews are now preserved at the North West Sound Archive, Clitheroe, Lancs, UK.

6. These papers were consulted by the author for preparing his M.Phil Dissertation "Labour Unrest in Assam: Some Aspects of the Labour Movement among the Non-plantation Workers (1919-39)", Jawaharlal Nehru University, New Delhi, 1984.
7. There is an urgent need of preservation of APCC papers as the papers are in a very poor state because of lack of proper preservation. Some documents, which have not been catalogued, are very important research materials. For example, Kedarnath Goswami and Fakhruddin Ali Ahmed's assessment report on Digboi strike.
8. Arthur Parcel and J. Hallsworth visited Assam in 1928 to study the labour situation in Assam and submitted their report at the Trade Union Congress General Council at London
9. Dipankar Banerjee, Brahmo Samaj and the North East India, Key-note address at the 111th. Session of All India Brahmo Conference, Guwahati, 2001.
10. David Kopf, *The Brahmo Samaj and the Shaping of Modern Mind*, Priceton, 1979, pp. 124-5.
11. Dipankar Banerjee, "Centenary of the publication of 'Coolie Kahini' – the role of Brahmo Samaj for the emancipation of plantation workers in Assam in retrospect", *Perspective*, Guwahati, 1987, pp. 6-15.
12. *Ibid.*, and Prabhat Chandra Ganguly, *Bharater Rastriya Itihasher Khasra*, Calcutta, 1960.

26

From the Margins: An Overview of the Alternative Sources on the History of North-East India

Indira Baptista Gupta

History in E.H. Carr's often quoted phrase is a dialogue between the past and the present. To address the past, conventional historians laid undue emphasis on the official record to write overwhelmingly narrative and descriptive accounts of historical events, which were usually centred on the actions and ideas of a few powerful men. Besides, traditional historians in western countries were interested only in their own civilisations seeing the rest of the world, if at all, in terms of interaction with western culture. The beginning of the 20th century saw the broadening of the conception of what constitutes a historical source and the methods for handling the new type of source. The surfacing of these new sources were the main impetus behind the assault on traditional historiography.[1] This led to the development of a "New History"[2] with a widened scope, encompassing new unexplored areas and attending to all spheres of life. It soon developed in the words of Geoffrey Barraclough, into an "attempt to discover on the basis of fragmentary evidence the significant things about the past."[3]

This paper is an attempt to dwell, rather briefly, on sources, apart from the official records, that could be used by the historian in the context of the North-East. However, the selection of a particular source would depend on the problem under study as well as the availability and authenticity of the sources.

Let me confess, that while recently editing a set of two books of articles on the partition of 1947,[4] I was struck by the multiplicity of sources and the different perspective these give to our perception of an event. One set of records enabled scholars to look at the complex interplay of historical events during the last years of British Raj in India and at the part played by the prominent leaders of the Congress, Muslim League and the British. But there were other sources used by scholars, like reminiscences in the form of eyewitness accounts, testimonials and narratives and also various genres of creativity, like films, T.V. serials, paintings, folk dramas and, most important of all, literature and poetry, which show the flip-side of partition. It mirrored the pain and anguish of partition while also highlighting the bond of oneness among the divided people. These vivid images would never have surfaced if only one genre of sources were used. This activated me to undertake this endeavour, which I believe will be useful because of the similarity of sources and its applicability to the practice of modern history, in any region of our country.

The first group of sources, which naturally fall within the purview of the historian are documents. No document, no history is the famous dictum of Langlois and Seignobos.[5] Medieval historians, to a greater degree, have the problem of making the most of minimal and fragmentary evidence: sometimes the discovery of one new document can be of critical importance. Modern historians, on the other hand, "tend to suffer from the converse problem of having too much evidence at their disposal though even so it does not always necessarily provide the answers to the particular questions they want to ask".[6]

The three forms of personal documents that are used by historians are autobiographies, diaries and letters.[7] Autobiographies, which are at least edited if not written sometime after the events recorded in them and which are almost invariably intended for publication, suffer from the propagandist motives and from the tendency to rationalise. The author from the vantage point of hindsight could select only those experiences and actions that he considers good for his image. Diaries, described as the personal document par excellence,[8] are often the most revealing and make for fascinating reading. But as source material they often disappoint, as they tend to exaggerate, leave gaps and are based on an individual's assumption. Letters are designed by the writer to convey to the recipient his impressions, but they vary with the culture in which the writer is immersed. In an age when correspondence takes a much smaller place in the peoples' lives and in politics when those who write letters and receive them rarely have the space to preserve them, the future historian will be much worse-off than those who work on the public figures of the 17th or the 18th centuries.[9]

Personal documents by their nature admit the possibility of distortion. There is no way in which the distortions in these documents can be measured, but Gottschalk has listed five kinds of circumstances,[10] which may help the user to find out the truthfulness of these sources: (1) when the truth of a statement is a matter of indifference to the witness, he is unlikely to be unbiased; (2) when the statement is prejudicial to the informant or his interests, it is likely to be unusually truthful; (3) when the facts at issue are so much matters of common knowledge that the informant would be unlikely to be mistaken or lie about them; (4) when the part of the statement of primary interest to the investigator is both incidental and intrinsically probable; and (5) when the informant makes statements, which are contrary to his expectations and anticipations as assured by the investigator.

A historian has to be careful when using these personal documents, so that his own biases and prejudices do not crop in while using his documents. The best use of these documents can be made by not relying on them entirely but by using them to supplement the data from other sources. One problem that a researcher faces and which he has to overcome while dealing with this source is that he has not only to locate such sources but also to have access to them.

A special class of the personal document belongs to this region. These are the accounts of the British administrators, foreign Christian missionaries and travellers, who were engaged in the purpose of colonial administration, historical study of culture and society, expansion of Christianity and the spread of Westernisation among the people, and memoirs of adventure seekers. In the course of their sojourns in the North-East, in the 19th and the 20th century, they have left behind many interesting accounts. To name a few, mention may be made of W. Robinson,[11] B.H. Hodgson,[12] John Butler,[13] E.T. Dalton,[14] Risley,[15] W.H.G. Cole[16] and J.H. Hutton.[17] The studies undertaken by these British scholars/ administrators were primarily to enable the rulers to take stock of their position and to see how they fared with the people committed to their charge. But the motive apart from these accounts provide rich data on the customs and peculiarities of the region and could be effectively used with other sources for the historical reconstruction of that period.

The North-East, which consists of seven states, inhabited by tribal groups of varied size, culture, language, etc. has been an area for intensive anthropological and ethnographical research.[18] The early anthropological studies were mainly government sponsored and this continued even into the 1950s and 1960s. An anthropologist works in the idiom of the eternal present and he moves from the present to the past, whereas a historian moves *vice versa*, from the past to the present. In spite of this basic difference, the monographs of anthropologists can be taken as a starting point and the data contained in them could be supplemented or verified from other sources. Each of the tribal groups of this region has their own history. A comparison of the growth-points of these will provide useful insights into the similarities and differences among them. These may also be handy to find out the factors, which helped in the development of different cultures. For instance, the anthropologist tells us that the Garos and Khasis are matrilineal groups, whereas the Nagas have different customs. A historian can take this as the base hypothesis and go into past factors, which led to these differences.

Apart from the above, another group of documents that can be put to use are editorials, speeches, pamphlets and letters to the editor. They reveal the clashing climates of opinion and provide an invaluable aid to direct observation. They also supplement observation and participation in retrospect by broadening the base of experience. But by themselves they tell an incomplete story and it is clearly unwise to stretch their adoption into contexts in which they can offer neither economy nor satisfaction.[19]

One particular type of source-material, which has given rise to much debate, is imaginative literature. The relationship between history and fiction has always been problematic. From a historian's viewpoint personal stories, steeped as they are in emotion and sentimentality, are difficult to lay down simply as "facts", because they bear the imprint of bias, distortion and even exaggeration. But if these texts are fiction, and in some sense they are, being literary compositions, the raw material of these fictions is veritable fact.[20] There is one basic rule for the historians handling imaginative literature: for the concrete facts of everyday existence he should prefer, if he could avoid it, not to take the word of a novelist, but to turn to other sources. Once he has established the record the historian may well use a vivid example culled from a novel or a poem to illustrate but not prove that record.[21]

Till the 19th century historians, often literate Europeans themselves, were content to reconstruct the past using the written remains of their heroes. But with the growth of interest in ordinary people and the advance of the disciplines of sociology and anthropology the focus of history shifted. If a historian is interested in ordinary people he cannot rely entirely on what they write because they write very little or even nothing at all. During the 1960s, therefore, more and more historians turned their attention to the spoken word. Oral traditions are accounts, which may or may not be historical in content, transmitted verbally from one generation to another. It is now thoroughly respectable to study "oral sources" and many historians do. Though not unproblematic these sources are nonetheless important.

Oral history could be a powerful tool for discovering, exploring and evaluating the nature of the process of historical memory, how people make sense of their past, how they connect individual experience and its social context, how the past becomes part of the present and how people use it to interpret their lives and the world around them.[22] It is true that memories are shifting, unreliable and changeable but as James Young wrote, "The fictiveness in testimony does not involve disputes about facts but the inevitable variance in perceiving and representing these facts witness by witness, language by language, culture by culture."[23]

The most important component of oral traditions are folklore, which is of principal interest to the social anthropologist. But in spite of increased recognition of the theoretical importance of popular behaviour very little is done by the historian to exploit this body of knowledge. For a region as rich and varied as the North-East in folk culture and traditions, which could comprise of myths, legends, folktales, songs, chants, etc. this source needs to be exploited more. There should be a coordinated, systematic and integrated exploration, collection and use of this source. For example, the legends surrounding Rani Gaidinliu could be collected and her role in the Non-cooperation Movement of 1932 analysed with the help of other sources.

All historical study is founded upon the critical evaluation of a wide range of evidence. The basic purpose of this paper is to show that the sources for the study of the modern period of any region are many and varied and the North-East is no exception. It is left to the practitioner of the past to first locate his sources, then scrutinise them and ultimately to synthesise them into a history that is authentic, interesting as well as multi-dimensional.

NOTES AND REFERENCES

1. Max Beloff, *An Historian in the Twentieth Century*, London 1992, p. 13.
2. For a discussion on 'New History' see Ernst Breisach, 'The American Quest for a New History: Observations on Developments and Trends' in Henry Kozchi (ed.), *Western and Russian Historiagraphy Recent Trends*, Macmillan, 1993, pp. 25-43.
3. Geoffrey Barraclough, *History in a Changing World*, Oxford, 1955, p. 29.
4. S. Settar and Indira B. Gupta (eds.), *The Pangs of Partition*, Vol. I and II, Manohar and ICHR, 2002.
5. V. Langlois and Seignobos, *Introduction to the Study of History* (1898), cited in John Madge, *The Tools of Social Science*, Longmans, 1953, p. 80.

6. Arthur Marwick, *The Nature of History,* Macmillan, 1970, p. 146.
7. See for details, John Madge, *The Tools of Social Science, op. cit.,* pp. 85-91.
8. G.W. Allport, *The Use of the Personal Documents in Psychological Science,* New York, 1942.
9. Max Beloff, *An Historian in the Twentieth Century, op. cit.,* p. 24.
10. L. Gottschalk, *The Historian and the Historical Document,* 1945, pp. 43-4. Cited in John Madge, *The Tools of Social Science, op. cit.,* p. 88.
11. W. Robinson, *A Descriptive Account of Assam,* London, 1841.
12. B.H. Hodgson, "The Aborigines of the Eastern Frontier", *Journal of the Royal Asiatic Society of Bengal,* Vol. XVIII, Part. II (1848).
13. John Butler, *Travels and Adventures in the Province of Assam During a Residency of Fourteen Years,* London, 1855; and idem, "Rough Notes on the Angami Nagas and the Language", *Journal of Asiatic Society of Bengal,* Vol. XCIV, Part 1, 1875.
14. E.T. Dalton, *Descriptive Ethnology of Bengal,* Calcutta, 1872.
15. H.H. Risley, "The Tribes and Castes of Bengal" (Official Edition, Circulated for Criticism), 1891; and idem, *The People of India,* Calcutta, 1905.
16. W.H.G. Cole, "Ethnographical Notes: The Lushais", *Census of India 1911,* Vol. III, Assam.
17. J.H. Hutton, *The Sema Nagas,* London, 1921; and idem, "The Connection of Different Nagas and Other Tribes in Assam", *Census of India 1921,* Vol. III, Assam.
18. Mention will only be made of two significant path-finding studies, though there are several others. Firstly, P.R.T. Gurdon, *The Khasis,* London, 1906; and secondly, after a fifty-year gap, Verrier Elwin who, in the course of about ten years in the 1950s, in a number of monographs brought the colourful Arunachal culture into the limelight.
19. John Madge, *The Tools of Social Science, op. cit.,* p. 116.
20. Eric Hobsbaum, *On History,* London, 1997, p. 211.
21. Arthur Marwick, *The Nature of History, op. cit.,* p. 147.
22. Robert Perks and Alistair Thomson (ed.), *The Oral History Reader,* London, 1998.
23. James E. Young, *Writing and Rewriting the Holocaust: Narrative and the Consequences of Interpretation,* Bloomington, 1990.

27

Dr. Fraser's Crusade and Bawi-Correspondences 1909-1923: Sources of Social History of the Lushai Hills District of Assam

Ranju Bezbaruah

At the time of the introduction of British administration in the Lushai Hills District (present Indian state of Mizoram) of the Province of Assam, a system approximating slavery prevailed. The system is generally described as the *Bawi* or *Boi* system. While the system was not exactly slavery, some of its attributes were nevertheless discernable. The first Superintendent of the Lushai Hills district, Major (later Lt. Col.) J. Shakespeare (1898-1899; 1904-1905) indicated the existence of a system approximating slavery in the following account:

.... His (the Chief's) house is the poor house of the village, and all orphans and others who have no means of support are received there, and get food in return for their labour. Formerly, a person who had committed some serious crime could enter the Chief's house and thus escape vengeance. When a child has been brought up in the Chief's house, it is in *some respect a slave.* Girls are released on marriage, but the chiefs received the marriage price. Boys have to *buy their release* at the cost of a *metna.* A Chief sometimes buys a wife for a favourite slave, and sets him up in a separate house, and three years after the man will be considered free, but his children are sometimes considered slaves. The Chief's slaves are very well off, they wear the Chief's ornaments and eat the best food to be got, and do no more work than they would have to do if they were slaves.[1]

Later on, at the height of the *bawi* controversy, Shakespeare, in a book,[2] published under the orders of the Government of Eastern Bengal and Assam'[3] classified the *bawis* into different categories: (i) *Inpuichhung (Inpui* = big house, *chhung* = within) *Lalchung* or *chhungte,* those who lived in the big house or the Chief's house. They consisted of those who took refuge in the Chief's house for want of food. When a person entered the Chief's house, he or she could 'only purchase freedom by paying one *mithun* or its equivalent; (ii) *Bawi* male children, married at the Chief's expenses, lived separately and were known as *Inhrang (in* = house, *hrang* = separate). Children of such *bawis* were also *bawis,* and in some cases only the youngest son inherited his father's property; (iii) *Chemshen (chem* = dao, *shen* = red) *bois* (*bawis*) were criminals who took refuge in the Chief's house to get protection; (iv) *Tuklut* (enter by promising) *Boi* (*bawis*) were those, who deserting the war, took side of the victor promising that they and their descendants would be *bawis.* Shakespeare stated that the *Chemshen bawis* were not recognised and the *tuklut bawis* had 'also not been formally recongnised'. According to Shakespeare, the *bawis* were 'miscalled slaves by those ignorant of their real condition'; and that the custom of the *impuichhung boi* (*bawi*) 'seems well-suited to the people and provides for the maintenance of the poor, old and destitute, and it would be extremely unwise to attempt to alter it'. It is, however to be borne in mind that Shakespeare's work reflected only the official point of view.[4]

Despite the Slavery Abolition Act of 1833, the *Bawi* system was left practically untouched until 1904 when a missionary conference held at Aijal arrived at a decision to appeal to the district administration for removing the more offensive elements of the system.[5]

By 1909-10, however, new controversies arose regarding the *Bawi* (*boi*) system as a result of Dr. P. Fraser's untiring crusade against it and his campaign for its removal. Dr. Fraser, a member of the Welsh Calvinistic Mission, was convinced, soon after his arrival in the Lushai Hills, that the *Bawi* system as it was prevalent then was nothing but slavery and therefore deserved removal. With that purpose in view, he not only tried to convince other missionaries in the district, but also the Superintendent of Lushai Hills, H.W.G. Cole, that the system was really slavery. He collected a number of statements from witnesses including Christian chiefs, ransomed *bawis,* and money-receipts of the District Administration to ransomed *bawis* in order to show that the system really amounted to slavery. Failing to convince the District Administration, he also appealed to the Imperial Government of Great Britain and the Anti-Slavery and Aborigines Protection Society for remedial action. Fraser's activities were restrained by the District Administration in late 1910 and he finally left the district in 1912. But he continued to pursue the cause of abolition of the system single-handed even at the expense of his isolation from other missionaries. Dr. Fraser got his correspondences on the *Bawi* question with fellow missionaries, the District Administration, the Imperial Government, and others, printed in the form of a book entitled *Slavery on British Territory: Assam and Burma*[6] and forwarded a copy to the India Office. This occasioned lengthy correspondences among the Imperial Government, the Government of India (GOI), the Government of Assam (GOA) and the Lushai Hills district administration between 1913 and 1923. These correspondences, together with Fraser's book, constitute invaluable source-materials for reconstructing the social history of the Lushai Hills district of Assam between 1909 and 1923. This paper is an attempt to bring to light and evaluate these source-materials for reconstructing the history of the district.

Fraser's Book

Fraser's book is a collection of letters, notes, statements and money-receipts in connection with the *bawi* question. It is evident from the correspondences and statements in the book that the missionaries, including Fraser, attempted to liberate the *bawis* from paying *bawimann* (redemption price) to the Chiefs. From the documents gathered, it can be inferred that the Christian chiefs were generally less hostile towards the liberation of the *bawis* and did not insist on *bawimann*. But from these documents, it also becomes clear that a freed *bawi* who had not paid *bawimann* was not recognised as free by other Chiefs. Fraser regarded the *bawi* system as slavery on the ground that (i) the *bawis* could become free only on payment of Rs. 40/- to the Chief as *bawimann*; (ii) the custom that when a *bawi* changed his Chief, his obligation to pay *bawimann* got transferred to the new Chief, the whole or part of which had to be given to the old Chief by the new Chief in the event of the *bawi's* redemption. Fraser felt that this system was nothing but the "sale" and "purchase" of "slaves"; (iii) the fact that children of *bawis* were also *bawis*, and that under the system many people were "born slaves".

In one of his letters to H.W.G. Cole, the Superintendent of the Lushai Hills, Fraser stated that the Imperial Government of Great Britain might be approached for a grant towards compensating the chiefs for liberating the "slaves".[7] Responding to the letter, Cole maintained that the so-called "slaves" were "not slaves at all" and that the abolition of the system "would deprive the poor and indignant of the right of food and shelter in the Chief's house".[8]

In a letter to several missionaries on 17 December 1909,[9] Fraser mentioned a case of a Christian Chief freeing his "slaves in the name of Jesus Christ and King Edward". But according to Paliana's statement, Major Cole is said to have told the Chiefs "that it was right that the *bawis* should be released according to the *Maharani's* custom, but that it was not a Lushai custom, and that the other chiefs might object as regards their slaves.... There is nothing to prevent your releasing your slaves, but if any other *Lal's* slaves come to you and claim is established against them, you will have to pay the usual ransom of 40 rupees each. Once a *bawi* has been released according to Lushai custom, no claim can be made against him by another Chief." In his letter of 17 December, cited above, Fraser observed that,

> ... it is clear that these British subjects are not enjoying the right to freedom (to) which every British subject is entitled. When a person contracts to purchase the life service of another and that of his helpless child or children and descendents, such an act can only be called slavery, and surely illegal within the British Empire. I cannot help thinking that if our King and the British people knew of the system which prevails here they would not tolerate it for a day, but would gladly make any sacrifice to do away with such a system, as our forefathers did in order to abolish slavery in the West Indies... As to the present system of slavery in Lushai I cannot help feeling that the only remedy for the evils of the present system is to "proclaim deliverance to the captives" by the Government, announcing to the Chiefs, their slaves, and the people of Lushai, the right to freedom which every British subject possesses.

Fraser invited the views of other missionaries and insisted on their requesting Major Cole to do away with "the present system of bondage."

Another important document incorporated in the book was a letter from J. Herbert Lorrain, one of the early missionaries in the Lushai Hills and an authority on the Lushai language, to Fraser.[10] Lorrain stated that before Fraser had broached the subject, he had always "sought to justify" the *bawi* system. "Careful enquiry" had however convinced him that "its abolition would be hailed as a blessing." Stating that the system "should not be allowed to exist under the British flag", he agreed to join Fraser in sending a petition to Cole.

F.W. Savidge, too, admitted in his letter to Cole[11] that he had revised his opinion on the *bawi* system, which was "most iniquitous", and that it would be good if it could be abolished "in toto". He, however, regretted Fraser's campaign which had been conducted without consulting either Cole or D.E. Jones, a senior missionary. Reginald A. Lorrain also wrote to Fraser[12] expressing his "full sympathy with any endeavour to abolish this system". Fraser's book includes a draft petition to the Superintendent of the Lushai Hills[13] January 1910, which was circulated among missionaries by him for signature. It stated:

> Since no slave system is legal within the British Empire, we felt it is our duty to earnestly protest against the further continuance of the system of slavery now existing in Lushai, and to respectfully ask you to be good enough to take action with a view of (*sic*) abolishing it.

The last paragraph of the draft read:

> As the question of slavery is an Imperial question, and as the name and honour of our King Edward are concerned, copies of this petition are sent to His Majesty King Edward and to the Secretary of State for India.

This paragraph was later on omitted at the advice of Herbert Lorrain who stated that it would result in a breach between Cole and the missionaries.[14] Fraser's book also incorporates a passage covering four pages, shown to be authored by D.E. Jones, a senior missionary. Jones stated that the interests of the Chiefs in respect of "legal contracts" should be safeguarded. Many of these were payments for wives, debts or ransom in the past. He stood for a gradual, not sudden, abolition of the system. While consenting to join fellow missionaries in approaching Cole to consider the abolition of the system, he felt that it was better to have the "approval of those in authority".

Cole ordered Fraser to confine his visits to villages west of the Sonai and Mat rivers on the ground that his "action regarding the *bawi* question should cause dissatisfaction among certain chiefs".[15] Further, he also demanded an undertaking from Fraser that he would not interfere in Lushai complaints or disputes.[16]

The Directors of the Welsh Calvinistic Methodists Foreign Missions, Liverpool, also insisted that Fraser give them an undertaking not to take any action on the *bawi* question to allow sufficient time to the Superintendent for removing the obnoxious features of the system.[17] In a defying tone, Fraser replied[18] that there was real danger of a system of slavery being perpetuated for generations with the sanction of the British officials. Further, the Church of Christ was in danger of being led into upholding a system of slavery. The question of rights of British citizens was a matter of far greater concern than the Mission. "I cannot believe that the Church of which I am a member requires that its missionaries in India should surrender the liberty of conscience for which it has always firmly stood in Wales."

In another letter,[19] Fraser indicated that he would inform the Anti-Slavery Society and the British public about the system. Fraser's book, however, has not incorporated any letter from him to the Society. But from the subsequent interest of the Society on the *bawi* question it can be assumed that Fraser must have informed it.

Cole's Note

Fraser's campaign for abolition of the *Bawi* system put the District Administration into the defensive. It defended the system with palliatives that there was not much hardship for the *bawis* in the system. A note prepared by the Superintendent of Lushai Hills, Lieut. Col. H.W.G. Cole in December 1910 justified the policy of the government to "gradually lightening the burdens of the *bawis*". Cole mentioned that the original translation of the word *bawi* by Messrs. Savidge and Lorrain in their dictionary as "slave or retainer" was recognised as unfortunate even by these authors, and that "retainer" or "pauper" would have been more suitable. He, however, acknowledged that before the British annexation some categories of *bawis* were "undoubtedly slaves". Cole, citing the authority of Jones, mentioned that before the annexation, *bawis* could be acquired generally in three ways: (i) those taken by capture; (ii) those who sought sanctuary in the Chief's house on account of their misdeeds; (iii) those who because of their poverty or seeking the Chief's assistance in some dispute. While the *bawis* were free to run away from one Chief to another, before the annexation they could never become free. "As regards their general well-being, much of course depended on the Chief, but under no circumstances could freedom be gained, and all the *bawis* children themselves became *bawi.*" Cole mentioned that while there were examples of *bawis* being buried alive with his master, on the whole they were often kindly treated. They formed part of the Chief's household, and were amply provided for. Wives were found for the men, and the women were allowed to marry. Personal restraint was very rare. No steps were taken to guard *bawis* except protecting them from raiding parties. It was even impossible for any outsider to know who was a *bawi* except by interrogation.

Cole justified government's tolerance of the *Bawi* system on the ground that for many years after annexation "the work of pacification of the Lushais did not allow our officers much opportunity for modifying local customs, and... any rash interference with these would have enormously increased the difficulties of peaceful government".

Cole's *Note* also mentioned the changes introduced into the system since annexation. "From a condition of perpetual serfdom they have been raised, to all intents and purposes, to complete freedom, subject to a civil liability of Rs. 40/- for a whole family, whatever may be the number of its members, and ample time...often years...is given for the payment of this amount". For this sum of Rs. 40/-, Cole pointed out, a Chief had to support several individuals, in some cases incapacitated ones, for years. Further, the work of a *bawi* for his Chief differed in no way from what he would have done for himself. In any case, *bawis* would have had to cultivate *jhums,* make clothes, and perform domestic duties, and they were precisely what the works they had to do for a Chief, "with the *additional advantage* that there was always the Chief's tribute rise to fall bank on, the share of the flesh and *zu* that find their way to the Chief's house and, above all, the Chief's protection and good offices".

Referring to Fraser's activities, Cole maintained that "the *system as it at present exists* has been robbed of *oppressive features*". Maintaining that his view on the question was "not a *special pleading, urged* in *justification of a system* that *Government* has thought *wise to modify rather than abolish*", he quoted from a letter of F.W. Savidge, thus:

> We call *bawis* slaves in English because we want a better word in our language. The Government has made easy for any *bawi* to redeem himself if he wishes. The condition of a *bawi* is not a hard one on the whole. I can say that many in the *South Lushai Hills hardly knew that they were bawis until they heard* Dr. Fraser's interpretation of it. I believe it will be an unfortunate day for many of these *bawis* when it will be proclaimed that they have to quit the home of their Chief willy-nilly. They will be like little orphan children when that day arrives, and they will die because they cannot look after themselves.[20]

Letter of Anti-Slavery and Aborigines Protection Society, 8 July 1913

In the meantime, as a result of Fraser's untiring campaign for the abolition of the *bawi* system, the Anti-Slavery and Aborigines Protection Society and the British Parliament became interested in the matter. On 16 July 1913 , Fraser forwarding his booklet to the India Office, drew attention to the "evidence of a system of slavery on British territory" and to the acknowledgment of even the Superintendent of Lushai Hills that "it was right" that the *bawis* should be released "according to the *Maharani's* custom."[21]

In the British Parliament too the Imperial Government was put into the defensive as a result of Fraser's campaign. In reply to a question of John Jardine (12 June 1913), the government maintained that "Fraser's action produced such acute discontent as was likely to result either in the murder of this missionary, or in a general rising".

The policy of the government is to gradually modify the local customs of these uncivilised people, who but a few years ago were fierce and independent savages. The success of this policy is endangered by persons who, with the best intentions, take action likely to provoke an armed rising with its punitive consequences. Dr. Fraser can, by giving the required undertaking, obviate the restriction of his actions considered necessary by the authorities responsible for the peace of the district, whose conduct is fully approved by the Secretary of State.[22]

On 8 July 1913, the Anti-Slavery and Aborigines Protection Society (Denison House, Vauxhall Bridge Road) in its letter to the India Office questioned the policy of the gradual modification of the *bawi* system, which it described as "undefined remedy", and demanded "an assurance that official recognition of a state of slavery will be withdrawn without any delay". The Society insisted, citing B.C. Allen's *District Gazetteer* (1906) that the *Boi (bawi)* system was "nothing but slavery", on the ground that in the system in which people were compelled by poverty to sell not only their freedom for maintenance, but of their children even yet unborn. Further, *bawis* had to purchase their freedom. It was argued that in the early 19th century the British authorities condemned identical systems, and that slavery was condemned and abolished in Coorg after its annexation in 1834. The letter drew attention of the British Government to the obligation of the Governor-General of India, under existing statutes to "take into consideration the means of mitigating the state of slavery and of ameliorating the condition of slaves". Discounting the "excuses" of the Government that "the slaves were very well off", the Society observed: "Slavery, however softened, is radically bad", and "repugnant to the sense of British justice and civilisation". Countering the government's plea that the *bawis* could "purchase their freedom at any time", the Society observed that without State relief in times of famine, savings for purchase of freedom was not possible for the *bawis*. "It seems to us intolerable that in an age when the obligation of the State to relieve distress in seasons of famine is so fully acknowledged, poverty should still be allowed in a small population in a district of Assam to fill the houses and farms of so-called Chiefs with unpaid labourers". The letter referred to the decision of the Court of Directors of the East India Company on 27 July 1842 for "removal of evils incidental to slavery" and the Indian Act of 1843 which forbade magistrates and judges to enforce rights arising out of an alleged property in slaves. The Society complained that the acts of the British officials in the Lushai Hills district, the acts of the Chiefs whom the government had conferred with authority, and even the "language of apology" in answer to the Parliamentary question on 12 June 1913 "constitute a marked departure from the policy pursued 70 years ago by the late

East India Company in 1843". Appealing to the Secretary of State in Council to take immediate action, the letter concluded thus:

It submits that evils incidental to slavery today exist in the British district of the Lushai Hills, that they are tolerated by the Government of Assam, that the law is defective, that not only past policy and traditions of former governments, but also the present sentiment of this country are repugnant to the continuance of the *Boi* (*bawi*) custom, and that, even if the present freedom of the Lushai slaves must be bought as a measure of relief at the public expense, that compensation should be paid, and the recurrence of the evil prohibited by legislation without further delay. At a time when abuses incidental to slavery in Portuguese and other foreign countries are attracting attention, it seems essential that anything of the nature of the *Boi* (*bawi*) system in a district of British India should be prohibited.[23]

On 15 August 1913, on behalf of the India Office, T.W. Holderness replied to the Secretary, Anti-Slavery and Aborigines Protection Society that the Marquees of Crewe was calling a report from GOI on the "difficult and important questions therein discussed".[24] Forwarding the letter from the Secretary of State to the Governor-General in Council (15 August 1913), to the Chief Commissioner of Assam, the Deputy Secretary to GOI, Foreign Department on 3 September 1913, wanted the GOA to furnish its "views on the question raised in paragraph 2 and 4 of the despatch (i.e. the nature of the *bawi* system, particularly how far redemption in practice was possible; verification and up-dating of H.W.G. Cole's *Note on the Bawi System,* and restrictions on the liberty of Dr. Fraser.[25]

Hezlett's Letter of 25 October 1913

This occasioned several correspondences among the Assam Government officials, which threw valuable insight into the *Bawi* system and the government's policy towards its modification. In answer to the letter of the Commissioner, Surma Valley and Hills District, who by his memorandum of 5 October 1913 forwarded the letter of the Under Secretary to the Chief Commissioner of Assam, dated 25 September 1913 (with enclosures), the Superintendent of Lushai Hills, J. Hezlett wrote a lengthy letter on 25 October 1913, together with a *Note on the Bawi System* by J. Hezlett, Esq., Superintendent, Lushai Hills, in continuation of Colonel Cole's Note, dated 10th December 1910. These two documents constitute invaluable source-materials for the study of the *Bawi* system and the government's policy towards it. Hezlett's letter to the Commissioner[26] showed that the government interpreted the *Bawi* system only as a contractual obligation. Since the Civil Codes of British India were not in force in the Lushai Hills, Hezlett stated that all disputes of civil nature were settled in accordance with Lushai customs which were not contrary to "principles of equity".

The *bawi* question has been dealt with in exactly the same way, and I think any fair-minded man will admit that the system *as now interpreted* (emphasis added) contains no trace of slavery whatever. All the objectionable features which existed in the system before our occupation of the district have been removed. Rupees 40/- has been fixed as the sum to be paid to the Chief as compensation when the *contract* (emphasis added) is ended. It has been held that only the son of a *bawi* who inherits his father's property is liable to carry out the obligations which his father entered into with the Chief, and is in that respect only *bawi.* It has been provided that any *bawi* who is discontented with his lot can appeal to the courts to have his *contract* cancelled, or can simply leave the Chief whose only remedy will be to realise his dues from the *bawi* through the courts.

Hezlett's letter also mentions about his meeting with three missionaries (Revd. J.C. Evans of Shillong, Revd. D.E. Jones of Aijal and Revd. J.H. Lorrain of Lungleh) on 7 October 1913. These missionaries met to discuss the *bawi* question by order of the Directors of the Welsh Calvinistic Mission. Hezlett claimed in his letter that these missionaries agreed with him "that all the objectionable features of the custom had been removed, and that certainly it was not slavery". From this letter it can be inferred that these missionaries, who had earlier agreed with Fraser that the *bawi* system was nothing but slavery, now played safe by shifting ground.

Referring to Cole's order (7 Nov. 1910) forbidding Fraser from touring east of Sonai and Mat rivers, Fraser's writings, and the views expressed by the Anti-Slavery and Aborigines Protection Society, Hezlett maintained that the "tendency to belittle the Chiefs" could not be entertained. "Otherwise, I need hardly point out that the administration in all departments of this huge district of 7,500 square miles by the Superintendent and two Assistants would be quite impossible." He also observed that apart from Dr. Fraser's "teaching and method", his attempt to belittle the Chiefs in effect was an attempt "to break down the village administration", and hence "regrettable".

Hezlett countered the views expressed by Fraser in his *Slavery on British Territory* as "one side of the story" and clarified on two points. It becomes evident that the government intended to give new interpretations to the *Bawi* system without wholly abolishing the old custom. Disputing Fraser's view that descendants of slaves were bound to serve their chiefs "generation after generation", Hezlett observed that the *bawis* were "not slaves properly so-called" and that only the heir to the *bawi* was "liable to carry out the *bawi* contract with the Chief".

He also clarified on the rule issued by Colonel Cole regarding the apportionment of *bawimann* (redemption price) between more than one Chief in case a *bawi* changed Chiefs. Disputing Fraser's interpretation that "when slaves move from one village to another, the new Chief is at once liable to the old Chief for the ransom money" in accordance with Colonel Cole's rule, which would mean buying and selling of *bawis,* Hezlett stated that it was only a matter of apportionment of liability arising out of the *"bawi* contract". He stated:

What Colonel Cole did lay down was this. When a *Bawi* changes his Chief and then pays his *bawimann,* thus ending the *bawi* contract, it was a question which should be decided in each case how much of the *bawimann* should go to the new Chief, and how much to the old Chief. He did not hold that the new Chief had to pay to the old Chief anything at the time of the transfer. It was only when the *Bawi* ended the contract that the question of apportionment of the *bawimann* could arise. It is absolutely immaterial, so far as the *bawi* is concerned, to which Chief he pays his *bawimann.* If he pays it to either or pays it to the court, the contract is ended. The Superintendent will decide who is entitled to the money.

Hezlett's Note of 1913

Hezlett's *Note on the Bawi System*[27] is another invaluable document for study of the transformation of the *Bawi* system. The *Note* makes it clear that the government interpreted the old custom to fit into the new requirements. Hezlett observed that a great deal of misunderstanding arose from the translation of the word *bawi* as "slave" and the expression *bawimann* as "price of the slave". On the authority of Revd. Lorrain, he expressed that *bawi* rather stood for English "pauper" than "slave". Hezlett also interpreted the term *bawimann* as different from its dictionary meaning of "price of the slave" in actual practice by citing the examples of the terms, wife's *man* (lit. price), *Niman* (lit. aunts' price), *Nauman* (lit. younger sister's price) and added:

... even Dr. Fraser will, I think, admit that the expressions *"Niman"* and *"Nauman"* do not mean that the bridegroom has to buy the bride's aunt and elder sister as well as the bride herself. Similarly, it is equally wrong to hold that the expression *"bawimann"* implies that the *bawi* is a person who can be bought and sold or who has to be ransomed.

Hezlett in his *Note* also elucidated that the obligations of the *bawi* to pay *bawimann* to the Chief for his release arose only out of implied contracts.[28] The only way "a new *bawi* contract" can arise under the British rule was when a Chief received a starving family into his house, and supported them. "When any family becomes *bawis,* they do so under an implied contract the terms of which are perfectly well understood on both sides." The implicit terms of the contract could be understood from Hezlett's *Note* as being: (i) The Chief had the obligation to support the *inchhung bawis;* (ii) The *bawis* had the obligation to work for the Chief both in his house and in his fields; (iii) When a girl (*bawi*) gets married, the Chief would be entitled to get her marriage price, as he had brought her up; (iv)

When a marriage price is paid, the girl and her husband are free from any obligation to the Chief; (v) As the male *bawis* grow up, the Chief buys them wives; (vi) If the wife is a *bawi,* the couple have to work for six years more in the Chief's house; if not a *bawi* then they work for three years; (vii) After that period they set up a house of their own, cultivate their own land and live independently of the Chief; (viii) The only obligation of the *inhrang bawis* to the Chief was to give him a leg of any animal that they killed; (ix) In any case, the *bawis* would have to pay the Chief his *bawimann,* which was fixed by the Government as Rs. 40/- if he wanted to be free, and thus terminate the contract; (x) The youngest son of an *inhrang bawi,* who inherited his father's property, also inherited the liabilities of his father to pay *bawimann* to his Chief on release.

Hezlett interpreted an *inhrang bawi* having to pay his father's *bawimann* as a reasonable contractual obligation on the ground that in the Lushai Hills all debts were hereditary and sons were liable even to pay his father's unpaid marriage price. Hezlett also interpreted the obligation of young male *bawis,* for whom wives were bought by the Chief, to work for the latter for 3 or 6 years, depending on the status of the wife as only a deferred payment for the cost of marriage which was estimated at about Rs. 80/-. He also interpreted the *bawimann* of Rs. 40/- only as a compensation to the Chief arising out of the "*bawi* contract" for maintenance by the Chief.

Hezlett admitted that a certain amount of stigma came to be attached to the word *bawi* ever since Dr. Fraser's agitation, but emphasised that the *Bawi* system was "neither unjust nor inequitable, and most certainly, not slavery in any shape or form". In his *Note,* Hezlett also proposed a set of new rules for the disposal of *bawi* cases. They were:

(*a*) The use of the word *bawi* will be abolished as far as possible.

(*b*) The claims for *bawimann* will generally be treated as claims for *chawmman,* i.e. boarding and lodging, and will continue to the hereditary.

(*c*) Claims for *bawis* other than which would fall under *chawmman* will not be entertained, unless there has been consideration, and will be limited to the amount of such consideration.

(*d*) The liabilities of *bawis* are not to be increased by the above rules, i.e. the claim for *chawmman* for any one family will not exceed Rs. 40/-.

(*e*) A Chief has no right to take any *bawi* back by force who leaves his service. All he can do is to appeal to the courts and ask that his claim against the *bawi* is settled. Thus, any *bawi* discontent with his lot can simply either leave the Chief's service and allow the latter to establish his claim in the courts, or can appeal to have his contract cancelled.

(*f*) Any other question arising in connection with the *bawi* contract will be decided according to the recognised Lushai customs applicable not only to Chiefs but to all Lushais.

W.J. Reid's Letter of 2 February 1914

The rules framed and the interpretations given by Hezlett were accepted by the GOA, and GOI was informed to that effect. In reply to GOI's letter,[29] W.J. Reid, Chief Secretary to the Chief Commissioner of Assam, wrote a lengthy letter to the Secretary to GOA, Foreign and Political Department on 2 February 1914.[30] This letter constitutes yet another valuable document on the *Bawi* system and the government's policy towards it. Reid's letter informed GOI of GOA's official seal of approval to the policy pursued by the Lushai Hills officials. It showed that GOA had accepted Hezlett's interpretation of the *Bawi* system as arising from a contract between the *bawi* and the Chief. It also endorsed the rules mentioned in Hezlett's *Note* describing them as "Principles". These six principles were incorporated in paragraph 4 of the letter, which were similar to the rules mentioned in Hezlett's *Note.* Reid mentioned the objectives of these principles in the following words:

> The present Superintendent of the Lushai Hills, who had independently been considering the question, enunciated certain principles which successive Superintendents had introduced in order to effect improvements, but the full effect had not up to date been completely realised or made generally known. These principles were communicated to the members of the Missionary Conference (Aizwal, October 1913), and it was agreed that, if it was made generally known that all cases arising out of the *"Bawi"* system would be decided on these lines, there would remain in the system no features to which objection could be taken.

Clarifying one of the six principles (No. 4), Reid stated that even if the obligations of a *bawi* to the Chief in terms of money was far greater, the Chief's claim against any one family of *bawis* must not exceed Rs. 40/-. While Colonel Shakespeare argued that it would be unfair that, where a Chief had paid Rs. 80/- or more to procure a wife for one of his *bawis,* the latter should be able immediately after to claim release from all his obligations on payment of Rs. 40/- only, the Chief Commissioner of Assam, Sir Archdale Earle was of the opinion that "no exception to this rule should be made, and that we must as heretofore, work in the direction of gradually lightening the burdens of the *bawis*".

The GOA also pleaded against the sudden abolition of the system on economic and administrative considerations. Citing the example of the scarcity of food during the preceding two years, Reid's letter stated that "the *bawi* system was of the greatest assistance". While many Chiefs let their *bawis* go because they were unable to feed them, the *bawis* "went off and attached themselves to other chiefs who had more rice". The sum of Rs. five and a half lakhs which the government distributed as loans and gratuitous relief were also utilised by the chiefs to feed their *bawis* along with the other members of their household. Reid also endorsed Hezlett's view that the sudden abolition of the system would strike a fatal blow to the position of the chiefs, without whose cooperation handful of Lushai Hills officials would be in no position to carry on the administration.

The letter also referred to Dr. Fraser's book and stated that in Colonel Shakespeare's opinion several petitions from *bawis* incorporated therein were of Chemshen *bawis*, which was not recognised by the Government. It also mentions that Sir Archdale Earle had approved the action taken by the Superintendent of the Lushai Hills against Dr. Fraser for his "unnecessary interference with the customs of a semi-savage people" which "might easily lead to grave political trouble". Reid's letter also stated that Sir Archdale Earle, Chief Commissioner of Assam, decided to give immediate effect to the six principles; and that he proposed to discuss the *bawi* question with local officials and missionaries during his proposed visit to the Lushai Hills in the following winter to see working of the principles, and to ascertain if the *Bawi* system was "susceptible of further modification".

Endorsing the GOA's policy towards the *Bawi* system, GOI forwarded its views to the Secretary of State for India on 5 March 1914.[31] This letter shows that the GOI was not in favour of upsetting the *status quo* on the ground that any drastic change in the system might cause individual hardship out of proportion to the benefits secured for the *bawis.* Further, it might also create a general condition of economic chaos. In the view of the GOI, pending personal inquiry into the matter by the Chief Commissioner, it was sufficient for the time being to adhere to "the working arrangement" (ie the principles mentioned in Reid's letter). Endorsing GOA's policy, it stated that principles enunciated in paragraph 4 of Reid's letter "if strictly followed, should suffice gradually to break down and weaken the *Bawi* system". The GOI also endorsed GOA's decision not to lift restrictions on Fraser without his giving the required undertaking.

Letter from the Secretary of State to the Governor-General, 26 June 1914 and Enclosures

In the wake of the GOI's endorsement of GOA's policy of implementing the principles mentioned in Reid's letter, several correspondences were exchanged between the India Office on the one hand, and Dr. Fraser and the Anti-Slavery and Aborigines Protection Society on the other. These documents were incorporated as enclosures to the letter from the Secretary of State for India to the Governor-General in Council, dated 26 June 1914[32]. This letter, together with seven enclosures, were forwarded by the GOI to GOA inviting its remarks.[33] These correspondences throw valuable light on the government's policy towards the *Bawi* system.

In one of his letters to the India Office (22 April 1914), Fraser and others, commenting on the "Working Arrangement" observed that a public proclamation should be made denying to the chiefs the right to keep "slaves", and that the right of the Chiefs to get compensation in the form of *bawimann* or *chawmman* should be done away with. Fraser insisted that if necessary, the chiefs should be compensated from public funds. According to his estimate, Rs. 1,333/- would suffice to compensate for 2,500 "slaves". He also maintained that the approval by the India Office of the "Working Arrangement" would amount to "direct sanctioning and maintaining of a slave system on British territory". He also appealed for an "impartial public inquiry" on the *bawi* question.

The Anti-Slavery and Aborigines Protection Society, in its letter to the India Office (18 May 1914), suggested the need for a definite time-frame for abolition of the *Bawi* system. It insisted that "hereditary debt" arising out of the *Bawi* system should be immediately done away with. The Society also queried as to the steps taken to make the decision of the government that freed *bawis* through court's intervention to treat them like ordinary judgment-debtors for their unpaid *bawi*-debt "generally known". It also proposed that a census of the *bawis* should be undertaken.

This Anti-Slavery letter seems to have exerted enormous impact in the thinking of the Assam Administration. In reply to GOI's letter forwarding the Secretary of State's despatch, B.C. Allen wrote that, "a report would be submitted after the Chief Commissioner's visit to the Lushai Hills and that time was inopportune for anything but the most cautious action", lest it should lead to "internal trouble".[34] Allen, indicating the lines on which the Chief Commissioner would review the *bawi* question during his visit to the Lushai Hills, wrote to the Commissioner, Surma Valley and Hill Districts[35] that: (a) a preliminary census without entailing "risk of trouble" should be undertaken indicating the number of males, females and children; (b) in line with the suggestion of the Anti-Slavery Society, it should be examined how the redemption price could be reduced within a time-frame after which no *bawi* debt would be recognised; (c) further proposals regarding hereditary debts (Rs. 40/- payable on release) might be examined, even while retaining the basic principle; (d) it should be ascertained whether the right of appeal by the *bawis* to courts for declaration of their freedom, was made "generally known", as insisted by the Anti-Slavery Society.

Another important source-material on the *bawi* question was the letter from Commissioner, Surma Valley to the GOA.[36] The letter mentions about the proposed "quiet inquiries" and not a "formal census" of the *bawis* by the gazetted officers only without calling up the *bawis* and "definitely" without asking "these people whether or not they wish to be released from their engagements. The letter also elucidated that proposed abolition of hereditary debts, according to Hezlett's analysis, would upset the "whole Lushai economic system" which was "based on the principle that all debts are hereditary." As regards publicity, the letter mentioned that orders were published in the semi-official Lushai monthly *Chan Chin Bu,* which was read out at the village assembly. Regarding the results of the new principles, the letter stated that according to Hezlett, "far from there being a general rush of *bois* to obtain an order from the courts after the modifications were published, the number of such cases has been extremely small". The Commissioner felt that "the system will gradually come to a natural end" and that no change in the system ought to be introduced at last till the European War was over.

Allen's Letter of 23 June 1915

Yet another very important document on the *bawi* question was B.C. Allen's letter to the GOI on 23 June 1915.[37] The letter was of the nature of a report on Sir Archdale Earle's visit to the Lushai Hills towards the end of the winter of 1915. It mentions that the Chief Commissioner held a conference at Aijal, at which five missionaries of the Welsh Calvinistic Mission and the English Baptist Mission, B.C. Allen, Mr. Hezlett, and Mr. Needham attended. The Chief Commissioner discussed with them, among others, the feasibility of bringing the *Bawi* system to an end. A consensus was reached that the principles laid down in paragraph 4 of Reid's letter to the GOI on 2 February 1914, which were enunciated with the object of putting into a clear light the modifications in the *Bawi* system introduced by successive Superintendents, might be amplified so as to make it clear (1) that, though the law permits imprisonment for non-liquidation of debt in those cases only in which the Superintendent of the Lushai Hills is satisfied that fraudulent disposal or concealment of property has taken place, in practice resort to imprisonment had not been taken; (2) that debts carry no interest; (3) that when it is ascertained that a *bawi* had rendered service to a Chief in excess of benefits received by him, the liability can be reduced to any sum less than Rs. 40/- or even to zero; (4) that debtors are treated with justice and consideration and that ample time is given to satisfy decrees passed against *ex-bawis;* and (5) that whether the decree is satisfactory or not, the Chief has no further claim on the judgment-debtor as a *bawi.*

The Chief Commissioner directed that these clarifications should be immediately adopted.

Allen's letter had also mentioned that there was no law of limitation according to Lushai custom. However, a limit of 10 years had been followed since the British occupation. Allen stated: "even that period is rather long, and it has been decided to fix 3 years from the date on which a *boi* (*bawi*) leaves a Chief's service but neglects to appeal to the courts to record an order that he is no longer a *boi* (*bawi*) as the period within which the Chief must, if he so wishes, put in a claim for the redemption price."

Allen's observation on the impact of missionary teaching on the *bawis* was also a revealing one: "He (the Chief Commissioner) is glad to find that one of the results of the teaching of the missionaries has been to awaken the people generally to their rights. Where missionary influence has not penetrated, everything tends to show that there is no feeling on the subject (ie *bawi*). On the contrary, the recent informal census has disclosed remarkable instances. In several cases the Superintendent reports that on his asking *bawis* if they wanted to be free or not, he was answered in the negative and in tones which implied that they were almost indignant at being asked such a question."

Allen's letter also throws light on the informal *bawi* census conducted shortly before the Chief Commissioner's visit. The estimated number of *bawis* was 1,369 out of the total population of 91,204 in the district.

Regarding the abolition of the *Bawi* system, several alternatives were examined. The Chief Commissioner was of the opinion that as a result of reforms, the "element of slavery" in the *Bawi* system "has been almost entirely eliminated". Two alternatives were examined for abolishing "what remains of the system". One alternative was that the government should compensate the Chiefs for releasing the *bawis.* It was estimated that out of the total 1369 *bawis,* 550 were in-dwellers, and 819 out-dwellers. The cost of liberating the 330 families to which these 550 in-dwelling *bawis* belonged to, was estimated at Rs. 13,200 (@ Rs. 40 per family), while the cost of releasing the 819 out-dwelling *bawis* was estimated at Rs. 32760). But, because of the conditions arising from the war and non-availability of fund, the expenses of Rs. 45,960 for releasing the *Bawis* was ruled out. The second alternative, which the Chief Commissioner preferred, was to let it be known that government would pay the required sum if any *bawi* asked for release. If the second alternative proved effective, it might be possible to proceed to the first alternative at a later stage.

Allen in his letter to the Commissioner, Surma Valley and Hill Districts,[38] instructed the local authorities to implement the proposed modification and to complete the informal census of the *bawis*. On 23 July 1915, the GOI informed the Secretary of State for India that consideration of abolishing the *Bawi* system was postponed until the war was over.[39]

The Secretary of State for India in his letter to the GOI[40] approved the reforms introduced into the *Bawi* system as being of "reasonable nature" and as "a marked advance towards entire abolition of this system." He, however, emphasised that the consideration of the Chief Commissioner's proposals should be taken up "as soon as return to normal conditions admits of it." The Secretary of State concluded with a general remark on "the survival of customs approximating to slavery" that "the principles of British Government cannot countenance the existence of slavery within its borders." It should be ensured that "steps taken to terminate all practices that in varying degrees approximate slavery do not produce consequences which may possibly be more immediately calamitous."

Post-War Recrudescence of the Bawi Question

In the wake of the First World War, on 25 August 1921, the despatch from the Secretary of State for India to the Governor-General[41] re-opened the *bawi* issue which was kept in abeyance by the GOI's despatch of 23 July 1915. The Secretary of State in his letter queried whether any progress had been made regarding the gradual abolition of the *bawi* custom. This occasioned another series of *bawi* correspondences.

GOA's answer to the above queries of the Secretary of State, forwarded to it on 30 September 1921, was sent to the GOI on 27 October 1921 by A.W. Botham.[42] The letter mentioned that in June 1921, the GOA issued instructions for the completion of the census of *bawis* so as to enable the Chief Commissioner to consider feasibility of the abolition of the custom.

After the completion of the informal census of *bawis,* the Commissioner, Surma Valley and Hill Districts had reported on the results of the census to GOA on 1 February 1923.[43] It also forwarded two enclosures.[44] Both the Confidential Note and the Commissioner's letter, after calculating only heads of the families arrived at the conclusion that in actual practice there would be 1,626 cases of actual redemption-payment for Rs. 65,040 only. Webster's statement was the following:

Statement Showing the Result of Bawi Census

Circle	No. of village	*In-dwelling bawis*				*Out-dwelling bawis*		
		No. of families	*No. of bawis*	*No. of males between 16 and 60*	*Females & children*	*No. of houses*	*Heads of families or youngest sons*	*No. of heads of families or youngest sons between ages 16 and 60*
1	2	3	4	5	6	7	8	9
				Aijal Subdivision				
I	7	10	10	6	4	83	83	82
II	5	4	5	—	5	16	16	16
III	14	77	78	18	60	306	319	289
IV	10	9	40	12	28	47	47	47
V	21	20	50	12	38	59	59	57
VI	11	31	31	5	26	105	105	103
VII	13	40	70	17	53	104	104	101
VIII	13	17	2	4	22	58	58	55
IX	10	8	8	5	3	40	40	38
X	7	20	20	11	9	43	43	40
XI	16	14	24	5	19	80	80	75
Total	127	250	362	95	267	911	954	903
				Lungleh Subdivision				
XII	17	20	30	10	20	50	50	45
XIII	13	7	7	2	5	33	33	30
XIV	8	14	16	3	13	14	14	14
XV	21	24	60	8	52	68	68	(a)
XVI	4	1	1	1	—	4	4	1
Total	63	66	114	21	90	169	169	158
District Total	190	316	476	119	357	1,110	1,123	1,061

(a) No. of *Bawi* is	Males between 16 to 60 years	78
	Females	77
	Children	97
	Total *Bawi*	252

J.E. Webster, Commissioner, Surma Valley and Hill District

In his letter to the GOI, A.W. Botham[45] reported on the results of the Census as reflected in W.L. Scott's *Note*, and Webster's *Statement*, and requested the GOI for financing the estimated cost of Rs. 65,00 for redemption of the *bawis* if "immediate execution was desired".

Signs of Modification Under the Influence of Christianity

In response to GOA's request for finance,[46] GOI on 22 March queried (1) whether GOA would be prepared to execute the reforms "in the absence of financial difficulty", (2) whether the *Bawi* system had shown any signs of modification or gradual disappearance under the civilising influence of Christianity, and (3) whether missionary opinion on the subject had undergone any change.

In response to GOI's queries, GOA reported[47] on the *bawis* on the basis of information received from the Superintendent of Lushai Hills,[48] the Commissioner of Surma Valley and Hill Division,[49] and a letter from Welsh Calvinistic Mission[50] that (1) The character of the *Bawi* system had materially changed by the acceptance of principles enunciated in para 4 of Reid's letter of 2 February 1914, and para 3 of Allen's letter of 23 June 1915, and in particular by liberty given to any man to convert his status as a *bawi* into a civil liability of by paying a sum of Rs. 40; (2) the system had also been further progressively modified "under the civilising influence of Christianity", which had "spread with great rapidity" in the Lushai Hills during the preceding ten years. By 1923, about 30 per cent of the population and 52 Chiefs were Christians. The tendency of the Christian Chiefs was either to release the *bawis* altogether or treat them on an entirely different footing; (3) the GOA, therefore, felt no necessity to put into effect further measures for abolition of the system apart from allowing the process of modification to continue until all objectionable features in the system had disappeared; (4) missionary opinion as a whole had not generally demanded drastic action for the out and out abolition of the *Bawi* system.

In this background, on 14 June 1923, the GOI in its despatch to London,[51] endorsing GOA's proposal, sought approval of the Secretary of State for India. The despatch stated:

> The Government of India agree with the views expressed by the Assam Government that it would be wiser to allow the process of modification which the system is now undergoing to continue until all objectionable features in it have disappeared, than to risk the serious disorganisation which might result from an attempt to uproot the system entirely. With the approval of His Majesty's Secretary of State for India, therefore, they do not propose to move further in this matter.

On 7 August 1923, the India Office through its despatch[52] stated that the Secretary of State for India in Council concurred in the view of the GOI that "it would be more advisable to allow the *Bawi* system to continue subject to the present process of modification than attempt to uproot it abruptly".

At least till 1926, while efforts to eradicate traces of slavery persisted, it was not fully removed. In this context, W.H. Vincent, and Indian representative to the Slavery Convention of the League of Nations on 25 September 1926, excluded operation of the Convention in several tracts in Assam including "a small tract in the south of the Lushai Hills district".[53]

The above materials which throw flood of light on the attitude of the British Government, GOI, GOA, and the Lushai Hills administration, the missionaries, not the least the *Bawi* system itself, have not been published till date. Neither have they been referred to by any scholar. Fraser's book deserves to be re-printed and the correspondences mentioned above need publication so as to enable scholars to go in for an in-depth study on an important segment of the social history of the Lushais (Mizos).

NOTES AND REFERENCES

1. B.C. Allen, *Assam District Gazetteers,* Vol. X, *The Khasi and Jaintia Hills, The Garo Hills and the Lushai Hills,* Part III, Lushai Hills District, 1906, pp. 41-42.
2. J. Shakespeare, *The Lushai Kuki Clans,* London, 1912, also, Aizawl (reprint 1988); also excerpted in *Annexure A* , W.J. Reid, Secy. to GOI, For. & Pol. Dept. No. 559 p. 2, Feb. 1914.
3. As mentioned in Reid, to Secy., *ibid.*
4. *Ibid.,* Annexure -A; Shakespeare, pp. 45-49.
5. Sangkima, "Bawi and its Abolition in Mizoram", *Proceedings of North East India History Association,* Imphal Session, p. 105.
6. P. Fraser, *Slavery on British Territory : Assam and Burma,* Carnarvon, 1913.
7. P. Fraser to Major Cole, 22 Feb. 1909.
8. H.W.G. Cole to Fraser, 23 Feb. 1909.
9. Fraser to "Brother in the Master's Service", December 1909. The same letter was sent to several missionaries. The date, 17 December, can be inferred from other correspondences.
10. J. Herbert Lorrain to Fraser, 17 January 1910.
11. Rev. F.W. Savidge to Superintendent, 26 January 1910.
12. Reginald A. Lorrain to Fraser, 27 January 1910.
13. Dated January 1910.
14. Lorrain to Fraser, 31 January 1910.

15. Order dated 7 November 1910.
16. Draft submitted by Major Cole, 16 December 1910.
17. R.J. Williams to Fraser, 16 March 1911.
18. Fraser to R.J. Williams, 27 April 1911.
19. Fraser to R.J. Williams, 26 May 1913.
20. Lieut. Col. Cole's *Note on the Bawi System,* forwarded with letter No. 265 IT, 30 Dec. 1910, from Commr. Surma Valley and Hill Districts to Ch. Commr. Assam; Also appended *Annexure B* in W.J. Reid, Secy. to GOI, For. & Pol. Dept, No 559, p. 2, Feb. 1914. The date of Cole's *Note* is mentioned as 10 Dec. in as J. Hezlett, Suptd. Lushai Hills to Commr. Surma Valley and Hill Districts, No. 970 G, dt. 25 Oct. 1913.
21. Encl. 4. Secy. of State for India to the Governor-General of India in Council, No. 217 Public, 15 August 1913. Forwarded to Deputy Secy. to GOI, Foreign Dept., to Ch. Commr., Assam, No. 2092 E.B. , 3 Sept. 1913.
22. *Ibid.,* Enclosure No. 3.
23. Enclosure No. l, Secy. of State for India to Governor-General of India in Council, No.217 Public, 15 August 1913, forwarded by Deputy Secretary to GOI, For. Dept, to Ch. Commr., Assam, No. 2092 E.B., 3 Sept. 1913.
24. Enclosure No. 2. *ibid.*
25. Deputy Secy. to GOI, For.Dept., to Ch. Commr. Assam, No.2092 E.B., 3 Sept. 1913. Forwarded by G.E. Soames, Under Secy. to Ch. Commr., Assam, Pol. Dept. to Commr., Surma Valley and Hill Districts, No. 5202 P, 23 Sept. 1913.
26. Hezlett to Commr. Surma Valley and Hills Districts, No. 970 G., 25 Oct. 1913. With Memo. No. 1646 T, pp. 5-14. Nov. 1913 from the Commr., Surma Valley and Hill District.
27. *Note on the Bawi System* by J. Hezlett, Esq., Superintendent, Lushai Hills, in continuation of Colonel Cole's *Note,* dated the 10th December 1910, enclosed with *ibid.*
28. Among the different types of *bawis* the government recognised only the *inchhung bawis* and the *inhrang bawis.*
29. Dy. Secy. to GOI, For. Dept, to C.C., Assam, No. 2092 E.B., 3 Sept. 1913.
30. W.J. Reid to Secy., to GOA, For. and Pol. Dept. No. 559P, 2 February 1914.
31. Governor-General of India, No.21 External, 5 March 1914, Copy forwarded by Memo., Deputy Secy. GOI, For. & Pol. Dept, No. 1358 D., 14 March 1914.
32. Secy. of State for India, to the Governor-General in Council, No. 98, Public, 26 June 1914.
33. A.H. Grant to C.C. Assam, No.728 E.B, 20 July 1914.
34. B.C. Allen to Secy. GOI, For & Pol. Dept, No. 5954 P. 24, Oct. 1914.
35. B.C. Allen to Commr. Surma Valley and Hill Districts, No. 5955 P. 24 October 1914.
36. W.J. Reid, C.C. Assam, No. 8242, 23 November 1914.

37. B.C. Allen, to Secy. GOI, For. and Pol. Dept, No. 5028 P. 23 June 1915.
38. B.C. Allen, to Commr. Surma Valley and Hill Districts, No. 5115 P. 30 June 1915.
39. Viceroy and Governor-General, to Secy. of State for India, 23 July 1915, No. 63. Forwarded to C. C. Assam, by Memo, Deputy Secy. GOI, For. and Pol. Dept. , No. 358 E.B, 23 July 1915.
40. Secy. of State for India, to Governor-General of India in Council, No. 186 Public, 29 October 1915, forwarded by Deputy Secy. GOI, For. and Pol. to C.C. Assam, No. 233 D, 24 November 1915.
41. Secretary of State for India, to Governor-General of India in Council, No. 130 Public, 25 August 1912, forwarded with F.H. Humphry (Deputy Secy., GOI, For.& Pol. Dept.) to Ch. Secy. GOA, No. 1256 E.B, 30 September 1921.
42. A.W. Botham, Ch. Secy. to GOA, to Secy, to GOI, For. & Pol. Dept, No. 6390 A.P, 27 October 1921.
43. J.E. Webster, to Secy. to GOA, No. 135, P. 1 February 1923.
44. Confidential No. 1850C, 10 January 1923 encl. to *ibid.* and a statement showing the result of Bawi Census, J.E. Webster, Commissioner, Surma Valley and Hill Division, encl. to Webster to Secy., No. 135, P. 1 Feb. 1923.
45. A.W. Botham, to Secy. to GOI, For. & Pol. Dept, 26 February 1923.
46. Deputy Secy. to GOI, For. & Pol. Dept, to Ch. Secy. to GOA, No. 337-522, Ext, 22 March 1923.
47. A.W. Botham, to Secy. to GOI, For. & Pol. Dept, No. 1142-2669 A.P., 28 May 1923.
48. S.N. Mackenzie, to Commr. Surma Valley and Hill Division, No. 245 G, 5 May 1923.
49. J. Hezlett, Off. Commr, Surma Valley and Hill Division, to Ch. Secy. to GOA, No. 483 P. 12 May 1923.
50. F.J. Sandy, Secy., Welsh Calvinistic Mission to Suptd., Lushai Hills, 4 May 1923. Encl. to *ibid*.
51. Secy. to GOI, For. & Pol. Dept, to Under-Secy. of State for India, No. 739-522 X, 14 June 1923. Forwarded to GOA, by Memo, Deputy Secy., GOI, For. & Pol. Dept, No. 522X, 30 August 1923.
52. Secy, Judicial and Public Dept, India Office, to Secy, to GOI, For. Dept, No. J. and P. 3818-23, 7 August 1923. Forwarded by Memo, Under Secy. to GOA, Appointment and Pol. Dept, No.Pol 1717-4016 A.P., 11 Sept 1923.
53. Slavery Convention signed at Geneva on 25 September 1926. Copy forwarded by Deputy Secy. to GOI, For. & Pol. Dept., to Ch. Secy. to GOA (and others), No. 264 [3], P. 25 August 1927.

28

An Analysis of American Baptist Missionary Sources for History Writing in North-East India

Sheila Bora

North-East India with a rich historical legacy, has been overlooked in general historical studies of the country. The oft-repeated explanation for this is that there is dearth of source-materials on this region with an all-India bearing. This argument no doubt, holds good to a certain extent because it was only after the 13th century that the hill areas of Manipur and parts of Meghalaya began to come within the reach of historiography. In the pre-independence period, most of the hill areas in the frontier region had been kept aloof from the outside world. Since the people in these areas were not literate, we are dependent only on British writers and anthropologists for first-hand information on them. Prior to extension of British rule in India, some of the earliest writings on the hill-tribes of North-East India are to be found in different volumes of the *Journal of the Asiatic Society*. However, it was only after the gradual extension of British rule in North-East India and their contact with the hill-tribes, that an era of historical writing by British civil and military officers was inaugurated. Captain Welsh, deputed to Assam in 1792 at the head of a detachment of troops, furnished a mass of information on the political, administrative and commercial interests of Assam. He was accompanied by John Peter Wade who not only compiled a valuable account of Assam, but also supplemented it with *A Geographical Sketch of Assam*. Thereafter followed a host of valuable works like Dr. Francis Hamilton's *Account of Assam*, John M. Cosh's *Topography of Assam*, W. Robinson's *A Descriptive Account of Assam*, W.W. Hunter's *Statistical Account of Assam*, David Scott's *An Account of Assam*, John Butler's *A Sketch of Assam with some Account of the Hill Tribes* and Edward Gait's *History of Assam*. A. Hamilton's *In Abor Jungles of North East India* is a sensational history of the gruesome and treacherous murder of the Assistant Political Officer and the Medical Officer in 1911 at Sadiya by the Abors. Haimendorf's series on *The Naked Nagas* is an anthropological work on the Konyak and other Naga tribes.

There is no doubt that the writings of British anthropologists gave a solid beginning to the historians of the North-East. However, it must be borne in mind that many of the administrator' anthropologists who served and wrote on the North-Eastern hills in the early modern period belonged to the 19th and early 20th century school. One such example is J.H. Hutton who has written volumes on the various Naga tribes. Very often they based their accounts on the information gathered from local informers on whom they were heavily dependent and who might not always have been representative of the entire community.

Under such circumstances a historian of this region is compelled to be unconventional in his methodology. It is here that the missionaries provide an important source for the historical study of the North-East in the modern period. The early heads of Baptist Missions were generally educated men and were trained for accurate observation and scholarly writing. However, it will do well to remember that preoccupied as they were with ideas of ameliorating what they considered to be the degraded conditions of the non-Christian population, their accounts were full of stories of oppression of the ethnic religions as compared to Christianity. This attitude of a superior civilisation was manifest in their writings, projecting Western culture as an agency of progress. Barring this, the usefulness of these records cannot be underestimated. They illustrate better than any other sources, the lives and surroundings of the people with whom they came into contact in the process of propagating their faith. We do not have in the accounts of these missionaries the chronicles of kings and warriors, their wars or conquests, or their successes and failures. On the contrary, they provide an account of the customs and prejudices and the hopes and aspirations of the people. Herein lies the importance of these accounts. In addition to these valuable reports, it will do well to remember that the missionaries have contributed greatly in unearthing old manuscripts and coins.

The sources available from the American Baptist Missionaries may be grouped under five broad categories:

(*a*) Manuscripts preserved and found in the possession of the missionaries;
(*b*) Coins preserved and found in the possession of missionaries;
(*c*) Ethnological works;
(*d*) Reports and correspondences of the missionaries, both official and private;
(*e*) Journals and periodicals published by missionaries.

Manuscripts Preserved and Found in the Possession of the Missionaries

The early American Baptist Missionaries in Assam had assiduously built up a rich collection of old manuscripts, primarily in Assamese and Sanskrit. Nathan Brown was reported to have collected up to forty manuscripts between 1840 and 1850.[1] S.K. Bhuyan, however, makes a more careful observation of this claim when he states that "the first attempt to collect Assamese manuscripts was made by Rev. Nathan Brown and other early workers of the American Baptist Mission stationed at Sibsagar. This was approximately between the years 1840 and 1850."[2] Though the exact number of manuscripts in this early collection is not known, the Mission published at least the *Chutia Rajar Bangshawali, Deodhai Asam Buranji, Kamrupar Asam Buranji, Kamrupar Buranji and Lakshmi Singhar Buranji* in their Assamese periodical, the *Orunodoi.*[3] Tamuli Phukan's *Asam Buranji* was brought out as a separate publication.

On May 13, 1925, Prof. S.K. Bhuyan visited the American Baptist Mission at Guwahati to consult certain volumes of the *Orunodoi* in the mission library. Mr. Stephens of the mission showed him a box of old Assamese *puthis* which were lying for years in the storeroom of the mission house, without anybody knowing what was inside. As Mr. Stephens removed the nails of the box in which these *puthis* were stored, it seemed to Dr. Bhuyan to be like "the opening of King Tut's tomb".[4] As the lid was removed, the *puthis*, dust-laden and scattered, emerged and to his delight Dr. Bhuyan discovered two significant manuscripts, *Manu Govinda* and *Biru Karji.* He then obtained permission from the Secretary of the American Baptist Mission to inspect and examine the *puthis.* Aided by Jagneswar Sarma and Madhab Chandra Barua, Dr. Bhuyan transcribed the valuable collection of Buranjis, religious and lyrical poems and treaties on astrology, working relentlessly for eighteen days. The mission manuscripts were thereafter exhibited at the anniversary of the *Kamrupa Anusandhana Samiti* in October of the same year. Of the fourteen *puthis* found, five were handed over by Miss Burnham in 1931 and the remaining nine in 1955, to the Department of Historical and Antiquarian Studies of the Government of Assam.[5]

Coins Preserved and Found in the Possession of Missionaries

A large number of coins, mostly belonging to the Ahom monarchs and the Muslim rulers, were also found in the possession of the missionaries. Most of these coins were reproduced in the *Orunodoi* with notes and observations.

Ethnological Works

Volumes of ethnological works have been published by missionaries both on the plains and hills of the North-Eastern region. William Carey's *A Garo Jungle Book* is a beautifully illustrated description of the people of the Garo Hills. Among the accounts of the various tribes, mention may be made of Herbert Anderson's *Among the Lushais,* Norola Rivenburg's *The Star of the Naga Hills,* Major A. Playfair's *The Garos,* Ruth Grimes Ewing's *Our life with the Garos of Assam,* Harriette Bronson Gunn's *In afar country: A Story of Christian Heroism and Achievement,* Grace R. Lewis' *The Lushai Hill: The Story of the Lushai Pioneer Mission,* Alva C. Bower's *Under Head Hunter's Eyes,* Eliza Whitney Brown's *The Whole World Kin: A Pioneer Experience Amongst Remote Tribes and other Labours of Nathan Brown* and Mary Mead Clark's *A Corner in India* and *The Ao-Naga Grammar with Illustrations, Phrases and Vocabulary.* Similar missionary writings on the plains of Assam also make interesting reading and provide valuable source materials. Special mention may be made of Elizath Vickland's book on *Women of Assam.* This was a book through which Vickland intended to introduce the women of Assam to her American friends and therefore tried to provide details of their religious faith, its role in their lives and the meaning of their customs. She writes that "both Hindu and Muslim women have been terribly handicapped, brazenly maligned, shamefully betrayed, sadly cheated."[6] Such contemporary accounts on women to Assam are rare and valuable. Mrs. P.H. Moore, a missionary working in Assam (Nowgong), also has to her credit four volumes, *Twenty years in Assam, Further Leaves From Assam, Autumn Leaves from Assam* and *Stray Leaves from Assam,* mainly based on her experience in Nowgong from 1879.

Reports and Correspondences of the Missionaries, both Official and Private

It was obligatory for mission-heads to send regular reports to their Home Board in America on the successes and failures of their missionary activities. Hence, the reports sent by the Baptist Missionaries in Assam contained both, details about their proposed operational programmes, as well as critical analyses of their successes and failures in this region. Many such reports are incorporated in the volumes of the Baptist Missionary Magazines available for the years 1834 to 1886 (Volume XIV-LXVI). These reports, together with the minutes, resolutions and reports of the annual Baptist Missionary Conference, form an invaluable source for the study of the modern history of Assam. In addition to the official reports mentioned above, the personal correspondences of the missionaries, especially those of the missionary wives, are useful documents for either confirming or contradicting the official reports. Most of the correspondences in this category is in the form of personal letters to friends and relatives at home, narrating one's experiences in a new and distant country. Hence, these letters depict the true opinions and personal observations of the writers. To cite a case in example, official missionary reports claim of having "successfully married off girls" in their boarding schools, have been referred to in private correspondence as cases of elopement.[7]

While reporting various obstacles at work, missionary reports described the existing society of the time. The position of women is an oft-repeated subject in such reports. Taking about the Miris, Mr. Whiting reported that it was customary among all Miris to get another woman in exchange for the one given in marriage. Thus a *Gam,* while talking a wife for himself or for his son, pledges his sister or daughter in return for the woman received, and if he has none to pledge, the first daughter born is promised as a compensation for her mother.[8] Whiting's observation on the systems was that, "... the Miris are polygamists. The more wives, the more slaves. And this explains the origin of the custom of exchanging a woman for a woman."[9]

Bronson, on the other hand, compared the status of Naga women as compared to that of Assamese women and noted that:

> Considerable respect appears to be paid to the female sex. In this particular case there is a striking contrast between the Nagas and the Assamese. The Assamese women are the most idle, worthless set of beings I ever saw. On the contrary, the Naga women are proverbial for their industrious and laborious habits. This remarkable difference in favour of the Naga women, is doubtless to be imputed to the anarchical state of the country, or rather to the number of independent chiefs, who formerly, for the slightest offence, were disposed to wage war, and the most of all wars, that which is covert and unsuspected. This made it necessary for the men to be always ready for an assault, and hence the custom that the women should cultivate the fields—the men prepare for the fight in battle (sic).[10]

Ella Marie Holmes, a missionary woman writing to her friend in the States, narrated a conversation which she had with Mr. Gopinath Bordoloi, the then Chief Minister of Assam. Gopinath Bordoloi, while delivering a public speech at Guwahati, had compared Japan's progress with that of India during the latter-half of the 19th century and had attributed all of India's failure to the British Government's policies. Ella Marie Holmes who had visited Japan four times and who had also spent nearly twenty years in India was well aware of the situation in both the countries in reference. Hence she felt impelled to call Mr. Bordoloi's attention to the baby in her arms and remark:

I found this baby in a zenana yesterday. It had been slowly starving for four months right here in Gauhati, where there are scores of Indian gentlemen very well able to supply milk for hungry children, but none of you are doing anything so mercifully humanitarian. You gentlemen of means are generally Brahmins and high caste co-religionists. Your only charity in this city of 20,000 people is hospital, not for the sick of humanity, but for sick cattle; a refuge, not for widows and orphans and the homeless sons and daughters of men, but hungry and wandering cows. You spend 20,000 rupees annually caring for these cows many of which should be mercifully put out of their misery. You give them an annual feast of five or six pounds of candy, but you do not give a half pint of milk a day for starving babies.[11]

While launching a crusade against both Hinduism and Animism, the Baptist Missionaries reported extensively on the state of religion prevalent both in the hills and plains of Assam. Reference to the celebration of *Durga Puja, Rash Jatra* or an occasional *Nam* or *Sabah* was common. The missionary journals refer to the principal *sattras* in Assam – *Auniati, Dakhinpat, Kamalabari* and *Moamara.* Talking about the oppressions by the priesthood in Assam, missionary magazines mention that,

Although the priests are indicted for collecting more than the government rates of land, there is little doubt but that twice that amount is exacted; indeed the ryots are mere slaves, and obliged to be at the call of the chief priest for any service he thinks proper to demand. So great is the oppression of the priests, that nearly two-thirds of their grants are perfectly waste. It would be well if their tyranny was confined to exacting the utmost produce of the land the ryots can give; but this is not all—they demand from the ryots on a variety of pleas, to defray present necessities—a general tax, a free gift or paddy, oil rice, etc, a fee on marriage-present on appointing their servants to conduct the fiscal duties of the sacred land. The chief priest likewise exercises the power of ex-communication for civil offences, and until the offenders pay a heavy fine to receive absolution, they are excluded from society and are perfect outcastes, no one daring to associate or eat, or to drink with them, or to lend them any assistance whatever.[12]

Simultaneously the missionaries predicted the process of transition in society and even in the forties Rev. Barker noted that the priests were losing their prosperity and their days appeared to be numbered. The policy adopted by the British Government resulted not only in the cancellation of a number of rent-free grants but in the emancipation of the *paiks* on whose services the priests were heavily dependent. Thus Rev. Barker felt that there was a gradual transfer of wealth from the hands of the priests into the hands of the cultivators and traders, consequently bringing about a decline in the position of the priestly classes. Barker's views were supported by Jenkins, who also believed that the minor religious heads were losing their respect and influence in society. However, Jenkins believed that this was mainly because of internal feuds and litigations in the civil courts. In a similar tone, Miles Bronson says that two-thirds of the cases pending in the Nowgong court were directly or indirectly connected with the *Gossains.*[13]

The literary activities of the American Baptist Missionaries, though primarily evangelistic, must be viewed in the context of the prevalent political scenario. It was a time when the government was committed to the policy of replacing Assamese with Bengali in the schools and courts of Assam. Initially, the missionaries accepted the British Government's explanation regarding the use of Bengali, but by 1840s they were no longer prepared to accept the validity of the government's arguments. Despite government instructions to use only Bengali in schools, they continued the use of Assamese as the principal means of instruction in the missionary schools. Neither did they hesitate to enter into public debate with the government on this issue. The first attack on the government's language policy was made by Miles Bronson in 1854 in the form of a petition to the Lt. Governor of Bengal. However, it was mainly after the death of Anandaram Dhekial Phukan in 1859, that the leadership of the movement passed on entirely into the hands of missionaries, particularly Bronson. During the period of the controversy he adopted the method of voicing public opinion through memoranda in addition to sending a number of reports to the Home Board supporting the continued use of Assamese in the schools of the province. His scholarly opinions and activities in this regard played an important role in influencing the government's decision to reintroduce Assamese in the schools and courts of Assam in 1873. Bronson's petitions, memoranda, reports and other materials about the Assamese language will tremendously add to the knowledge of any scholar working on this subject. Even Maheswar Neog has admitted that:

> The Baptists held the line of this 'agitation' as is evident from such facts as that of the continuation of their publication programme in Assamese and their Assamese medium schools and that of Bronson's leading a representation of 216 educated Assamese on 9th March 1872. In fact, the Commissioner, Colonel Henry Hopkinson, makes special mention in his letter of 11th December 1873 to the Director of Public Instruction of 'the Sibasagar missionaries to whom we are chiefly indebted for agitation in favour of the creation of the Assamese language'.[14]

Christian contribution to the development of literature in hill areas, especially in matters of creating a script and of publishing a literature where none had existed, is also remarkable. Hence, for any scholar working on the development of literature of the North-East, the missionary sources, especially the Bronson papers, are of immense help.

The habit of opium smoking amongst the native population shocked Nathan Brown on his arrival at Jaipur in 1836 and he reported with horror that:

> The greatest curse of this country, at present is opium. A large portion of the inhabitants are completely besotted by it. It carries off immense numbers to an untimely grave. The disease, which attacks opium chewers, is commonly dysentery and is almost sure to be fatal, no medicine being of any avail.[15]

As the American missionaries were not involved in the political fortunes of Great Britain, they were often critical of the government's policies and actions. Attacking the government's opium policy, a Baptist resident in India in his article entitled *Devastation of India's Millions by Opium Under British Rule – Will God Permit its Continuance?* unhesitatingly pointed out how a government, Christian in name, tended to thwart the work of the ambassadors of Christ. In this connection he wrote:

> In Great Britain, legal precautions are taken to prevent the sale of opium for common use .... It is unlawful for opium to be sold except by a duly qualified and registered chemist, or druggist, and then 'unless the box, bottle, vessel, wrapper, or cover in which such poison is contained be distinctly labelled with the name of the article and the word "Poison", and with the name and address of the seller of the poison' (Pharmacy Act, 1868, Sec. 17). Who can contrast without shame the action of the British Government in England with the action of the British Government in India?[16]

Mr. Whiting wrote to the Board in a similar tone in 1858:

> The government, as it maintains, in order to destroy the cultivation of the plant in Assam, and so gradually to discourage its use, introduced its own drug, and it is now sold from our government treasuries. The result is, as might be expected, a perfectly alarming demand for the article. This act of the government has done more than anything else to spread the use of opium, and put far off the day of fat things. It is almost hopeless that a confirmed opium eater will ever leave off the use of the article.[17]

The government's policy of justice and police also came under missionary attack. In this regard their views were corroborated by A.D. Phukan in his *Observation on the Administration of Assam.* The missionaries attributed the origin of the Phularguri Revolt of 1862 to the multiplication of taxes by the British Government, the more objectionable ones being the licence tax and the income tax.

Often the missionaries reported about important historical findings in the region to the Board, as early as 1871. Mr. Brown reported from Makum that:

He could not leave Makum till the following morning as Captain Vetch has been getting out some brass cannons, that have lately been discovered here. They were secreted in a thick wood, about a mile from the river. These guns were brought in, it is supposed, during the Mohammedan invasion of India. This is the most eastern point which the Moslem army reached, sickness breaking out, and the inhabitants of the hills pouring down upon them in all directions, they were obliged to retreat, leaving their artillery behind them. The guns are twenty in number, some of them highly ornamented and so large as to be drawn with great difficulty by an elephant. Ten more are said to be secreted near Ningru. The Persian inscriptions upon them shown to be about 200 years old.[18]

Journals and Periodicals Published By the Missionaries

The American Baptist Missionaries were pioneers in publishing the first periodical in Assamese language in 1846. The *Orunodoi* as it was called, contained articles of varied nature and provided important source-materials for writing history. It contained descriptive articles on numerous tribes like the Singphos and the Garos. An account of the Garos with a full page picture of a Garo man in his warrior dress appeared in the issue of May 1847.[19] Similarly, the issue of August 1848 contains a vivid description of the Singpho tribe with the picture of Ningrula Singpho woman, a Singpho hat and a Singpho knife.[20]

Through the *Orunodoi* the missionaries called for social reforms, such as promotion of widow remarriage, prevention of child marriage and the abolition of *Sati.* Though Assam boasts of the absence of the degrading practice of *Sati,* the *Orunodoi* makes one of the first reference to an attempted case of *Sati.* The paper refers to a case from Kalugaon in the South of Sibsagar district where the widow of the elder brother of Lambodar *Mauzadar,* was willing to prove her purity by offering to perform *Sati* after the death of her husband. However, when the matter was brought to the notice of Mr. Dowerah, the *Daroga,* she was prevented from performing the act.[21] It must be noted that missionary reports on the gruesome practice of *Sati* were admirably balanced statements. Though the ritual had already been declared illegal in British India, the missionaries did not fail to take note of the exceptions permitted by the scriptures to this practice. It may therefore be assumed that their criticisms were often made in terms of the higher intentions of the native scriptures.

The missionaries, with their characteristic zeal for collection of historical relics, accumulated a large number of Assamese curious coins and images. In their possession was found a bronze lion forming the pedestal of the royal throne of the Ahoms. A picture of this pedestal was reproduced in the *Orunodoi.*[22]

Beside the *Orunodoi* the missionaries published numerous other journals for their readers. Magazines such as *The Helping Hand* and the *Heathen Women's Friend* were published essentially for middle-class women readers. Such magazines featured stories, poems and graphic visual materials in addition to reports and letters from the field. These magazines were used primarily in attempting to improve women's lives and relieve them from their sheer commitment to domestic chores.

Foreign missionary activities by American Baptist Missionaries began in 1812 and by 1820 these missionaries began to provide their supporters at home with first-hand descriptions of social life of the people whom they were attempting to convert. Though anthropological studies in America began to have scientific and scholarly credence only in the last decades of the 19th century, it is creditable that the American missionaries with only the slightest notions of scientific methodology began a study of ethnology as early as the 1820s. Though the evangelical was not professional anthropology, it is important for its distinctive focus on manners, family-life and culture of the people amongst whom they lived. However, the missionaries often ignored the complexities of inter-cultural contact and hence developed a formulaic vocabulary in describing the condition of the people in the lands where they came to preach the Gospel.

Certain sections of the last three categories of missionary documents mentioned in the paper are not readily available for consultation in the country. Apart from the United Theological College in Bangalore which houses the above-mentioned documents and papers, the bulk of the missionary papers are preserved in the Franklin Trask Library of the Andover Newton Theological School at Andover Newton and in the Baptist Missionary Archives at Valley Forge in Pennsylvania. However, since most of the documents are now available on microfilm, it may do well for the various libraries and institutions of the North-Eastern region to acquire the microfilms in order to make available to scholars a valuable and additional source for reconstructing the history of the region.

NOTES AND REFERENCES

1. *Indian Church History Review*, Gillespie George, Missionaries and Manuscripts, Vol. XIII, No. 2, Mysore, 1979, p. 157.
2. Bhuyan, S.K., *Studies in the Literature of Assam*, Gauhati, 1956, p. 58.
3. *Indian Church History Review*, *loc. cit*, p. 3.
4. *Ibid.*, p.58.
5. A typescript marked, "Old Assamese manuscripts in possession of the American Baptist Mission at Gauhati, Assam", contains a receipt for the manuscripts signed by the Director of Historical and Antiquarian Studies in Assam dated 27.6.55 to be found in the Gauhati library of the C.B.C.N.E.I.
6. Vickland, E. Elizabeth, *Women of Assam*, Philadelphia, 1928, Preface.
7. *Baptist Missionary Mazagine* (B.M.M.), Vol XV, 1861, W. Ward to Bronson, 31 October 1861, Franklin Trask Library.

8. *Ibid.*
9. *Ibid.*, Journal of Mr. Whiting, Vol. XXXVI, July 1866, p.395.
10. *Ibid.*, December 1839, Journal of Mr. Bronson, p.286.
11. Letter from Ella Marie Holmes to a friend, Gauhati, 1948, Missions collections, Yale Divinity School Library.
12. B.M.M., Vol. XV, 1855, Journal of Mr. Whiting, p. 448.
13. *Ibid.*, Vol. XIII, May 1841, Nowgong Report by Mr. Bronson, p. 210.
14. Cf. Fredrick, S. Downs, *Christianity in North East India,* 1983, p. 248.
15. B.M.M., Vol. XIII, May 1837, Journal of Mr. Brown, p. 172.
16. *Devastation of India's Millions by Opium under British Rule,* p. 12, Missions Pamphlets Collection, Manuscripts Group No. XXXI, Special Collection, Yale Divinity School Library, India Monograph.
17. B.M.M., Vol. VL, August 1858, Letter from Mr. Whiting, p.292.
18. B.M.M., Vol. XXI, February 1841, p. 31.
19. *Ibid.*, Vol. II, No. 5, Sibsagar, May 1847, pp. 138-40.
20. *Orunodoi,* Vol. III, No.8, Sibsagar, August 1848, pp. 225-57.
21. *Ibid.*, Vol. I, No. 5, Sibsagar, May 1846, p.36.
22. *Ibid.*, Vol. V, No. 11, November 1850, p.490.

APPENDIX

Extract taken from, *Indian Church History Review*, George Gillespie, Missionaries and Manuscripts, Vol. XIII, No. 2, Mysore, 1979, pp. 157-167.

Rajar Maidam Khana

An article about the digging-up of the tombs of Ahom kings appeared in the first issue of *Orunudoi* (January 1846, Vol. I, No.l). It is a contemporary report on the digging-up of the tombs entitled "Rajar Maidam Khana". Dimembeawar Neog refers to a book called *Ahom Rajar Maidam,* which is supposed to be a republished form of the *Orunudoi* article. It does not appear to have been published as a book later by the mission, though an English translation of the article appeared in the Baptist Missionary Magazine, September 1846, pp. 290-292.

Assam Buranji

This *Assam Buranji* is a history of Assam from the rule of Svargadeo Jayadhvaja Singha to the Kachari wars of Rudra Singha, covering the period AD 1648 -1770. The manuscript consists of 54 folios and is incomplete. It was one of the manuscripts found in 1925 at the Baptist Mission in Guwahati and handed over to the D.H.A.S. in 1931, probably by Rev. A.J. Tuttle. This manuscript was used by S.K. Bhuyan as a part of the 1932 D.H.A.S. Assamese publication, *Tangkhungia Buranji,* which he later edited. A part of this *buranji* was also included in the last pages of the D.H.A.S. edition of the old *Kachari Buranji* (edited by S.K. Bhuyan, and published in 1936 and 1951). The manuscripts also form most of the *Assam Buranji,* 1648 -1681 (edited by S.K. Dutta and published by the D.H.A.S. in 1938).

Bhagavata Purana

Popularly known as *Ekadasa,* this section of the *Bhagavata Purana* was translated by Sankaradeva at the order of King Naranarayana of Koch Behar. It is in Assamese verse. This manuscript was with the group found in 1925 on the mission compound, Guwahati. It has 62 folios and is incomplete. On its cover is the simple Assamese verse written by Sankaradeva as a child, that begins, *Karatala Kamala.* The manuscript was donated to the D.H.A.S. in 1955.

Chanakya's Aphorisms

Among the Guwahati mission manuscripts found in 1925 was one of only two folios. This is a very incomplete Assamese version of what is probably Chanakya's *aphorisms*. The two folios are numbered 14 and 17. The manuscript was given to the D.H.A.S. in 1955.

Chutia Rajar Bangshawala

An article in English called "Ancient Chronicle of the Chutias", appeared in the December 1850 issue (Vol. V, No. 12) of the *Orunodoi,* wherein it is explained that the Chutia have also decried their royal family history *bangsawali.* The name of William Robinson, Inspector of the Government Schools in Assam (and an ex-British Missionary), is associated with the original finding and publishing of this manuscript. This chronicle was later published as part of the *Deodhai Assam Buranji* (edited by S.K. Bhuyan, D.H.A.S., 1932).

Deodhai Assam Buranji

This is a complete Assamese manuscript of 30 folios narrating the history of the Ahom kings, beginning with the ancestors of Sukhapha (the first Ahom king who ruled Assam from AD 1228 -1268) to the reign of Naria Raja (1648). It is a translation, probably by Jajnaram Deodhai Barua, from a chronicle written in the Ahom language. In addition to a list of Ahom kings beginning from Khunlung to Khunlai (the ancestors of Sukhapha) to the time of the kingdom's annexation by the East India Company, there is also an appendix showing Hindu Saka equivalents of Ahom *laklis* (Ahom calendar years). In the D.H.A.S. edition of the Buranji, it is claimed that "the whole manuscript was prepared for Rev. Nathan Brown somewhere between 1840 and 1850, which in fact is recorded in a fly-leaf."

This Buranji was published by the mission in the *Orunodoi* in 21 installments, excluding the appendix, under the name *Purani Assam Buranji.* The manuscript still shows directions in it for press preparation. This manuscript was discovered among the Guwahati mission *puthis* in 1925 and handed over to the D.H.A.S. by 1931. The *Deodhai Assam Buranji,* edited by S.K. Bhuyan, was published by the D.H.A.S. in 1932 along with some short chronicles. This edition includes the appendix.

Jaduram Deka Baruah's Bengali-Assamese Dictionary

Jaduram Deka Baruah prepared a Bengali-Assamese Dictionary which he gave to Col. Jenkins Commissioner of Assam in 1839. It gave Bengali words with Assamese definitions. Col. Jenkins gave this manuscript to the mission. Its spellings influenced not only the *Orunodoi* but also Miles Bronson's *A Dictionary in Assamese and English.* But it was never published and its whereabouts are not known.

Kamrupar Buranji

The *Kamrupar Buranji,* with 78 sanch bark folios, complete and preserved, is in three parts. Folios 1-56 is a history of Assam (mostly western Assam) from the time of king Biswa Singha of Koch Behar (1603) to the battle of Itakhuli in 1682, with emphasis on the Mogul-Koch Behar wars and the Mogul-Assam wars. Folios 57-68 contain copies of 18 letters of correspondence between Ahom kings and Mogul representatives. Folios 69-78 are chapters dealing with Jahangir, Shah Jahan and others, along with observations of the Mogul court, written by an Assamese living among with the Moguls.

Though the present manuscript could not have been copied earlier than 1973, the original chronicle 'was complied beyond doubt during the later part of the 17th century'. The missionaries published a part of it (folios 1-56) in the *Orunodoi* in eight issues, January through July, and October 1853 (Vol. VIII), calling it *Kamrupar Buranji.* Bhuyan says, 'There are directions here and there in the manuscript for preparing the press-copy for publication in the journal; and the manuscript also bears traces of the handiwork of Rev. Nidhi levi Farwell, the first Assamese convert of Christianity and a distinguished worker in the field of Assamese literature'.

The manuscript, after being found by Bhuyan, was turned over to the D.H.A.S. by 1931. Folios 1-56 were published as the major part of *Kamrupar Buranji* (D.H.A.S. 1930 and 1958), with folios 57-68 interspersed in its text. Folios 69-78 are included as a minor part of *Annals of the Delhi Badshahate* (D.H.A.S., 1947). Both books are edited by Dr. Bhuyan.

Kitabata Manjari

The *Kitabata Manjari* is a work on arithmetic, land-surveying and book-keeping in Assamese poetry, translated by Vakula Kayastha in 1434 or 1508 AD from the Sanskrit original of Lilavati. Dimbeswar Neog, Birinchi Kumar Barua and others claim that Nathan Brown published the *Kitabata Manjari* in two parts in 1645.

Lakshmi Singhar Buranji

The *Lakshmi Singhar Buranji* is an incomplete manuscript of 140 folios, giving a daily record of events during the last part of the reign of Svargadeo Lakshmi Singha (AD 1769-1775). The author is not known. When these folios were found by Bhuyan in 1925, they were for some time considered to be two separate manuscripts of and 23 folios each, but they are now generally accepted as one. It is reported to have been published in the *Orunodoi*, probably in 1860. In addition to having the maximum number of folios, each folio is very long, as a result of which it is a voluminous body of writing. It seems improbable, then, that all of the *buranji* could have appeared in the *Orunodoi.* Its ink is often faded. Its Assamese language is free from archaisms.

This manuscript (then considered as two manuscripts) was given to the D.H.A.S. by 1931.

Manu Chandra Ghosh

Manu Chandra Ghose is a popular Assamese verse translation of part of the *Vanaparva* of the *Mahābhārata.* It was written by the Assamese poet Rama Sarasvati at the command of King Nararnaryana of Koch Behar in the 16th century. This manuscript is of 57 folios written only on one side and is incomplete. This copy was written no earlier than 1825. It was found with the mission manuscripts in 1925 and turned over to the D.H.A.S. in 1955.

Sisupal Vadh

Sisupal Vadh is an Assamese poem about the killing of Sisupal, the king of the Chedis by Sri Krishna. The *tulapat* (paper made of cotton) manuscript is incomplete, containing folios no. 77 - 101. Dr. Bhuyan does not mention having found this with the mission manuscripts in 1925. However, it was handed over to the D.H.A.S. by the mission in 1955.

Syamantakaharana

In 1975, 15 folios of an Assamese *puthi* of bark were sent to the Baptist Historical Library, Rochester, New York State, by someone in the U.S.A. Fourteen of the folios (numbered 1-3, 5, 7-16) belong together and the other folio is written on only one side with a different hand. Of the 14, one had writing on the back, "Hindu Shaster, 1878, Stoddard, Assam". Rev. I.J. Stoddard was in Nowgong, from 1848 to 1855 and in Goalpara from 1867 to 1873. In 1878 he was residing in America.

Dr. Maheswar Neog of Gauhati University identified the group as a section of Sankaradeva's Kritana-Ghosha called *Syamantaka-Harana,* a popular poem, whose manuscripts are often to be found.

Tamuli Phukan Asam Buranji

The Ahom king, Purandar Singha (1833-1838) ordered Kasinath Tamuli Phukan to compile an *Asam Buranji* in Assamese from old sources, particularly from old *buranjis* written in the Ahom language. Radhanath Barbarua, who knew the Ahom language, probably collected and deciphered the Ahom texts, thus making an important contribution to the work. The resulting *buranji* normally goes by Tamuli Phukan's name, but a number of writers attribute to the *buranji* a dual authorship.

This manuscript was eventually prepared as publication by Rev. Nathan Brown and the first edition was published by the American Baptist Mission Press in Sibsagar in 1844, with the title, *Asam Buranji Puthi,* along with the words, *indrabangsi asam maharaja Sakalar bibaran. Shri Radhanath Barbarua duara sangsodhi mate Kasinath Tamuli Phukan kartrik grantha prastut hai* (witten by Kasinath Tamuli Phukan and corrected by Radhanath Barbarua). There were 1500 copies printed of this first published Assamese *buranji*. The books were "issued for the benefit of the schools at the expense of the resident magistrate".

Harakanta Sarma Barua Sadar Amin's *Asam Buranji,* edited by S.K. Bhuyan and published by the D.H.A.S. in 1930 and 1962, is an enlarged version of the *Tamuli Phukan Asam Buranji.*

SANSKRIT

Bhagavata, Fifth and Sixth Skandhas

The Sanskrit text of the Bhagavata, along with the commentary of Sridhara Svami is commonly read aloud in the *sattras* (monasteries) of Assam, by a reader called Bhagavati, who follows the reading with an explanation in Assamese. On each folio of this well-preserved manuscript, the commentary accompanies the text. There are wooden covers, one having a painting. There are 55 folios of the fifth *Skandha* and 35 of the sixth. The manuscript was found with others at the Baptist Mission in 1925, and was given to the D.H.A.S. in 1955.

Jyotish-Samkshep

Jyotish-Samkshep is a work on astrology by Harideva Sarma mainly for the use of Brahmins. This manuscript was written soon after 1825 and is complete, consisting of 33 folios. Found in 1925 by Bhuyan at the Baptist Mission, it was given to the D.H.A.S. in 1955.

Jyotish-Tattva

This astrology work is by Raghunanda, the founder of a school of rituals practiced mainly in Bengal. This manuscript of 11 folios is incomplete and was prepared soon after 1825. It was with the *puthis* in 1825, and was turned over to the D.H.A.S. in 1955.

Svarodaya

This Sanskrit *puthi* is on astrology. There are 29 folios and the manuscript is incomplete. The author's name is not given. However, Bhuyan says, "from the eulogy paid to Prince Sukladhvaja of Koch Bihar, and the brief description of

Kamrupa, Kamakhya, Kamapitha and Ratnapitha, we conjecture this book to be eminently an Assamese product." It was found with the other *puthis* in 1925 and donated to the D.H.A.S. in 1955.

Tulasi Duta Kavyam

Tulasi Duta Kavyam was written in 1784 by the Assamese writer, Vaidyanath Dvija of Kamakhya (Gauhati). The manuscript was copied in 1799 by Maniram. There are 13 folios and it is incomplete. The poem narrates the love between Sri Krishna and the *gopis.* There is also an invocation to Kamakhya. This *puthi* was found in 1925 at the mission and turned over to the D.H.A.S. in 1955.

Manipuri

Manipuri Manuscripts

Not long before 1928, American Baptist missionaries in Manipur found several old Manipuri manuscripts dealing with Assam-Manipur relations of ancient times. Mr. J.C. Higgins, the British Political Agent of Manipur suggested that the compilation and the publication of the manuscripts be done by the D.H.A.S. Finally, this responsibility was entrusted to Mr. William Pettigrew of Manipur, though the work was interrupted when Pettigrew left India permanently in 1933.

Shan

Shan Chronicle

In 1835, Captain R. Boileau Pemberton, an English officer, found an ancient Shan chronicle in Manipur. The manuscripts chronicled the ancient history of the Shan kingdom which centred around Mogaung in northern Burma. Since the manuscript was found in the possession of an old Shan it may be assumed that it was originally a Shan manuscript which Capt. Pemberton got it translated into Manipuri. This manuscript was extensively used by Captain Pemberton in preparing his *Report on the Eastern Frontier of British India.* It is probable that Pemberton also had an English translation of the manuscript made for his use.

In November 1835, the Brown's claim that while in Calcutta on their way to Assam, they had received from Capt. Pemberton "a copy of an interesting old Shan manuscript purporting to be an abstract of the history of the people from the first century to their subjection by the Burmese conqueror Alompra and ascribing to the ancient Shans a powerful empire, called the kingdom of Pong." Dr. S.K. Bhuyan is of the opinion that the manuscript given to Rev. Brown by Pemberton was the same, which the latter had discovered in Manipur.

KHAMTI

Khamti Sacred Book

While Miles Bronson was travelling in the Singppho area in March 1838, he was informed about a priest residing at Iagando village, who was conversant with the Burman, Khamti, Singppho, and Assamese language. Bronson visited the priest and presented him a paper in return for which the priest gifted him "one of their large Khamti sacred books".

BLANK

Blank and Unused Folios

Among the manuscripts discovered in 1925 were 35 blank and unused *sanchipat* folios in two sizes, the large ones being reportedly very beautifully made. They were given to the D.H.A.S. in 1925.

Select Bibliography

BOOKS

Acharya, N.N., *North East as Viewed by Foreigners*, Omsons Press, New Delhi, 1985.

Agarwal, A.K., *North East India: An Economic Perspective*, Chugh Publications, Allahabad, 1985.

Agarwal, D.P., *Archaeology of India*, Curzon Press, London, 1982.

Agrawala, V.S., *India as Known to Panini* (2nd ed.), Prithvi Prakashan, Varanasi, 1963.

Aier, L., IMTI, *Ao Naga: Social and Customary Genealogy*, Mokokchung (Nagaland), Published by the Author, 1967.

Alien, B.C., *Assam District Gazetteers*, Vol. IX Pt. 17, 'Naga Hills and Manipur: Socio-Economic History', British Baptist Mission, Calcutta, 1905.

——, *Gazetteer of Naga Hills and Manipur*, Assam Secretariat Press, Shillong, 1905.

——, *Assam Report 1901*, Shillong, Assam Secretariat Printing Press, 1901.

Alien, B.C., (*et al.*), *Gazetteer of Bengal and North East India* (Reprint), Mittal Publications, Delhi, 1977.

Altekar, A.S., *Education in Ancient India*, Benaras, 1948.

——, *Position of Women in Hindu Civilization*, Delhi, 1973.

Ansari, S.A., *Economic Geography of Manipur*, P. Tikendrajit Singh, Imphal, 1976.

Anand, V.K., *Nagaland in Transition*, Associated Publications, Delhi, 1985.

A.O.M. Alemchiba, *A Brief Historical Account of Nagaland*, Naga Institute of Culture, Kohima, 1970.

——, *The Arts and Crafts of Nagaland*, Naga Institute of Culture, Kohima, 1968.

A.O., Shilu, 'The Nagas', *Vanyajati*, Vol. 1 No. 3, March 1953.

Aram, M., *Evolution of Naga Politics*, Nagaland Peace Centre, Kohima, 1972.

——, *Peace in Nagaland*, Arnold-Heinemann, New Delhi, 1974.
——, *Peace has come to study in Nagaland*, Sarvodaya Friends, Coimbatore, 1968.
——, *Prospects of Peace in Nagaland*, Sarvodaya, Thanjaur, 1965.
Awasthy, Indira, *Between Sikkra and Bhutan*, B.R. Publishing Corporation, New Delhi, 1978.
Badem-Powell, *The Indian Village Community*, London, 1897.
Bagchi, G.G. and S. Sinha, *Census of India 1961: West Bengal Upper Pedong, A Village Survey Monograph*, Govt. of West Bengal, Calcutta, 1972.
Balwan, M., *Lalung Dictionary: Catholic Church*, Nongpoh, 1965.
Bandyopadhayay, P.K., *Leadership among the Mizos*, B.R. Publishing Corporation, Delhi, 1985.
Banerjea, J.N., *Development of Hindu Iconography*, Calcutta University, Calcutta, 1956.
Bareh, Hamlet, *The History and Culture of the Khaki People*, Naba Mudran (Pvt.) Ltd., Calcutta, 1967.
Barkakti, S., *Assam*, National Book Trust, New Delhi, 1969.
Barpujari, H.K., *American Missions and North East India 1836-1900 AD. A Documentary Study*, Spectrum, Guwahati, 1986.
——, *A Comprehensive History of Assam* (in 5 vols.), Publication Board Assam, Guwahati, Assam, 1990.
Barrett, E. (ed.), *World Christian Encyclopedia*, New York, 1982.
Barch, H., *Gazetteer of India*, Nagaland: Government of Nagaland, Kohima, 1970.
——, *Nagaland's Prehistory* (Highlander Vol. 1, No. l, Kohima, March 1973).
Barua, B.K., *History of Asssamese Literature*, Sahitya Akademi, New Delhi, 1978.
——, *Sankaradeva, Vaisnava Saint of Assam*, Assam Academy for Cultural Relations, Guwahati, 1960.
——, *Temples and Legends of Assam*, Bhartiya Vidya Bhawan, Bombay, 1965.
Barua, Beni Madhav, *Asoka and his Inscriptions* (Reprint), New Age Publications, Calcutta, 1969.
Barua, Beni Madhav & G.N. Sinha, *Old Brahmi Inscriptions and Udaigiri and Khandagiri Caves*, Calcutta University, 1929.
Barua, B.M., *History of Pre-Buddhistic Indian Philosophy* (Reprint), Motilal Banarsidass, Delhi, 1998.
——, *Studies in the Buddhist Jatakas* (Reprint), Saraswati Library, Calcutta, 1989.
Barua, G.R., *Asom Buranji*, Calcutta, 1876.
Barua, Hem, *Assam Literature*, NBT, New Delhi, 1965.
——, *The Red River and the Blue Hill*, Lawyer's Book Stall, Guwahati, 1956.
Barua, H.C., *Notes on the Marriage System of the People of Assam*, Sibsagar, 1908.
Barua, Jishnu, *Hundred Years of Halfong*, Delhi, 1995.
Barua, Jishnu, Arun Bhuyan (*et al.*), *Nationalist Upsurge in Assam*, Pub. by Govt. of Assam, Guwahati, 2000.
Barua, H.K., *Hemakosha: Assamese-English-Dictionary*, Guwahati, 1900.
Barua, K.L., *Early History of Kamarupa*, Shillong, 1933.
Baruah, S.L., *A Comprehensive History of Assam*, Munshiram Manoharlal, 1985.
——, *Last Days of Ahom Monarchy: A History of Assam from 1769 to 1825*, Munshiram Manoharlal, New Delhi, 1993.

Baruah, T.K.M., *The Singphos and their Religion*, Research Deptt., Govt. of Arunachal Pradesh, Shillong, 1977.
——, *'The Indu Mishrni', North East Frontier Agency*, Shillong, 1960.
Barthakur, J.K., *Census of India, 1971*, Directorate of Census Operation, Arunachal Pradesh, Shillong, 1972.
Bharathakur, Pulin Behari, *Assam*, Pub. Division, New Delhi, 1971.
Basak, R.G., *History of North Eastern India*, Calcutta, 1934.
Basnet, L.B., *Sikkim: A Short Political History*, S. Chand & Co., New Delhi, 1974.
Basu, N.K., *Assam in Ahom Age*, Sanskrit Pustak Bhandar, Calcutta, 1970.
Bhadra, Madhumita, *Sikkim, Democracy and Social Change*, Minerva Associates, Calcutta, 1992.
Bhattacharjee, J.B., *Cachar under British Rule in North East India*, Radiant Publishers, New Delhi, 1977.
Bhattacharjee, T.K., *The Myths of the Shimongs of the Upper Siang*, Research Deptt., Govt. of Arunachal Pradesh, Shillong, 1965.
Bhattacharya, J., 'Patterns of Economic Change in Garo Society', *Garo Hills Land and People*, L.S. Gassah (ed.), Omsons Publications, New Delhi, 1984.
Bhattacharya, J.B., *The Garos and the English*, New Delhi, 1978.
——, *World War II and India: A Fifty Years Perspective*, Presidential Address, Modern Section, Indian History Congress, Gorakhpur, 1990.
Bhattacharya, J.N., *Hindu Castes and Sects* (Reprint), Calcutta, 1968.
Bhattacharya, K.K., *Tripurana: A Select and Annotated Bibliography on Tripura*, Tripura Library Association, Agartala, 1970.
——, *North East India*, Cosmo Publications, 1983.
Bhattacharya, N., *Bhartiya Jati Varna Pratha*, Firma, K.L. Mukhopadhaya, Calcutta, 1987.
Bhattacharya, N.N., *Religious Culture of North-Eastern India*, Manohar Publication, New Delhi, 1995.
Bhattacharya, P.K., 'Forests and the Naga Tribes (Highlander)', *Bulletin of Cul. Res. and State Museum*, Government of Nagaland, Kohima, 1973.
Bhattacharya, P.N., 'ABO Blood Groups of the Angami Naga', *The Eastern Anthropologist*, Vol. IV, XI, 1:42-46, 1957.
——, *Kamarupa Sasanavali*, Benaras, 1931.
Bhattasali, N.K., *Iconography of the Buddhist and Hindu Sculptures in the Dacca*, Museum, 1929.
Bhowmik, K.K. (*et al.*), *Fertility of Zemi Women in Nagaland*, Institute of Social Studies, Calcutta, 1971.
Bista, D.B., *People of Nepal*, Ratna Pustak Bhawan, Kathmandu, 1972.
Bordoloi, M., *Land of the Hornhill and Myna*, Research Deptt., Govt. of Arunachal Pradesh, Shillong, 1964.
Boruah, B.K., *Nagamese: The Languages of Nagaland*, Mittal Publications, New Delhi, 1993.
Bose, K. Sisir, *Beacon Across Asia: A Biography of Subhas Chandra Bose*, Orient Longman, New Delhi, 1973.
Bose, S.C., *Land and People of the Himalayas*, Indian Publication, Calcutta, 1968.
Bour, Ursula G., *The Naga Path*, John Murray, London, 1950.
Brouson, M., *Phrases in English and Naga*, ABM Press, Jaipur, 1867.

Brown, R., *Statistical Account of Manipur*, Govt. Press, London, 1874.

——, *Statistical Account of the Native State of Manipur and the Hill Territory under its Rule*, Govt. Printing Press, Calcutta, 1874.

Butler, J. (Major), *Travels and Adventures with the Province of Assam*, London, 1855.

Carey, P.S. and H.N. Truck, *The Chin Hills*, Firma, K.L. Mukhopadhayaya, Calcutta, 1932.

Chaki-Sircar, *Feminism in a Traditional Society*, Shakti Books, New Delhi (Reprint), 1932.

Chanana, S.M., *Nagaland: A Contemporary Ethnography*, Cosmo Publication, New Delhi, 1992.

Chanda, R., *The Indo-Aryan Races: A Study of the Origin of Indo-Aryan People and Institutions*, Part I, Rajshahi (now Bangladesh), 1916.

Chakrabarti, D.K., *Archaeology of Eastern India, Chhota Nagpur Plateau and West Bengal*, Munshiram Manoharlal, New Delhi, 1993.

Chakravarti, C., *The Tantras: Studies on their Religion and Literature*, Calcutta, 1963.

Chakravarti, R., *People of Manipur*, B.R. Publishing Corporation, New Delhi, 1986.

Chakravarty, L.N., *Glimpses of the Early History of Arunachal Pradesh*, Research Deptt., Arunachal Pradesh Administration, Shillong, 1973.

Chari, R.B., *Census of India - Scheduled Castes and Tribes*, Series I, Govt. of India, New Delhi, 1971.

Chatterjee, Suhas, *Mizo Chiefs and Chiefdom*, M.D. Publications, New Delhi, 1995.

——, *Mizoram under the British Rule*, Mittal Publications, New Delhi, 1985.

Chatterjee, S., *Mizoram Encyclopedia in 3 vols*, Jaico Publication, Bombay, 1990.

Chatterjee, S.P., *India—A Physical Geography*, Gazetter of India, (p. 40), Publication Division, Govt. of India, New Delhi, 1968.

——, *Meghalaya: Garo and Khasi Jaintia*, Paris, 1936.

Chatterji, N., *Status of Women in the Earlier Mizo Society*, Tribal Research Institute, Aizawl, 1975.

——, *Zawlbuck as a Social Institution in the Mizo Society*, Tribal Research Society, Aizawl, 1975.

Chatterji, S.K., *Kirat Jana-Kriti : Asiatic Society of Bengal*, Calcutta, 1950.

Chatterji, S.K., *Kirat-Janakrti: The Indo-Mongoloids*: 'Their Contribution to the History & Culture of India', Calcutta, *The Asiatic Survey*, Rev. Ed. 1974.

Chattopadhayaya, K., *Tribalism in India*, Vikas, New Delhi, 1978.

Chaube, S.K., *Hill Politics in North-East India*, Calcutta, 1973.

—— (ed.), *The Himalayas: Profiles of Modernisation and Adaptation*, Sterling Publishers, New Delhi, 1985.

Chaudhuri, D.P., *North East Frontier of India*, 1865-1914, Asiatic Society of Bengal, Calcutta, 1978 (Reprint).

Chaudhuri, J.C., *Tripura: Land and its People*, Concept Publication, Delhi, 1980.

Chaudhuri, R.D.S., *Source Book of the Numismatic Studies in North East India*, Directorate of Museums, Assam, Guwahati, 1988.

Chaudhury, B.N., *The Cultural and Linguistic Aspects of the Garos*, Guwahati, 1968.

Chaudhury, J.N., *Arunachal Through the Ages*, Jaya Choudhury, Shillong, 1982.

Chemjong, I.S., *History and Culture of the Kirat People* (2 vols.), Tumang-Hang, Kathmandu, 1966.

Chib, S.S., *Sikkim*, Light and Life Publishers, 1977.

Chodhury, P.C., *The History and Civilization of the People of Assam upto Twelfth Century AD*, Deptt. of Historical and Antiquarian Studies, Government of Assam, Guwahati, 1939.
Chopra, P.N., *Sikkim*, S. Chand & Co., New Delhi, 1979.
Choudhury, P.P., *Assam - Bengal Relations: From the Earliest Times to the Twelfth Century AD*, Spectrum Publication, Guwahati, 1988.
Choudhury, R.O., *Assam: State Museum*, Catalogue of Inscriptions in the Assam State Museum, Directorate of Museum, Assam, 1987.
Coelho, V.N., *Sikkim and Bhutan*, Indian Council for Cultural Relations, Delhi, 1967.
Cooke, Hope, *Time Change: An Autobiography*, Simon and Schuster, New York, 1981.
Constantine, R., *Manipur Maid of the Mountains*, Lancers Publishers, New Delhi, 1981.
Crawford, G.C., *Handbook of Kuki Customers*, Manipur, 1927.
Dalton, E.T., *Descriptive Ethnology of Bengal*, Calcutta, 1872.
Damant, G.H., *Administrative Report of Naga-Hills*, Govt. Press, Shillong, 1878-79.
Dami, A.H., *Prehistory and Proto-History of Eastern India*, Calcutta, 1960.
Das, B.M. (ed.), *Contemporary Anthropology in North East India*, Dibrugarh University Press, Dibrugarh, 1974.
Das, B.M., *Microevolution* (Ranchi, Anthropology Series 4), Concept Publishing House, New Delhi, 1981.
——, *Variations in Physical Characteristics in the Khasi Population of North East India*, D.K. Publications, New Delhi, 1978.
Das, B.S., *Sikkim Saga*, Vikas Publications, New Delhi, 1982.
Das, N.K., *The Emergence and Role of Naga Hills in Independent India in the Emergence and Role of Middle Class in North East India*, B. Dutta Ray (ed.), Uppal Publication, New Delhi, 1983.
Das, R.K., *Manipur Tribal Scene* (Studies in Society and Change), Inter-India Publications, New Delhi, 1985.
Das, T.C., *The Purames: An old Kuki Tribe of Manipur*, Calcutta University, Calcutta, 1945.
Das Gupta, K., *An Introduction to the Gallong Language*, Research Deptt., Govt. of Arunachal Pradesh, Shillong, 1963.
Das Gupta, P.K., *Life and Culture of Matrilineal Tribe of Meghalaya*, Inter-India Publications, New Delhi, 1984.
Das Gupta, P.K. and N.K. Das, *Socio-Cultural Aspects of Cultivation and Soil Conservation in North East India*.
Dash, A.J., *Bengal District Gazetters*, Darjeeling District, Bengal Govt. Press, Calcutta, 1907.
Datta, Amal, *Sikkim Since Independence : A Study of Impact of Education and Emerging Class Structure*, Mittal Publication, 1991.
Datta, P.S., *North East as I See it*, Omsons Press, New Delhi, 1994.
—— (ed.), *North East and the Indian State: Paradoxes of A Periphery*, Vikas Publications, New Delhi, 1995.
——, *North East: A Study of Mobility and Political Behaviour*, Omsons Press, Guwahati, 1991.
Dave, R.K. (Comp), *Manipur including Who's Who?*, Surya Prakashan, Jodhpur, 1980.
Davis, A.W., *Naga Tribes: Assam Census Report*, Govt. Press, Shillong, 1981.
Deb, Barma R., *The Tribes of Tripura*, Directorate of Tribal Research, Tripura.
Dev Barman, T.J.M., *Origin of Tripura and its People*, Vanjatiya Vol. VI.

Deori, D., *Deori Sanskrit*, Janam Bhumi Press, Jorhat, 1964.

Dev, Bimal and Dilip K. Lahiri, *Manipur: Culture and Politics*, Mittal Publication, 1987.

Deuri, R.K., *Festivals of Kameng*, Directorate of Research, Arunachal Pradesh, Shillong, 1983.

Dihingia, Hemashwar, *Assam Struggle against British Rule 1826-63*, Asian Publication Services, New Delhi, 1980.

Dutta, Anuradha, *Assam in the Freedom Movement*, Darbari Prakashan, Calcutta, 1991.

Dun, Capt. E.W., *Gazetter of Manipur*, (Reprint) Vivkek Publication House, New Delhi, 1975.

Dubey, S.M., *Modernisation and Elites in Arunachal Pradesh* (Census of India, 1971), Delhi, Govt. of India Publication, 1975.

Edgar, J.W., Report on a visit to Sikkim and the Tibetan Frontier in Oct, November and December 1873, Bengal Secretariat Press, Calcutta, 1874.

Elwin, Verrier, *The Art of North East Frontier of India*, North East Frontier Agency, Shillong, 1959.

——, *India's North East Frontier in the Nineteenth Century*, Oxford University, Bombay, 1959.

——, *The Nagas in the Nineteenth Century*, Oxford University Press, 1969,

Evans-Wentz, W.Y., *The Tibetan Book of the Dead*, Oxford University Press, London, 1957.

Fergusson, J., *A History of Indian and Eastern Architecture*, London, 1910.

Fick, R., *The Social Organisation in North East India in Buddha's Time*, Calcutta, 1920.

Fleet, J.F., *Corpus Inscriptionum Indicarum*, Vol. III (Gupta Inscriptions), Calcutta, 1888.

Furer-Haimendorf, C. Von, *Highlanders of Arunachal Pradesh*, Vikas Publishing House, Delhi, 1982.

——, *The Naked Nagas Head Hunters of Assam in Peace and War*, Thacker Spink & Co., Calcutta, 1946.

Gailt, Edward, A., *Manipur in History of Assam*, Thacker Spink & Co., Calcutta, 1933.

Gait, E.A., *History of Assam*, Calcutta, 1906.

Garden, E., *Nepal, Sikkim and Bhutan in Pictures,* Oxford and IBH, Calcutta, 1972.

Ghose, B.B., *History of Nagaland*, S. Chand & Co., New Delhi, 1980.

Gopal Krishanan, R., *North East India: From a Geographical Expression to Regional Accommodation*, Har-Anand Publisher, Delhi, 1995.

——, *North East India: Land Economy and People*, Har-Anand Publisher, Delhi, 1995.

Gorer, G., *Himalayan Village*, An Account of the Lepchas of Sikkim, Thomas Nelson & Sons (2nd ed.), London, 1967.

Goswami, B.B., *Mizo-unrest: A Study of Politicisation of Culture*, Aalekh Publication, Jaipur, 1979.

Goswami, M.C. and D.N. Majumdar, *Social Institutes of the Garo of Meghalaya*, Calcutta, 1972.

Goswami, P., *Assam in the 19th Century: Industrialization and Colonial Penetration*, Guwahati, 1999.

Gougin, T., *History of Zomi*, Zomi Press, Manipur, 1984.

Govt. of India, *Census of India*, Tripura (General Report) Vol. XXVI, Part I (i), 1961.

Govt. of India, *Census of India of 1981*, Special Report on Jhum Series 14, Paper 12, 1983, Meghalaya.

Govt. of India, *Census of India*, Series 19, Sikkim: District Hand Book, 1981.

Govt. of India, *Census of India 1981: Provisional Population Tables Paper-I of 1981*. Reporter General of Census Commission for India, New Delhi, 1981.

Govt. of Mizoram, *Statistical Hand Book*, Mizoram, 1987, Deptt. of Economics and Statistics, Aizawl.

Goyal, N., *Political History of Himalayan States Tibet, Nepal, Sikim and Nagaland* since 1947, Cambridge Book & Stationary Store, New Delhi, 1966.

——, *Prelude to India: A Study of India's Relation with Himalayan States*, Cambridge Book & Stationery Store, New Delhi, 1966.

Grierson, G.A., *The Linguistic Survey of India*, Vol. III Pt. I, Calcutta, 1903.

——, *Linguistic Survey of India*, Vol. II & III, Govt. Printing Press, Calcutta, 1904.

——, Report on the *Linguistic Survey of India*, Vols. 2 & 3, Calcutta, 1923.

Grimwood, E., St. Claire, *My Three Years in Manipur*, Richard Bentley and Sons, London, 1891.

Grover, B.S.K., *Sikkim and India: Storm and Consolidation*, Jain Brothers, New Delhi, 1974.

Guha, Amalendu, *Planter Raj to Swaraj: Freedom Struggle and Electoral Politics*, New Delhi, 1977.

Gundevia, Y.D., *War and Peace in Nagaland*, Palit and Palit Publishers, Dehradun, 1975.

Gupta, K.K., *Copper-Plates of Sylhet*, Sylhet, 1967.

Gurdon, P.R.T., *The Khasi*, David Scott, London, 1907.

Gupta, P. and P.C. Dutta, *Anthropology in India 1868-1961*, Anthropological Survey of India, Calcutta, 1966.

Gupta, P.L. and T.R. Hardeker, 'Ancient Indian Silver Punched Marked Coins of the Magdh-Maurya Karshapana Series', *Indian Institute of Research in Numismatic Studies*, Anjaneri, 1985.

Haldipur, K., *Around the Hills and Dales of Arunachal Pradesh*, North Eastern Hill University, Shillong, 1985.

Hazarika, Bisweswar, *Assam Language: Origin and Development*, Aya Prakashan, Guwahati.

Hazarika, Sanjoy, *Strangers of the Mist*, New Delhi, 1994.

Helfley, James and Marti, *God's Tribesman, The Rochunga Pudaite Story*, Victor Books, 1976.

Hodson, T.C., *The Naga Tribes of Manipur*, Macmillan & Co., London, 1911.

——, *The Meitheis*, David Natt, London, 1908.

Hooker, J.D., *Himalyan Journals: Notes of a Naturalist in Bengal, the Sikkim and Nepal*, Himalayas, the Khasia Mountains, etc (2 vols.), John Murray, London.

Horam, M., *Naga Polity*, B.R. Publication, New Delhi, 1975.

Hunter, W.W., *A Statistical Account of Assam*, Vol. 11, B.R. Publishing Corporation, Delhi (Reprint), 1982.

——, *A Statistical Account of Bengal*, Vol. VI, B.R. Publishing Corporation, Delhi (Reprint) 1973.

Hussain, M., *The Assam Movement: Class, Ideology and Identity*, Manak Publications, New Delhi, 1993.

Huttan, J.H., *The Angami Nagas*, Macmillan & Co., London, 1921.

——, *The Sema Nagas*, Oxford University Press, London, 1921.

Jain, Ajit Prasad, *Sikkim: Retrospects and Prospects*, New Delhi, 1973.

Jain, Rekha, *Ancient Indian Coinage*, New Delhi, D.K. Printwell, 1995.

Jayaswel, K.P., *Imperial History of India*, Lahore, 1934.

Jha, J.C., 'Aspects of Indentured Inland Emigration to North-East India 1859-1918' (H.K. Barpujari endowment lecture), Indus Publication, New Delhi, 1996.

Jha, S.D., *Arunachal Pradesh: Rich and Poor Peoples*, Omsons, Delhi, 1986.

Johnstone, J., *Manipur and Naga Hills*, Gyan Publication, Delhi, 1997.

——, *My Experiences in Manipur and Naga Hills* (Reprint), Vivek Publication House, Delhi, 1971.

Jolly, J. (ed.), *Narada Smrti*, Calcutta, 1885.

Joykumar Singh, N., *Social Movements in Manipur*, Mittal Publication, New Delhi, 1992.

Kabui, Gangmumei, *Anal a Transborder of Manipur*, Mittal Publication, Delhi, 1985.

Kamkhenthang, H., *The Paite* (A Transborder tribe of India), Mittal Publication, Delhi, 1988.

Kandell, A.S. and C.Y. Salibury, *Mountaintop Kingdom, Sikkim*, Vikas Publication, New Delhi, 1977.

Kar, Parimal Chandra, *Garos in Transition*, Cosmo Publications, New Delhi, 1982.

Karam, P.P., *Nepal - A Cultural and Physical Geography*, University of Kentucky Press, Lexington, 1960.

Karan, P.P. and Jenkines, W.M., *Himalayan Kingdoms, Bhutan, Sikkim, Nepal*, D. Van Nostrand, New Jersey, 1963.

Karpurkar, Pushpa, *Tripura Phonetic Reader*, Central Institute of Indian Languages, Mysore, 1972.

Kashyap, T.S., *Sikkim, A Himalayan Realm*, Atma Ram & Sons, Delhi, 1988.

Kaviraj Chiranjiv (Tr.), *Tripura Ties with Tagore: A Compilation of Selected Speeches, Letters and Songs of Tagore*, Govt. Press, Agartala, 1969.

Kisor, S.B., *Tripura: Historical Documents*, Firma, K.L. Mukhopadhayaya, Calcutta, 1994.

Kotturen, G., *Folk Tales of Sikkim* (Folk Tales of India, No. 2), Sterling Publishers, New Delhi, 1979.

Kotturen, G., *The Himalayan Gateway: History & Culture of Sikkim*, Sterling Publishers, New Delhi, 1983.

Kyndiah, P.R., *Meghalaya: Yesterday & Today*, Har-Anand Publication, New Delhi, 1990.

——, *Mizo Freedom Fighters*, Sanchar, New Delhi, 1994.

Lahiri, Nayanjot, *Pre-Ahom Assam: Studies in the Inscriptions of Assam before the 5th and 13th Centuries AD.*, New Delhi, Munshiram Manoharlal, 1991.

Laitanga (ed.), *Know Your Own Land* (Mizoram Series I-III), Firma, K.L. Mukhopadhyaya, Calcutta, 1981.

Lal, C., *Mizoram, Politics of Regionalism and National Integration*, Reliance Publishers, New Delhi 1994.

Lal Dena, *History of Modern Manipur 1826-1949*, Orbit Publishers & Distributors, New Delhi, 1991.

Lal, J.S., *The Himalya: Aspects of Change*, Oxford University Press, New Delhi, 1981.

Lal, P. and B.K. Das Gupta, *Lower Siang People*, Anthropological Survey of India, Calcutta, 1979.

Lall, K., *The Thami in Rising Nepal*, Kathmandu, 1966.

Lallanji Gopal, *Early Medieval Coin-Types of Northern India*, Numismatic Society of India, Varanasi, 1966.

Lehman, F.K., Review of Lalthanglian's book, *History of Mizo in Burma* (in Thu Leh Hia, Sept. 1979).

Lewin, T.H., *The Hill Tracts of Chittagong and the Dwellers Therein*, Calcutta, 1896.
——, *Wild Races of South-Eastern India*, (p. 197).
Little, C.B. and J. Wert, *Gazetteer of Manipur*, Calcutta, 1984.
Luthra, P.N., *Constitutional and Administrative Growth of North East Frontier Agency*, Research Deptt., Govt. of Arunachal Pradesh, Shillong, 1964.
Mackenzie, Alexander, *North East Frontier of India* (Reprint, Mittal Publication), New Delhi, 1995.
Maculay, C., *Report of A Mission to Sikkim and Tibetan Frontier*, Bengal Secretariat Press, Calcutta, 1884.
Mahanta, P.N. (ed.), 'Assam in 2001 AD: Proceedings of the Workshop on Futurology Awareness', Dibrugarh University 1990.
Maitreya, A.K., *Gauda-Lekhmala*, Rajshahi, 1919.
Majumdar, B.C., *Elements of Social Anthropology*, University of Calcutta, 1936.
Majumdar, N.G., *Inscriptions of Bengal*, Rajshahi, Vol. III, 1929.
——, *Glimpses of Bengal in the 19th Century*, Firma, K.L. Mukhopadhyaya, Calcutta, 1960.
—— (ed.), *History and Culture of the Indian People*, The Classical Age: Bombay, Bhartiya Vidya Bhawan, 1970.
——, *History of Ancient Bengal* (in 2 vols.), G. Bhardwaj, Calcuta, 1981.
Majumdar, S.N. (ed.), *Ancient India as Described by Ptolemy*, Calcutta, 1927.
Male, P.F., *Sikkim*, Oxford and I.B.N., Calcutta, 1971.
Mathur, P.R.G., *The Khasi of Meghalaya*, Cosmo Publications, New Delhi, 1979.
McCrindle, J.W., *Ancient India as Described in Classical Literature Western Minister*, 1901.
McCall, A.G., *Lushai Chrysalis*, Luzac & Co. Ltd., London, 1947.
Mills, J.P., *The Lhota Nagas*, Macmillan & Co., London, 1922.
Misra, R.C., *Sikkim Joins the Motherland*, Ajay Bandhu Fort, Bharatpur, 1977.
Misra, Udayam, *North-East India: Quest for Identity*, A Collection of Essays on Socio-Political Topic, Omsons, Guwahati, 1988.
Morris, C.J., *The Gurkhas: An Anthology*, B.R. Publishing Corporation, Delhi, 1985.
——, *Living with the Lepchas*, A Book about the Sikkim Himalayans, William Heinemann, London, 1938.
Mukherjee, B.N., *East Indian Art-Styles*, Calcutta, 1980.
——, *Coins and Currency System in Gupta Bengal – (AD 320-550 AD)*, Harman Publishers, New Delhi, 1992.
——, *Coins and Currency System in Post-Gupta Bengal – (AD 550-700 AD)*, Munshiram Manoharlal, New Delhi 1993.
——, *External Trade of Early North-Eastern India*, Vikas Publishers, New Delhi 1992.
Mukherji, R. & S.K. Maity, *Corpus of Bengal Inscriptions: Bearings on History and Civilization of Bengal*, Calcutta, Firma, KLM, 1967.
Munshi, S.& Lama U., *The Tamangs of Darjeeling, A Study of A Group Identity*, Journal of Indian Anthropological Society, Vol. 13 No. 2, p. 1978.
Nag, Chittaranjan, *Mizo Society in Transition*, Vikas Publications, New Delhi, 1993.
Nair, P.T., *Tribes of Arunachal Pradesh*, Spectrum Publication, Guwahati.
Nakane, Chie., *Garo and Khasi, A Comparative Study in Materialineal Systems*, Mount & Co., Paris, 1967.

Nakani, C., 'Plural Society in Sikkim: A Study of Interrelations of Lepches, Bhutias and Nepalis' in F. Haimendorf C. (ed.), *Caste and Kin in Nepal, India & Ceylon*, Anthropological Studies in Hindi - Buddhist Contact Jones: Asia, Pub., 1966.

Natarajan, Naline, *The Missionary Among the Khasi*, United Publishers, Guwahati, 1977.

Nepali, G.S., *The Newars: An Enthno-Sociological Study of A Himalayan Community*, United Area Bombay, 1965.

Nunthara, C., *Mizoram: Society and Polity*, Indus Publications, New Delhi, 1996.

Oldfield, H.A., *Sketches from Nepal*, London, 1880.

Panchani, C.S., *Arunachal Pradesh: Religion, Culture and Society*, Konark Publishers, Delhi, 1989.

Pandey, B.B., *Arunachal Pradesh: Village State to Statehood*, Himalaya Publications, Bomdila, 1996.

——, *The Hill Miris*, Govt. of Arunachal Pradesh, Shillong, 1974.

Pandeya, S.N. (ed.), *Sources of the History of Manipur*, National Publishing House, New Delhi, 1985.

Pandey, V. (ed.), *Assam: The Land of Sankaradeva-History, Art, Literature, Philosophy & Religion*, Bombay, The Author, 1979.

Pargitetr, F.E., *The Purana Text of the Dynasties of the Kali Age*, Oxford University Press, 1913.

Parry, N.E., *A Monograph on Lushai Customs and Ceremonies*, Assam Govt. Press, Shillong, 1982.

Pathak, L.P., *Meghalaya, Manipur and Tripura: A Select Bibliography with Context, Documentation and Data Analysis*, Shillong, 1982.

Pemberton, R.B., *Report on the Eastern Frontier of British India* (Reprint), Deptt. of Historical and antiquarian Studies, Assam, Guwahati, 1966.

Phukon, G., *Assam: Attitude of Federalism*, Sterling Publications, New Delhi, 1984.

Playfair, A., *The Garos*, Calcutta, 1909.

Porter, A.E., *Census of India 1931: West Bengal & Sikkim*, Usha Publications, New Delhi, 1987 (Reprint).

Pudaite, Rocheenga, *The Education of Hmar People*, Sielmat, Indo-Burma Pioneer Mission, Manipur, 1963.

Puri, B.N., *Studies in Early History and Administration in Assam*, Guwahati, 1967.

Rafiabadi, H.N., *Assam from Agitation to Accord*, Genuine Publications, New Delhi, 1989.

Rai, M.B., *Census of India, 1981*, District Hand Book – West Kameng District, Arunachal Pradesh, Series No. 25, Directorate of Census Operations, Arunachal Pradesh, Shillong, 1987.

Ram, R., *The Himalayan Borderland*, Vivek Publication, Delhi, 1969.

——, *The Himalayas as A Frontier*, Vikas Publication, New Delhi, 1978.

Rammuny, M., *The World of Nagas*, Northern Book Centre, New Delhi, 1988.

Rana, Capt, B.S., *The People of Meghalaya: Study in the People and Their Religio-Cultural Life*, Punthi Pustak, Calcutta, 1989.

Rao, P.R. *Sikkim: The Story of its Integration with India*, Cosmo, New Delhi, 1978.

——, *India and Sikkim 1814-1970*, Sterling Publications, New Delhi, 1972.

Ray, Animesh, *Mizoram, Dynamics of Change*, Pearl Publications, Calcutta, 1982.

——, *Mizoram*, N.B.T., New Delhi, 1993.

Ray, Burman, B.K. (ed.), *Census of India, 1961*, Demographic and Socio-Economic Profiles of the Hill Area of North East India, Govt. of India, New Delhi, 1961.

Ray Choudhury, N.R., *Tripura Through the Ages*, Sterling Publicatons, New Delhi., 1982.
Ray, Datta, *North East India 2000 A.D.*, Deep & Deep, Delhi, 1987.
Ray, Jyatirmery, *History of Manipur*, Firma, L.K. Mukhopadhyaya, Calcutta, 1958.
Ray, Sunil, C., *Coins and Culture: An Archaeological Approach*, Angkor Publisher, New Delhi, 1996.
Reid, R., *History of the Frontier Area Bordering on Assam 1833-1941*, Govt. Press, Shillong, 1942.
Risley, H.H., *Gazeteer of Sikkim* (Reprinted), B.R. Publishing Corporation, New Delhi, 1985.
——, *Tribes and Castes of Bengal: Ethnographic Glossary* (Reprinted), Firma K.L. Mukhopadhyaya, Calcutta, 1981.
——, *The Tribes and Castes of Bengal* (Reprint), West Bengal Secretariat Press, 1981.
Risley, Sirherbert, *The People of India*, (Reprint), Oriental Books Corporation, Delhi, 1969.
Rizvi, S.H.M. & Shibani Ray, *Nicotine Water to Heroin: A Case Study of Manipur*, D.K. Publishers, New Delhi, 1986.
Rizvi, S.H.M. & S.K. Mukherjee, 'Tribes in Contemporary India – A Study of Paiti Tribes of Manipur South', *Anthropological Survey of India*, Calcutta, 1984.
Robinson, W., *Descriptive Account of Assam*, Ostell & Lepage, London, 1841.
Roland, Y.L., *Comparative History of the Nagas (From Ancient Period)*, D.K. Publishers, Delhi, 1988.
Ronaldshay, L., *Lands of the Thunderbolt Sikkim Chumbi and Bhutan*, Constable, London, 1923.
Rowney, H.B., *The Wild Tribes of India*, B.R. Publishing Corporation, New Delhi, 1974 (Reprinted).
Roy, Sachin, 'Dress, Ornaments and Decoration of the Adis', *Vanyajati*, Vol. 6 No. 1, pp. 4-21, 1958.
Roy, T.N., *A Study of Northern Black Polished Ware Culture: An Iron Age Culture of India*, Ramanand Vidya Bhawan, Delhi, 1986.
Rustomji, Nari, *Enchanted Frontier: Sikkim, Bhutan and India's North-Eastern Borderlands*, OUP, Bombay, 1971.
——, *Sikkim, A Himalayan Tragedy*, Allied Publishers 1987.
Rymbai, R.T., 'Some Aspects of the Religion of Khasi-Pnar ', *Religion and Society of North East India*, S. Miri (ed.), Vikas Publishers, New Delhi, 1980.
Saingal, Omesh, *Tripura – Its History and Culture*, Concept Publishing House, Delhi, 1978.
Samajaoba, Naorem, *Manipur Past & Present: Roots Beyond the Root*, Mittal Publications, New Delhi, 1985.
Sangkima, *Mizo's Society and Social Change 1890-1947*, Spectrum, Gauhati, 1992.
Sangma, Milton, 'History and Culture of the Garos', *Garo Hills Land People*, L.S. Gassah (ed.), Omsons Publications, New Delhi, 1984.
Saraswati, B.N., 'Material Culture Studies – A Trend Report', *A Survey of Research in Sociology and Social Anthropology*, Vol. III, New Delhi, ICSSR, 1972.
Sardeshpande, S.C., *The Patkoi Nagas*, D.K. Publishers, Delhi, 1987.
Sarkar, N., *Buddhism among the Monpas and Sherdukpens*, Research Deptt., Govt. of Arunachal Pradesh, Shillong, 1980.
——, *Tawang Monastery*, Research Deptt., Govt. of Arunachal Pradesh, Shillong, 1981.
Sarma, G. (ed.), *Asamiya Jatoi Itibritta*, Jorhat, 1974.

Sarma, Ramanimohan, *Political History of Tripura*, Patliputra, Calcutta, 1987.

Sastri, H.G. (ed.), *Amarkosha of Amarasmiha*, Varanasi, 1970.

Schoff, W.H. (tr.), *Periplus of the Erythraeian Sea*, London, 1912.

Seal, Samud, *Buddhist Records of the Western World*, Calcutta, 1957-58 (Reprint).

Seiger, Halfden, *The Lepches: Culture and Religion of Himalayan People*, Pts. I & II, National Museum of Denmark, Copenhagen, 1967.

Sengupta, N., *Politics and Government of Sikkim*, Sterling New Delhi, 1985.

Shakespeare, J., *The Lushai Kuki Clans*, Macmillan & Company, London, 1912.

Shamasastri, R. (ed.), *Arthasastra*, Mysore, 1919.

Sharma, A.K., 'Emergence of Early Culture in North East India' (A Study Based on Excavations at Bhaitbari, Meghalaya), Aryan Books International, New Delhi, 1993.

——, *Manipur: The Glorious Past*, Aryan Books International, 1994.

Sharma, H.C., *Stone Age Culture of the Garo Hills* (Ph.D. Thesis), Gauhati University, 1972.

Sharma, J.L, *Hamro Samaj: Ek Adhyayan*, Sajha Prakashan, Kathmandu, 1982.

Sharma, M.M. (ed.), *Inscriptions of Ancient Assam*, Gauhati, 1977.

Sharma, Rajesh, *The Images of Sikkim: The Land, People and Culture*, Regium Publications, Gangtok, 1983.

Shastri, Ajay Mitra, *Ancient North-East India (Pragjyotisha): A Pan India Perspective (Upto Seventh Century AD)*, Aryan Books International, New Delhi, 2002.

——, *India as Seen in the Kuttani-mata of Damodargupta*, Moti Lal Banarasidass, New Delhi, 1975.

Shimray, R.R., *Origin and Culture of Nagas*, Aruna Printing Press, New Delhi, 1985.

Shukla, B.K., *The Daflas of Subansiri Region*, North-East Frontier Agency, Shillong, 1965.

Shukla S.R., *Sikkim: The Story of Integration*, S. Chand & Co., New Delhi, 1976.

Shyam Chaudhuri, N.K. and M.M. Das, 'The Haleng Society: A Theme for Analytical Ethnography', *Anthropological Survey of India*, Calcutta.

Singh, Chandrika, *Emergence of Arunachal Pradesh as A State*, Mittal Publications, Delhi, 1989.

Singh, Jai Prakash and Gautam Sengupta (eds.), *Archaeology of North-Eastern India*, Har-Anand Publications, Delhi, 1991.

Singh, Jai Prakash, *Coinage and Economy of North-Eastern States of India* (Memoir Series No. 7), Varanasi, Numismatic Society of India, 1978.

Singh, Inder, *Manipur Phonetic Reader*, Central Institute of Indian Languages, Mysore, 1975.

Singh, K.M., *Hijaim Irabot Singh and the Political movements in Manipur*, D.K. Publishers, 1989.

Singh, K. Suresh, *Tribal Movement in India* (in 2 Vols.), Manohar Publications, New Delhi, 1982.

—— (ed.) *Tribal Situation in India*, Indian Institute of Adv. Studies, Simla, 1972.

Singh, K.S. (Gen. Ed.), *Arunachal Pradesh* (People of India series. Vol. XIV) Anthropological Survey of India, Calcutta, 1995.

—— (Gen. Ed.), *Assam* (People of India Series No. XV), Anthropological Survey of India, Calcutta, 2002.

—— (Gen. Ed.), *Manipur* (People of India Series, No. XXXI), Anthropological Survey of India, Calcutta, 1998.

—— (Gen. Ed.), *Meghalaya* (People of India Series, No. XXXII), Anthropological Survey of India, Calcutta, 1994.

—— (Gen. Ed.), *Mizoram* (People of India Series, No. XXXIII), Anthropological Survey of India, Calcutta, 1995.

—— (Gen. Ed.), *Nagaland* (People of India Series, No. XXXIV), Anthropological Survey of India, Calcutta, 1994.

—— (Gen. Ed.), *Sikkim* (People of India Series, No. XXXIX), Anthropological Survey of India, Calcutta, 1993.

—— (Gen. Ed.), *Tripura* (People of India Series, No. XLI), Anthropological Survey of India, Calcutta, 1996.

Singh, N. Tombi, *Manipur - A Study*, Rajesh Printing Press, Delhi, 1972.

Singh, O.P., *Strategic Sikkim*, B.R. Publishing Corp., Delhi, 1985.

Singh, Prakash, *Nagaland*, National Book Trust, New Delhi, 1970.

Singh, S., *The Beautiful India, Sikkim and Life*, New Delhi, 1977.

Sinha, A.C., *Politics of Sikkim: A Sociological Study*, Thomson Press, Faridabad.

Sinha, B.P., *The Decline of the Kingdom of Magdha*, Motilal Banarsidass Patna, 1954.

Sinha, Kamaleshwar, *Meghalaya: Triumph of the Tribal Genius*, Indian School, Supply Depot, Delhi, 1970.

Sinha, Raghuvir, *The Akas*, Researsch Department, Government of Arunachal Pradesh, Shillong, 1962.

Sircar, D.C., *Early Indian Numismatic and Epigraphic Studies*, Calcutta, 1977.

——, *Select Inscriptions Bearing on Indian History & Civilization*, Calcutta University, 2nd ed., 1965.

——, *Studies in the Geography of Ancient and Medieval India*, 2nd ed., Motilal Banarsidass, Delhi, 1972.

Soppitt, C.A., *A Short Account of the Kuki Lushai Tribes on the North-East Frontier District*, Cachar, Sylhet Naga Hills, etc. and North Cachar Hills, Shillong, 1887.

Sougate, Hranglien, *Hmar History*, Mmar Chanchin Mao Press, Imphal, 1956.

Srivastava, L.R.N., *Among the Wanchos*, Research Deptt., Govt. of Arunachal Pradesh, Shillong, 1973.

——, *The Gallongs*, Research Deptt., Govt. of Arunachal Pradesh, Shillong, 1962.

Stracey, P.D., *Nagaland Nightmare*, Allied Publisher, 1968.

Subha, Tanka, B., *The Nepalis in Darjeeling and Sikkim Himalayas: Dynamics of a Hill Society*, Mittal Publication, Delhi, 1989.

Syiemlieh, D.R., *British Administration in Meghalaya: Policy and Pattern*, Heritage Publishers, New Delhi, 1989.

Sykes, M., *North East Frontier: Sarva Seva Sangh*, Varanasi, 1963.

Taleyarkhdn, H.J.H., *Splendour of Sikkim*, Impression Printer, Gangtok, 1982.

Tarakratna, P. (ed.), *Kalika Purana*, Bombay, 1829 (ed. B.N. Sastri), Chowkhambha Sansrkit Series, Varanasi, 1972.

Teyeng, J., *'Census of India' Meghalaya*, Directorate of Census Operation, 1971.

Thanga, L.B., *The Mizos: A Study in Racial Personality*, United Publishers, Gauhati, 1978.

Thompson, P.C.M., *Assam Valley: Beliefs and Customs of the Assamese Hindus*, London, 1948.

Touche, Tom D. La., *Note on the Geology of the Lushai Hill Records of the Geological Survey of India*, Vol. XXIV, pt. 2., 1891.

Urmila Sant, *Neolithic Settlement Pattern of North-Eastern and Northern India*, Sarita Book House, Delhi, 1991.

Vaiphei, S.P., *Who We are/ Who are We? In Search of Identity*, Kuki Chin Baptist Mission, Imphal, 1986.

Verma, A.K., *Neolithic Cultures of Eastern India*, Delhi, 1988.

Vidyasagar, J. (ed.), *Harsa Carita*, Calcutta, 1892.

Waddell, L.A., *Among the Himalayas* (Reprint), Mittal Publication, Delhi, 1979.

——, *Lamaism in Sikkim* (Reprint), Cosmo, Delhi, 1973.

Ward, Kingdom, *Plant Hunter in Manipur*, Jonathan Cape, London, 1952.

Watters, T., *On HuenTsiang Travels in India* (ed.), Rhys Davids in 2 vols., London, 1904-05.

Wavell, Stewart, *The Naga King's Daughter*, George Allen & Unwin Ltd., London, 1964.

White, J.C., *Himalayan Bhutan, Sikkim and Tibet* (Reprint), Ess Publications, Delhi, 1977.

——, *Sikkim and Bhutan: Twentyone Years on the North-East Frontier 1886-1908*, Edward Arnold, London, 1909.

Wilson, H.H. (tr.), *Vishnu-Purana* in 5 vols., London, 1864-70.

Yadav, B.N.S, *Society and Culture in Northern India in the Twelfth Century*, Allahabad, 1973.

Younu, Asoso, *The Rising Nagas (A Historical and Political Study)*, Vivek Publication, Delhi, 1974.

Zawala, K., *Mizo Pi Pute Leh on Thalahte Chanchin*, Modern Printing Press, Aizawl, 1964.

ARTICLES

Abbot, A.K., 'Notes on the Naga Hills and the Narrative of a Military into Kacha Naga Country during Feb-April 1881', *Journal of the United Service Institute of India*, No. 49.50, 1881-1882.

Acharya, N.N., 'Source Materials for the Early History and Culture of North-Eastern States of India: A Historical Approach', *Bulletin, Assam State Museum*, No. IV, pp. 14-19, 1982.

Aier, Yajin, 'The Nagaland of Tomorrow and Her Educated Youth', *The Thinker*, Vol. I, No. I, 1973.

A.O, M. Alemchiba, 'Significance of Cultural Research in Nagaland', *The Thinker*, Vol. I, No. I, Feb. 1973.

——, 'Divergence in Political and Social System among the Naga Tribes, Highlander', (*Res. Bull. Of Deptt of Cultural Res. & State Museum*), Nagaland Vol. I, No. I March 1973.

Aram, M., 'Nagaland Problem: Some Blocks to Emotional Integration', *Cohesion*, Vol. I, Jan. 1970 - 71.

——, 'Social Change and Political Tension in Nagaland', *North Eastern Research Bulletin*, No. 3, Department of Sociology, Dibrugarh University, Summer of 1972.

Archer, W.G., 'The Attitude of Sewa Nagas to Dancing by Women', *Man in India*, Vol. 28, 1948.

Avery, J. 'The Ao Naga Language of Southern Assam', *American Journal of Philology*, Vol. VIII, No. 27, 1886.

Bacon, Elizabeth E., 'Naga', *Encyclopedia Americana*, Vol. 19, p. 679, 1965.

Balfour, Henry, 'Some Types of Natives Hoes, Naga Hills', *Man*, Vol. 17, No. 24, 1917.

Banerjee, R.D., 'Neulpur Plate of Subhakara, The 8th Year', *E.I.* XV, pp. 1-8, 1919-20.

Banerjee, S., 'Tripura and the Cognate Dialects – A Study of Bodo Group of Dialects', *Educational Miscellany*, Vol. III (Pt. I & II), 1966.

Barpujari, H.K., 'North-East India: The Problems and Policies since 1947', (General Presidential Address at Indian History Congress, Rabindra Bharati University, Calcutta), 1996.

Barua, K.L., 'Prehistoric Culture in Assam', *Journal of Assam Research Society,* Vol. VII, 1939.

Basak. R.G., 'Five Damodarpar Copper Plate Inscriptions of the Gupta Period', *E.I.* XV, pp. 113-45, 1919-20.

Basnet, B.S., 'Sikkim, New Thrust on Agriculture', *Himalyan Today,* March-May, 1989.

Basu, Amitabha (*et al.*), 'Demography and Demographical Genetics of Two Isolated Mountain Villages of Northern Sikkim Eastern Himalaya', *Journal of Indian Anthro-Phijical Society,* Vol. 17, No. 2, 1982.

Basu, S., 'Bhots of Northern Sikkim', *Man in India* 46-2, April-June 1966.

Bhandarkar, D.R., 'A List of Inscriptions of Northern India in Brahmi and its Derivative Scripts from about 200 B.C. (Appendix to *E.I.* XIX-XXII).

Bhattacharya, P.N. & D.K. Nanda, 'Blood Groups of the Paite of Manipur' *Journal of Indian Anthropological Society,* Vol. 15, No. 2-3, p. 1980.

Bhuiyan, M.C., 'Natural Environment and Pattern of Human Geography in Brahmaputra Valley', *Journal of the University of Gauhati,* Vol. 20-22, No. 2, Science, 1969-71.

Bose, K.K., 'Social Organisation of Aimol-Kukis', *Journal Deptt. of Letters,* University of Calcutta, 1934.

Bose, N.K., 'Prehistoric Research in Mayarbhanj', *Science and Culture,* Vol. 6, pp. 75-79, Calcutta, 1940.

Burling, Robbins & P.C. Bhattacharya, 'Lexicostatistic Dating Method of Boro-Garolinguistic Separation', *Journal of the University of Guwahati* (67-73), 1956.

Chakravarti, M.R. & D.P. Mukhrjee, 'Dermatoglyphic Study on the Tribes and Castes of Nagaland and Manipur', Bulletin Anthropological Survey of India II: 3-4: 233-34, 1962.

——, 'Dermatoglyphic Study of Tribes and Castes of the State of Assam' *Science and Culture,* 27: 584-85, 1961.

Chakravarti, K.R., 'Verdict in Sikkim - 1979-85', *A Sikkim Express Study,* May 1988.

Chakladar, H.C. & T.C. Roy Choudhuri, 'The Kabui', *Man in India,* 37: 192-98, 1957.

Chandra, P.R., 'Sikkim: Its Customs in North Bengal', *Lawsland University Review Humanities & Social Sciences,* 2 (1-2) June-Dec. 1981.

Chaudhuri Pratap, 'Neolithic Culture in Kamarupa', *Journal of Assam Res. Society,* Vol. XI, 1944.

Chisti, S.M.A.W., 'Christian Mission in Manipur 1926-29', *Social Research,* Vol. 2, No. 1, pp. 48-51.

Das, A.K., 'Analysis of the Social System of the Kharias', *Bulletin of the Cultural Research Institute,* Vol. VII (I & II). pp. 85-88, 1968.

Das, A.R. 'Linguistic Traits of Some Arunachal Languages' *Janajati Bhashayam Aur Hindi Sikhshan,* by N.B. Rajagopalam (ed.), (pp. 17-25), Kendrya Hindi Sansthan, Agra, 1980.

Das, N.K., 'Agrarian Structure and Economic Development', *Highlander,* Vol. IV, No. I & II. Bulletin of the Deptt. of Art & Culture, Govt. of Nagaland, 1976.

Datta Chaudhuri, S.S. & G.C. Ghosh, 'Indigenous Health practices among the Idu Mishmi of Arunachal Pradesh', *Human Science,* Vol. 33, No. 1, pp. 24-34, 1984.

Dikshitar, V.R.R. "Aryanisation of East India (Assam), *Indian Historical Quarterly,* XXI, pp. 29-30, 1945.

Ering, O., 'Adi Belief and Faith', *Arunachal News*, Vol. 12, No. 5, pp. 25-26, 1983.

Ete, Tumpak, 'Gomko Agam Adi Sacred Literature Series', Vol. III, *Adi Folklore Literature Research Centre*, Along, 1984.

Gangmumei, Kabui, 'Social and religious reform movements in Manipur 19th 20th Centuries", *Bulletin of the Division of History*, J.N.U., Imphal, 1974.

Ganguly, D.C., 'Political Condition of Bengal during HiuenTsiang's Visit', *Indian Historical Quarterly*, XV, pp. 122-26, 1939.

Gimson, C., 'Some Notes on the Maring Nagas of Manipur', *Man in India*, Vol. 6, 1926.

Gohain, B.K., 'Myth and Ritual', *Journal of North-East Indian Council for Social Sciences*, p. 151, April, 1991.

Goswami, M.C., 'Peasants and non-Peasants in North-East India and their New Dimension', *Social Anthropology of Peasantry*, (ed. J.P. Menchar), Bombay, 1983.

Gyaltschen, T., 'Note on Buddhist Communities of Sikkim', *Orient*, Vol. 6, No. 1-2, 1977.

Husain, Zahid, 'Human Adaptation to Extreme Climate: A Case Study of Arunachal Pradesh' (Presented in workshop on human adaptation to extreme climate Abstracts, pp. 5-6), *Anthropological Survey of India*, Calcutta, 1984.

Hutton, J.H., "Thadu-Kuki" terms of relationship, *Man in India*, Vol. 2, No. 1-2, pp. 108-10, 1922.

Jaswal, Susma (*et al.*), 'Anthropometry of the Apa Tanis of Arunachal Pradesh', *Human Science*, Vol. 32, No. 4, pp. 292-302, 1983.

Lal, B.B., 'Proto-historic Investigation of Eastern India', *Ancient India*, No. 9, 1953.

Misra, Binayak, 'Hindol Plate of Subhakaradev', *Journal of Bihar & Orissa Research Society*, XVI, pp. 69-83, 1930.

Peal, S.E., 'Eastern Nagas of the Tirap and Namtsik', *Journal of the Asiatic Society of Bengal*, 1, 1986.

——, 'Fading Histories', *Journal of the Asiatic Society of Bengal*, Calcutta, 1894.

Rhodes, N.G., 'Earliest Coins of Assam', *The Numismatic Chronicle*, Oct., 1973.

Roy Sachin, 'Domestic Animals and Their Role in Life of the Adi', *Vanjajati*, Vol. 6, No. 4, pp. 146-152, 1958.

Sen, Kranti, 'Break-up of Naga Background', *Mainstream*, No. 30, Vol. 21-22, 1968.

Shakespear, J., 'Kabul Notes', *Man*, Vol. 12, No. 37, p. 1912.

Sharma, T.C., 'Archaeological Chronology of North-Eastern India', Int. Congress Papers No. 0359, *International Cong. Anth. And Ethno Sc., Chicago*, 1973.

Sharma, T.C., 'Recent Archaeological Discoveries in North-Eastern India', *Puratattava*, Bulletin Ind. Arch. Soc., New Delhi, 1974.

Sharmathakur, G.C., 'A Cultural Profile of a Less Known Tribes the Lalungs', Bulletin of Tribal Research Institute, Vol. I, No. I, Assam, 1983.

Shaw, William, 'Notes on the Thadous Kulds', *Journal of Asiatic Society of Bengal*, 1-175, 1928.

Singh, K.B., 'Slavery in Manipur', *Folklore*, XVIII: 7-9, 1975.

Singh, Madan Mohan, 'Stone Age Economy of Eastern India', *Journal of Bihar & Orissa Research Society*, Vol. 50, pp. 8-15, 1964.

Singh, R.P., 'Geomorphology of the Shillong Plateau of Assam', Proco Pre-cong Sys. On Meghalaya, II Guwahati, I.G.U., 1968.

Sircar, D.C., 'Asvamedhas Celebrated by 1983 Kamampa Kings', *Indian Historical Quarterly,* XXI, pp. 143-45, 1945.

——, 'Gauda-Kamarupa Struggle in the 6-7th Century AD.', *Indian Historical Quarterly,* XXVI, pp. 241-46, 1950.

Sircar, D.C., & P.D. Choudhary, 'Umacal Book Inscription of Surendravarman', Vol. XXXI, 1955-56.

Stonor, C.R., 'The Sulung Tribe of the Assam Himalayas', *Anthropos*-47, 1952.

Thapar, B.K., 'Problems of the Neolithic Cultures in India: A Restrospect', *Puratattava* - No. 7, New Delhi, 1974.

Tripathi, Narayan, 'Chaurasi Grant of Sivakaradeva', *Journal of Bihar & Orissa Research Society,* XIV, pp. 292-306, 1929.

Verma, B.S., 'Excavations at Chirand', *Puratattava* - No. 4, New Delhi, 1970-71.

Venis, A, 'Copper Plate Grant of Vaidyadeva King of Kamrupa', *Epigraphic Indica,* Vol. II, 1894.

Watt, G., 'Aboriginal Tribes of Manipur', *Journal of Anthropological Institute,* Vol. 16, No. 346-70, 1887.

——, 'The Nagas of Manipur - In the Nagas in the Nineteenth Century', (ed.) Verrier, Elwin, Oxford University Press, pp.447-463, London, 1887.

Yambem, Sanamahi, 'Manipur Women's Agitation 1939', *Economic and Political Weekly,* Vol. X, No. 8, pp. 325-330, 1976.

Index